LibreOffice Writer 4.2

A catalogue record for this book is available from the Hong Kong Public Libraries.

Published by Samurai Media Limited.

Email: info@samuraimedia.org

ISBN 978-988-14435-4-0

Contents

Preface

Who is this book for?

Anyone who wants to get up to speed quickly with LibreOffice Writer will find this book valuable. You may be new to word processing software, or you may be familiar with another office suite.

What's in this book?

This book introduces some of the main features of Writer, the word processor component of LibreOffice:

- Text entry, editing, and formatting (Chapter 3)
- Page-layout methods, including frames, columns, and tables (Chapter 4)
- Export to PDF, including bookmarks (Chapter 5)
- Templates and styles (Chapters 6, 7, and 10)
- Embedding or linking of graphics, spreadsheets, and other objects (Chapter 8)
- Built-in drawing tools (Chapter 8)
- Tables of data (Chapter 9)
- Mail merge (Chapter 11)
- Tables of contents, indexes, and bibliographies (Chapter 12)
- Master documents, to group a collection of shorter documents into a single long document (Chapter 13)
- Fields and forms (Chapters 14 and 15)
- Database integration, including a bibliography database (Chapters 11, 12, 15)
- And many more

Where to get more help

This book, the other LibreOffice user guides, the built-in Help system, and user support systems assume that you are familiar with your computer and basic functions such as starting a program, opening and saving files.

Help system

LibreOffice comes with an extensive Help system. This is your first line of support for using LibreOffice.

To display the full Help system, press *F1* or go to **Help > LibreOffice Help** on the Menu bar. In addition, you can choose whether to activate **Tips**, **Extended tips**, and the **Help Agent** by going to **Tools > Options > LibreOffice > General** on the Menu bar.

If *Tips* are enabled, hover the mouse pointer over any of the icons to see a small box (tooltip) with a brief explanation of the icon's function. For a more detailed explanation, select **Help > What's This?** on the Menu bar and hover the pointer over the icon.

Free online support

The LibreOffice community not only develops software, but provides free, volunteer-based support. See Table 1 and this web page: http://www.libreoffice.org/get-help/

You can get comprehensive online support from the community through mailing lists and the Ask LibreOffice website, http://ask.libreoffice.org/en/questions/.

Other websites run by users also offer free tips and tutorials. This forum provides community support for LibreOffice: http://en.libreofficeforum.org/

This site provides support for LibreOffice, among other programs: http://forum.openoffice.org/en/forum/

Table 1: Free support for LibreOffice users

Free LibreOffice support	
Ask LibreOffice	Questions and answers from the LibreOffice community http://ask.libreoffice.org/en/questions/
Documentation	User guides, how-tos, and other documentation. http://www.libreoffice.org/get-help/documentation/ https://wiki.documentfoundation.org/Documentation/Publications
FAQs	Answers to frequently asked questions http://wiki.documentfoundation.org/Faq
Mailing lists	Free community support is provided by a network of experienced users http://www.libreoffice.org/get-help/mailing-lists/
International support	The LibreOffice website in your language. http://www.libreoffice.org/international-sites/ International mailing lists http://wiki.documentfoundation.org/Local_Mailing_Lists
Accessibility options	Information about available accessibility options. http://www.libreoffice.org/get-help/accessibility/

Paid support and training

Alternatively, you are able to pay for support services. Service contracts can be purchased from a vendor or consulting firm specializing in LibreOffice.

What you see may be different

Illustrations

LibreOffice runs on Windows, Linux, and Mac OS X operating systems, each of which has several versions and can be customized by users (fonts, colors, themes, window managers). The illustrations in this guide were taken from a variety of computers and operating systems. Therefore, some illustrations will not look exactly like what you see on your computer display.

Also, some of the dialogs may be different because of the settings selected in LibreOffice. You can either use dialogs from your computer system or dialogs provided by LibreOffice (default). Follow these steps to change to using LibreOffice dialogs if settings have been altered:

1) On Linux and Windows operating systems, go to **Tools > Options > LibreOffice > General** on the Menu bar to open the dialog for general options.
2) On a Mac operating system, go to **LibreOffice > Preferences > General** on the Menu bar to open the dialog for general options.
3) Select **Use LibreOffice dialogs** in **Open/Save dialogs** to display the LibreOffice dialogs on your computer display.
4) Click **OK** to save your settings and close the dialog.

Icons

The icons used to illustrate some of the many tools available in LibreOffice may differ from the ones used in this guide. The icons in this guide have been taken from a LibreOffice installation that has been set to display the Tango set of icons.

You can change your LibreOffice software package to display Tango icons as follows:

1) On Linux and Windows operating systems, go to **Tools > Options > LibreOffice > View** on the Menu bar to open the dialog for view options.

2) On a Mac operating system, go to **LibreOffice > Preferences > View** on the Menu bar to open the dialog for view options.

3) In **User interface > Icon size and style**, select **Tango** from the options available in the drop-down list.

4) Click **OK** to save your settings and close the dialog.

Note	Some Linux operating systems, for example Ubuntu, include LibreOffice as part of the installation and may not include the Tango icon set. You should be able to download the Tango icon set from the software repository for your Linux operating system.

Using LibreOffice on a Mac

Some keystrokes and menu items are different on a Mac from those used in Windows and Linux. The table below gives some common substitutions for the instructions in this chapter. For a more detailed list, see the application Help.

Windows or Linux	Mac equivalent	Effect
Tools > Options menu selection	**LibreOffice > Preferences**	Access setup options
Right-click	Control+click and/or right-click depending on computer setup	Opens a context menu
Ctrl (Control)	⌘ (Command)	Used with other keys
F5	Shift+⌘+F5	Open the Navigator
F11	⌘+T	Open the Styles and Formatting window

What are all these things called?

The terms used in LibreOffice for most parts of the user interface (the parts of the program you see and use, in contrast to the behind-the-scenes code that actually makes it work) are the same as for most other programs.

For example, a dialog is a special type of window. Its purpose is to inform you of something, or request input from you, or both. It provides controls for you to use to specify how to carry out an action. The technical names for common controls are shown in Figure 1. In most cases we do not use the technical terms in this book, but it is useful to know them because the Help and other sources of information often use them.

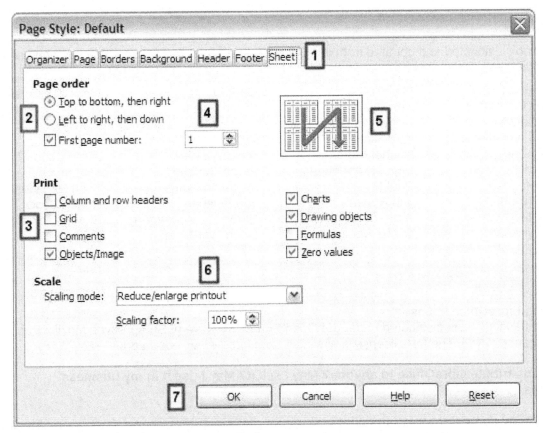

Figure 1: Dialog showing common controls

1) Tabbed page (not strictly speaking a control).
2) Radio buttons (only one can be selected at a time).
3) Checkbox (more than one can be selected at a time).
4) Spin box (click the up and down arrows to change the number shown in the text box next to it, or type in the text box).
5) Thumbnail or preview.
6) Drop-down list from which to select an item.
7) Push buttons.

In most cases, you can interact only with the dialog (not the document itself) as long as the dialog remains open. When you close the dialog after use (usually, clicking **OK** or another button saves your changes and closes the dialog), then you can again work with your document.

Some dialogs can be left open as you work, so you can switch back and forth between the dialog and your document. An example of this type is the Find & Replace dialog.

Who wrote this book?

This book was written by volunteers from the LibreOffice community. Profits from sales of the printed edition will be used to benefit the community.

Acknowledgements

This book is adapted and updated from the *OpenOffice.org 3.3 Writer Guide*. The contributors to that book are:

Jean Hollis Weber	Michele Zarri	Gary Schnabl	Magnus Adielsson
Agnes Belzunce	Ken Byars	Bruce Byfield	Daniel Carrera
Dick Detwiler	Alexander Noël Dunne	Laurent Duperval	Martin Fox
Katharina Greif	Tara Hess	Peter Hillier-Brook	Lou Iorio
John Kane	Rachel Kartch	Stefan A. Keel	Jared Kobos
Michael Kotsarinis	Sigrid Kronenberger	Peter Kupfer	Ian Laurenson
Alan Madden	Paul Miller	Vincenzo Ponzi	Scott Rhoades
Carol Roberts	Iain Roberts	Joe Sellman	Robert Scott
Janet M. Swisher	Barbara M. Tobias	Catherine Waterman	Sharon Whiston
Bob Wickham	Claire Wood	Linda Worthington	

Frequently asked questions

How is LibreOffice licensed?

LibreOffice 4.2 is distributed under the Open Source Initiative (OSI) approved Mozilla Public License (MPL). The MPL license is available from http://www.mozilla.org/MPL/2.0/.

May I distribute LibreOffice to anyone? May I sell it? May I use it in my business?

Yes.

How many computers may I install it on?

As many as you like.

Is LibreOffice available in my language?

LibreOffice has been translated (localized) into over 40 languages, so your language probably is supported. Additionally, there are over 70 *spelling, hyphenation*, and *thesaurus* dictionaries available for languages, and dialects that do not have a localized program interface. The dictionaries are available from the LibreOffice website at: www.libreoffice.org.

How can you make it for free?

LibreOffice is developed and maintained by volunteers and has the backing of several organizations.

How can I contribute to LibreOffice?

You can help with the development and user support of LibreOffice in many ways, and you do not need to be a programmer. To start, check out this web page: http://www.documentfoundation.org/contribution/

May I distribute the PDF of this book, or print and sell copies?

Yes, as long as you meet the requirements of one of the licenses in the copyright statement at the beginning of this book. You do not have to request special permission. We request that you share with the project some of the profits you make from sales of books, in consideration of all the work we have put into producing them.

What's new in LibreOffice Writer 4.2?

LibreOffice 4.2 offers many new features, in addition to those in the 4.1 release. These new features are listed on these wiki pages:

https://wiki.documentfoundation.org/ReleaseNotes/4.1

https://wiki.documentfoundation.org/ReleaseNotes/4.2

Here are some of the features (not a full list):

- Images embedded in Writer can now be rotated easily in 90 degree increments.
- Writer text frames now support having a gradient as background.
- The Comments bar now can easily be toggled using a button in the ruler.
- Footnote and footer comment handling has been improved.
- Comments to text ranges can now include multiple paragraphs.
- Embedding fonts in a Writer document.
- Media file types Windows Media Audio (WMA), Windows Media Video (WMV), Advanced Audio Coding (AAC), Flash Video (FLV), Multiplexed OGG Video (OGX), RMI MIDI Audio and SND (SouND) Audio are now accessible from **Insert > Movie and Sound**.
- Support for legacy Mac word processor documents:
    Microsoft Word for Mac 5.1
    Write Now 4.0
    MacWrite Pro 1.5
    AppleWorks 6.0
- Match Case option has been added to the search bar.
- The Find hotkey *Ctrl+F* is a toggle.
- **File > Recent Documents > Clear List** feature has been added.
- Recent Documents can now be accessed directly from the toolbar using the arrow on the **Open** button.
- Multiple styles can be deleted at the same time.
- Embedding images into HTML files enables sending merge emails with images in HTML format.
- Character border: format one or more characters with a border.
- Spelling checker popup menu now allows change tracking operations.
- Multiple styles can be selected in the Style and Formatting window to delete or hide them.
- A new default template has been designed for Writer.
- RTF import has added initial support for group shapes.
- Writer can now create *.DOT files.
- Graphical bullets are imported and exported in the DOC, DOCX and RTF filters.
- The DOCX import filter now handles non-bitmap drawing shapes.
- Further improvements for DOCX interoperability.

Chapter 1
Introducing Writer

What is Writer?

Writer is the word processor component of LibreOffice. In addition to the usual features of a word processor (spelling check, thesaurus, hyphenation, autocorrect, find and replace, automatic generation of tables of contents and indexes, mail merge, and others), Writer provides these important features:

- Templates and styles (see Chapters 6 and 7)
- Page-layout methods, including frames, columns, and tables (Chapter 4)
- Embedding or linking of graphics, spreadsheets, and other objects (Chapter 8)
- Built-in drawing tools (Chapter 8)
- Master documents, to group a collection of shorter documents into a single long document (Chapter 13)
- Change tracking during revisions (Chapter 3)
- Database integration, including a bibliography database (Chapters 11, 12, 15)
- Export to PDF, including bookmarks (Chapter 5)
- And many more

Parts of the main Writer window

The main Writer workspace is shown in Figure 2. Its features are described in this section.

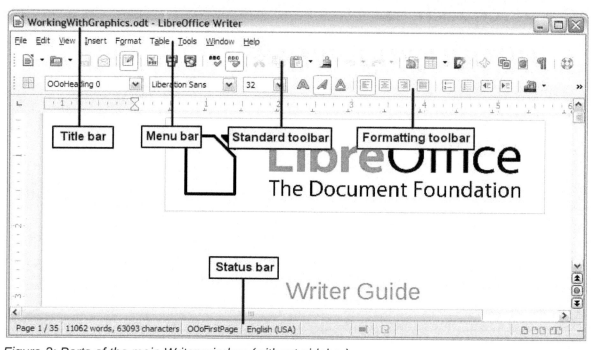

Figure 2: Parts of the main Writer window (without sidebar)

Title bar

The Title bar is located at the top of the Writer window, and shows the file name of the current document. When the document is newly created, the document name will appear as *Untitled X*, where *X* is a number.

Menus

The Menu bar is located just below the Title bar. When you select one of the menus, a submenu drops down to show further options such as:

- Executable commands, such as **Close** or **Save**, found in the **File** menu.
- Commands to open dialogs, indicated by the command being followed by an ellipsis (...), such as **Find** or **Paste Special** found in the **Edit** menu.
- Further submenus, indicated by a right-pointing black arrow, such as **Toolbars** and **Zoom** found in the **View** menu. Moving the cursor onto these causes them to open.

Toolbars

Writer displays toolbars in different ways: docked (fixed in place), or floating. Some toolbars have sections which you can tear off. Docked toolbars can be moved to different locations or made to float, and floating toolbars can be docked.

The top docked toolbar, just under the Menu bar, is called the *Standard Toolbar*. It is consistent across all the LibreOffice applications (Writer, Calc, Draw, Impress).

The second toolbar at the top is context sensitive. For example, when working with text, the Formatting toolbar is displayed. When the cursor is on a graphic (image type), the Graphics toolbar is displayed, and the Pictures toolbar is displayed docked at the bottom of the screen. An additional toolbar (Bullets and Numbering) is displayed next to the Formatting toolbar, when for example, the cursor is in a numbered/bulleted list.

Displaying or hiding toolbars

To display or hide toolbars, choose **View > Toolbars**, then click on the name of a toolbar in the list. An active toolbar shows a check mark beside its name. Tear-off toolbars are not listed in the View menu.

Submenus and tear-off toolbars

Combination toolbar buttons having a down arrow will display *submenus*, *tear-off toolbars*, and other ways of selecting things, depending on the toolbar.

Figure 3 shows a tear-off toolbar from the Drawing toolbar. Once removed from the parent toolbar it displays a title bar.

Tear-off toolbars can be floating or docked along an edge of the screen or in one of the existing toolbar areas. To move a floating tear-off toolbar, drag it by the title bar, as shown in Figure 5.

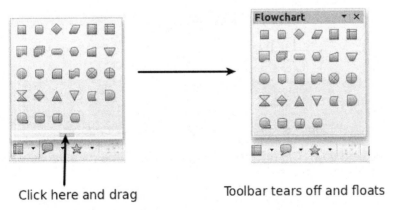

Click here and drag   Toolbar tears off and floats

Figure 3: Example of a tear-off toolbar

Moving toolbars

To move a docked toolbar, place the mouse pointer over the toolbar handle (the small vertical bar to the left of the toolbar), hold down the left mouse button, drag the toolbar to the new location, and then release the *mouse button.*

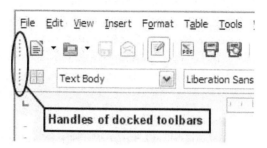

Figure 4: Moving a docked toolbar

To move a floating toolbar, click on its title bar and drag it to a new location.

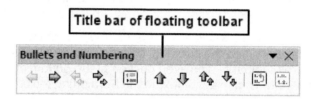

Figure 5: Moving a floating toolbar

Floating toolbars

Some toolbars activated from the View menu may appear as floating toolbars, for example the Insert toolbar. Writer also includes several additional context-sensitive toolbars, whose defaults may appear as floating toolbars in response to the cursor's current position or selection. You can dock these toolbars to the top, bottom, or side of the window, if you wish (see "Moving toolbars" above).

Docking/floating windows and toolbars

Toolbars and some windows, such as the **Navigator** and the **Styles and Formatting** window, are dockable. You can move, resize, or dock them to an edge.

To dock a window or toolbar, hold down *Ctrl* and double-click on the frame of the floating window (or in a vacant area near the buttons at the top of the floating window) to dock it in its last position.

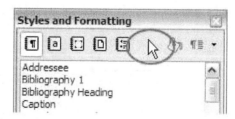

Figure 6: Ctrl+double-click to dock or undock

To undock a window, hold down *Ctrl* and double-click on the frame (or a vacant area near the buttons at the top) of the docked window.

Docking (AutoHide)

On any window edge where another window is docked you will see a button which allows you to show or hide the window.

- If you click the button on the window edge to show the window, the window will remain visible until you manually hide it again (with the same button).
- If you show the window by clicking the window border, but not the button, you activate the **AutoHide** function. The AutoHide function allows you to temporarily show a hidden window by clicking on its edge. When you click in the document, the docked window hides again.

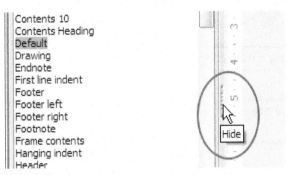

Figure 7: The Hide button

Figure 8: Show button and Autohide

Customizing toolbars

You can customize toolbars in several ways, including choosing which buttons are visible and locking the position of a docked toolbar.

To access a toolbar's customization options, right-click between the buttons on the toolbar to open a context menu.

The context menu lists the buttons defined for the selected toolbar but not visible on it. To show or hide buttons defined for the selected toolbar, choose **Visible Buttons** from the context menu. Visible buttons are indicated by being highlighted (Figure 9) or by a check mark beside the button, depending on your operating system. Click on buttons to hide or show them on the toolbar.

You can also add buttons and create new toolbars, as described in Chapter 16, Customizing Writer.

Note	In earlier versions of LibreOffice, these options were accessed by clicking on an arrow at the end of the toolbar. The arrow is still present on floating toolbars, but not on docked ones. However, the arrow has no effect.

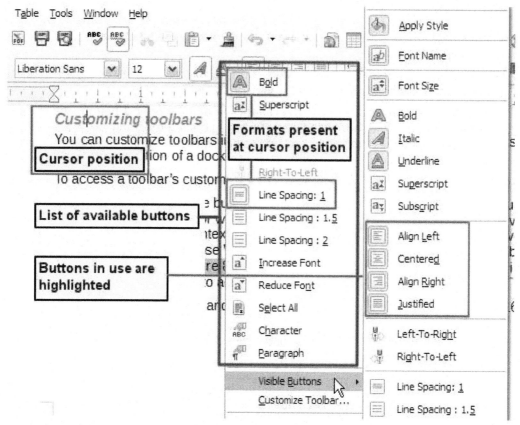

Figure 9: Selection of visible toolbar buttons

Right-click (context) menus

Right-click on a paragraph, graphic, or other object to open a context menu. Often the context menu is the fastest and easiest way to reach a function. If you're not sure where in the menus or toolbars a function is located, you can often find it by right-clicking.

Rulers

Rulers are enabled by default. To show or hide the rulers, choose **View > Ruler**. To disable the rulers, choose **Tools > Options > LibreOffice Writer > View** and deselect either or both rulers. The horizontal ruler has a comments button on its right side to show or hide comments.

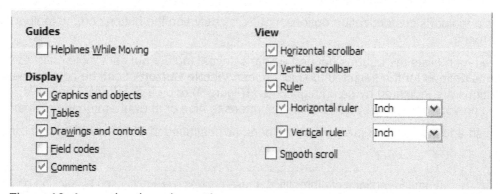

Figure 10: Accessing the ruler settings

Status bar

The Writer status bar is located at the bottom of the workspace. It provides information about the document and convenient ways to quickly change some document features. It can be hidden by deselecting it in the View menu.

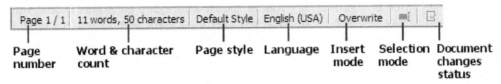

Figure 11: Left end of Status bar

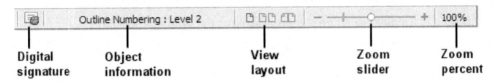

Figure 12: Right end of Status bar

Page number

Shows the current page number, the sequence number of the current page (if different), and the total number of pages in the document. For example, if you restarted page numbering at 1 on the third page, its page number is 1 and its sequence number is 3.

If any bookmarks have been defined in the document, a right-click on this field pops up a list of bookmarks; click on the required one.

To jump to a specific page in the document, double-click on this field. The **Navigator** opens (see page 35). Click in the **Page Number** field in the **Navigator,** type the *sequence* number of the required page, and press *Enter*.

Word and character count

The word and character count of the document is shown in the status bar, and is kept up to date as you edit. Any text selected in the document will be counted and this count will replace the displayed count.

To display extended statistics such as character counts excluding spaces, double-click the word count in the status bar, or choose **Tools > Word Count**.

Page style

Shows the style of the current page. To change the page style, right-click on this field. A list of page styles pops up; click on one to select a different style.

To edit the current page style, double-click on this field. The Page Style dialog opens. See Chapters 6 and 7 for more information about styles.

Language

Shows the language at the cursor position, or for the selected text, that is used for checking spelling, hyphenation, and thesaurus. Click to open a menu where you can choose another language for the selected text or for the paragraph where the cursor is located. You can also choose **None (Do not check spelling)** to exclude the text from a spelling check or choose **More** to open the **Character** dialog. Any directly formatted language settings can be reset to the default language from this menu. See Chapter 3, *Working with Text*, for more information.

Insert mode

This area is blank when in Insert mode. Double-click to change to *Overwrite* mode; single-click to return to Insert mode. In Insert mode, any text after the cursor position moves forward to make room for the text you type; in Overwrite mode, text after the cursor position is replaced by the text you type. This feature is disabled when in **Edit > Changes > Record** mode.

Selection mode

Click to choose different selection modes. The icon does not change, but when you hover the mouse pointer over this field, a tooltip indicates which mode is active.

When you click in the field, a context menu displays the available options.

Mode	Effect
Standard selection	Click in the text where you want to position the cursor; click in a cell to make it the active cell. Any other selection is then deselected.
Extending selection (*F8*)	Clicking in the text extends or crops the current selection.
Adding selection (*Shift+F8*)	A new selection is added to an existing selection. The result is a multiple selection.
Block selection (*Ctrl+Shift+F8*)	A block of text can be selected.

On Windows systems, you can hold down the *Alt* key while dragging to select a block of text. You don't need to enter the block selection mode.

See Chapter 3, Working with Text, for more information about these modes.

Document changes status

The icon that is displayed here changes from this one (☑) if the document has no unsaved changes, to this one (☐*) if it has been edited and the changes have not been saved.

Digital signature

If the document has been digitally signed, this icon (🖻) is displayed here; otherwise, it is blank. To view the certificate, double-click the icon.

Section or object information

When the cursor is in a section, heading, or list item, or when an object (such as a picture or table) is selected, information about that item appears in this field. Double-clicking in this area opens a relevant dialog.

Object	Information shown	Dialog opened
Picture	Size and position	Picture
List item	Level and list style	Bullets and Numbering[1]
Heading	Outline numbering level	Bullets and Numbering[1]
Table	Name or number and cell reference of cursor	Table Format
Section	Name of section	Edit Sections
Other	(Blank)	Fields

---

1   If a *list style* was used with a list item or heading, no dialog appears.

View layout

Click an icon to change between single page, side-by-side, and book layout views (see Figure 13). You can edit the document in any view. Zoom settings (see below and next page) interact with the selected view layout and the window width to determine how many pages are visible in the document window.

Zoom

To change the view magnification, drag the Zoom slider, or click on the + and − signs, or right-click on the zoom level percent to pop up a list of magnification values from which to choose.

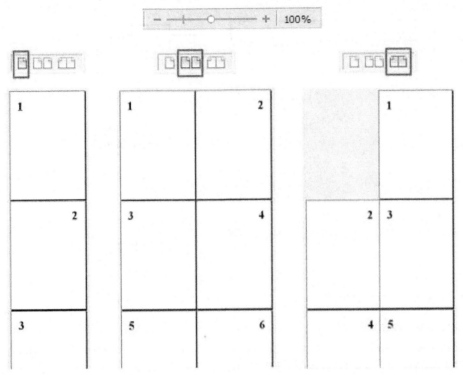

Figure 13: View layouts: single, side-by-side, book

Sidebar

To activate the Sidebar, select **View > Sidebar** from the Menu Bar. The sidebar is located on the right side of the edit view. The sidebar (Figure 14) contains four decks: Properties, Styles and Formatting, Gallery, and Navigator. Each deck has a corresponding icon on the Tab bar to the right of the sidebar, allowing you to switch between them.

Each deck consists of a title bar and one or more content panels. A panel is like a combination of toolbar and dialog. Toolbars and sidebar panels share many functions. For example, the buttons for making text bold or italic exist in both the Formatting toolbar and the Character panel of the Properties deck.

Some panels contain a **More** button (🗔) which when clicked opens a dialog to give greater choice of editing controls. The dialog that opens locks the document for editing until the dialog is closed.

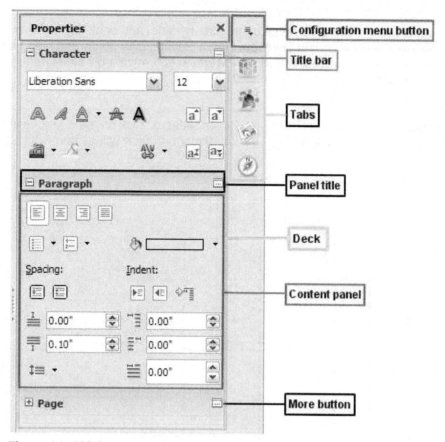

Figure 14: Sidebar Properties deck and text context panels

The decks are described below.

- **Properties**: Contains tools for direct formatting within the document. The tools are separated into three panels for text editing:
    - *Character*: Modify text by the font type, size, color, weight, style and spacing.
    - *Paragraph*: Style the paragraph by alignment, lists or bullets, background color, indent, and spacing.
    - *Page*: Format the page by orientation, margin, size, and number of columns.

    If a graphic is selected, then the following panels open:
    - Graphic: Modify the graphic's brightness, contrast, color mode and transparency.
    - Position: Modifications to width and height.
    - Wrap: Permits wrap modifications where these are available.

    If a drawing object is selected, then the following panels are available;
    - Area: Fill and transparency edits are available.
    - Line: Permits edits to the line style, width, color, arrows, corners and cap styles.
    - Position and Size: Enables edits to width, height, rotation and flip attributes.

    If a frame is selected, then the wrap panel opens but may be grayed-out if frame wrap is not available.

Caution	Be aware that by changing the options on the Page panel you will change the page style in use, modifying not only the current page but all pages using the same page style.

- **Styles and Formatting**: Manage the styles used on the document, applying existing styles, creating new ones or modifying them. This deck is also a floating toolbar that can be accessed from **Format > Styles and Formatting** from the Menu bar.

- **Gallery**: Add images and diagrams included in the Gallery themes. The Gallery displays as two sections; the first lists the themes by name (Arrows, Background, Diagrams, etc.) and the second displays the images in the selected category. Select the **New Theme** button to create new categories. To insert an image, or add a new image to the gallery, drag and drop the selected image. This deck is also a docked toolbar that can be accessed from **Tools > Gallery** or the **Gallery** button on the Standard Toolbar.

- **Navigator**: Browse the document and reorganize its content by selecting different content categories, such as headings, tables, frames, graphics, etc. The Sidebar Navigator does not contain a **List Box On/Off** button. This deck is also a floating toolbar that can be accessed from **View > Navigator** or the **Navigator** button on the Standard Toolbar.

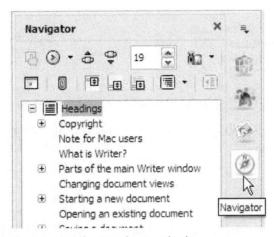

Figure 15: The Navigator deck

The Sidebar has on its left edge a Hide button (see Figure 16); click this button to hide the panel by collapsing it to the right edge of the window. Click the button on a collapsed panel to reopen it.

To adjust the width of the panel, place the cursor on the left edge of the panel, click and drag to right or left depending on the starting width. With the Properties deck selected, you cannot drag to less than a certain width. With any of the other decks selected, you can drag the panel width to a minimum useable width; an arrow then indicates that when you release the mouse button, the Sidebar will collapse to the width of the Tab bar (see Figure 17).

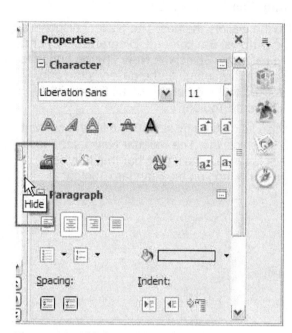

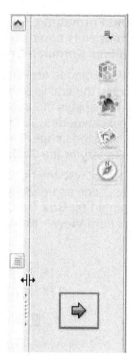

Figure 16: Sidebar Hide button

Figure 17: Panel dragged past minimum useable width showing arrow

Changing document views

Writer has three ways to view a document: *Print Layout*, *Web Layout*, and *Full Screen*. To change the view, go to the **View** menu and click on the required view.

Print Layout is the default view in Writer. In this view, you can use the Zoom slider and the View Layout icons on the Status bar to change the magnification.

You can also choose **View > Zoom > Zoom** from the Menu bar to display the **Zoom & View Layout** dialog, where you can set the same options as on the Status bar.

In Web Layout view, you can use only the Zoom slider; the View Layout buttons on the Status bar are disabled, and most of the choices on the **Zoom & View Layout** dialog are not available.

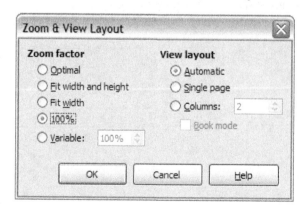

Figure 18: Choosing Zoom and View Layout options

In Full Screen view, the document is displayed using the zoom and layout settings previously selected. To exit Full Screen view and return to either Print or Web Layout view, press the *Esc* key or toggle the **Full Screen** button on the floating toolbar in the top left-hand corner. You can also use *Ctrl+Shift+J* to enter or exit Full Screen view.

Starting a new document

You can start a new, blank document in Writer in several ways. If a document is already open in LibreOffice, the new document opens in a new window.

From the Start Center

When LibreOffice is open but no document is open, the **Start Center** is shown. Click the **Create: Writer Document** button to create a new text document, or click the **Templates** button to start a new document using a template.

Figure 19: LibreOffice Start Center

From the Quickstarter

When LibreOffice is installed on computers running Windows or Linux, a Quickstarter feature may also be installed. Computers with a Mac operating system do not have a Quickstarter.

The Quickstarter is an icon that is placed in the system tray during system startup. It indicates that LibreOffice has been loaded and is ready to use. The Quickstarter must be enabled in **Tools > Options > LibreOffice > Memory** by selecting the checkbox.

Right-click the **Quickstarter** icon (Figure 20) in the system tray to open a pop-up menu from which you can create a new document, or open the **Template Manager** dialog. You can also double-click the **Quickstarter** icon to display the **Template Manager** dialog.

See Chapter 1, *Introducing LibreOffice*, in the *Getting Started* guide for more information about starting Writer and using the Quickstarter.

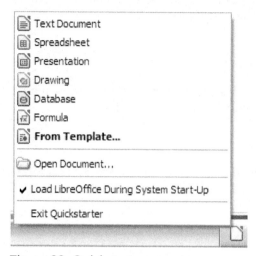

Figure 20: Quickstarter pop-up menu

From the operating system menu

You can open the LibreOffice Start Center or the Writer component from the operating system menu in the same way that you start other programs. When LibreOffice was installed on your computer, in most cases a menu entry for each component was added to your system menu. If you are using a Mac, you should see the LibreOffice icon in the Applications folder. When you double-click this icon, LibreOffice opens at the Start Center (Figure 19).

From the menu bar, toolbar, or keyboard

When LibreOffice is open, you can also start a new document in one of the following ways.

- Press the *Ctrl+N* keys.
- Use **File > New > Text Document**.
- Click the **New** button on the Standard Toolbar.

From a template

You can use templates to create new documents in Writer. A template is a set of predefined styles and formatting. Templates serve as the foundation of a set of documents, to make sure they all have a similar layout. For example, all the documents of the *Writer Guide* are based on the same template. As a result, all the documents look alike; they have the same headers and footers, use the same fonts, and so on.

A new LibreOffice installation does not contain many templates. It is possible for you to add new templates to your installation and use them for new documents. This is explained in Chapter 10, *Working with Templates*. More templates can be downloaded from http://templates.libreoffice.org/ and other websites.

Once you have templates on your system, you can create new documents based on them by using **File > Templates > Manage** (*Ctrl+Shift+N*), **File > New > Templates** or click the arrow button next to the New Document button on the Standard Toolbar and select **Templates** from the drop-down list. This opens the Template Manager dialog where you can choose the template you want to use for your document.

The example shown in Figure 21 uses a template in the **Documents > My Templates** folder. Double-click on the required template. A new document is created based on the styles and formats defined in the template.

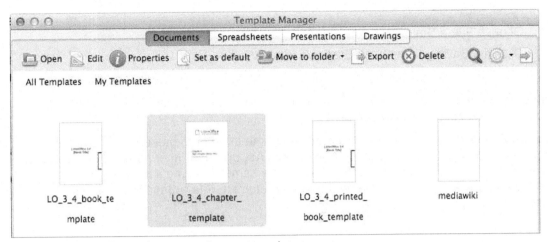

Figure 21: Creating a document from a template

Opening an existing document

When no document is open, the **Start Center** (Figure 19) provides an **Open File** button for navigating to saved files. It also displays, in the right pane, recently opened documents; click one to open it.

You can also open an existing document in one of the following ways. If a document is already open in LibreOffice, the second document opens in a new window.

- Choose **File > Open**.
- Click the **Open** button on the Standard Toolbar.
- Click the down-arrow on the **Open** button on the Standard Toolbar to select a recent document.
- Press *Ctrl+O* on the keyboard.
- Use **File > Recent Documents** to make a selection.
- Use **Open Document** on the Quickstarter.

Except for the selection of recent documents, the actions above launch the **Open** dialog. Select the file you want, filtering by version if required and available, and then click **Open**. If a document is already open in LibreOffice, the second document opens in a new window.

In the Open dialog, you can reduce the list of files by selecting the type of file you are looking for. For example, if you choose **Text documents** as the file type, you will only see documents Writer can open (including ODT, DOC, TXT). This method opens Word (DOC and DOCX) files as well as LibreOffice files and other formats.

You can also open an existing Writer document using the same methods you would use to open any document in your operating system.

If you have associated Microsoft Office file formats with LibreOffice, you can also open these files by double-clicking on them.

Saving a document

To save a new document in Writer, do one of the following:

- Press *Ctrl+S*.
- Choose **File > Save.**
- Click the **Save** button on the Standard Toolbar.

When the Save As dialog appears, enter the file name, verify the file type, and click **Save**.

To save an opened document with the current file name, select one of the above options. This will overwrite the last saved state of the file.

To save an opened document with a different file name in order to preserve the original and have edits saved in another version, choose **File > Save As,** give it another name and/or select a different file type. A document can be saved with the same file name if the file type is changed, but must have a different name if the same file type is retained. **File > Save a Copy** behaves in a similar fashion.

Saving a document automatically

You can choose to have Writer save your document automatically in a temporary file at regular intervals. Automatic saving, like manual saving, overwrites the last saved state of the target file in the temporary file. To set up automatic file saving:

8) Select **Tools > Options > Load/Save > General**.
9) Click on **Save AutoRecovery information every** and set the time interval. The default value is 15 minutes. Enter the value you want by typing it or by pressing the up or down arrow keys.

Saving as a Microsoft Word document

If you need to exchange files with users of Microsoft Word who are unwilling or unable to receive Open Document Format (ODF) files, you can save a document as a Microsoft Word file.

1) **Important**—First save your document in the file format used by LibreOffice Writer, ODT. If you do not, any changes you made since the last time you saved will only appear in the Microsoft Word version of the document.
2) Then click **File > Save As**.
3) On the Save As dialog, in the **File type** (or **Save as type**) drop-down menu, select the type of Word format you need. You may also choose to change the file name.
4) Click **Save**.

From this point on, *all changes you make to the document will occur only in the new (Microsoft Word) document*. You have changed the name and file type of your document. If you want to go back to working with the ODT version of your document, you must open it again.

Tip	To have Writer save documents by default in the Microsoft Word file format, go to **Tools > Options > Load/Save > General**. In the section named *Default file format and ODF settings*, under **Document type**, select **Text document,** then under *Always save as*, select your preferred file format.

Caution

It is recommended that if you use a Microsoft Word format, you use the DOC and not the DOCX (XML) format. There is anecdotal evidence that the DOCX format experiences problems even within native Microsoft applications. Saving in ODF format gives you the option to redo the document if the recipient of your document experiences trouble with the Microsoft format.

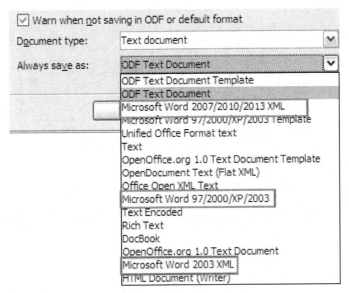

Figure 22: Saving a file in Microsoft Word format

Password protection

Writer provides two levels of document protection: read-protect (file cannot be viewed without a password) and write-protect (file can be viewed in read-only mode but cannot be changed without a password). Thus you can make the content available for reading by a selected group of people and for reading and editing by a different group. This behavior is compatible with Microsoft Word file protection.

1) Use **File > Save As** when saving the document. (You can also use **File > Save** the first time you save a new document.)

2) On the Save As dialog, select the **Save with password** option, and then click **Save**.

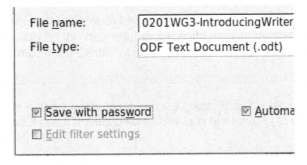

3) The Set Password dialog opens.

Figure 23: Two levels of password protection

Here you have several choices:

- To read-protect the document, type a password in the two fields at the top of the dialog.

- To write-protect the document, click the **More Options** button and select the **Open file read-only** checkbox.

- To write-protect the document but allow selected people to edit it, select the **Open file read-only** checkbox and type a password in the two boxes at the bottom of the dialog.

4) Click **OK** to save the file. If either pair of passwords do not match, you receive an error message. Close the message box to return to the Set Password dialog and enter the password again.

In LibreOffice 3.5, a different encryption was introduced to replace the previously used one. In consequence, files encrypted with LibreOffice 3.5 or later can not be opened by earlier versions of LibreOffice. Files with the old encryption can be used in LibreOffice 3.5 and later.

Caution	LibreOffice uses a very strong encryption mechanism that makes it almost impossible to recover the contents of a document if you lose the password.

Changing the password for a document

When a document is password-protected, you can change the password while the document is open. Choose **File > Properties > General** and click the **Change Password** button.

Closing a document

If only one document is open and you want to close that document, go to **File** > **Close** on the Menu bar or click on the X on the Title bar. The X may be located on either the right or left end of the Title bar.

If more than one document is open and you want to close one of them, go to **File** > **Close** on the Menu bar or click on the X on the Menu bar of that document's window. When only the last document is open, the X on the Menu bar disappears.

If the document has not been saved since the last change, a message box is displayed. Choose whether to save or discard your changes.

Closing LibreOffice

To close LibreOffice completely, go to **File** > **Exit** on the menu bar in Windows and Linux operating systems. In a Mac operating system, go to **LibreOffice** > **Quit LibreOffice** on the menu bar.

When you close the last document using the X on the Title bar of the window, then LibreOffice will close completely. A Mac operating system does not have this function; instead, you need to go to **LibreOffice** > **Quit LibreOffice** on the menu bar.

You can also use a keyboard shortcut as follows:

- In Windows and Linux – *Ctrl+Q*
- In Mac OS X – *Command ⌘+Q*

If any documents have not been saved since the last change, a message box is displayed. Choose whether to save or discard your changes.

Using the Navigator

In addition to the Page Number field on the Status bar (described on page 23), Writer provides other ways to move quickly through a document and find specific items by using the many features of the **Navigator**, the Navigation toolbar, and related buttons.

The **Navigator** lists all of the headings, tables, text frames, graphics, bookmarks, and other objects contained in a document.

To open the **Navigator** do one of the following;

- Click its button ( ) on the Standard Toolbar.
- Press *F5.*
- Choose **View > Navigator** on the Menu bar.
- Double-click on the Page number field on the status bar.
- Click the Navigator tab ( ) on the Sidebar (**View > Sidebar** to open it).

You can dock the **Navigator** to either side of the main Writer window or leave it floating, even from the Sidebar, (see "Docking/floating windows and toolbars" on page 20).

To hide the list of categories and show only the buttons at the top, click the **List Box On/Off** button ( ). Click this button again to show the list. The Sidebar Navigator does not have this button.

Click the + sign or triangle by any of the lists to display the contents of the list.

Table 2 summarizes the functions of the buttons at the top of the **Navigator**.

Note	The **Navigator** has different functions in a master document. See Chapter 13, *Working with Master Documents*.

Figure 24: The Navigator

Table 2: Function of buttons in the Navigator

	Toggle: Not active in ordinary documents (left image). In a master document (right image), switches between the master document file and its subdocuments.
	Navigation: Opens the Navigation toolbar (see page 37).
	Previous, Next: Jumps to the previous or next item in the selected category (page, graphic, hyperlink, comment, and so on). To select the category of items, see "Using the Navigation toolbar" on page 37.
	Page number: Jumps to the page sequence number showing in the box. Type the required page number or select it using the up and down arrows.
	Drag Mode: Select Hyperlink, Link, or Copy. See "Choosing drag mode" on page 39 for details.
	List Box On/Off: Shows or hides the list of categories. (Not Sidebar).
	Content View: Switches between showing all categories and showing only the selected category.
	Set Reminder: Inserts a reminder (see page 39).
	Header/Footer: Jumps between the text area and the header or footer area (if the page has them).
	Anchor <–> Text: Jumps between a footnote anchor and the corresponding footnote text.
	Heading Levels Shown: Choose the number of heading levels to be shown.

Moving quickly through a document

The Navigator provides several convenient ways to move around a document and find items in it:

- To jump to a specific page in the document, type its *sequence* number in the box at the top of the **Navigator** and press *Enter*. The sequence number may be different from the page number if you have restarted numbering at any point.

- When a category is showing the list of items in it, double-click on an item to jump directly to that item's location in the document. For example, you can jump directly to a selected heading, graphic, or comment by using this method.

    To see the content in only one category, highlight that category and click the **Content View** button. Click the button again to display all the categories. You can also change the number of heading levels shown when viewing Headings.

- Use the **Previous** and **Next** buttons to jump to other objects of the type selected in the **Navigation** toolbar. (See next page for details.)

Note	A hidden section (or other hidden object) in a document appears gray in the **Navigator**, and displays the word "hidden" as a tooltip. For more about hidden sections, see Chapter 4, Formatting Pages.

Tip	Objects are much easier to find if you have given them names when creating them, instead of keeping LibreOffice's default names of graphics1, graphics2, Table1, Table2, and so on—which may not correspond to the position of the object in the document. To rename an image, right-click on the image, select **Picture > Options**, and then edit the name in the dialog. Similarly, to rename a table, right-click on the table, select **Table > Table**, and then edit the name.

Using the Navigation toolbar

To display the **Navigation** toolbar (Figure 25), click the **Navigation** button (⊙ ▾) (second button from the left at the top of the **Navigator**, Figure 24) or the small **Navigation** button near the lower right-hand corner of the document window below the vertical scroll bar (Figure 26).

Figure 25: Navigation toolbar

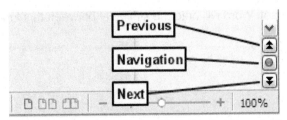

Figure 26: Previous, Navigation, and Next buttons

The Navigation toolbar has buttons for all the object types shown in the Navigator, plus some extras (for example, the results of a **Find** command).

Click a button to select that object type. Now all the **Previous** and **Next** buttons (in the **Navigator** itself, in the **Navigation** toolbar, and on the scroll bar) will jump to the previous or next object of the selected type. This is particularly helpful for finding items like index entries, which can be difficult to see in the text. The names of the buttons (shown in the tooltips) change to match the selected category; for example, **Next Graphic**, **Next Bookmark**, or **Continue search forward**.

Rearranging chapters using the Navigator

You can rearrange chapters and move headings in the document by using the **Navigator**.
1) Click the **Content View** button to expand the headings, if necessary.
2) (Optional) If you have several subheading levels, you can more easily find the headings you want, by changing the Heading Levels Shown selection to show only 1 or 2 levels of headings.
3) Click on the heading of the block of text that you want to move and drag the heading to a new location on the **Navigator**, or click the heading in the **Navigator** list, and then click either the **Promote Chapter** or **Demote Chapter** button. All of the text and subsections under the selected heading move with it.

To move only the selected heading and not the text associated with the heading, hold down *Ctrl*, and then click the **Promote** or **Demote** button.

Tip	The tooltips **Promote Chapter** and **Demote Chapter** can be misleading; all headings—whether at Level 1 (chapter) or lower—can be rearranged using this function; and the feature might be better described as Move Up or Move Down (within the document, without changing the heading level) to distinguish it more clearly from **Promote Level** and **Demote Level**, which change the heading level within the document (see below).

4) To quickly change the outline level of a heading and its associated subheadings, select the heading in the **Navigator**, and then click either the **Promote Level** or **Demote Level** button. This action does not change the location of the heading, only its level.

To increase the outline level of only the selected heading, but not its associated subheadings, hold down *Ctrl*, and then click the button.

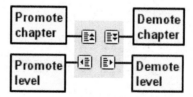

Figure 27: Reorganizing with the Navigator

Note	Users of Microsoft Word will note the similarity between this functionality and Word's Outline View.

Setting reminders

One of the little-known features of Writer that you may find quite useful is the possibility of jumping between reminders. *Reminders* let you mark places in your document that you want to return to later on, to add or correct information, make some other change, or simply mark where you finished editing. The possible uses of reminders are limited only by your imagination.

To set a reminder at the cursor's current location, click on the (📖) button in the Navigator. You can set up to 5 reminders in a document; setting a sixth causes the first to be deleted.

Reminders are not highlighted in any way in the document, so you cannot see where they are, except when you jump from one to the next—the location of the cursor then shows the location of the reminder.

To jump between reminders, first select the **Reminder** button on the **Navigation** toolbar. Then click the **Previous** and **Next** buttons. Reminders are not saved with the document.

Choosing drag mode

To select the drag and drop options for inserting items such as other documents and images, into a document using the **Navigator**, choose one of the following from the drop-down menu of the **Drag Mode** button.

Insert As Hyperlink
> Creates a hyperlink when you drag and drop an item into the current document.

Insert As Link
> Inserts the selected item as a link where you drag and drop in the current document. Text is inserted as protected sections. However, you cannot create links for graphics, OLE objects, references, or indexes using this method.

Insert As Copy
> Inserts a copy of the selected item where you drag and drop in the current document. You cannot drag and drop copies of graphics, OLE objects, or indexes.

Undoing and redoing changes

When a document is open, you can undo the most recent change by pressing *Ctrl+Z,* or clicking the **Undo** button (↩ ▾) on the Standard Toolbar, or choosing **Edit > Undo** from the Menu bar.

The **Edit** menu shows the latest changes that can be undone.

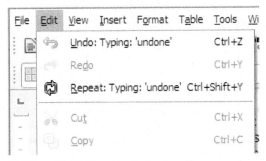

Figure 28: Edit > Undo last action

Click the down arrow button of the **Undo** combination button to get a list of all the changes that can be undone. You can select multiple changes and undo them at the same time (see Figure 29).

Figure 29: List of actions that can be undone

After changes have been undone, **Redo** becomes active. To redo a change, select **Edit > Redo**, or press *Ctrl+Y* or click on the **Redo** button ( ). As with **Undo**, click on the down arrow button of the combination button to get a list of the changes that can be restored.

Chapter 2
Setting up Writer

Choosing options to suit the way you work

Choosing options that affect all LibreOffice components

This section covers some of the settings that apply to all the components of LibreOffice and are particularly important when using Writer. Other general options are discussed in Chapter 2, Setting up LibreOffice, in the *Getting Started* guide.

Click **Tools > Options**. The list on the left-hand side of the Options – LibreOffice dialog varies depending on which component of LibreOffice is open. The illustrations in this chapter show the list as it appears when a Writer document is open.

Click the marker (+ or triangle) by **LibreOffice** on the left-hand side. A list of pages drops down. Selecting an item in the list causes the right-hand side of the dialog to display the relevant page.

Note	The **Revert** button (located in the lower right of the full Options dialog) has the same effect on all pages of the dialog. It resets options to the values that were in place when you opened the dialog.

If you are using a version of LibreOffice other than US English, some field labels may be different from those shown in the illustrations.

User Data options

Because Writer can use the name or initials stored in the **LibreOffice – User Data** page for several things, including document properties (created by and last edited by information) and the name of the author of comments and changes, you will want to ensure that the correct information appears here.

Fill in the form (not shown here) or amend or delete any existing incorrect information. If you do not want user data to be part of the document's properties, clear the box at the bottom.

General options

The options on the **LibreOffice – General** page are described below.

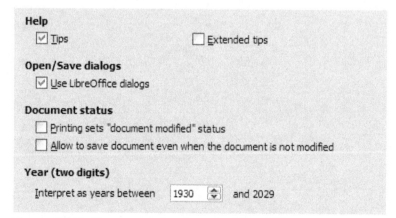

Figure 30: Setting general options for LibreOffice

Help – Tips

When **Tips** is active, one or two words will appear when you hold the mouse pointer over an icon or field, without clicking.

Help – Extended tips

When **Extended tips** is active, a brief description of the function of a particular icon or menu command or a field on a dialog appears when you hold the mouse pointer over that item.

Open/Save dialogs – Use LibreOffice dialogs

To use the standard Open and Save dialogs for your operating system, deselect the **Use LibreOffice dialogs** option. When this option is selected, the Open and Save dialogs supplied with LibreOffice will be used. See Chapter 1, *Introducing Writer*, for more about the LibreOffice Open and Save dialogs. This book uses the LibreOffice Open and Save dialogs in illustrations.

Document status – Printing sets "document modified" status

If this option is selected, then the next time you close the document after printing, the print date is recorded in the document properties as a change and you will be prompted to save the document again, even if you did not make any other changes.

Document status – Allow to save document even when the document is not modified

Normally when a document has not been modified, the **File > Save** menu option and the **Save** button on the Standard Toolbar are disabled and the keyboard shortcut *Ctrl+S* has no effect. Select this option to allow documents to be saved even when they have not been modified.

Year (two digits)

Specifies how two-digit years are interpreted. For example, if the two-digit year is set to 1930, and you enter a date of 1/1/30 or later into your document, the date is interpreted as 1/1/1930 or later. An "earlier" date is interpreted as being in the following century; that is, 1/1/20 is interpreted as 1/1/2020.

Memory options

The options on the **LibreOffice – Memory** page control how LibreOffice uses your computer's memory and how much memory it requires.

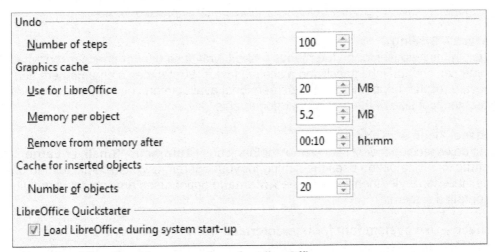

Figure 31: Choosing Memory options for LibreOffice

Before changing these options, you may wish to consider the following points:

- More memory can make LibreOffice faster and more convenient (for example, more undo steps require more memory); but the trade-off is less memory available for other applications and you could run out of memory altogether.

- If your documents contain a lot of objects such as images, or the objects are large, LibreOffice's performance may improve if you increase the memory for LibreOffice or the memory per object. If you find that objects seem to disappear from a document that contains a lot of them, increase the number of objects in the cache. (The objects are still in the file even if you cannot see them on screen.)

- To load the Quickstarter when you start your computer, select the option near the bottom of the dialog. This makes LibreOffice start faster; the trade-off is that LibreOffice uses some memory even when not being used. This option (called **Enable systray Quickstarter** on Linux) is not available on Mac OS X or on systems where the Quickstarter module has not been installed.

View options

The options on the **LibreOffice – View** page affect the way the document window looks and behaves. Some of these options are described below. Set them to suit your personal preferences.

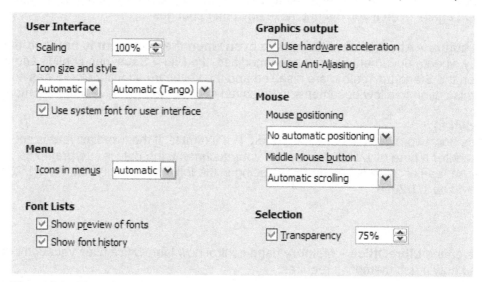

Figure 32: Choosing View options for LibreOffice applications

User Interface – Scaling
 If the text in the help files or on the menus of the LibreOffice user interface is too small or too large, you can change it by specifying a scaling factor. Sometimes a change here can have unexpected results, depending on the screen fonts available on your system. However, it does not affect the font size of the text in your documents.

User Interface – Icon size and style
 The first box specifies the display size of toolbar icons (**Automatic**, **Small**, or **Large**); the **Automatic** icon size option uses the setting for your operating system. The second box specifies the icon style (theme); here the **Automatic** option uses an icon set compatible with your operating system.

User Interface – Use system font for user interface
 If you prefer to use the system font (the default font for your computer and operating system) instead of the font provided by LibreOffice for the user interface, select this option.

User interface – Screen font Anti-Aliasing
 (Not available in Windows; not shown in Figure 32.) Smooths the screen appearance of text. Enter the smallest font size to apply anti-aliasing.

Menu – Icons in menus
 Causes icons as well as words to be visible in menus. Choice of **Automatic**, **Hide** or **Show**.

Font Lists – Show preview of fonts

Causes the font list to look like Figure 33, Left, with the font names shown as an example of the font. With the option deselected, the font list shows only the font names, not their formatting (Figure 33, Right). The fonts you will see listed are those that are installed on your system.

Fonts which are tuned for use with a specific script, such as Arabic, Hebrew, Malayalam, and so on, now show an additional preview of some sample text in the target script.

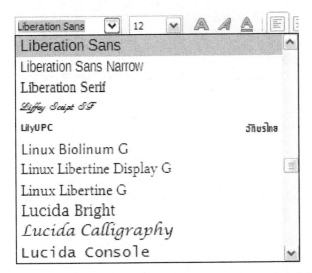 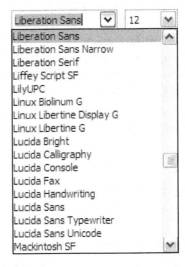

Figure 33: Font list (Left) showing preview; (Right) without preview

Font Lists – Show font history

Causes the last five fonts you have assigned to the current document to be displayed at the top of the font list.

Graphics output – Use hardware acceleration

Directly accesses hardware features of the graphical display adapter to improve the screen display. Not supported on all operating systems and LibreOffice distributions.

Graphics output – Use Anti-Aliasing

Enables and disables anti-aliasing, which makes the display of most graphical objects look smoother and with fewer artifacts. Not supported on all operating systems and LibreOffice distributions.

Tip	Press *Shift+Ctrl+R* to restore or refresh the view of the current document after changing the anti-aliasing settings, to see the effect.

Mouse positioning

Specifies if and how the mouse pointer will be positioned in newly opened dialogs.

Middle mouse button

Defines the function of the middle mouse button.

- **Automatic scrolling** – dragging while pressing the middle mouse button shifts the view.
- **Paste clipboard** – pressing the middle mouse button inserts the contents of the "Selection clipboard" at the cursor position.

The "Selection clipboard" is independent of the normal clipboard that you use by **Edit > Copy/Cut/Paste** or their respective keyboard shortcuts. Clipboard and "Selection clipboard" can contain different contents at the same time.

Function	Clipboard	Selection clipboard
Copy content	**Edit > Copy** or *Ctrl+C*	Select text, table, or object.
Paste content	**Edit > Paste** or *Ctrl+V* pastes at the cursor position.	Clicking the middle mouse button pastes at the mouse pointer position.
Pasting into another document	No effect on the clipboard contents.	The last marked selection is the content of the selection clipboard.

Selection – Transparency

Determines the appearance of selected text or graphics, which appear on a shaded background. To make the shaded background more or less dark, increase or decrease the Transparency setting.

If you prefer selected material to appear in reversed color (typically white text on a black background), deselect this option.

Print options

On the **LibreOffice – Print** page, set the print options to suit your default printer and your most common printing method.

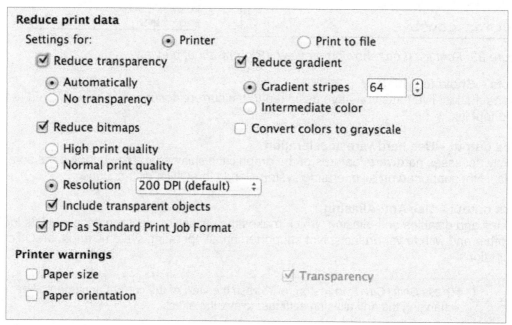

Figure 34: Choosing general printing options to apply to all LibreOffice components

The option **PDF as Standard Print Job Format** is not available on Windows. Select this option to change the internal print job format from a Postscript document description to a PDF description. This format has a number of advantages over Postscript. For more information, see http://www.linuxfoundation.org/collaborate/workgroups/openprinting/pdf_as_standard_print_job_format

Deselecting this option reverts to the Postscript document workflow system.

In the *Printer warnings* section near the bottom of the page, you can choose whether to be warned if the paper size or orientation specified in your document does not match the paper size or orientation available for your printer. Having these warnings turned on can be quite helpful, particularly if you work with documents produced by people in other countries where the standard paper size is different from yours.

Tip	If your printouts are incorrectly placed on the page or chopped off at the top, bottom, or sides or the printer is refusing to print, the most likely cause is page-size incompatibility.

Paths options

On the **LibreOffice – Paths** page, you can change the location of files associated with, or used by, LibreOffice to suit your working situation. In a Windows system, for example, you might want to store documents by default somewhere other than My Documents.

To make changes, select an item in the list shown in Figure 35 and click **Edit**. On the Select Paths dialog (not shown), add or delete folders as required, and then click **OK** to return to the Options dialog. Note that many items can have at least two paths listed: one to a shared folder (which might be on a network) and one to a user-specific folder (normally on the user's personal computer). Items with more than one path allowed will use an Edit Paths dialog (not shown).

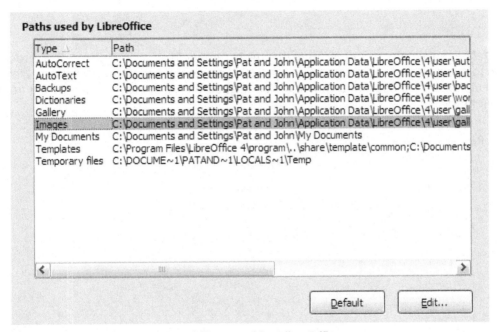

Figure 35: Viewing the paths of files used by LibreOffice

Tip	You can use the entries in the **LibreOffice – Paths** dialog to compile a list of files, such as those containing AutoText, that you need to back up or copy to another computer.

Colors options

On the **LibreOffice – Colors** page, you can specify colors to use in LibreOffice documents. You can select a color from a color table or selection list, edit an existing color, or define new colors. These colors will then be available in color selection lists in LibreOffice.

For details on how to modify a color or create a new color, see Chapter 14, Customizing LibreOffice, in the *Getting Started* guide.

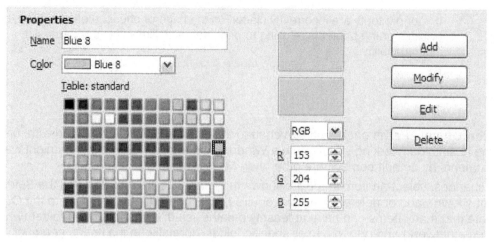

Figure 36: Defining colors to use in color lists in LibreOffice

Fonts options

You can define replacements for any fonts that might appear in your documents. If you receive from someone else a document containing fonts that you do not have on your system, LibreOffice will substitute fonts for those it does not find. You might prefer to specify a different font from the one the program chooses.

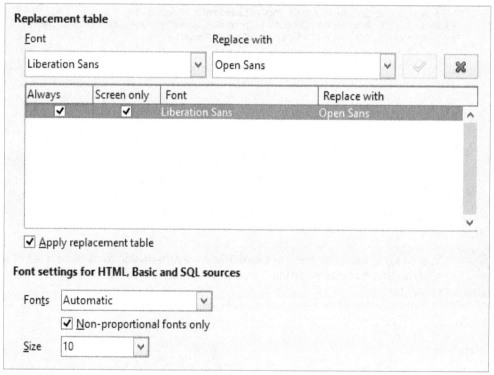

Figure 37: Defining a font to be substituted for another font

On the **LibreOffice – Fonts** page:

1) Select **Apply Replacement Table** option.
2) Select or type the name of the font to be replaced in the **Font** box. (If you do not have this font on your system, it will not appear in the drop-down list in this box, so you need to type it in.)

3) In the **Replace with** box, select a suitable font from the drop-down list of fonts installed on your computer.

4) The check mark to the right of the **Replace with** box turns green. Click on this check mark. A row of information now appears in the larger box below the input boxes. Select **Always** to replace the font, even if the original font is installed on your system. Select **Screen only** to replace the screen font only and never replace the font for printing. The results of combining these selections are given in Table 3. A listing in the display pane can be removed by selecting it and clicking the red cross.

5) In the bottom section of the page, you can change the typeface and size of the font used to display source code such as HTML and Basic (in macros).

Table 3: Font substitution replacement actions

Always checkbox	Screen only checkbox	Replacement action
checked	blank	Font replacement on screen and when printing, whether the font is installed or not.
checked	checked	Font replacement only on screen, whether the font is installed or not.
blank	checked	Font replacement only on screen, but only if font is not available.
blank	blank	Font replacement on screen and when printing, but only if font is not available.

Security options

Use the **LibreOffice – Security** page to choose security options for documents containing hidden information and for opening documents that contain macros.

Figure 38: Choosing security options for opening and saving documents

Security Options and warnings

If you record changes, save multiple versions, or include hidden information or notes in your documents, and you do not want some of the recipients to see that information, you can set warnings to remind you to remove it, or you can have LibreOffice remove some of it automatically. Note that (unless removed) much of this information is retained in a file whether the file is in LibreOffice's default Open Document format, or has been saved to other formats, including PDF.

Click the **Options** button to open a separate dialog with specific choices (Figure 39).

Passwords for web connections

You can enter a master password to enable easy access to websites that require a user name and password. If you select the **Persistently save passwords for web connections** option, a new dialog opens where you can specify the password. LibreOffice will securely store all passwords that you use to access files from web servers. You can retrieve the passwords from the list after you enter the master password.

Macro security

Click the **Macro Security** button to open the **Macro Security** dialog, where you can adjust the security level for executing macros and specify trusted sources.

Certificate Path

Note	This option appears only on Linux and Mac systems. On Windows, LibreOffice uses the default Windows location for storing and retrieving certificates.

Users can digitally sign documents using LibreOffice. A digital signature requires a personal signing certificate. Most operating systems can generate a self-signed certificate. However, a personal certificate issued by an outside agency (after verifying an individual's identity) has a higher degree of trust associated with it than does a self-signed certificate. LibreOffice does not provide a secure method of storing these certificates, but it can access certificates that have been saved using other programs. Click **Certificate** and select which certificate store to use.

Security options and warnings

The following options are on the **Security options and warnings** dialog (Figure 39).

Remove personal information on saving

Select this option to always remove user data from the file properties when saving the file. To manually remove personal information from specific documents, deselect this option.

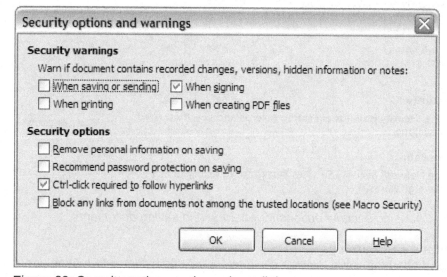

Figure 39: Security options and warnings dialog

Ctrl-click required to follow hyperlinks

The default behavior in LibreOffice is to *Ctrl+click* on a hyperlink to open the linked document. Many people find creation and editing of documents easier when accidental clicks on links do not activate the links. To set LibreOffice to activate hyperlinks using an ordinary click, deselect this option.

The other options on this dialog should be self-explanatory.

Personalization

Using Personalization, you can add a theme to your LibreOffice installation. Choices on this page are to not use a Theme, use a pre-installed Theme if one is available, select a Theme from the Mozilla Firefox site, or add your own design. This option defaults to **Pre-installed Theme** at installation time.

Figure 40: Personalization options

To install a Theme, click the **Select Theme** button to open the install dialog (Figure 41). From here you can enter an address (URL) to the theme or click the **Visit Firefox Themes** button. An internet connection is required for this process. Installation instructions are on this dialog.

Figure 41: Theme installation dialog

Full details about Themes are on the website: https://addons.mozilla.org/en-US/firefox/themes/

Figure 42: An example of an installed theme

Appearance options

Writing, editing, and (especially) page layout are often easier when you can see the page margins (text boundaries), the boundaries of tables and sections, grid lines, and other features. In addition, you might prefer to use colors that are different from LibreOffice's defaults for such items as comment indicators or field shadings.

On the **LibreOffice – Appearance** page, you can specify which items are visible and the colors used to display various items.

- To show or hide items such as text boundaries, select or deselect the options next to the names of the items.

- To change the default colors for items, click the down-arrow in the *Color setting* column by the name of the item and select a color from the list box. Note that you can change the list of available colors as described in Chapter 14, Customizing LibreOffice, in the *Getting Started* guide.

- To save your color changes as a color scheme, click **Save…** and you will be prompted for a name.

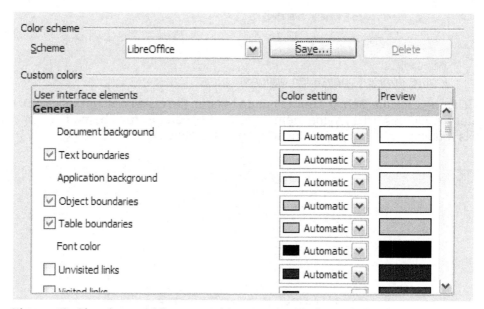

Figure 43: Showing or hiding text, object, and table boundaries

Accessibility options

Accessibility options include whether to allow animated graphics or text, how long help tips remain visible, some options for high contrast display, and a way to change the font for the user interface of the LibreOffice program.

Accessibility support relies on the Java Runtime Environment for communication with assistive technology tools. The *Support assistive technology tools* option is not shown on all LibreOffice installations. See *Assistive Tools in LibreOffice* in the Help for other requirements and information.

Select or deselect the options as required.

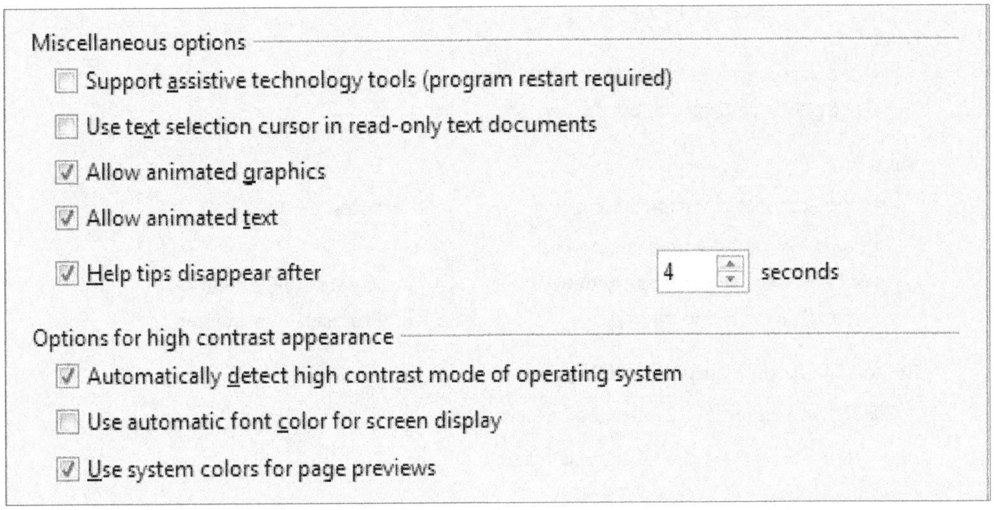

Figure 44: Choosing accessibility options

Advanced options

Java options

If you install or update a Java Runtime Environment (JRE) after you install LibreOffice, or if you have more than one JRE installed on your computer, you can use the *LibreOffice – Advanced options* page to choose the JRE for LibreOffice to use.

Optional (unstable) options

Enable experimental features

Selecting this option enables features that are not yet complete or contain known bugs. The list of these features is different version by version.

Enable macro recording (limited)

This option enables macro recording, with some limitations. Opening a window, switching between windows, and recording in a different window to that in which the recording began, is not supported. Only actions relating to document contents are recordable, so changes in Options or customizing menus are not supported.

Expert Configuration button

Permits detailed changes to the LibreOffice configuration. Most users will have no need to use this.

Choosing options for loading and saving documents

You can set the Load/Save options to suit the way you work.

If the Options dialog is not already open, click **Tools > Options**. Click the marker (+ or triangle) to the left of **Load/Save**.

General

Most of the choices on the **Load/Save – General** page are familiar to users of other office suites. Some items of interest are described below.

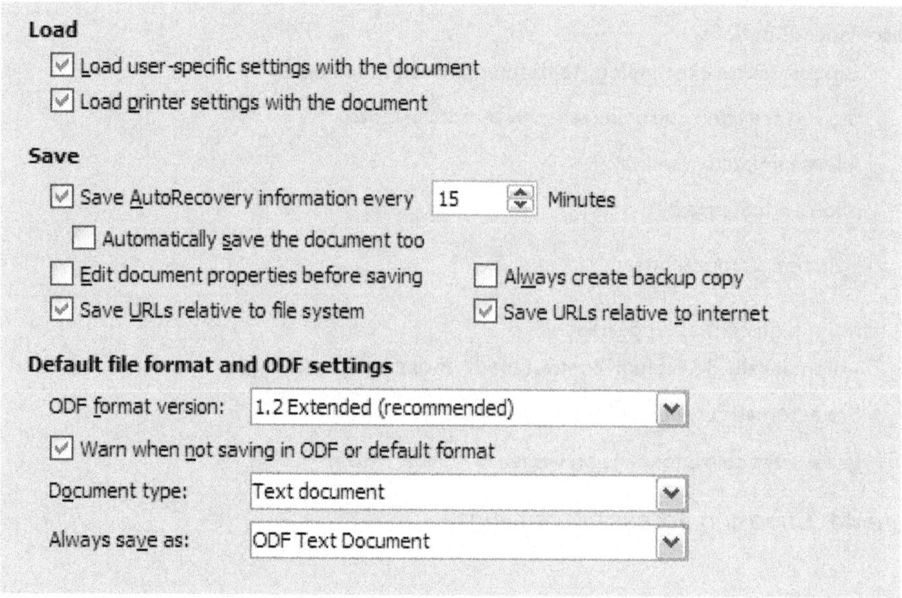

Figure 45: Choosing Load and Save options

Load user-specific settings with the document

A LibreOffice document contains certain settings which are read from the user's system. When you save a document, these settings are saved with it.

Select this option so that when a document loads, it ignores the stored settings in favor of the settings on your computer.

Even if you do not select this option, some settings are taken from your LibreOffice installation:

- Settings available in **File > Print > Options**
- Name of Fax
- Spacing options for paragraphs before text tables
- Information about automatic updating for links, field functions and charts
- Information about working with Asian character formats.

The following settings are **always** loaded with a document, whether or not this option is marked:

- Data source linked to the document and its view.

If you deselect this option, the user's personal settings do not overrule the settings in the document. For example, your choice (in the options for LibreOffice Writer) of how to update links is affected by the **Load user-specific settings** option.

Load printer settings with the document

If enabled, the printer settings will be loaded with the document. This can cause a document to be printed on a distant printer (perhaps in an office setting), if you do not change the printer manually in the Print dialog. If disabled, your standard printer will be used to print this document. The current printer settings will be stored with the document whether or not this option is selected.

Save AutoRecovery information every ___ Minutes

Choose whether to enable AutoRecovery and how often to save the information used by the AutoRecovery process.

AutoRecovery in LibreOffice saves the information needed to restore all open documents in case of a crash. If you have this option set, recovering your document after a system crash will be easier.

Automatically save the document too
Specifies that LibreOffice saves all open documents when saving auto recovery information. Uses the same time interval as AutoRecovery does.

Edit document properties before saving
If this option is selected, the document's **Properties** dialog pops up to prompt you to enter relevant information the first time you save a new document (or whenever you use **Save As**).

Always create backup copy
Saves the previous version of a document as a backup copy whenever you save a document. Every time LibreOffice creates a backup copy, the previous backup copy is replaced. The backup copy gets the extension **BAK**. Authors whose work may be very lengthy should always consider using this option.

Save URLs relative to file system / to internet
Use these options to select the default for relative addressing of URLs in the file system and on the Internet. Relative addressing is only possible if the source document and the referenced document are both on the same drive.

A relative address always starts from the directory in which the current document is located. In contrast, absolute addressing always starts from a root directory. The following table demonstrates the difference in syntax between relative and absolute referencing:

Examples	File system	Internet
relative	../images/img.jpg	../images/img.jpg
absolute	file:///c/work/images/img.jpg	http://myserver.com/work/images/img.jpg

If you choose to save relatively, the references to embedded graphics or other objects in your document will be saved relative to the location in the file system. In this case, it does not matter where the referenced directory structure is recorded. The files will be found regardless of location, as long as the reference remains on the same drive or volume. This is important if you want to make the document available to other computers that may have a completely different directory structure, drive or volume names. It is also recommended to save relatively if you want to create a directory structure on an Internet server.

If you prefer absolute saving, all references to other files will also be defined as absolute, based on the respective drive, volume or root directory. The advantage is that the document containing the references can be moved to other directories or folders, and the references remain valid.

Default file format and ODF settings
ODF format version. LibreOffice by default saves documents in Open Document Format (ODF) version 1.2 Extended. While this allows for improved functionality, there may be backwards compatibility issues. When a file saved in ODF 1.2 is opened in an earlier version of LibreOffice (using ODF 1.0/1.1), some of the advanced features may be lost. Two notable examples are cross-references to headings and the formatting of numbered lists. If you plan to share documents with people who are still using older versions of LibreOffice, you may wish to save the document using ODF version 1.0/1.1, even though some information will be lost.

Document type: The default is **Text document**. If you routinely share documents with users of Microsoft Word, you might want to change the **Always save as** attribute for text documents to one of the Word formats. Current versions of Microsoft Word can open ODF files, so this may no longer be needed.

Caution	If you need to save in Microsoft Word format, it is good practice to save in LibreOffice (OpenDocument) format (**ODT**) first and then do a **Save As** from your finished document to a Microsoft Word format. For best results, save to the **DOC** and not the **DOCX** format. Saving first in **ODT** format gives you the option to redo the document if the recipient of your document experiences trouble with the Microsoft format.

VBA Properties

On the **Load/Save – VBA Properties** page, you can choose whether to keep any macros in Microsoft Office documents that are opened in LibreOffice. These macros are disabled in LibreOffice.

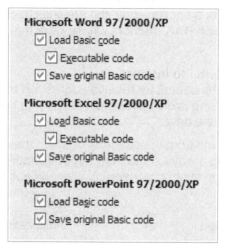

Figure 46: Choosing Load/Save VBA Properties

If you choose **Load Basic code**, you can edit the macros in LibreOffice. The changed code is saved in an LibreOffice document but is not retained if you save into a Microsoft Office format.

If you are importing a Microsoft Word or Excel file containing VBA code, you can select the option **Executable code**. Whereas normally the code is preserved but rendered inactive, with this option the code is ready to be executed.

If you choose **Save original Basic code**, the macros are retained unchanged if you save the file into Microsoft Office format.

Save original Basic code takes precedence over **Load Basic code**. If both options are selected and you edit the disabled code in LibreOffice, the original Microsoft Basic code will be saved when saving in a Microsoft Office format.

To remove any possible macro viruses from the Microsoft Office document, deselect **Save original Basic code**. The document will be saved without the Microsoft Basic code.

Microsoft Office

On the **Load/Save – Microsoft Office** page, you can choose what to do when importing and exporting Microsoft Office OLE objects (linked or embedded objects or documents such as spreadsheets or equations).

Select the [L] check boxes to convert Microsoft OLE objects into the corresponding LibreOffice OLE objects when a Microsoft document is loaded into LibreOffice (mnemonic: "L" for "load").

Select the [S] check boxes to convert LibreOffice OLE objects into the corresponding Microsoft OLE objects when a document is saved in a Microsoft format (mnemonic: "S" for "save").

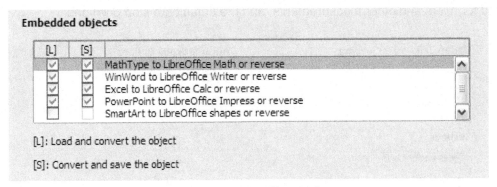

Figure 47: Choosing Load/Save Microsoft Office options

HTML compatibility

Choices made on the **Load/Save – HTML Compatibility** page (not shown) affect HTML pages imported into LibreOffice and those exported from LibreOffice. See *HTML documents; importing/exporting* in the Help, and the *Getting Started* book, for more information.

Choosing options for Writer

Settings chosen on the pages in the LibreOffice Writer section of the Options dialog determine how your Writer documents look and behave while you are working on them.

If the Options dialog is not already open, click **Tools > Options**.

Click the marker (+ or triangle) by LibreOffice Writer on the left-hand side of the dialog. A list of pages drops down (see Figure 48).

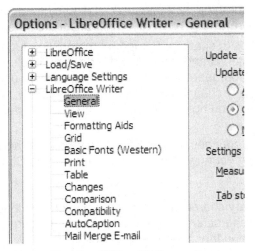

Figure 48: LibreOffice Writer options

The choices on the **LibreOffice Writer – General** page affect the updating of links and fields, the units used for rulers and other measurements, and the default tab stop positions.

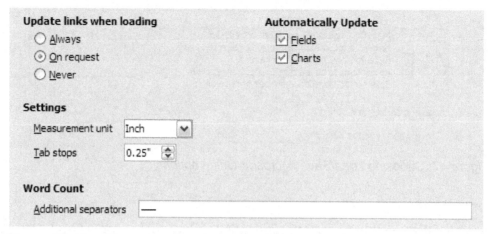

Figure 49: Choosing general options for Writer

Update links when loading
Depending on your work patterns, you may not want links to be updated when you load a document. For example, if your file links to other files on a network, you won't want those links to try to update when you are not connected to the network.

Update fields and charts automatically
You may not want fields or charts to update automatically when you are working, because that slows down performance.

Settings – Tab stops
The *Tab stops* setting specifies the distance the cursor travels for each press of the *Tab* key. This setting is also used for the indent distance applied by the **Increase Indent** and **Decrease Indent** buttons on the **Formatting Toolbar**, which affect the indentation of entire paragraphs.

Using the default tab stops to space out or indent material on a page is not recommended. If you use the default tab interval and then send the document to someone who uses a different default tab interval, then your tabbed material will be displayed using the other person's default tab settings. In addition, any changes to the default tab stops will change the existing default tab stops in any document you open afterward, as well as tab stops you insert after making the change.

To avoid these unwanted changes, define your own tabs in paragraph styles or individual paragraphs (see "Defining your own tab stops and indents" in Chapter 3, Working with Text).

Word Count
Allows extra word boundary characters. This feature overrides long dash (—) and short dash (–) to be word boundary characters for the purposes of counting words, and allows the user to specify additional word boundary characters

View options

Two pages of options set the defaults for viewing Writer documents: **View** (described here) and **Formatting Aids** (described below).

Enabling the Guides helps you to precisely position a drawing object on a page by providing horizontal and vertical parallel lines the height and width of the object, across the complete working area of the screen as the object is moved.

If the remaining items on the **LibreOffice Writer – View** page are not self-explanatory, you can easily test their effects in a blank document.

This is a good page to check if, for example, you cannot see graphics on the screen or you see field codes instead of the text or numbers you are expecting.

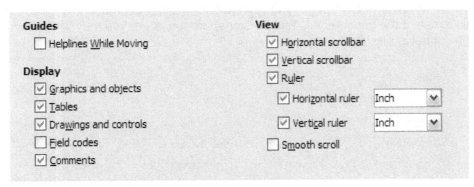

Figure 50: Choosing View options for Writer

Formatting Aids options

The display of symbols such as paragraph ends and tabs helps you when writing, editing, and doing page layout. For example, you might want to know if any blank paragraphs or tabs are included or if any tables or graphics are too wide and intrude into the margins of the page. Selections here determine which symbols show when you select the **Nonprinting Characters** button in the Standard Toolbar.

On the **LibreOffice Writer – Formatting Aids** page, select the required options.

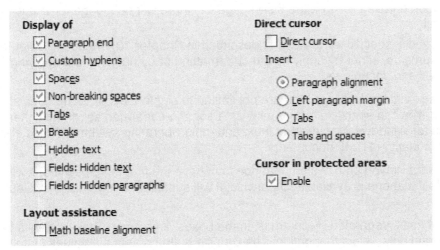

Figure 51: Choosing Formatting Aids options

Note	*Direct cursor* lets you enter text, images, tables, frames, and other objects in any blank area in your document. Writer inserts blank paragraphs and tabs to position the text or objects.
	This feature is incompatible with rigorous use of styles and can lead to many formatting oddities, so it should be avoided by professional writers.

Grid options

Specifying **snap to grid** can be very helpful when you are trying to align several objects such as graphics or tables.

On the **LibreOffice Writer – Grid** page, you can choose whether to enable this feature and what grid intervals to use. If the grid intervals (subdivisions) are too large, you may find that you do not have enough control in placing the objects.

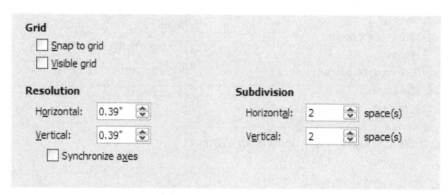

Figure 52: Choosing Grid options

Basic Fonts (Western) options

The default fonts specified on the **LibreOffice Writer – Basic Fonts (Western)** page (Figure 53) apply to both Writer documents and HTML (Web) documents. They define the basic fonts for the predefined templates. If you want to change the defaults, do so on this page. If you have Asian language support enabled (see Figure 61 on page 67) there will be a page for **Basic Fonts (Asian)** as well.

You can also modify specific templates (as described in Chapter 10) or choose other fonts for use in specific documents, either by applying direct formatting or by defining and applying styles in those templates and documents.

When choosing fonts on this page, you are not limited to single fonts or to the ones shown in the drop-down list. You can specify a "font family" as a comma-separated set of fonts that includes those suitable for Windows, Macintosh, Linux, and other operating systems. These choices are particularly important in HTML documents.

If the document is viewed on a system that does not have the first font specified, it will use one of the other fonts if that one is available. Otherwise, it will substitute a font that is available on the system.

Type the list of fonts, separated by commas, in the boxes. If you want these defaults to apply to the current document only, select that option. The **Default** button resets the values on this page to the defaults installed with LibreOffice.

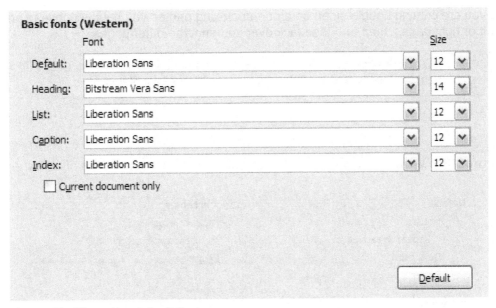

Figure 53: Choosing default fonts

Print options

On the **LibreOffice Writer – Print** page, you can choose which items are printed with the document by default. These options are in addition to those on the **LibreOffice – Print** page (Figure 37).

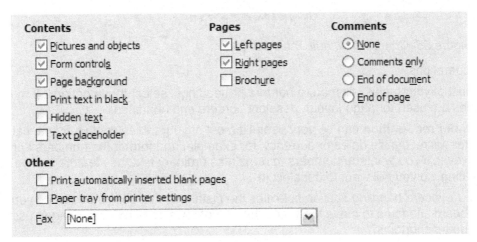

Figure 54: Choosing Print options for Writer

Some considerations:

- When you are working on drafts and you want to save printer ink or toner, you might want to deselect some of the items in the *Contents* section.

- The **Print text in black** selection causes color text (but not graphics) to print as black on a color printer; on a black-and-white printer, this option causes color text to print as solid black instead of shades of gray (dithered).

- The **Print text in black** option has a different effect than the **Convert colors to grayscale** option on the **Options – LibreOffice – Print** page (Figure 34), which prints all graphics as grayscale on color printers. (On black-and-white printers, color in graphics normally prints as grayscale.)

- If you are printing double-sided on a non-duplexing printer, you might choose to print only left or right pages, then turn the stack over and print the other pages.

Tip	You can override any of these defaults when printing a document. Click **File > Print**, then use the options on the various pages of the Print dialog.

Table options

On the **LibreOffice Writer – Table** page, you can specify the default behavior of tables.

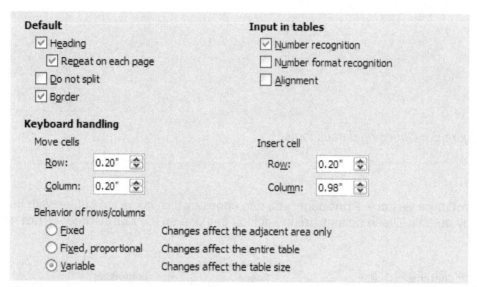

Figure 55: Choosing default Table options

Some considerations:

- If most of your tables will require borders or headings, select those options. If most of your tables are used for page layout, deselect borders and headings.

- **Number recognition** can be very useful if most of your tables contain numerical data; Writer will recognize dates or currency, for example, and format the numbers appropriately. However, if you want the numbers to remain as ordinary text, this feature can be quite irritating, so you will want to deselect it.

- The *Keyboard handling* section specifies the distances that cells move when you use keyboard shortcuts to move them and the size of rows and columns inserted using keyboard shortcuts.

- The choices in the *Behavior of rows/columns* section determine the effects that changes to rows or columns have on adjacent rows or columns and the entire table. You might need to test these selections to fully understand the effects.

Changes options

If you plan to use the change-tracking feature of Writer, use the **LibreOffice Writer – Changes** page to choose the way inserted and deleted material is marked, whether and how attribute changes are marked, and whether and how change bars are marked in the margins.

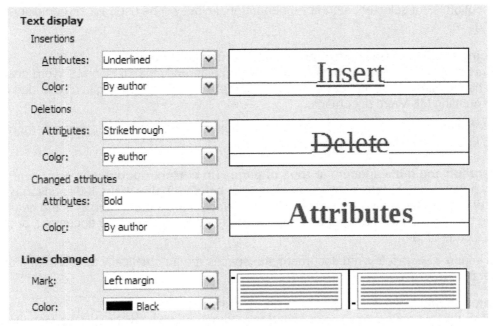

Figure 56: Choosing options for tracking changes

Compatibility options

Do you need to import Microsoft Word documents into LibreOffice Writer? If so, you might want to select some or all of the settings on the **LibreOffice Writer – Compatibility** page (Figure 57). If you are not sure about the effects of these settings, leave them as the defaults provided by LibreOffice. For information about the settings not described below, see the Help. All settings selected will apply to the current document.

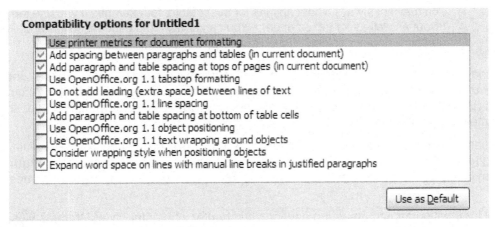

Figure 57: Choosing compatibility options

Use printer metrics for document formatting

If this option is selected, the printer specified for the document determines how the document is formatted for viewing on screen. The line breaks and paragraph breaks you see on screen match those that apply when the document is printed on that printer.

This setting can be useful when several people are reviewing a document that will eventually be printed on a specific printer or when the document is exported to PDF (a process that uses "Adobe PDF" as the printer).

If this option is not selected, a printer-independent layout will be used for screen display and printing.

Add spacing between paragraphs and tables (in current document)
In LibreOffice Writer, paragraph spacing is defined differently than it is in MS Word documents. If you have defined spacing between two paragraphs or tables, spacing is also added in the corresponding MS Word documents.

If this option is selected, Microsoft Word-compatible spacing is added between paragraphs and tables in LibreOffice Writer documents.

Add paragraph and table spacing at tops of pages (in current document)
You can define paragraphs to have space appear before (above) them. If this option is selected, any space above a paragraph will also appear if the paragraph is at the beginning of a page or column, if the paragraph is positioned on the first page of the document, or after a manual page break.

If you import a Microsoft Word document, the spaces are automatically added during the conversion.

Add paragraph and table spacing at bottom of table cells
Specifies that the bottom spacing is added to a paragraph, even when it is the last paragraph in a table cell.

Use as Default
Click this button to use the current settings on this page as the default in LibreOffice.

AutoCaption options

Do you want LibreOffice to automatically insert captions for tables, pictures, frames, and OLE objects that have been inserted in a Writer document?

Note	You may not always want captions for every table, for example, if you use tables for layout as well as for tables of data. You can always add captions to individual tables, graphics, or other objects (right-click > **Caption**).

If you do want automatic captions on one or more object types, use the options on the **LibreOffice Writer > AutoCaption** page. Enable the check box next to an object you want to be automatically captioned (**LibreOffice Writer Picture** in the example shown).With the item highlighted, specify the characteristics of the caption.

The supplied categories for captions are **Drawing**, **Illustration**, **Table**, and **Text**. However, you are not limited to the supplied categories. If you want to use another name (for example, **Figure**) for the caption label, type the required term in the box. In the example shown, **Figure** has been added to the list.

Additional information about numbering captions by chapter, character styles, frame styles, and other items on the **AutoCaption** page, is given in later chapters in the Writer Guide.

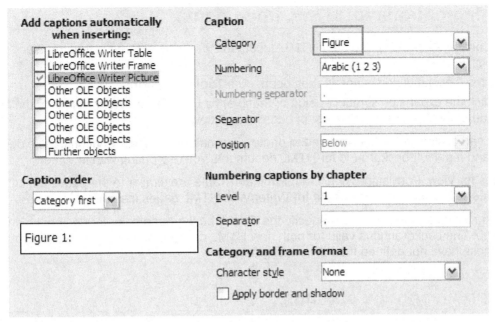

Figure 58: Setting up a new category for automatic captions on graphics

Mail Merge E-mail options

You can produce form letters using Writer and then use the mail merge function to personalize those letters and send them to a number of addresses taken from a data source, such as an address book. Mail merged documents can be printed and mailed, or sent by e-mail. (See Chapter 11, Using Mail Merge, for details.)

Use the **LibreOffice Writer – Mail Merge E-mail** page to set up the user and server information for sending form letters by e-mail. If you are not sure what information to put in any of the fields, consult your e-mail program or your Internet service provider.

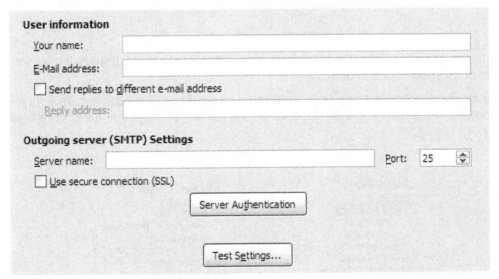

Figure 59: Specifying settings for use when e-mailing mail-merged form letters

Choosing options for HTML documents

You can configure LibreOffice to treat HTML documents in Writer differently than regular documents.

1) If the Options dialog is not already open, click **Tools > Options**.
2) Click the expansion symbol (+ sign or triangle) by **LibreOffice Writer/Web** on the left-hand side of the Options dialog. A list of pages drops down.

Here you can customize settings related to printing, formatting aids, view options, table defaults, the grid, and a default background for HTML documents you're working with in Writer.

The pages for View, Formatting Aids, Grid, Print, and Table are similar to the pages described above under LibreOffice Writer, but are for Writer/Web HTML pages instead.

The Background page allows you to specify the default background color for documents in Writer/Web. The background is valid for both new HTML documents and for those that you load, as long as these have not defined their own background.

Choosing language settings

You may need to do several things to set the language settings to what you want:

- Install the required dictionaries
- Change some locale and language settings
- Choose spelling options

Install the required dictionaries

LibreOffice automatically installs several dictionaries with the program. To add other dictionaries, be sure you are connected to the Internet, and then use **Tools > Language > More Dictionaries Online**. LibreOffice will open your default web browser to a page containing links to additional dictionaries that you can install. Follow the prompts to select and install the ones you want.

Change some locale and language settings

You can change some details of the locale and language settings that LibreOffice uses for all documents or for specific documents.

In the Options dialog, choose **Language Settings > Languages**. Click the expansion symbol (+ sign or triangle). The exact list shown depends on the *Enhanced language support* settings (see Figure 61).

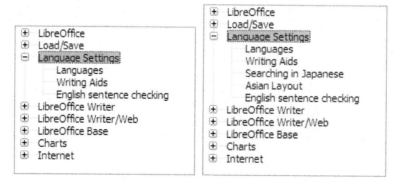

Figure 60: LibreOffice language options, with Asian language options enabled on the right side

On the right-hand side of the **Language Settings – Languages** page (Figure 61), change the **User interface**, **Locale setting**, **Default currency**, and the settings under *Default languages for documents* as required. In the example, English (USA) has been chosen for all the appropriate settings.

If you want the language setting to apply to the current document only, instead of being the default for all new documents, select **For the current document only**.

If necessary, select the options to enable support for Asian languages (Chinese, Japanese, Korean) and support for CTL (complex text layout) languages such as Hindi, Thai, Hebrew, and Arabic. If you choose either of these options, the next time you open the Options dialog, you will see some extra pages under **Language Settings**, as shown in the right side of Figure 60. These pages (Searching in Japanese, Asian Layout, and Complex Text Layout) are not discussed here.

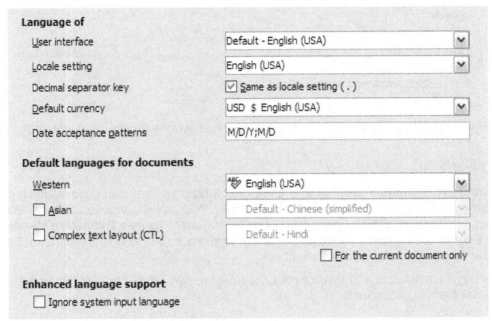

Figure 61: Choosing language options

Choose spelling options

To choose the options for checking spelling, choose **Language Settings > Writing Aids**. In the *Options* section of the page, choose the settings that are useful for you.

Some considerations:

- If you do not want spelling checked while you type, deselect **Check spelling as you type**. This option can also be deselected using the **AutoSpellcheck** button on the Standard Toolbar.

- If you want grammar to be checked as you type, you must have **Check spelling as you type** enabled too.

- If you use a custom dictionary that includes words in all uppercase and words with numbers (for example, AS/400), select **Check uppercase words** and **Check words with numbers**.

- **Check special regions** includes headers, footers, frames, and tables when checking spelling.

Here you can also check which of the user-defined (custom) dictionaries are active, or you can add or remove user installed dictionaries by clicking the **New** or **Delete** buttons. Dictionaries installed by the system cannot be deleted.

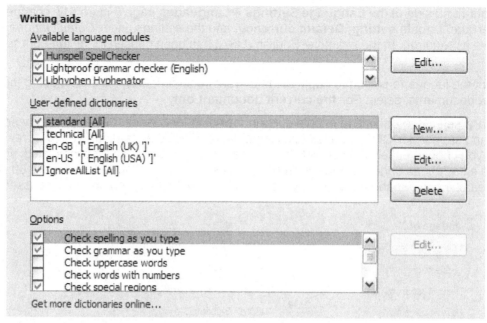

Figure 62: Choosing languages, dictionaries, and options for checking spelling

English sentence checking

On the **Language Settings > English sentence checking** page, you can choose which items are checked for, reported to you, or converted automatically. This menu is also found in the English dictionaries extension installed by default by LibreOffice. Select **Tools > Extension Manager**, select the English spelling dictionaries and click the **Options** button to reveal the menu. Select which of the optional features you wish to check.

After selecting the additional grammar checks, you must restart LibreOffice, or reload the document, for them to take effect.

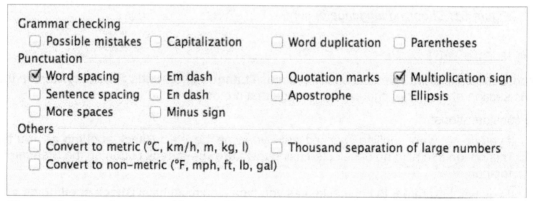

Figure 63: Choosing options for checking sentences in English

Grammar checking

Possible mistakes
　　Checks for things such as; *with it's, he don't, this things* and so on.

Capitalization
　　Checks for the capitalization of sentences. The sentence boundary detection depends on abbreviations.

Word duplication

Checks for all word duplication, increased from the default number of words checked.

Parentheses

Checks for pairs of parentheses and quotation marks.

Punctuation

Word spacing

This option is selected by default. It checks for single spaces between words, indicating instances of double or triple spaces, but not of more than that.

Sentence spacing

Checks for single spacing between sentences, indicating when one or two extra spaces are found.

More spaces

Checks word and sentence spacing for more than two extra spaces.

Em dash; En dash

These options force a non-spaced em dash to replace a spaced en dash, or force a spaced en dash to replace a non-spaced em dash, respectively.

Quotation marks

Checks for correct typographical double quotation marks.

Multiplication sign

This option is selected by default. It replaces an 'x' used as a multiplication symbol with the correct typographical symbol.

Apostrophe

Replaces an apostrophe with the correct typographical character.

Ellipsis

Replaces three consecutive periods (full stops) with the correct typographical symbol.

Minus sign

Replaces a hyphen with the correct minus typographical character.

Others

Convert to metric; Convert to non-metric

Converts quantities in a given unit to quantities in the other type of unit: metric to imperial or imperial to metric.

Thousands separation of large numbers

Converts a number with five or more significant digits to a common format, that is one which uses the comma as a thousands separator, or to the ISO format which uses a narrow space as a separator.

Controlling Writer's AutoCorrect functions

Some people find some or all of the items in Writer's AutoCorrect feature annoying because Writer changes what you type when you do not want it changed. Many people find some of the AutoCorrect functions quite helpful; if you do, then select the relevant options. But if you find unexplained changes appearing in your document, this is a good place to look to find the cause.

To open the AutoCorrect dialog, choose **Tools > AutoCorrect Options**. (You need to have a document open for this menu item to appear.) In Writer, this dialog has five tabs. Many of the options are described in Chapter 3, Working with Text, in this book.

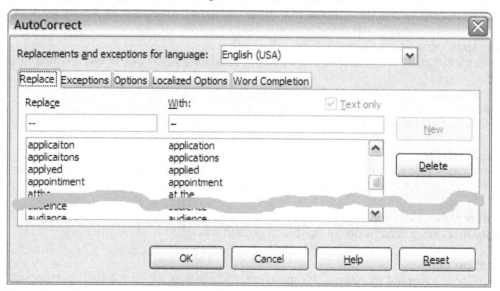

Figure 64: The AutoCorrect dialog in Writer

Chapter 3
Working with Text

Introduction

This chapter covers the basics of working with text in Writer, the word-processing component of LibreOffice. It assumes that you are familiar with the use of a mouse and keyboard and that you have read about Writer's menus and toolbars and other topics covered in Chapter 1, Introducing Writer.

We recommend that you also follow the suggestions in Chapter 2, Setting up Writer, about displaying formatting aids, such as end-of-paragraph marks, and selecting other setup options.

When you have read this chapter, you should know how to:

- Select, cut, copy, paste, and move text
- Find and replace text
- Insert special characters
- Format paragraphs and characters
- Create numbered or bulleted lists
- Check spelling and grammar, use the thesaurus, and choose hyphenation options
- Use the autocorrection, word completion, autotext, and line numbering features
- Track changes, undo and redo changes, and insert comments
- Link to other parts of a document

Selecting text

Before you can do anything with text, you need to select it. Selecting text in Writer is similar to selecting text in other applications.

In addition to selecting blocks of text, you can select items that are not consecutive, and columns (vertical blocks) of text.

Selecting items that are not consecutive

To select nonconsecutive items (as shown in Figure 65) using the mouse:

1) Select the first piece of text.
2) Hold down the *Ctrl* key and use the mouse to select the next piece of text.
3) Repeat as often as needed.

Now you can work with the selected text (copy it, delete it, change the style, and so on).

To select nonconsecutive items using the keyboard:

1) Select the first piece of text. (For more information about keyboard selection of text, see the topic "Navigating and Selecting with the Keyboard" in the LibreOffice Help (*F1*).)
2) Press *Shift+F8*. This puts Writer in "Adding selection" mode.
3) Use the arrow keys to move to the start of the next piece of text to be selected. Hold down the *Shift* key and select the next piece of text.
4) Repeat as often as required.

Now you can work with the selected text.

Press *Esc* to exit from this mode.

> Around the World in 80 Days - Jules Verne
>
> A puzzled grin overspread Passepartout's round face; clearly he had not comprehended his master.
> "Monsieur is going to leave home?"
> "Yes," returned Phileas Fogg. "We are going round the world."
> Passepartout opened wide his eyes, raised his eyebrows, held up his hands, and seemed about to collapse, so overcome was he with stupefied astonishment.
> "Round the world!" he murmured.
> "In eighty days," responded Mr. Fogg. "So we haven't a moment to lose."
> "But the trunks?" gasped Passepartout, unconsciously swaying his head from right to left.
> "We'll have no trunks; only a carpet-bag, with two shirts and three pairs of stockings for me, and the same for you. We'll buy our clothes on the way. Bring down my mackintosh and traveling-cloak, and some stout shoes, though we shall do little walking. Make haste!"

Figure 65: Selecting items that are not next to each other

Selecting a vertical block of text

You can select a vertical block or "column" of text that is separated by spaces or tabs (as you might see in text pasted from e-mails, program listings, or other sources), using LibreOffice's block selection mode. To change to block selection mode, use **Edit > Selection Mode > Block Area**, or press *Ctrl+F8*, or click on the **Selection** icon in the status bar and select **Block selection** from the list.

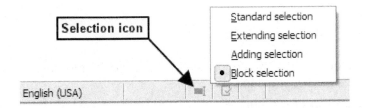

Now you can highlight the selection, using mouse or keyboard, as shown in Figure 66.

January	February	March
April	May	June
July	August	September
October	November	December

Figure 66: Selecting a vertical block of text

Cutting, copying, and pasting text

Cutting and copying text in Writer is similar to cutting and copying text in other applications. You can copy or move text within a document, or between documents, by dragging or by using menu selections, icons, or keyboard shortcuts. You can also copy text from other sources such as Web pages and paste it into a Writer document.

To *move* (drag and drop) selected text using the mouse, drag it to the new location and release it. To *copy* selected text, hold down the *Ctrl* key while dragging. The text retains the formatting it had before dragging.

To *move* (cut and paste) selected text, use *Ctrl+X* to cut the text, insert the cursor at the paste-in point and use *Ctrl+V* to paste. Alternatively, use the buttons on the Standard toolbar.

When you paste text, the result depends on the source of the text and how you paste it. If you click on the **Paste** button, then the pasted text keeps its original formatting (such as bold or italics). Text pasted from Web sites and other sources may also be placed into frames or tables. If you do not like the results, click the **Undo** button or press *Ctrl+Z*.

To make the pasted text take on the formatting of the surrounding text:

- Choose **Edit > Paste Special**, or
- Click the arrow on the combination **Paste** button, or
- Click the **Paste** button without releasing the left mouse button.

Then select **Unformatted text** from the resulting menu.

The range of choices on the Paste Special menu varies depending on the origin and formatting of the text (or other object) to be pasted. See Figure 67 for an example with text on the clipboard.

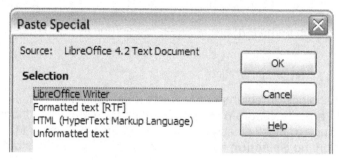

Figure 67: Paste Special menu

Finding and replacing text and formatting

Writer has two ways to find text within a document: the Find toolbar for fast searching and the Find & Replace dialog. In the dialog, you can:

- Find and replace words and phrases
- Use wildcards and regular expressions to fine-tune a search
- Find and replace specific attributes or formatting
- Find and replace paragraph styles

Using the Find toolbar

If the Find toolbar is not visible, you can display it by choosing **View > Toolbars > Find** from the Menu bar or by pressing *Ctrl+F*. The Find toolbar is shown docked at the bottom of the LibreOffice window (just above the Status Bar) in Figure 68, but you can float it or dock it in another location. For more information on floating and docking toolbars, see Chapter 1, Introducing Writer.

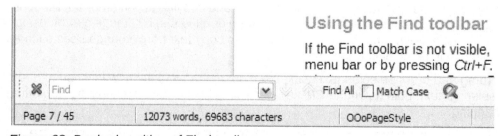

Figure 68: Docked position of Find toolbar

To use the Find toolbar, click in the text input box and type your search text, then press *Enter* to find the next occurrence of that term from the current cursor position. Click the **Find Next** or **Find Previous** buttons as needed.

Click the **Find All** button to select all instances of the search term within the document. Select **Match Case** to find only the instances that exactly match the search term. Click the button next to Match Case (🔍) to open the Find & Replace dialog and still keep the Find toolbar open.

The Find toolbar can be closed by clicking the red X button on the left, or by pressing Esc on the keyboard when the text cursor is in the search box. *Ctrl+F* toggles the Find toolbar off and on.

Using the Find & Replace dialog

To display the Find & Replace dialog, use the keyboard shortcut *Ctrl+H*, or choose **Edit > Find & Replace** from the Menu bar, or click the Find and Replace button (🔍) on the Find toolbar. Once opened, optionally click the **Other Options** symbol to expand the dialog (see Figure 69). Click the button again to reduce the dialog options.

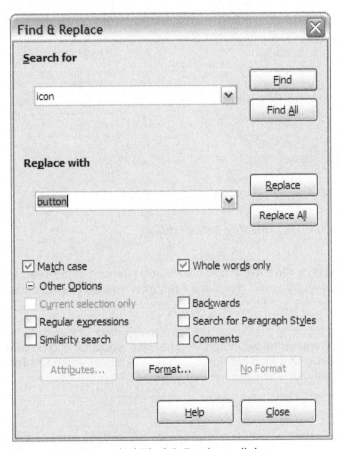

Figure 69: Expanded Find & Replace dialog

To use the Find & Replace dialog:

1) Type the text you want to find in the *Search for* box.
2) To replace the text with different text, type the new text in the *Replace with* box.
3) You can select various options, such as matching the case or matching whole words only.
   Among the Other Options, choices include searching only in selected text, searching from the current cursor position backwards toward the beginning of the file, or searching for similar words.

- Select **Similarity search** and click the button to the right to open a dialog in which you can modify the text search by length and number of characters different from the search term (see Figure 70).
- Select **Combine** to combine settings to modify the search.
- Select **Comments** to enables searching in comments text.

See the following sections for some other options choices.

4) When you have set up your search, click **Find**. As the document view moves to each found instance, replace the text by clicking **Replace**.

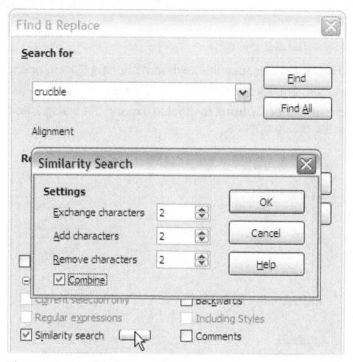

Figure 70: Similarity search dialog

Tip	If you click **Find All**, Writer selects all instances of the search text in the document. Similarly, if you click **Replace All**, Writer replaces all matches.

Caution	Use **Replace All** with caution; otherwise, you may end up with some highly embarrassing (and hilarious) mistakes. A mistake with **Replace All** might require a manual, word-by-word, search to fix.

Finding and replacing specific attributes and formatting

A very powerful use of Find & Replace takes advantage of the *Attributes* and *Format* options. For example, you might want to replace underlined words with italics.

To find document attributes:

1) On the Find & Replace dialog (with **Other Options** displayed, as in Figure 69), click the **Attributes** button.

2) Select the attribute you wish to search for from the list in the Attributes dialog and click **OK**. The names of the selected attributes appear under the *Search for* box. For example, to search for text that has been changed from the default font color, select the **Font Color** attribute.

3) Click **Find** to search the document.

To find specific formatting, open the Find & Replace dialog (with **Other Options** displayed, as in Figure 69):

1) To search for text with specific formatting, enter the text in the *Search for* box. To search for specific formatting only, delete any text in the *Search for* box.

2) Click **Format** to display the Text Format (Search) dialog. The tabs on this dialog are similar to those on the Paragraph and Paragraph Style dialogs.

3) Choose the formats you want to search for and then click **OK**. The names of the selected formats appear under the *Search for* box. For example, you might search for all text in 14-point bold Times New Roman. The option **Search for Paragraph Styles**, changes to **Including Styles**.

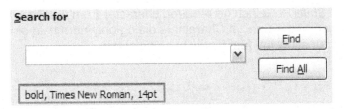

4) To replace the format, click in the **Replace with** text box, choose the format to use, and then click **OK**. The format selected will be displayed below this text box. To replace text as well as formatting, type the replacement text in the *Replace with* box.

To search for specific text with specific formatting (for example, the word **hello** in bold), specify the formatting, type the text in the *Search for* box and leave the *Replace with* box blank.

To remove specific character formatting, click **Format**, select the **Font** tab, then select the opposite format (for example, No Bold). The **No Format** button on the Find & Replace dialog clears all previously selected formats.

5) Click **Find, Find All**, **Replace**, or **Replace All.**

Tip	Unless you plan to search for other text using those same attributes, click **No Format** to remove the attributes after completing your search. If you forget to do this, you may wonder why your next search fails to find words you know are in the document.

Finding and replacing paragraph styles

If you combine material from several sources, you may discover that lots of unwanted paragraph styles have suddenly shown up in your document. To quickly change all the paragraphs from one (unwanted) style to another (preferred) style:

1) On the expanded Find & Replace dialog (Figure 69), select **Search for Paragraph Styles**. (If you have attributes specified, this option is labeled *Including Styles*. Select No Format to remove any attributes and return the option to Search for Paragraph Styles.) The *Search for* and *Replace with* boxes now contain a list of styles in use in the document.

2) Select the styles you want to search for and replace.

3) Click **Find, Find All**, **Replace**, or **Replace All**.

Repeat steps 2 and 3 for each style that you want to replace.

Finding and replacing special characters

To enter special characters into the *Search for* and *Replace with* text input boxes, select the text box and press *Ctrl+Shift+S*. Select the required character from the Special Characters dialog and click **OK**. This version of the Special Characters dialog only permits a single character to be selected and does not allow the font family to be selected.

Using wildcards and regular expressions

Most users will be familiar with the concept of a *wildcard*—a special character that represents one or more unspecified characters. Wildcards make text searches more powerful but often less specific. LibreOffice enables you to use combinations of characters known as *regular expressions* which are more specific than simple wildcards but less so than a literal string. Regular expressions are very powerful but not very intuitive. They can save time and effort by combining multiple finds into one.

Table 4 shows a few of the regular expressions used by LibreOffice.

Tip	The online help describes many more regular expressions and their uses.

To use wildcards and regular expressions when searching and replacing:

1) On the Find & Replace dialog, click **Other Options** to see more choices. On this expanded dialog (Figure 69), select the **Regular expressions** option.

2) Type the search text, including the wildcards, in the *Search for* box and the replacement text (if any) in the *Replace with* box. Not all regular expressions work as replacement characters; the line break (**\n**) is one that does work.

3) Click **Find, Find All**, **Replace**, or **Replace All** (not recommended).

Note	To search for a character that is defined as a wildcard, type a backslash (\) before the character to indicate that you are using it literally. For example, to find the text **$5.00**, you would conduct a search using **\$5\.00**.

Table 4: Examples of search wildcards (regular expressions)

To find	Use this expression	Examples and comments
Any single character	. (a period or full stop)	b.d finds *bad*, *bud*, *bid*, and *bed*.
One of the specified characters	[xyz]	b[iu]n finds *bin* and *bun*.
Any single character in this range	[x-y]	[r-t]eed finds *reed*, *seed*, and *teed*; ranges must be in alphabetically ascending order.
Any single character except the characters inside the brackets	[^x]	p[^a]st finds *post* and *pest*, but not past.
The beginning of a word	\<start	\<log finds *logbook* and *logistics*, but not *catalog*.
The end of a word	end\>	log\> finds *catalog*, but not *logistics*.
A paragraph marker	$	Does not work as a replacement character. Use **\n** instead.
A line break	\n	Finds a line break that was inserted with *Shift+Enter*. When used as a replacement character, it inserts a paragraph marker.

Inserting special characters

A *special character* is one not found on a standard English keyboard. For example, © ¾ æ ç Ł ñ ö ø ¢ are all special characters. To insert a special character:

1) Place the cursor in your document where you want the character to appear.
2) Click **Insert > Special Character** to open the Special Characters dialog (Figure 71).
3) Select the characters (from any font or mixture of fonts) you wish to insert, in order; then click **OK**. The selected characters are shown in the lower left of the dialog. As you select each character, it is shown on the right, along with the numerical code for that character.

Tip	Different fonts include different special characters. If you do not find a particular special character you want, try changing the *Font* selection.

Inserting non-breaking spaces and hyphens

Non-breaking spaces

To prevent two words from being separated at the end of a line, press *Ctrl+Shift* when you type the space between the two words.

Non-breaking hyphen

You can use a non-breaking hyphen in cases where you do not want the hyphen to appear at the end of a line, for example in a number such as 123-4567. To insert a non-breaking hyphen, press *Shift+Ctrl+minus sign*.

These are also available through **Insert > Formatting Mark.**

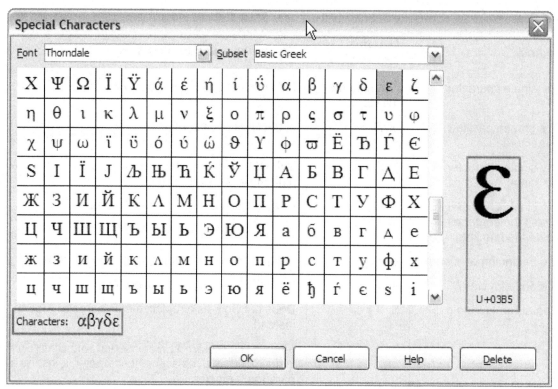

Figure 71: The Special Characters dialog, where you can insert special characters

Inserting en and em dashes

To enter en and em dashes, you can choose the *Replace dashes* option under **Tools > AutoCorrect Options** (Figure 83 on page 87). This option replaces two hyphens, under certain conditions, with the corresponding dash.

In Table 5, the A and B represent text consisting of letters A to z or digits 0 to 9.

Table 5: Inserting dashes

Text that you type	Result
A - B (A, space, hyphen, space, B)	A – B (A, space, en dash, space, B)
A -- B (A, space, hyphen, hyphen, space, B)	A – B (A, space, en dash, space, B)
A--B (A, hyphen, hyphen, B)	A—B (A, em dash, B)
A-B (A, hyphen, B)	A-B (unchanged)
A -B (A, space, hyphen, B)	A -B (unchanged)
A --B (A, space, hyphen, hyphen, B)	A –B (A, space, en dash, B)

Another means of inserting en or em dashes is through the **Insert > Special Characters** menu. Select the **U+2013** or **U+2014** character (found in the *General punctuation* subset), respectively.

A third method uses keyboard shortcuts. These shortcuts vary depending on your operating system, as described on the next page.

Tip	You can also record macros to insert en and em dashes and assign those macros to unused key combinations, for example *Ctrl+Shift+N* and *Ctrl+Shift+M*. For more information, see Chapter 17, Customizing Writer.

Windows

On most non-Asian installations of Windows, hold down one of the *Alt* keys and type on the numeric keypad: 0150 for an en dash or 0151 for an em dash. The dash appears when you release the *Alt* key.

Tip	On a keyboard with no numeric keypad, use a *Fn* (*Function*) key combination to type the numbers. (The *Fn* key is usually to the right of the left-hand *Ctrl* key on the keyboard.) For example, on a US keyboard layout, the combination for an en dash should be *Alt+Fn+mjim* and for an em dash it should be *Alt+Fn+mjij*.

Linux

Hold down the *Compose* key and type two hyphens and a period for an en dash, or three hyphens for an em dash. The dash appears when you release the *Compose* key.

Tip	The key that operates as a *Compose* key varies with the Linux distribution. It is usually one of the *Alt* or *Win* keys, but may be another key, and should be user-selectable.

Mac OS X

Hold down the *Option* (*Alt*) key and type a hyphen for an en dash. For an em dash, the combination is *Shift+Option+Hyphen*.

Formatting paragraphs

You can apply many formats to paragraphs using the buttons on the *Formatting* toolbar. Figure 72 shows the *Formatting* toolbar as a floating toolbar, customized to show only the buttons for paragraph formatting. If you have Asian or Complex Text Layout language support enabled, two additional buttons are available: Left-to-Right and Right-to-Left. The appearance of the icons may vary with your operating system and the selection of icon size and style in **Tools > Options > LibreOffice > View**.

Tip	The use of *paragraph styles* is highly recommended as an alternative to manually formatting paragraphs, especially for long or standardized documents. For information on styles and how to use them, see Chapters 6 and 7 in this book.

Caution	Manual formatting (also called *direct formatting*) overrides styles, and you cannot get rid of the manual formatting by applying a style to it. To remove manual formatting, select the text, right-click, and choose **Clear Direct Formatting** from the context menu. Alternatively, use *Ctrl+M*.

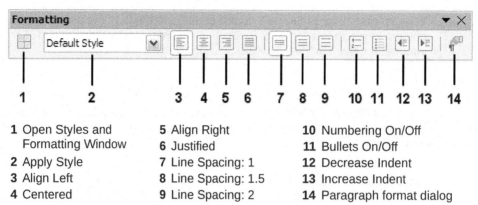

1 Open Styles and Formatting Window	**5** Align Right	**10** Numbering On/Off
	6 Justified	**11** Bullets On/Off
2 Apply Style	**7** Line Spacing: 1	**12** Decrease Indent
3 Align Left	**8** Line Spacing: 1.5	**13** Increase Indent
4 Centered	**9** Line Spacing: 2	**14** Paragraph format dialog

Figure 72: Formatting toolbar, showing icons for paragraph formatting

Formatting can also be carried out using the Sidebar (**View > Sidebar**). The Sidebar opens with the *Properties* deck selected by default. Click the **Panel Open (+)** button to open the panels if necessary.

The Paragraph panel contains most of the controls that are described above for the Formatting toolbar. Figure 73 shows the Paragraph panel on the Properties deck containing those formatting controls. Clicking the down-arrow of a composite button opens the control for further choices, such as fixed line spacing, or color palette. The Line Spacing submenu is shown in Figure 74.

Click the **More Options** button to open the Paragraph Style dialog.

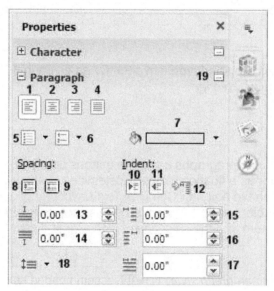

1 Align Left	**8** Increase Spacing	**15** Indent From Left
2 Align Center	**9** Decrease Spacing	**16** Indent From Right
3 Align Right	**10** Increase Indent	**17** Indent First Line
4 Align Justified	**11** Decrease Indent	**18** Line Spacing composite button
5 Bullets composite button	**12** Hanging Indent	**19** More Options button – opens Paragraph dialog
6 Numbering composite button	**13** Above Paragraph Spacing	
7 Paragraph Background Color	**14** Below Paragraph Spacing	

Figure 73: Paragraph panel of the Properties deck in the Sidebar

Figure 74: Line spacing submenu

Figure 75 shows examples of the alignment options applied to text.

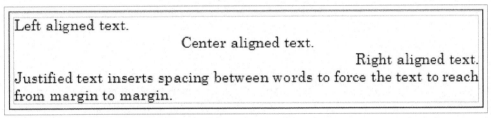

Figure 75: Text alignment options

When using justified text, the last line is by default aligned to the left. However, you can also align the last line to the center of the paragraph area or justify it so that spaces are inserted between the words in order to fill the whole line. If you select the **Expand single word** option, then whenever the last line of a justified paragraph consists of a single word, this word is stretched by inserting spaces between characters so that it occupies the full length of the line. Figure 76 shows an example of the effect obtained when setting each of these options.

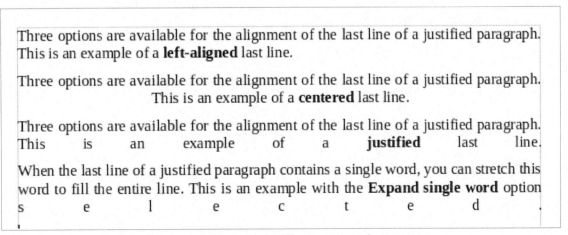

Figure 76: Four choices for the last line of a justified paragraph

These options are controlled in the *Alignment* page of the Paragraph dialog, reached by choosing **Format > Paragraph** from the Menu bar, or by *right-clicking* in the paragraph and selecting **Paragraph** from the context menu, or by clicking the **More Options** button on the Paragraph panel in the Properties deck of the Sidebar.

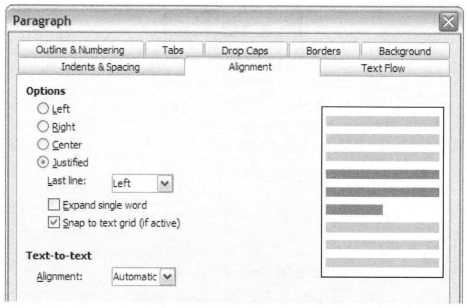

Figure 77: Options for the last line of a justified paragraph

Setting tab stops and indents

The horizontal ruler shows the tab stops. Any tab stops that you have defined will overwrite the default tab stops. Tab settings affect indentation of full paragraphs (using the **Increase Indent** and **Decrease Indent** buttons on the Formatting toolbar) as well as indentation of parts of a paragraph (by pressing the *Tab* key on the keyboard).

Using the default tab spacing can cause formatting problems if you share documents with other people. If you use the default tab spacing and then send the document to someone else who has chosen a different default tab spacing, tabbed material will change to use the other person's settings. Instead of using the defaults, define your own tab settings, as described in this section.

To define indents and tab settings for one or more selected paragraphs, double-click on a part of the ruler that is not between the left and right indent icons to open the *Indents & Spacing* page of the Paragraph dialog. Double-click anywhere between the left and right indent icons on the ruler to open the *Tabs* page of the Paragraph dialog.

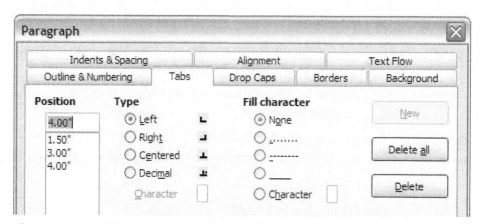

Figure 78: Specifying tab stops and fill characters

A better strategy is to define tabs for the paragraph style. Refer to Chapters 6 and 7 for more about paragraph styles.

Tip	Using tabs to space out material on a page is not recommended. Depending on what you are trying to accomplish, a table is usually a better choice.

Changing the default tab stop interval

Note	Any changes to the default tab setting will affect the existing default tab stops in any document you open afterward, as well as tab stops you insert after making the change.

To set the measurement unit and the spacing of default tab stop intervals, go to **Tools > Options > LibreOffice Writer > General**.

Figure 79: Selecting a default tab stop interval

You can also set or change the measurement unit for rulers in the current document by right-clicking on the ruler to open a list of units, as shown in Figure 80 for the horizontal ruler. Click on one of them to change the ruler to that unit. The selected setting applies only to that ruler.

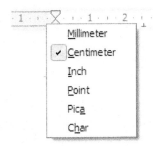

Figure 80: Changing the measurement unit for a ruler

Formatting characters

You can apply many formats to characters using the buttons on the Formatting toolbar, or those in the Characters panel of the Properties deck of the Sidebar. Figure 81 shows the Formatting toolbar customized to show only the buttons for character formatting. Figure 82 Shows the Character panel in the Properties deck of the Sidebar. Clicking the down-arrow of a composite button opens the control for further choices, such as line styles or color palette. The appearance of the buttons may vary with your operating system and the selection of icon size and style in **Tools > Options > LibreOffice > View**.

It is highly recommended that you use character styles rather than manually formatting characters. For information on styles and how to use them, see Chapters 6 and 7.

Tip	To remove manual formatting, select the text and choose **Format > Clear Direct Formatting** from the Menu bar, or right-click and choose **Clear Direct Formatting** from the context menu, or use *Ctrl+M* from the keyboard.

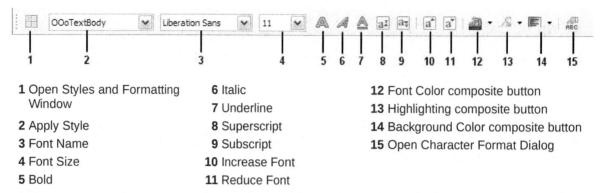

1 Open Styles and Formatting Window	**6** Italic	**12** Font Color composite button
	7 Underline	**13** Highlighting composite button
2 Apply Style	**8** Superscript	**14** Background Color composite button
3 Font Name	**9** Subscript	**15** Open Character Format Dialog
4 Font Size	**10** Increase Font	
5 Bold	**11** Reduce Font	

Figure 81: Formatting toolbar, showing buttons for character formatting

1 Font name	**6** Strikethrough	**11** Highlight – composite button
2 Font size	**7** Shadow	**12** Character Spacing composite button
3 Bold	**8** Increase Font	**13** Superscript
4 Italic	**9** Reduce Font	**14** Subscript
5 Underline composite button	**10** Font Color composite button	**15** More Options – opens Character dialog

Figure 82: Character panel in the Properties deck of the Sidebar

Autoformatting

You can set Writer to automatically format parts of a document according to the choices made on the *Options* page of the AutoCorrect dialog (**Tools > AutoCorrect Options**).

The Help describes each of these choices and how to activate the autoformats. Some common unwanted or unexpected formatting changes include:

- Horizontal lines. If you type three or more hyphens (- - -), underscores (_ _ _) or equal signs (===) on a line and then press *Enter* the paragraph is replaced by a horizontal line as wide as the page. The line is actually the lower border of the preceding paragraph.

- Bulleted and numbered lists. A bulleted list is created when you type a hyphen (-), asterisk (*), or plus sign (+), followed by a space or tab at the beginning of a paragraph. A numbered list is created when you type a number followed by a period (.), followed by a space or tab at the beginning of a paragraph. Automatic numbering is only applied to paragraphs formatted with the *Default*, *Text body* or *Text body indent* paragraph styles.

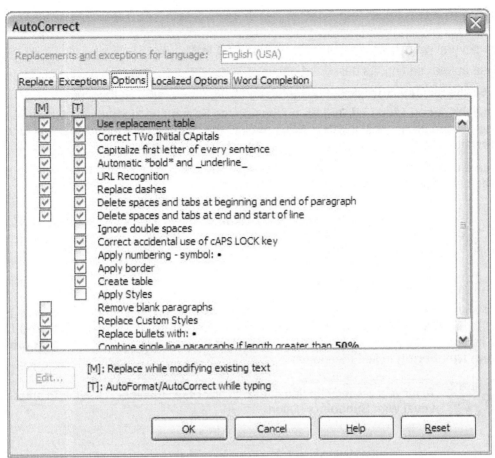

Figure 83: Autoformat choices on the Options page of the AutoCorrect dialog

Tip	If you notice unexpected formatting changes occurring in your document, this is the first place to look for the cause.

To automatically format the file according to the options you have set, choose **Format > AutoCorrect** and select or deselect the items on the submenu.

While Typing
Automatically formats the document while you type.

Apply
Automatically formats the document.

Apply and Edit Changes
Automatically formats the file and then opens a dialog where you can accept or reject the changes.

AutoCorrect Options
Opens the AutoCorrect dialog (Figure 83).

Creating numbered or bulleted lists

There are several ways to create numbered or bulleted lists:

- Use autoformatting, as described above.
- Use list (numbering) styles, as described in Chapters 6 and 7 in this book.
- Use the **Numbering** and **Bullets** buttons on the Formatting toolbar (see Figure 72) or on the Paragraph panel of the Properties deck of the Sidebar (see Figure 73). This method is described here.

To produce a numbered or bulleted list, select the paragraphs in the list and then click on the appropriate button on the Paragraph panel or the toolbar.

Note	It is a matter of personal preference whether you type your information first, then apply Numbering/Bullets or apply these as you type.

Using the Bullets and Numbering toolbar

You can create a nested list (where one or more list items has a sub-list under it, as in an outline) by using the buttons on the Bullets and Numbering toolbar (Figure 84). You can move items up or down the list, or create subpoints, and even change the style of bullets. Use **View > Toolbars > Bullets and Numbering** to see the toolbar.

Tip	To move a list entry up, together with all of its sub-entries, click the **Promote One Level With Subpoints** button.

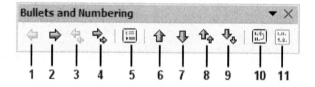

1 Promote One Level	**5** Insert Unnumbered Entry	**8** Move Up with Subpoints
2 Demote One Level		**9** Move Down with Subpoints
3 Promote One Level with Subpoints	**6** Move Up	**10** Restart Numbering
4 Demote One Level with Subpoints	**7** Move Down	**11** Bullets and Numbering

Figure 84: Bullets and Numbering toolbar

If you create a nested list using the buttons on this toolbar, all the levels of the list (up to 10) apply the same numbering (or bullet). However, in many circumstances you will want to use a combination of numbering formats and bullets when creating nested lists. Such lists, with a mixture of numbering formats and bullets, can be easily configured as described in the following example. Additional information on lists, in particular the technique to create your own list style, is described in Chapter 7, Working with Styles.

	When creating nested lists, one option is to enter all the list paragraphs first and apply the levels afterwards.
	You can use keyboard shortcuts to move paragraphs up or down the outline levels. Place the cursor at the beginning of the numbered paragraph and press:
Tip	*Tab* Down a level
	Shift+Tab Up a level
	To insert a tab stop at the beginning of a numbered paragraph (that is, after the number but before the text), press *Ctrl+Tab*.

Example: configuring a nested list

We will use a numbering style to produce the following effect:

I. Level-1 list item

   A. Level-2 list item

      i. Level-3 list item

         a) Level-4 list item

This example uses one of the supplied styles, *Numbering 1*. If you intend to reuse this type of nested list, you can also create a new style as illustrated in Chapter 7, Working with Styles.

1) Open the Styles and Formatting window (*F11*) and click the *List Styles* button at the top. Specify *All* in the drop-down list at the bottom of the window. Right-click on the *Numbering 1* style and choose **Modify** from the context menu.

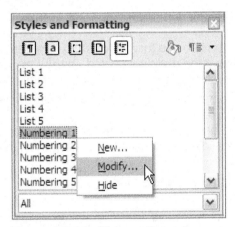

Figure 85: Modifying a list style

2) On the Numbering Style dialog, go to the *Outline* page, where you will find that one style matches our requirements. Click once on that style.

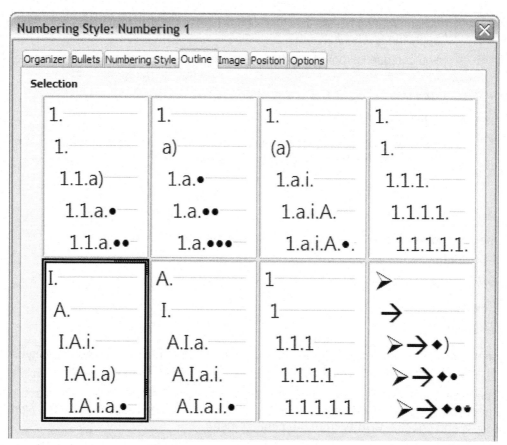

Figure 86: Choosing a predefined outline-numbering style

3) To modify the layout of the list, use the *Options* tab (Figures 87 and 88). Notice that the preview on the right shows the outline selected. In the *Level* box on the left, select **1**, then **2**, **3**, and **4** and see how the information in the *Numbering* and *After* boxes changes.

Use the *Options* page to set different punctuation; for example, a period (full stop) after "a" on level 4 instead of a parenthesis.

To make the indentation at each level greater or less than the default, change it on the *Position* page. Select the level, then make any changes in the indentation, spacing, or numbering alignment.

4) Repeat for each level as required, then click **OK**.

Tip	With outline numbering you can define different bullet styles for the different levels of a bullet list. Use the *Bullets* tab of the Bullets and Numbering dialog (not shown) to select the basic style. Return to the *Options* tab to customize the bullet for each indent level. Here you can set bullets to any character. See the *Image* tab for more bullets.

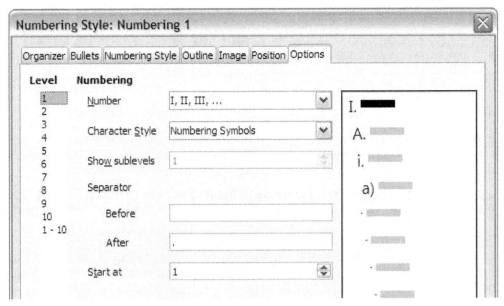

Figure 87: Checking the outline numbering for level-1 list items

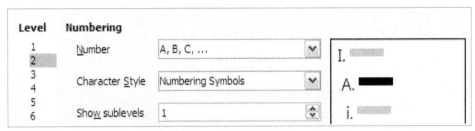

Figure 88: Numbering style for level-2 list items

Using footnotes and endnotes

Footnotes appear at the bottom of the page on which they are referenced. Endnotes are collected at the end of a document.

To work effectively with footnotes and endnotes, you need to:

- Insert footnotes.
- Define the format of footnotes.
- Define the location of footnotes on the page, and the color and line styles for separator lines.

Inserting footnotes/endnotes

To insert a footnote or an endnote, put the cursor where you want the footnote/endnote marker to appear. Then select **Insert > Footnote/Endnote** from the Menu bar or click the **Insert Footnote/Endnote Directly** or **Insert Endnote Directly** button on the *Insert* toolbar.

A footnote or endnote marker is inserted in the text and, depending on your choice, the cursor is relocated either to the footnote area at the bottom of the page or to the endnote area at the end of the document. Type the footnote or endnote content in this area.

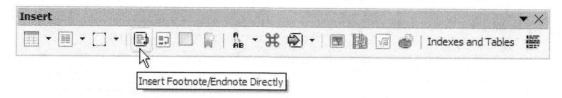

Figure 89: Using the Insert Footnote Directly icon on the toolbar

If you use **Insert > Footnote/Endnote**, the Insert Footnote/Endnote dialog (Figure 90) is displayed. Here you can choose whether to use the automatic numbering sequence specified in the footnote settings and whether to insert the item as a footnote or an endnote.

If you use the **Insert Footnote/Endnote Directly** or **Insert Endnote Directly** icon, the footnote or endnote automatically takes on the attributes previously defined in the Footnote Settings dialog.

You can edit an existing footnote or endnote the same way you edit any other text.

To delete a footnote or endnote, delete the footnote marker. The contents of the footnote or endnote are deleted automatically, and the numbering of other footnotes or endnotes is adjusted automatically.

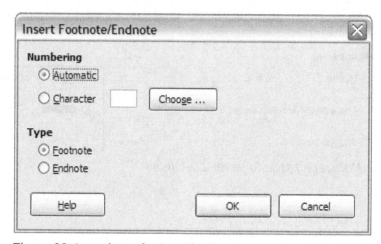

Figure 90: Inserting a footnote/endnote

Defining the format of footnotes/endnotes

To format the footnotes themselves, click **Tools > Footnotes/Endnotes**. On the Footnotes/Endnotes Settings dialog (Figure 91), choose settings as required.

Defining footnote location and separator line

The location of footnotes on the page, and the color and style of the line that separates the footnotes from the text, are defined in the page style. If you are using several page styles, and may have footnotes on any of them, you need to define the footnote location and separator line on each of the page styles.

Choose **Format > Page** from the Menu bar or right-click on a page and choose **Page** from the context menu, to display the **Page Style** dialog. Go to the *Footnote* tab (Figure 92) and make your selections, then click **OK** to save the changes.

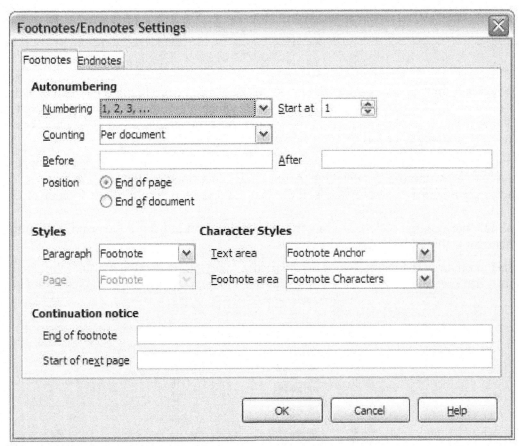

Figure 91: Defining footnote formatting

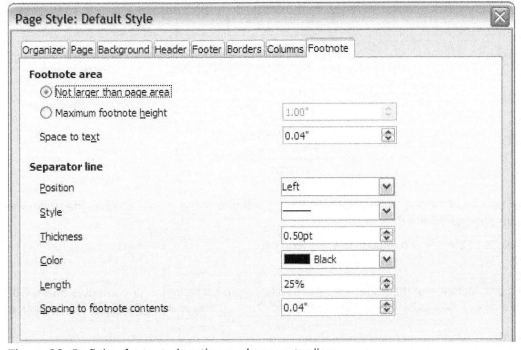

Figure 92: Defining footnote location and separator line

Spelling

Writer provides a spelling checker, which checks to see if each word in the document is in the installed dictionary. This can mean that proper names which are correctly spelled but which do not appear in the dictionary will be flagged as misspelled. Also provided is a grammar checker, which can be used separately or in combination with the spelling checker.

If it is enabled before entering text, **AutoSpellcheck** checks each word as it is typed. If it is enabled after text is inserted it checks the text already in the document. A wavy red line is displayed under any unrecognized words. It can be enabled from the Standard Toolbar by clicking the AutoSpellcheck button ( ), or from **Tools > Options > Language Settings > Writing Aids** and selecting it in the **Options** list.

Right-clicking on an unrecognized word brings up the AutoCorrect context menu. If the document has change tracking enabled, then the context menu contains options relating to changes in the text.

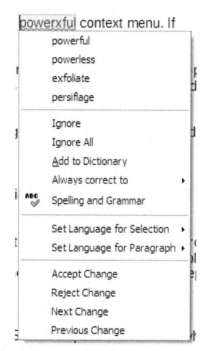

Figure 93: AutoCorrect context menu

Clicking on one of the suggested words in the top section of the menu replaces the underlined word with the one selected.

The choices in the second section of the menu are:

Ignore

This one instance of the underlined word will be ignored while the document is open. Other instances, if they exist, will still be underlined. This setting is not stored with the document.

Ignore All

All instances of the word in the document will be ignored, and the word will be added to the **IgnoreAllList** user-defined dictionary.

Add to Dictionary

The word is added by default to the **Standard** dictionary.

Always correct to

Selecting this opens the submenu, which repeats the suggestions for the word from the top section listing. Selecting a replacement word here stores the word pair in the replacement table under **Tools > AutoCorrect Options > Replacement**. The underlined word is replaced with the selected word.

Spelling and Grammar

This opens the **Spelling and Grammar** checker. See the explanations for this which follow.

In the third section of the context menu, language settings for the text can be set. These settings can be applied to the text, or to the paragraph containing the text.

The fourth section is only visible when change tracking has been enabled and further edits are carried out after saving the document. If the spelling error was in the saved document, then only **Next** and **Previous Change** are shown. If the spelling error is in the newly added text, then the content shown in Figure 93 is displayed.

Spelling and grammar

To perform a combined spelling and grammar check on the document (or a text selection), click the **Spelling and Grammar** button on the Standard Toolbar (ABC ✔), or press *F7*. In order to use this, the appropriate dictionaries must be installed. By default, four dictionaries are installed: a spellchecker, a grammar checker, a hyphenation dictionary, and a thesaurus. In operation the **Spelling and Grammar** tool checks either the document from the cursor point onwards, or the text selection. It opens the **Spelling and Grammar** dialog if any unrecognized words are found, or if any of the built-in grammar rules are broken. The option to restart from the beginning of the document is offered on reaching the end of the document.

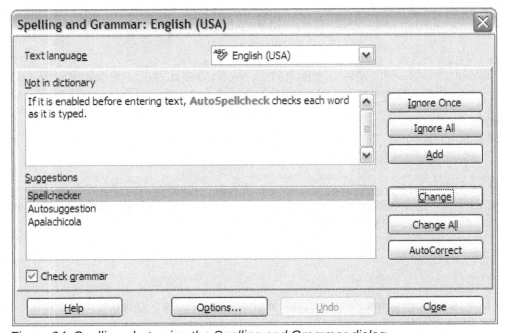

Figure 94: Spelling alert using the Spelling and Grammar dialog

The elements of the Spelling and Grammar dialog are as follows.

Not in dictionary

The sentence containing the error is displayed in the pane. If an unrecognized word is found it is highlighted.

If the error is grammatical, then it is indicated in a pale colored bar below the **Text language** setting (Figure 95). The sentence or the word can be edited in the pane.

Suggestions

The pane contains suggested replacement words for the highlighted word. Select a word and then select **Change** or **Change All** to replace it.

For grammatical errors there is no multiple choice. Select **Change** to accept the suggestion.

Text language

The language to be used for the spell and grammar checking can be selected from this list. If the spell check is enabled for this language, a check mark is displayed in front of it.

Ignore Once, Ignore All, and Add

Selecting one of these buttons has the same effect as the item in the **AutoCorrect** context menu detailed above.

Change

Replaces the unknown word with the suggested word. If the sentence was edited, the whole sentence is changed.

For grammar, the suggested replacement is used to correct the text.

Change All

This replaces all instances of the word with the selected replacement word.

AutoCorrect

This behaves in a similar fashion to **AutoCorrect** described above. *However*, the word is not replaced and you must select one of the Change buttons.

Undo

This button is enabled when a change has been made to the sentence, in case you wish to reverse the change. The button is not accessible if you use a **Change** button to replace a word.

Options

Selecting this opens the **Options** dialogue box where you can select user defined dictionaries and set the spell checking rules.

Note	It is recommended you run the Spelling and Grammar checker twice on your document. A minor software problem may prevent it detecting all the grammatical errors in a single pass.

Grammar

By default, **Check grammar as you type** is enabled in **Tools > Options > Language Settings > Writing Aids > Options**.

AutoSpellcheck must be enabled for this to work.

If any errors are detected, they are shown underlined by a wavy blue line. Right clicking on this line brings up a context menu which may be similar to one of those below.

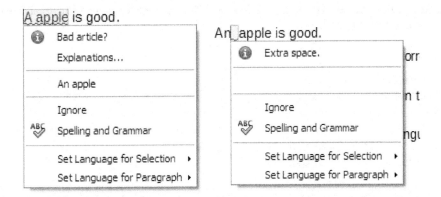

The first entry in the menu informs you of the suspected broken grammatical rule.

The second menu item in the left example is **Explanations**, which if selected opens your browser and takes you to a web page offering more information about the error. This entry is not always present in the context menu, as seen in the right example.

In the second section of the menu is the suggested correction. Clicking this changes the text to the suggestion. The example to the right appears blank, but clicking here removes the extra space causing the error.

In the third section of the menu you can select to ignore the indicated error, or to open the Spelling and Grammar checker. This dialog is shown below. This example displays the URL which will take you to a web site for more information on the error indicated.

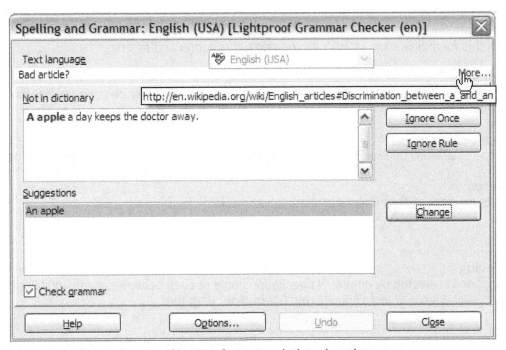

Figure 95: Dialog showing the URL for expanded explanation

In the final section of the menu, you can set the language for the selection or the paragraph.

English sentence checking

Additional grammar checking rules can be selected through **Tools > Options > Language Settings > English sentence checking**, or through **Tools > Extension Manager > English spelling dictionaries > Options**.

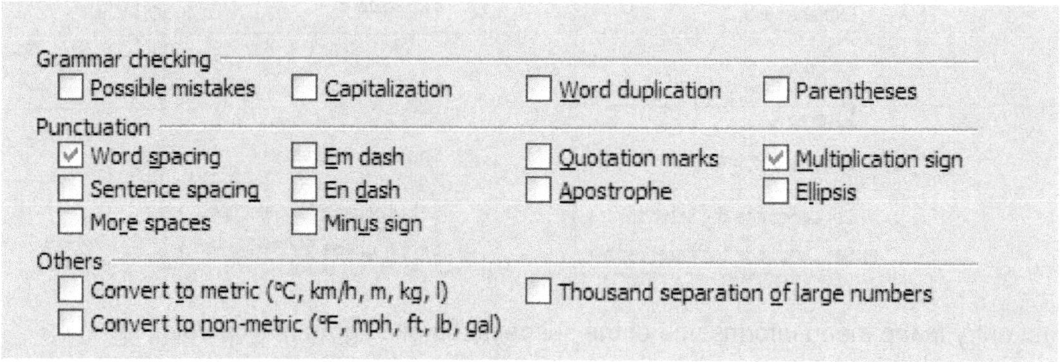

Figure 96: Additional grammar checking options

On the **Language Settings > English sentence checking** page, you can choose which items are checked for, reported to you, or converted automatically. Select which of the optional features you wish to check.

After selecting the additional grammar checks, you must restart LibreOffice, or reload the document, for them to take effect.

Grammar checking

Possible mistakes
Check this for things such as; *with it's, he don't, this things* and so on.

Capitalization
Checks for the capitalization of sentences. The sentence boundary detection depends on abbreviations.

Word duplication
Checks for all word duplication, rather than just the default words 'and', 'or', 'for' and 'the'.

Parentheses
Checks for pairs of parentheses and quotation marks.

Punctuation

Word spacing
This option is selected by default. It checks for single spaces between words, indicating instances of double or triple spaces, but not of more than that.

Sentence spacing
Checks for a single space between sentences, indicating when one or two extra spaces are found.

More spaces
Checks word and sentence spacing for more than two extra spaces.

Em dash; En dash

These options force a non-spaced em dash to replace a spaced en dash, or force a spaced en dash to replace a non-spaced em dash, respectively.

Quotation marks

This checks for correct typographical double quotation marks.

Multiplication sign

This option is selected by default. It replaces an 'x' used as a multiplication symbol with the correct typographical symbol.

Apostrophe

Replaces an apostrophe with the correct typographical character.

Ellipsis

Replaces three consecutive periods (full stops) with the correct typographical symbol.

Minus sign

Replaces a hyphen with the correct minus typographical character.

Others

Convert to metric; Convert to non-metric

Converts quantities in a given type of unit to quantities in the other type of unit: metric to imperial or imperial to metric.

Thousands separation of large numbers

Converts a number with five or more significant digits to a common format, that is one which uses the comma as a thousands separator, or to the ISO format which uses a narrow space as a separator.

Using built-in language tools

Writer provides some tools that make your work easier if you mix multiple languages within the same document or if you write documents in various languages:

- Selection of paragraph and character styles
- The functions in **Tools > Language**
- The use of language settings in Options
- The functions available on the status bar

The main advantage of changing the language for a text selection is that you can then use the correct dictionaries to check spelling and apply the localized versions of AutoCorrect replacement tables, thesaurus, and hyphenation rules. A grammar checking dictionary may be available for the selected language.

You can also set the language for a paragraph or a group of characters as **None (Do not check spelling)**. This option is especially useful when you insert text such as web addresses or programming language snippets that you do not want to check for spelling.

Using paragraph and character styles

Specifying the language in character and paragraph styles can be problematic unless you use a particular style for a different language. Changing the Language on the Font tab of the Paragraph Styles dialog will change the language for all paragraphs that use that paragraph style. You can set certain paragraphs to be checked in a language that is different from the language of the rest of the document by putting the cursor in the paragraph and changing the language on the Task Bar. See Chapter 7, Working with Styles, for information on how to manage the language settings of a style.

Using Tools > Language

You can also set the language for the whole document, for individual paragraphs, or even for individual words and characters, from **Tools > Language** on the Menu bar.

For Selection
Applies a specified language to the selected text.

For Paragraph
Applies the specified language to the paragraph where the cursor is located.

For all Text
Applies the specified language to all of the document, including text inserted after making the change.

Using language settings in Options

Another way to change the language of a whole document is to use **Tools > Options > Language Settings > Languages**. In the *Default languages for documents* section (Figure 97), you can choose a different language for all the text that is not explicitly marked as a different language.

Caution	Unlike the menu tool that applies to the individual document, a change in the default language from the **Options** dialog is a general change of settings of LibreOffice and will therefore apply to all the documents created in the future. If you want to change the language for the current document only, be sure to select the *For the current document only* option.

Figure 97: Options available in the Languages settings

The spelling checker works only for those languages in the list which have the symbol next to them. If you do not see this symbol next to your preferred language, you can install the dictionary using **Tools > Language > More dictionaries online**.

Using the status bar

The language used for checking spelling is also shown in the status bar, next to the page style in use. You can change the language for the paragraph or the entire document; click on the language in the status bar to pop up a menu of choices.

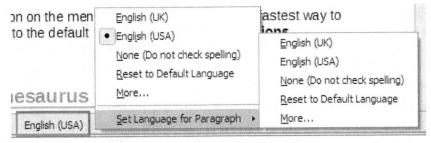

Figure 98: Language choices on the status bar

Notice the *Reset to Default Language* option on the menu and submenu. This is the fastest way to return a paragraph or the entire document to the default language set in **Tools > Options** (described above).

Using synonyms and the thesaurus

You can access a short list of synonyms from the context menu (Figure 99).

1) Select a word or phrase, right-click, and point to **Synonyms** on the context menu. A submenu of alternative words and phrases is displayed.

2) Click on a word or phrase to select it and replace the highlighted word or phrase in the document.

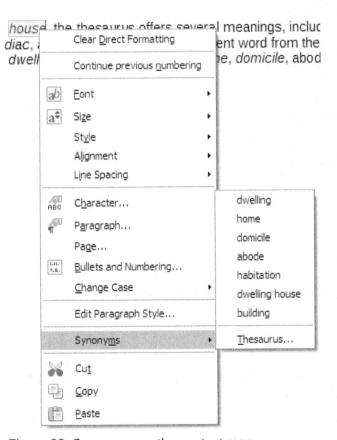

Figure 99: Synonyms on the context menu

The thesaurus gives a more extensive list of alternative words and phrases. To use the thesaurus:

1) Select a word or phrase, and then choose **Tools > Language > Thesaurus**, or press *Ctrl+F7*, or right-click and choose **Thesaurus** from the **Synonyms** submenu.

2) In the dialog, click on a word or phrase within the numbered list of meanings to select it.

3) Click **Replace** to make the substitution.

For example, when given the word *house*, the thesaurus offers several meanings, including *dwelling*, *legislature*, *sign of the zodiac*, and others. Select a replacement word from the list under the relevant meaning, so for *dwelling*, you will see *dwelling*, *home*, *domicile*, abode, and other alternatives, as shown in Figure 100.

Note	If the current language does not have a thesaurus installed, this feature is disabled.

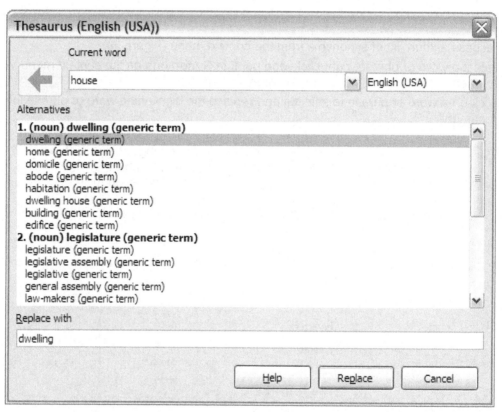

Figure 100: The thesaurus offers alternatives to words

Hyphenating words

You have several choices regarding hyphenation: let Writer do it automatically (using its hyphenation dictionaries), insert conditional hyphens manually where necessary, or don't hyphenate at all. Each choice has its pros and cons.

Automatic hyphenation

To turn automatic hyphenation of words on or off:

1) Press *F11* to open the Styles and Formatting window. On the *Paragraph Styles* page, right-click on **Default** and select **Modify**.

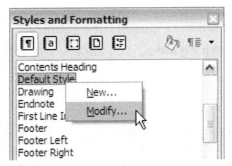

Figure 101: Modifying a paragraph style

2) On the Paragraph Style dialog, select the *Text Flow* tab.

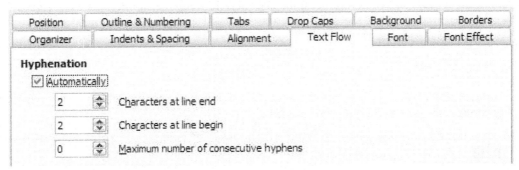

Figure 102: Turning on automatic hyphenation

3) Under *Hyphenation*, select or deselect the **Automatically** option.

4) Click **OK** to save.

Note	Turning on hyphenation for the *Default* paragraph style affects all other paragraph styles that are based on *Default*. You can individually change other styles so that hyphenation is not active; for example, you might not want headings to be hyphenated. Any styles that are not based on *Default* are not affected. For more on paragraph styles, see Chapters 6 and 7 in this book.

You can also set hyphenation choices through **Tools > Options > Language Settings > Writing Aids**. In *Options*, near the bottom of the dialog, scroll down to find the hyphenation settings.

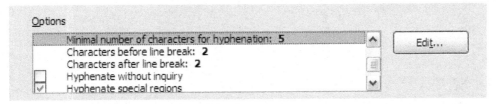

Figure 103: Setting hyphenation options

To change the minimum number of characters for hyphenation, or the minimum number of characters before or after a line break, select the item, and then click the **Edit** button in the Options section.

Hyphenate without inquiry

Specifies that you will never be asked to manually hyphenate words that the hyphenation dictionary does not recognize. If this box is not selected, when a word is not recognized, a dialog will open where you can manually enter hyphens.

Hyphenate special regions

Specifies that hyphenation will also be carried out in footnotes, headers, and footers.

Hyphenation options set in the **Writing Aids** dialog are effective only if hyphenation is turned on through paragraph styles.

Manual hyphenation

To manually hyphenate words, *do not* use a normal hyphen, which will remain visible even if the word is no longer at the end of a line when you add or delete text or change margins or font size. Instead, use a *conditional hyphen*, which is visible only when required.

To insert a conditional hyphen inside a word, click where you want the hyphen to appear and press *Ctrl+hyphen* or use **Insert > Formatting Mark > Optional hyphen**. The word will be hyphenated at this position when it is at the end of the line, even if automatic hyphenation for this paragraph is switched off.

Using AutoCorrect

Writer's AutoCorrect function has a long list of common misspellings and typing errors, which it corrects automatically. For example, "hte" will be changed to "the".

AutoCorrect is turned on when Writer is installed. To turn it off, uncheck **Format > AutoCorrect > While Typing**.

Select **Tools > AutoCorrect Options** to open the AutoCorrect dialog. There you can define what strings of text are corrected and how. In most cases, the defaults are fine.

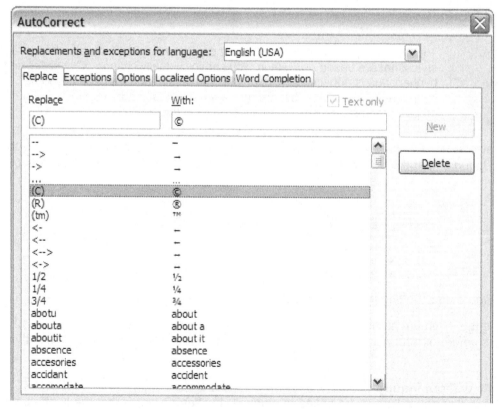

Figure 104: Replace tab of AutoCorrect dialog

To stop Writer replacing a specific spelling, go to the **Replace** tab, highlight the word pair, and click **Delete**.

To add a new spelling to the list, type it into the *Replace* and *With* boxes on the Replace tab, and click **New**.

See the different pages of the dialog for the wide variety of other options available to fine-tune AutoCorrect.

Tip	AutoCorrect can be used as a quick way to insert special characters. For example, (c) will be automatically corrected to ©. You can add your own special characters.

Using word completion

If Word Completion is enabled, Writer tries to guess which word you are typing and offers to complete the word for you. To accept the suggestion, press *Enter*. Otherwise, continue typing.

To turn off Word Completion, select **Tools > AutoCorrect Options > Word Completion** and deselect **Enable word completion**.

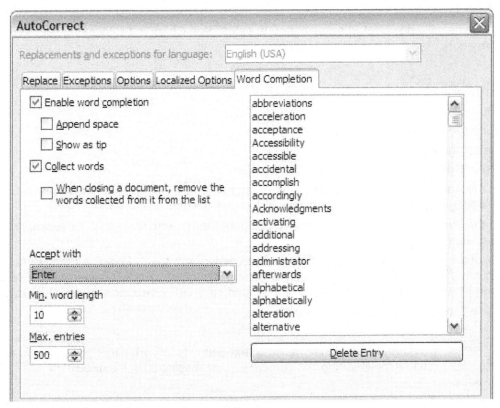

Figure 105: Customizing word completion

You can customize word completion from the *Word Completion* page of the AutoCorrect dialog (Figure 105).

*   Add (append) a space automatically after an accepted word.
*   Show the suggested word as a tip (hovering over the word) rather than completing the text as you type.

- Collect words when working on a document, and then either save them for later use in other documents or select the option to remove them from the list when closing the document.
- Change the maximum number of words remembered for word completion and the length of the smallest words to be remembered.
- Delete specific entries from the word completion list.
- Change the key that accepts a suggested entry—the options are *right arrow*, *End* key, *Enter* (*Return*), *Space bar*, and *Tab*.

Note	Automatic word completion only occurs after you type a word for the second time in a document.

Using AutoText

Use AutoText to store text, tables, fields, and other items for reuse and assign them to a key combination for easy retrieval. For example, rather than typing "Senior Management" every time you use that phrase, you can set up an AutoText entry to insert those words when you type "sm" and press *F3*.

AutoText is especially powerful when assigned to fields. See Chapter 14, Working with Fields, for more information.

Creating AutoText

To store some text as AutoText:

1) Type the text into your document.
2) Select the text.
3) Go to **Edit > AutoText** (or press *Ctrl+F3*).
4) In the AutoText dialog (Figure 106), type a name for the AutoText in the *Name* box. Writer will suggest a one-letter shortcut, which you can change.
5) In the large box to the left, choose the category for the AutoText entry, for example *My AutoText*.
6) Click the **AutoText** button on the right of the dialog and select from the menu either **New** (to have the AutoText retain specific formatting, no matter where it is inserted) or **New (text only)** (to have the AutoText take on the existing formatting around the insertion point..
7) Click **Close** to return to your document.

Tip	If the only option under the **AutoText** button is **Import**, either you have not entered a name for your AutoText or there is no text selected in the document.

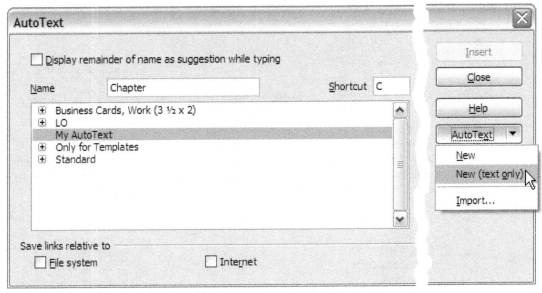

Figure 106: Defining a new AutoText entry

To save a table as AutoText:

1) Create a table and format it the way you want.
2) Select the table.
3) Go to **Edit > AutoText** (or press *Ctrl+F3*).
4) Type a name for the AutoText, optionally amend the suggested shortcut, and choose the category for the AutoText entry.
5) Click the **AutoText** button and select **New** (because you want the formatting of the table preserved).
6) Click **Close** to return to your document.

Inserting AutoText

To insert AutoText, type the shortcut and press *F3*.

Printing a list of AutoText entries

To print a list of AutoText entries:

1) Choose **Tools > Macros > Organize Macros > LibreOffice Basic**.
2) In the *Macro from* list, expand **LibreOffice Macros > Gimmicks**.
3) Select **AutoText** and then click **Run**. A list of the current AutoText entries is generated in a separate text document. You can then print this document.

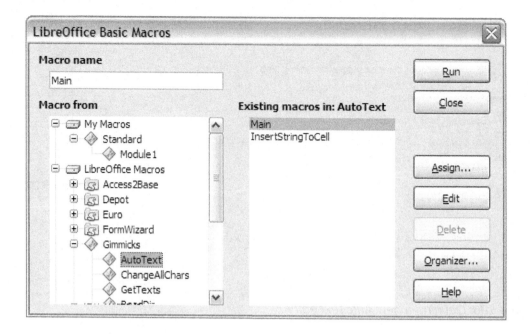

Line numbering

Line numbering puts line numbers in the margin. The line numbers are displayed on screen and are also printed. Figure 107 shows an example with numbering on every line.

> 1 Line numbering
>
> 2 Line numbering puts line numbers in the ma
> 3 also printed. Figure 1 shows an example wit
>
> 4 Click **Tools > Line Numbering** and select th
> 5 Line Numbering dialog (Figure 2). Then click
>
> 6 You can choose how many lines are number
> 7 numbering type, and whether numbers resta
> 8 choose) can be set on a different numbering

Figure 107: Line numbering example

Click **Tools > Line Numbering** and select the **Show numbering** option in the top left corner of the Line Numbering dialog (Figure 108). Then click **OK**.

You can choose how many lines are numbered (for example, every line or every tenth line), the numbering type, and whether numbers restart on each page. In addition, a text separator (any text you choose) can be set on a different numbering scheme (one every 12 lines, for example).

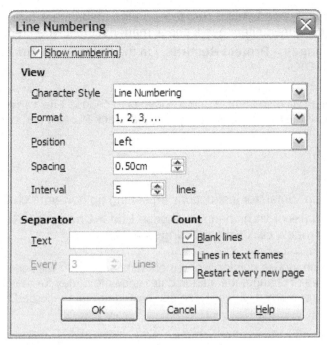

Figure 108: The Line Numbering dialog

Tracking changes to a document

You can use several methods to keep track of changes made to a document.

- Make your changes to a copy of the document (stored in a different folder, under a different name, or both), then use Writer to combine the two files and show the changes you made. Click **Edit > Compare Document**. This technique is particularly useful if you are the only person working on the document, as it avoids the increase in file size and complexity caused by the other methods.

- Save versions that are stored as part of the original file. However, this method can cause problems with documents of nontrivial size or complexity, especially if you save a lot of versions. Avoid this method if you can.

- Use Writer's change marks (often called "redlines" or "revision marks") to show where you have added or deleted material or changed formatting. Later, you or another person can review and accept or reject each change.

Note	Not all changes are recorded. For example, changing a tab stop from align left to align right and changes in formulas (equations) or linked graphics are not recorded.

Preparing a document for review

When you send a document to someone else to review or edit, you may want to prepare it first so that the editor or reviewer does not have to remember to turn on the revision marks. After you have protected the document, any user must enter the correct password in order to turn off the function or accept or reject changes.

1) Open the document. To check whether it contains multiple versions, click **File > Versions**. If multiple versions are listed, save the current version as a separate document with a different name and use this new document as the review copy.

2) With the review copy open, make sure that change recording is turned on. The **Edit > Changes > Record** menu item has a check mark next to it when recording is turned on.

3) Click **Edit > Changes > Protect Records**. On the Enter Password dialog, type a password (twice) and click **OK**.

Tip	An alternative to steps 2 and 3 above is to choose **File > Properties > Security** tab, select the **Record changes** option, then click **Protect** and enter the password.

Recording changes

See Chapter 2, Setting up Writer, for instructions on setting up how your changes will be displayed.

1) To begin tracking (recording) changes, choose **Edit > Changes > Record**. To show or hide the display of changes, click **Edit > Changes > Show**.

Tip	Hold the mouse pointer over a marked change; you will see a *Help Tip* showing the type of change, the author, date, and time of day for the change. If *Extended Tips* are enabled, you will also see any comments recorded for this change.

2) To enter a comment on a marked change, place the cursor in the area of the change and then click **Edit > Changes > Comment**.

In addition to being displayed as an extended tip, the comment is also displayed in the list in the Accept or Reject Changes dialog (Figure 110).
To move from one marked change to the next, use the arrow buttons. If no comment has been recorded for a change, the *Text* field is blank.

3) To stop recording changes, click **Edit > Changes > Record** again.

Tip	See also "Adding other comments" on page 113 for a way to annotate text that is not associated with a recorded change.

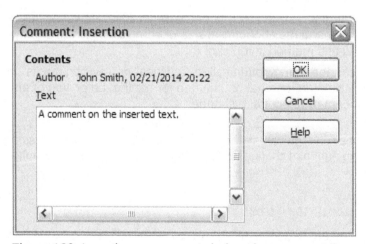

Figure 109: Inserting a comment during change recording

Accepting or rejecting changes

To accept or reject recorded changes, use either of these methods:

- Right-click (context) menu
- Accept or Reject Changes dialog

The results of accepting or rejecting a change are as follows:

- Accepting a change incorporates the alteration into the document and removes the change indication marking.
- Rejecting a change reverts the document to its original state and removes the change indication marking.

Right-click (context) menu

1) If recorded changes are not showing, click **Edit > Changes > Show**.
2) Hover the mouse pointer over a recorded change. A box appears with information about the type of change, who made it, and the date and time.
3) Right-click on the changed text. In the context menu, choose **Accept Change** or **Reject Change**.

Accept or Reject Changes dialog

1) Click **Edit > Changes > Accept or Reject**. The Accept or Reject Changes dialog (Figure 110) opens, showing changes that have not yet been accepted or rejected.
2) When you select a change in the dialog, the actual change is highlighted in the document, so you can see what the editor changed.
3) Click **Accept** or **Reject** to accept or reject the selected change. You can also click **Accept All** or **Reject All** if you do not want to review the changes individually.

To show only the changes of certain people or only the changes on specific days or various other restrictions, use the *Filter* page (Figure 111) on the Accept or Reject Changes dialog. After specifying the filter criteria, return to the *List* page to see those changes that meet your criteria.

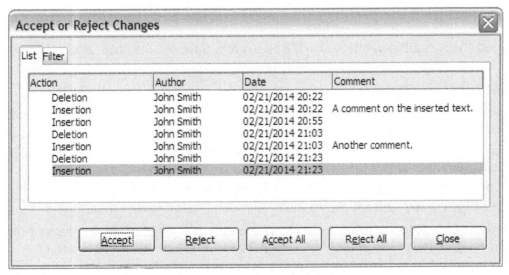

Figure 110: The List tab of the Accept or Reject Changes dialog

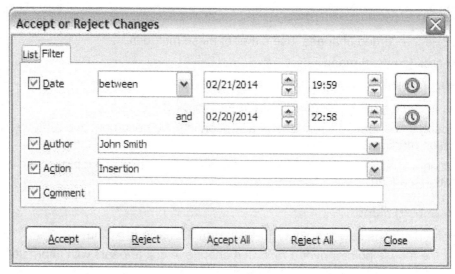

Figure 111: The Filter page of the Accept or Reject Changes dialog

Merging modified documents

The processes discussed to this point are effective when you have one reviewer at a time. Sometimes, however, multiple reviewers all return edited versions of a document at the same time. In this case, it may be quicker to review all of these changes at once, rather than one review at a time. For this purpose, you can merge documents in Writer.

To merge documents, all of the edited documents need to have recorded changes in them.

1) Open one copy.
2) Click **Edit > Changes > Merge Document** and select and insert another copy of the document to be merged with the first.
3) After the documents merge, the Accept or Reject Changes dialog opens, as in Figure 110, showing changes by more than one reviewer. If you want to merge more documents, close the dialog and then repeat step 2.
4) Repeat until all copies are merged.

All recorded changes are now included in the open copy. Save this file under another name.

Comparing documents

Sometimes reviewers may forget to record the changes they make. This is not a problem with Writer because you can find the changes if you compare documents.

In order to compare documents, you need to have the original document and the one that is edited. To compare them:

1) Open the edited document. Select **Edit > Compare Document**.
2) The Insert dialog appears. Select the original document and click **Insert**.

Writer finds and marks the changes and displays the Accept or Reject Changes dialog. From this point, you can go through and accept or reject changes procedure as described earlier.

Adding other comments

Writer provides another type of comments (formerly called "notes"), which authors and reviewers often use to exchange ideas, ask for suggestions, or brainstorm during the review process.

You can select a block of text, including multiple paragraphs, to be highlighted for a comment, or insert a comment at a single point. To insert a comment, select the text, or place the cursor in the place the comment refers to, and choose **Insert > Comment** or press *Ctrl+Alt+C*.

The anchor point of the comment is connected by a dotted line to a box on the right-hand side of the page where you can type the text of the comment. Writer automatically adds at the bottom of the comment the author's name and a time stamp indicating when the comment was created. Select **Tools > Options > LibreOffice > User Data** to configure the name you want to appear in the Author field of the comment, or to change it.

Click somewhere on the page to finish your comment. Otherwise, you will not be able to move away from this location.

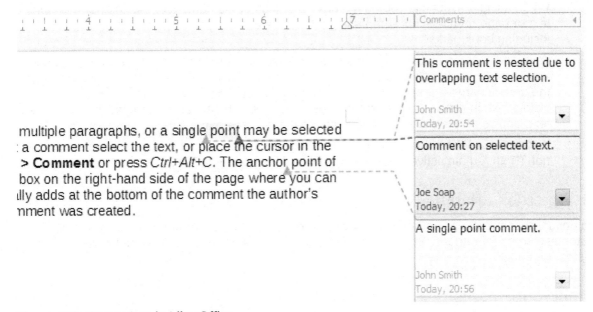

Figure 112: Comments in LibreOffice

If more than one person edits the document, each author is automatically allocated a different background color. Figure 112 shows an example of text with comments from two different authors. If an author selects text that overlaps another author's comments, then the comments from the second author are nested with those of the first author.

Right-clicking on a comment pops up a menu where you can delete the current comment, all the comments from the same author, or all the comments in the document. This part of the menu is also available by clicking the down-arrow in the comment. From this menu, you can also apply some basic formatting to the text of the comment. You can also change font type, size, and alignment from the Menu bar.

To navigate from one comment to another, open the Navigator (*F5*), expand the Comments section, and click on the comment text to move the cursor to the anchor point of the comment in the document. Right-click on the comment to quickly edit or delete it.

You can also navigate the comments using the keyboard. Use *Ctrl+Alt+Page Down* to move to the next comment and *Ctrl+Alt+Page Up* to move to the previous comment.

Inserting a comment causes the Comments button to appear on the right-hand end of the ruler (see Figure 112). Toggling the button hides or shows all the comments.

Linking to another part of a document

If you type in cross-references to other parts of the document, those references can easily get out of date if you reorganize the order of topics, add or remove material, or reword a heading, Writer provides two ways to ensure that your references are up to date, by inserting links to other parts of the same document or to a different document:

- Hyperlinks
- Cross-references

The two methods have the same result if you *Ctrl+click* the link when the document is open in Writer: you are taken directly to the cross-referenced item. However, they also have major differences:

- The text in a hyperlink does **not** automatically update if you change the text of the linked item (although you can change it manually), but changed text does automatically update in a cross-reference.

- When using a hyperlink, you do not have a choice of the content of the link (for example text or page number), but when using a cross-reference, you have several choices, including bookmarks.

- To hyperlink to an object such as a graphic, and have the hyperlink show useful text such as *Figure 6*, you need to either give such an object a useful name instead of leaving it as the default name ("Graphics6"), or you need to use the Hyperlink dialog to modify the visible text. In contrast, cross-references to figures with captions automatically show useful text, and you have a choice of several variations of the name.

- If you save a Writer document to HTML, hyperlinks remain active but cross-references do not. (Both remain active when the document is exported to PDF.)

Using cross-references

To ensure that references update if you reword a heading, caption, or other linked item, use automatic cross-references. See "Using automatic cross-references" in Chapter 14, Working with Fields, for details.

Using bookmarks

Bookmarks are listed in the Navigator and can be accessed directly from there with a single mouse click. In HTML documents, bookmarks are converted to anchors that you can jump to by hyperlink. For more about bookmarks, see "Using bookmarks" in Chapter 14, Working with Fields.

Using hyperlinks

When you type text (such as website addresses or URL) that can be used as a hyperlink, and then press the spacebar or the *Enter* key, Writer automatically creates the hyperlink and applies formatting to the text (usually a color and underlining).

If this does not happen, you can enable this feature using **Tools > AutoCorrect Options > Options** and selecting the **URL Recognition** option.

If you do not want Writer to convert a specific URL to a hyperlink, choose **Edit > Undo Insert** from the Menu bar or press *Ctrl+Z* immediately after the formatting has been applied.

You can also insert hyperlinks using the Navigator and the Hyperlink dialog, and you can modify all hyperlinks using the Hyperlink dialog, as described in this section.

Note	Hyperlinks between documents can be set as relative or absolute, using the **Save URLs relative to** option in **Tools > Options > Load/Save > General**.
	Relative linking is only possible when the document you are working on and the link destination are on the same drive, and you need to create the same directory structure on your hard disk as will apply on the destination website.
	LibreOffice uses absolute path names internally, so when you move your mouse cursor over a hyperlink, the tooltip displays the absolute reference even when it is set to be a relative link.

Inserting hyperlinks using the Navigator

The easiest way to insert a hyperlink to another part of the same document is by using the Navigator:

1) Open the document containing the items you want to cross-reference.
2) Open the Navigator (by clicking its icon, choosing **View > Navigator**, pressing *F5*, or selecting the Navigator Tab on the open Sidebar).
3) Click the arrow next to the **Drag Mode** icon, and select **Insert as Hyperlink**.
4) In the list at the bottom of the **Navigator**, select the document containing the item that you want to cross-reference.
5) In the **Navigator** list, select the item that you want to insert as a hyperlink.
6) Drag the item to where you want to insert the hyperlink in the document. The name of the item is inserted in the document as an active hyperlink.

Figure 113: Inserting a hyperlink using the Navigator

Inserting hyperlinks using a dialog

To display the Hyperlink dialog (Figure 114), click the **Hyperlink** icon ( ) on the Standard Toolbar or choose **Insert > Hyperlink** from the Menu bar. To turn existing text into a link, select it before opening the dialog.

On the left hand side, select one of the four types of hyperlink:

- **Internet**: a web address, normally starting with http://
- **Mail & News**: for example an email address.
- **Document**: the hyperlink points to another document or to another place in the presentation.
- **New document**: the hyperlink creates a new document.

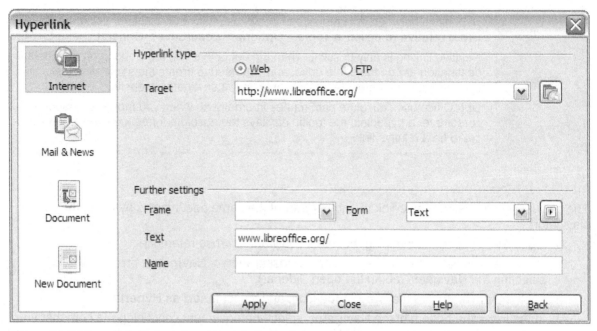

Figure 114: Hyperlink dialog showing details for Internet links

The top right part of the dialog changes according to your choice for the hyperlink type. A full description of all the choices, and their interactions, is beyond the scope of this chapter. Here is a summary of the most common choices used in presentations.

For an *Internet* type hyperlink, choose the type of hyperlink (choose between Web, FTP or Telnet), and enter the required web address (URL).

For a *Mail and News* type hyperlink, specify whether it is a mail or news link, the receiver address and for email, also the subject.

For a *Document* type hyperlink, specify the document path (the **Open File** button opens a file browser); leave this blank if you want to link to a target in the same presentation. Optionally specify the target in the document (for example a specific slide). Click on the **Target** icon to open the Navigator where you can select the target, or if you know the name of the target, you can type it into the box.

For a *New Document* type hyperlink, specify whether to edit the newly created document immediately or just create it (**Edit later**) and the type of document to create (text, spreadsheet, and so on). For a text document, **Edit now** is the more likely choice. The **Select Path** button opens a directory picker.

The *Further settings* section in the bottom right part of the dialog is common to all the hyperlink types, although some choices are more relevant to some types of links.

- Set the value of **Frame** to determine how the hyperlink will open. This applies to documents that open in a Web browser.
- **Form** specifies if the link is to be presented as text or as a button.
- **Text** specifies the text that will be visible to the user.
- **Name** is applicable to HTML documents. It specifies text that will be added as a NAME attribute in the HTML code behind the hyperlink.
- **Event** button: this button will be activated to allow LibreOffice to react to events for which the user has written some code (macro). This function is not covered in this book.

Editing hyperlinks

To edit a hyperlink, click anywhere in the link text and then open the Hyperlink dialog by clicking the **Hyperlink** icon on the Standard Toolbar or choosing **Edit > Hyperlink** from the Menu bar. Make your changes and click Apply. If you need to edit several hyperlinks, you can leave the Hyperlink dialog open until you have edited all of them. Be sure to click **Apply** after each one. When you are finished, click **Close**.

The standard (default) behavior for activating hyperlinks within LibreOffice is to use *Ctrl+click*. This behavior can be changed in **Tools > Options > LibreOffice > Security > Options**, by deselecting the option **Ctrl-click required to follow hyperlinks**. If clicking in your links activates them, check that page to see if the option has been deselected.

To change the color of hyperlinks, go to **Tools > Options > LibreOffice > Appearance**, scroll to *Unvisited links* and/or *Visited links*, select those options, pick the new colors and click **OK**. Caution: this will change the color for *all* hyperlinks in *all* components of LibreOffice—this may not be what you want.

In Writer and Calc (but not Draw or Impress), you can also change the *Internet link* character style or define and apply new styles to selected links.

Switching between insert and overwrite mode

In insert mode, any text after the cursor position moves forward to make room for the text you type; in overwrite mode, text after the cursor position is replaced by the text you type. Only the Overwrite mode is displayed on the Status Bar. The shape of the cursor does not change.

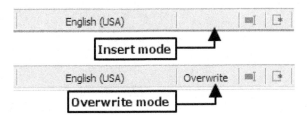

With the keyboard, press *Insert* to toggle between overwrite mode and insert mode. With the mouse, click in the area on the Status Bar that indicates the current mode in order to switch to the other mode. Overwrite mode cannot be used with **Edit > Changes > Record** enabled.

Counting the words in a selection

Word and character count for the document, or for any selected text, is displayed on the Status bar. Word count and character count can be viewed by choosing **Tools > Word Count** or double-clicking on the word count field in the Status bar; this information updates as you edit the document. See Chapter 2, Setting up Writer, for information on setting word counting boundaries.

You can also see the number of words and characters (and other information including the number of pages, tables, and graphics) in the entire document in **File > Properties > Statistics**.

Changing the case of selected text

To quickly change the case of text, select it, choose **Format > Change Case** from the Menu bar, and then choose one of the following:

- Sentence case, where only the first word is capitalized (together with any proper nouns)
- lower case, where no words (except proper nouns) are capitalized
- UPPER CASE, where all letters are capitalized
- Capitalize Every Word, where every word is capitalized
- tOGGLE cASE, which changes every letter to the opposite case

There are also several options that are used with Asian text. These are not strictly "Case" changes, but are lumped together in the broader sense of replacing characters with different forms of the same letter. These options are hidden when Asian language support is not enabled.

Writer does not have an automated way to do Title Case, where all words are capitalized except for certain subsets defined by rules that are not universally standardized. To achieve this affect, you can use *Capitalize Every Word* and then restore those words that were incorrectly capitalized.

Chapter 4
Formatting Pages

Using Page Styles, Tables, Frames, Columns, and Sections

Introduction

Writer provides several ways for you to control page layouts:

- Page styles
- Columns
- Frames
- Tables
- Sections

This chapter describes these methods and some associated functions:

- Headers and footers
- Numbering pages
- Changing page margins

Tip	Page layout is usually easier if you select the options to show text, object, table, and section boundaries in **Tools > Options > LibreOffice > Appearance** and the options for paragraph ends, tabs, breaks, and other items in **Tools > Options > LibreOffice Writer > Formatting Aids**.

Choosing a layout method

The best layout method depends on what the final document should look like and what sort of information will be in the document. Here are some examples. Do not worry if all this does not mean much to you now. The techniques mentioned are all described in this chapter.

For a book similar to this user guide with one column of text, some figures without text beside them, and some other figures with descriptive text, use page styles for basic layout, and use tables to place figures beside descriptive text, where necessary.

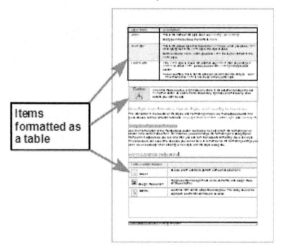

Items formatted as a table

Use page styles (with two columns) for an index or other document with two columns of text where the text continues from the left-hand column to the right-hand column and then to the next page, all in sequence (also known as *snaking columns* of text). If the title of the document (on the first page) is full-page width, put it in a single-column section.

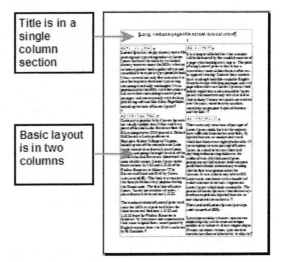

For a newsletter with a complex layout, two or three columns on the page, and some articles that continue from one page to some place several pages later, use page styles for basic layout. Place articles in linked frames and anchor graphics to fixed positions on the page, if necessary.

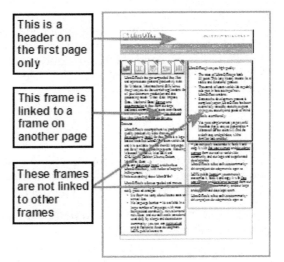

For a document with terms and translations to appear side-by-side in what appear to be columns, use a table to keep items lined up so you can type in both "columns".

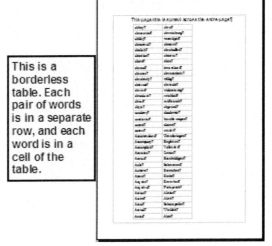

Setting up basic page layout using styles

In Writer, *page styles* define the basic layout of all pages, including page size, margins, the placement of headers and footers, borders and backgrounds, number of columns, and so on.

Writer comes with several page styles, which you can build on or modify, and you can define new (custom) page styles. You can have one or many page styles in a single document.

Note	All pages in a Writer document are based on styles. If you do not specify a page style, Writer uses the *Default* page style.

To change the layout of individual pages, either define a new page style or use one of the techniques (sections, frames, or tables) described later in this chapter.

This chapter describes some uses of page styles. Some other uses are discussed in Chapter 6, Introduction to Styles. The Page Style dialog is covered in detail in Chapter 7, Working with Styles.

Tip	Any modifications of page styles, including the *Default* page style, apply only to the document you are working on. If you want the changes to be the default for all documents, you need to put the changes into a template and make that template the default template. See Chapter 10, Working with Templates, for details.

Inserting a page break without switching the style

In many documents (for example, a multi-page report), you may want the text to flow from one page to the next as you add or delete information. Writer does this automatically, unless you override the text flow using one of the techniques described earlier.

If you do want a page break in a particular place, for example, to put a heading at the top of a new page, here is how to do it:

1) Position the cursor at the point you want to start the next page. Select **Insert > Manual Break**.
2) In the *Type* section, *Page break* is preselected, and **Style** is set at *[None]*.
3) Click **OK** to position the paragraph at the start of the next page.

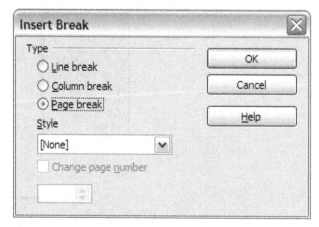

Figure 115: Inserting a manual page break

Breaks

☑ Insert   Type Page ▾   Position Before ▾

☐ With Page Style   Page number 0 ▾

Defining a different first page for a document

Many documents, such as letters and reports, have a first page that is different from the other pages in the document. For example, the first page of a letterhead typically has a different header, as shown in Figure 116, or the first page of a report might have no header or footer, while the other pages do. This is simple to achieve with Writer.

Using the Default (or any other) page style for your document, you can add a header/footer as you wish to the first page by deselecting the **Same content on first page** option on the header/footer pages in the Page Style dialog, and then adding the header/footer. You can then add a different header/footer to the other pages of the document.

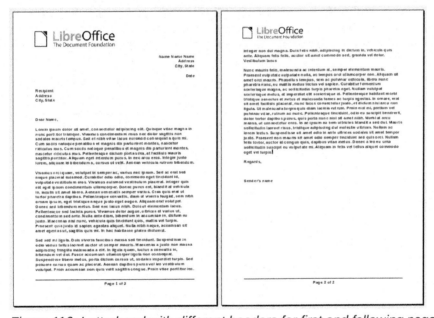

Figure 116: Letterhead with different headers for first and following pages

Changing page orientation within a document

A document can contain pages in more than one orientation. A common scenario is to have a landscape page in the middle of a document, whereas the other pages are in a portrait orientation. Here are the steps to achieve it.

1) If you wish to keep the margins the same as on other pages, then note the margin settings of the current page style. (You can find the margin settings on the Page Style dialog, by selecting the Page tab as shown in Figure 118.)

2) In the Styles and Formatting window, right-click on **Landscape** in the list of page styles and choose Modify from the pop-up menu (Styles and Formatting can also be accessed from the Sidebar, **View > Sidebar**).

3) On the *Organizer* page of the Page Style dialog (Figure 117), make sure the *Next Style* property is set to **Landscape** (to allow for having more than one sequential landscape page).

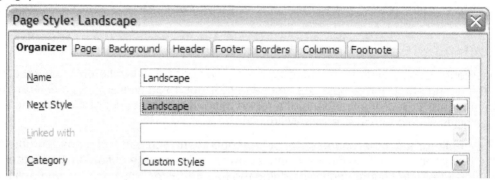

Figure 117: Name the new style and set the next page style to Landscape

4) On the *Page* page of the Page Style dialog (Figure 118), make sure the *Orientation* is set to **Landscape**. Change the margins so that they correspond with the margins of the portrait page. That is, the portrait top margin becomes the landscape left margin, and so on.

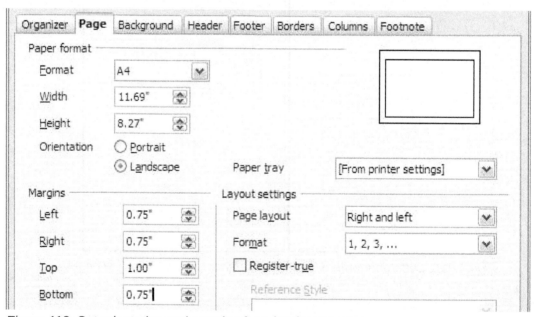

Figure 118: Set orientation and margins for a landscape page

5) Click **OK** to save the changes.

Inserting a landscape page into a portrait document

Now that you have defined the *Landscape* page style, here is how to apply it.

1) Position the cursor in the paragraph or table at the start of the page that is to be set to landscape. Right-click and choose **Paragraph** or **Table**, respectively, in the pop-up menu.

2) On the *Text Flow* page of the Paragraph dialog (Figure 119) or the Table Format dialog (Figure 120), select **Insert** (or **Break** for a table) and **With Page Style**. Set the *Page Style* property to **Landscape**. Click **OK** to close the dialog and to apply the new page style.

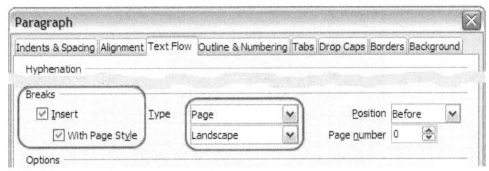

Figure 119: Specifying a page break before a paragraph

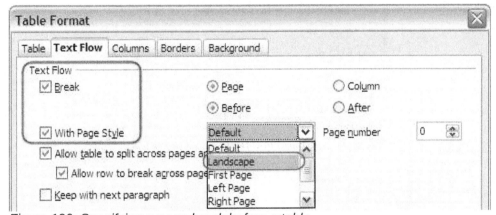

Figure 120: Specifying a page break before a table

3) Position the cursor in the paragraph or table where the page is to return to portrait orientation and change the paragraph properties or table properties so that *With Page Style* is the portrait page style that was used before the *Landscape* page style.

4) Click **OK** to return to the previous portrait page style.

Tip	If you need the headers or footers on the landscape pages to be in portrait orientation, see "Portrait headers on landscape pages" on page 147.

Adding title pages

Writer provides a fast and convenient way to add one or more title pages to a document and optionally to restart the page number at 1 for the body of the document.

To begin, choose **Format > Title Page** from the Menu Bar. On the Title Page dialog (Figure 121), you can make a variety of choices:

- Convert existing pages to title pages, or insert new title pages
- How many pages to convert or insert

- Where those pages are located
- If and where to restart page numbering, and what number to start with
- What page style to use for the title page

Using this technique, you can insert several "title pages" at different points in your document, for example to add decorative pages between chapters as well as title, copyright, and other pages at the beginning of a book.

Figure 121: Adding title pages to a document

Changing page margins

You can change page margins in three ways:
- Using the page rulers—quick and easy, but does not have fine control.
- Using the Page Style dialog—can specify margins to two (fractional) decimal places.
- Using the Page panel of the Properties deck in the Sidebar.

Note	If you change the margins using the rulers or the Sidebar, the new margins affect the page style and will be shown in the Page Style dialog the next time you open it.

To change margins using the rulers:
1) The shaded sections of the rulers are the margins (see Figure 122). Put the mouse cursor over the line between the gray and white sections. The pointer turns into a double-headed arrow and displays the current setting in a tool-tip.
2) Hold down the left mouse button and drag the mouse to move the margin.

Caution	The small arrows on the ruler are used for indenting paragraphs. They are often in the same place as the page margins, so you need to be careful to move the margin marker, not the arrows. The double-headed arrows shown in Figure 122 are actual mouse cursors placed in the correct position.

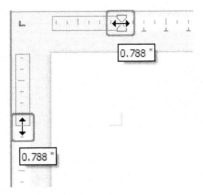

Figure 122: Moving the margins

To change margins using the Page Style dialog (Figure 118):

1) Right-click anywhere on the page and select **Page** from the context menu.

2) On the *Page* page of the dialog, type the required distances in the *Margins* boxes.

To change margins using the Page panel of the Properties deck of the Sidebar:

1) On the open Sidebar (**View > Sidebar**) select the **Properties** tab.

2) Open the Page panel if is not open by clicking the plus (**+**) symbol in the panel title

3) Click the **Margin** button to open the sub-panel and enter the required dimensions in the **Custom** size boxes (clicking the **More Options** button will open the Page Style dialog).

Using columns to define the page layout

You can use columns for page layout in the following ways:

- By defining the number of columns and their layout on a page, using page styles.

- By changing the number of columns for existing text.

Defining the columns on a page

It is a good idea to define your basic page style (such as *Default*) with the most common layout to be used in your document, either single-column or multiple-column. You can then either define extra page styles for pages with different numbers of columns or use sections (described in "Using sections for page layout" starting on page 138) for pages or parts of pages with different numbers of columns.

To define the number of columns on a page:

1) Choose **Format > Columns** to go to the Columns dialog (see Figure 123), or go to the *Columns* page of the Page Style dialog, or click the **More Options** button on the Page panel of the Properties deck of the Sidebar.

2) In the *Settings* section, choose the number of columns and specify any spacing between the columns and whether you want a vertical separator line to appear between the columns. You can use one of Writer's predefined column layouts, or you can create a customized column layout. The preview pane, located to the right of the *Settings* section, shows how the column layout will look.

   Notice the *Apply to* box in the dialog of Figure 123. In this instance, the changes are being applied to the *Default* page style.

3) Click **OK** to save the changes.

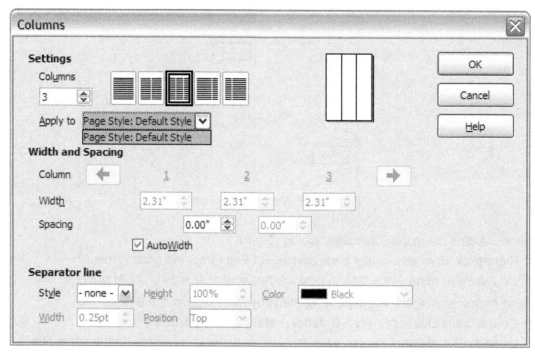

Figure 123: Defining the number of columns on a page

Specifying the number of columns

In the *Settings* section, enter the number of columns into the **Columns** selection box, or select one of the column layout icons.

Formatting column width and spacing

Select the **AutoWidth** option in the *Width and spacing* section to create columns of equal width.

To customize the width and spacing of the columns:

1) In the *Width and spacing* section, deselect the **AutoWidth** option.
2) In the *Width* selection boxes, enter a width for each column.
3) On the *Spacing* line, enter the amount of space that you want between each pair of columns.

If you specify more than three columns, use the arrow keys on the *Column* line to scroll among the columns.

Formatting separator lines

To display separator lines between the columns:

1) Using the *Style* drop-down list, select the line style from the three styles available.
2) Using the *Width* control, select the width of line to use, settable from 0.25pt to 9.0pt. (1 pt = 1 point = 1/12 pica = 1/72 inch = 127/360 mm = 0.3527 mm.)
3) Using the *Height* control, select the height of line required, as a percentage of the column height. Variable from 25% to 100%.
4) If you entered a height of less than 100%, use the *Position* drop-down list to select a vertical alignment for the separator lines. The vertical-positioning options are: **Top**, **Centered**, or **Bottom**.
4) The line color can be selected from the *Color* drop-down list's palette of colors.

Tip	To quickly input the maximum or minimum allowed value in an input box, click the current value and press *Page Up* or *Page Down* respectively.

Reverting to a single-column layout

To revert to a single-column layout for the page style, go to the *Settings* section and either reset the number in the *Columns* box to **1** or click the single-column layout icon.

Changing the number of columns for existing text

You might want some parts of a page to have one column and other parts of the page to have two or more columns. For example, you might have a page-width headline over a three-column news story.

You can create columns and then type or paste text into them, or you can select some existing text and change the number of columns for displaying it.

When you select text and change the number of columns for that text (**Format > Columns**), Writer turns the selected text into a *section*, as described in "Using sections for page layout" on page 138.

Figure 124 shows the Columns dialog for a selection. The *Apply to* box has **Selection** highlighted and an extra option (**Evenly distribute contents to all columns**) appears in the Settings section.

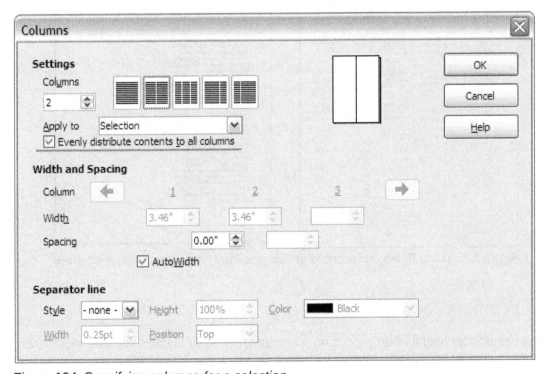

Figure 124: Specifying columns for a selection

Tip	You cannot select text on a two-column formatted page and change it to a single column using this method. Instead, you need to define a single-column page and then select the text you want to be in a two-column section on that page.

Distributing text across columns

As you add text to the section, you will see that the text flows from one column to the next. You can distribute text across the columns in one of two ways:

Evenly—Writer adjusts the length of the columns to the amount of text, so that all the columns are approximately the same height. As you add or delete text, the columns readjust.

Newspaper-style—Writer fills the columns one at a time, beginning with the first column. The last column may be shorter than the others.

To distribute text evenly, select the **Evenly distribute contents to all columns** option in the *Settings* area. Deselect this option if you want to distribute text newspaper-style.

Tip	Choose **View > Nonprinting Characters** (or press *Ctrl+F10*) to display end of paragraph markers (¶). Often, unexpected behavior of columns is due to extra paragraphs that are normally invisible to the user but are taking up space.

Figure 125: (Left) Evenly distributed columns; (Right) Newspaper-style columns.

Using frames for page layout

Frames can be very useful when producing a newsletter or other layout-intensive documents. Frames can contain text, tables, multiple columns, pictures, and other objects.

Use frames when you need to:

- Position something in a particular place on a page, for example, a logo or a "stop press" news box in one corner of a page.

- Allow text on one page to continue on another page, somewhere more distant than the next one, by linking the content of one frame to another so the contents flow between them as you edit the text.

- Wrap text around an object, such as a photograph.

Because LibreOffice does not allow you to define page styles with recurring frames, consider doing some quick sketches of the basic page layouts you need, indicating the approximate positions of different frames and their purposes. Try to keep the number of different page layouts as low as possible in order to avoid chaos in your design.

Pay special attention to the positioning of frames. Many of the predefined styles default to a center alignment. Although centering all frames looks reasonably good in most cases, it is rarely the best choice.

One of the most visually effective ways to position a frame is to align its left margin with that of the paragraph above it. To achieve this effect, the frame is inserted in a blank paragraph of the same style as the paragraph above. Select **Insert > Frame**; in the *Position* section of the *Type* page, select **From Left** in the *Horizontal* selection box to position the frame exactly where you want it.

You also should think about the type of wrap and the spacing between the frame and text. Instead of cramming a frame close to the text, use the *Wrap* tab to place some white space between them.

You can format frames individually or define and apply frame styles; see Chapter 7, Working with Styles.

Example: Using a frame to center text on a page
Although you can center text horizontally as part of a paragraph style or by using manual formatting, those methods do not work for vertical centering. To center text vertically, you need to place the text in a frame, anchor the frame to a page or a paragraph, and then center the frame vertically on the page. See "Anchoring frames" on page 133.

Creating frames

You can create a frame in several ways, depending on your needs.

- Choose **Insert > Frame** to create an empty frame. The Frame dialog (Figure 127) appears. You can click **OK** and come back to customize it later, or you can set the frame's characteristics at this stage.

- Select text or a graphic, choose **Insert > Frame**, and click **OK** to create a frame containing the selection. The selected text is automatically deleted from the normal text flow and inserted into the frame, and the Frame dialog appears.

- Insert a picture or other object by selecting **Insert > Image > From file** or **Insert > Object > [type of object]** to start the process to insert a picture or object. The item inserted automatically appears in a frame, but the Frame dialog does not appear.

- Select the **Insert Frame Manually** button on the Insert toolbar (go to **View > Toolbars > Insert** to display it), select the number of frames in the drop-down menu, the mouse cursor changes to a plus (+) symbol, click and drag the mouse to draw the frame.

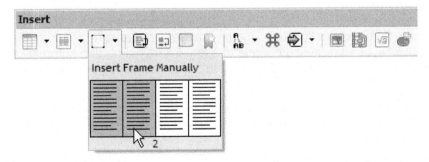

Figure 126: Using a button on the Insert toolbar to create a frame

Releasing the mouse button creates the frame: an area isolated from the main document.

To add content to a frame, first deselect the frame by clicking somewhere else on the page. Then, click inside the frame to place the text cursor there. Now add content just like you would on the main page. When you are done, deselect the frame.

Moving, resizing, and changing frame attributes

When an object is added to Writer, it is automatically enclosed in a frame of a predetermined type. The frame sets how the object is placed on the page, as well as how it interacts with other elements in the document. You can edit the frame by modifying the frame style it uses or by using a manual override when a frame is added to the document. Frame styles are discussed in Chapter 7, Working with Styles.

To change the size or location of a frame, first select the frame, then use either the mouse or the Frame dialog (Figure 127). Using the mouse is quicker but less accurate. You might want to use the mouse for gross layout and the dialog for fine-tuning.

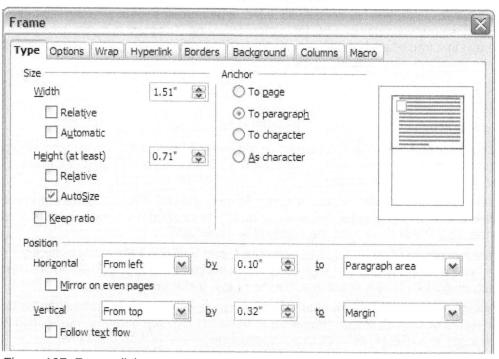

Figure 127: Frame dialog

You can re-size the frame manually by clicking on the green squares (sizing handles) and dragging to the appropriate size, or start adding content to it (the frame will re-size automatically if, for example, you add a large picture to it) or go back to the Frame dialog and set the size and other characteristics.

To change the location of the frame using the mouse, drag and drop one of the edges or put the cursor anywhere within the frame. (The I-bar cursor changes to a four-headed arrow when properly positioned for a drag-and-drop move.)

To change the size of the frame, drag one of the sizing handles. Drag a handle on one of the sides to enlarge or reduce the text frame in one dimension only; drag a corner handle to enlarge or reduce it in both dimensions.

These resizing actions distort the proportions of the frame. Holding down the *Shift* key while dragging one of the handles makes the frame keep the same proportions.

You can open the Frame dialog at any time by selecting the frame, right-clicking, and choosing **Frame** from the context menu.

To remove the default border on a newly created frame, open the Frame dialog, go to the *Borders* page, and in the **Style** box under *Line*, select **None**. Alternatively, you can assign a borderless style to the frame; see Chapter 7, Working with Styles, for information on frame styles.

Note	Do not confuse a frame's border with the text boundaries that are made visible using the View menu (by selecting **View > Text Boundaries**).

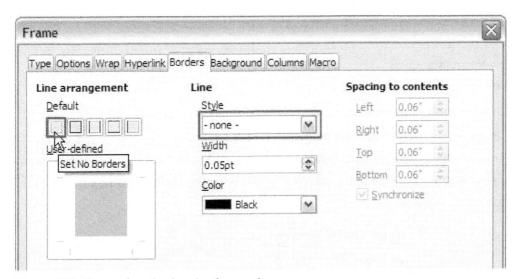

Figure 128: Removing the border from a frame

Anchoring frames

Using the Frame dialog (or by right-clicking and pointing to **Anchor**), you can anchor a frame to a page, paragraph, or character, or you can anchor it as a character.

To Page
> The frame keeps the same position in relation to the page margins. It does not move as you add or delete text. This method is useful when the frame does not need to be visually associated with a particular piece of text. It is often used when producing newsletters or other documents that are very layout-intensive. This method is also used to center text on a page.

To Paragraph
> The frame is associated with a paragraph and moves with the paragraph. It may be placed in the margin or another location. This method is useful as an alternative to a table for placing icons beside paragraphs. It is also used to center text on a page in documents which will be used in a master document (frames anchored to pages will disappear from the master document).

To Character
> The frame is associated with a character but is not in the text sequence. It moves with the paragraph but may be placed in the margin or another location. This method is similar to anchoring to a paragraph.

As Character
The frame is placed in the document like any other character and, therefore, affects the height of the text line and the line break. The frame moves with the paragraph as you add or delete text before the paragraph. This method is useful for adding a small icon in sequence in a sentence. It is also the best method for anchoring a graphic to an empty paragraph so it does not move around the page in unexpected ways.

Linking frames

You can link frames to each other even when they are on different pages of a document. The contents will automatically flow from one to the next. This technique is very useful when designing newsletters, where articles may need to be continued on a different page.

Note	You cannot link from a frame to more than one other frame.

To link one frame to another:

1) Select the frame to be linked from.

2) Click the **Link Frames** button (🗇) on the Frames toolbar.

3) Click the next frame in the series (which must be empty).

When a linked frame is selected, any existing links are indicated by a faint connecting line, as shown in Figure 129. Frames can be unlinked by selecting the **Unlink Frames** button (🗇) on the Frames toolbar.

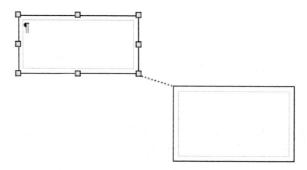

Figure 129: Linked frames

The height of a frame that is being linked from is fixed; you can change this height manually or by using the Frame dialog, but it does not automatically adjust to the size of the contents (that is, the AutoHeight attribute is disabled). Only the last frame of a chain can adapt its height to the content.

The *Options* page of the Frame dialog (Figure 130) shows the names of the selected frame and any frames it is linked to or from. You can change this information here. On this page, you can also select options to protect the contents, position, and size of the frame.

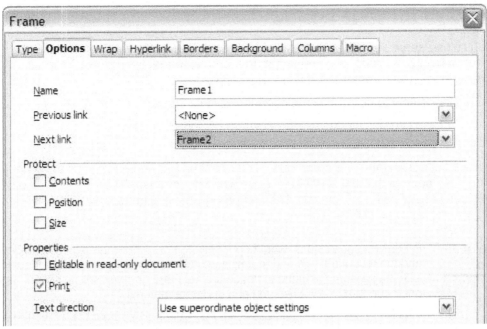

Figure 130: Options page of the Frame dialog

On the *Hyperlink* page (Figure 131), you can specify the file for the hyperlink to open. This file can be on your machine, a network, or the Internet.

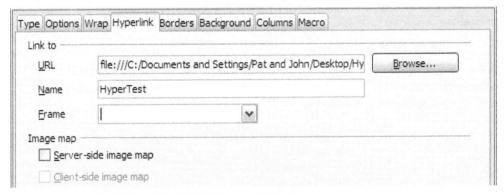

Figure 131: Hyperlink page of the Frame dialog

To open this file, you must *Ctrl+click* in the area between the border and the text boundary. Note that as the mouse cursor moves over any area within the frame boundary the hyperlink tooltip will be displayed, but it will only be active at the edges.

The *Wrap*, *Borders*, *Background*, *Columns*, and *Macro* pages of the Frame dialog are the same as those for frame styles. Refer to the Chapter 7, Working with Styles, for details.

Using tables for page layout

Writer's tables can serve several purposes, such as holding data as you might see it in a spreadsheet, lining up material, and creating more complex page layouts. For information about using tables of data, see Chapter 9, Working with Tables.

This topic describes how to achieve some common layouts by using tables.

Example: Creating sideheads using tables

Sideheads and marginal notes are commonly used in documents from resumes to computer user guides. The main body of the text is offset to leave white space (usually on the left-hand side) in which the sideheads or notes are placed. The first paragraph is aligned beside the sidehead, as in Figure 132.

Example of a sidehead	In some cases you may want to put only one or two paragraphs in the table itself and the rest of the text and graphics in ordinary paragraphs (formatted to line up with the paragraphs in the table) so that text and graphics will flow more easily from one page to another when you add or delete material.
	In other cases, you might put each paragraph in a separate row of the table and allow the table to break between pages.

Figure 132: Example of a sidehead

Note	Sideheads can also be created by placing text in a frame using the *Marginalia* frame style, as described in Chapter 7, Working with Styles.

To create a table for use with a sidehead:

1) Place the cursor where you want the table to appear and choose **Insert > Table** (*Ctrl+F12*).
2) In the Insert Table dialog, define a one-row, two-column table with no border and no heading. Click **Insert** to create the table.

Figure 133: Defining a two-column borderless table with no header

3) Right-click on the table and choose **Table** from the context menu. On the *Columns* page of the Table Format dialog, make the columns the required width.

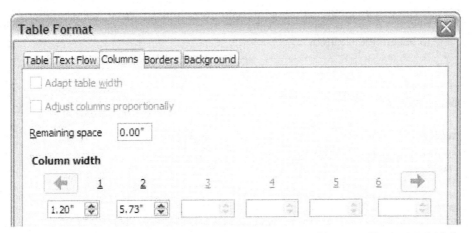

Figure 134: Defining a two-column table to line up with text offset at 1.2 inches

4) On the *Table* page of the Table Format dialog (Figure 135), in the *Spacing* section, make the *Above* and *Below* values the same as the *Top* and *Bottom* spacing you have defined for ordinary paragraphs of text. Click **OK** to save your settings.

Tip	To check the top and bottom spacing for ordinary paragraphs: 1) Position the cursor in a paragraph and press *F11* (unless the Styles and Formatting window is already open). Check that the Styles and Formatting window shows paragraph styles (top left button). 2) The current style should be highlighted. If no paragraph style is highlighted, select **All Styles** in the bottom drop-down list. Right-click on it and select **Modify** from the pop-up list. 3) Go to the *Indents & Spacing* page and look in the *Spacing* area for the values in *Above paragraph* and *Below paragraph*.

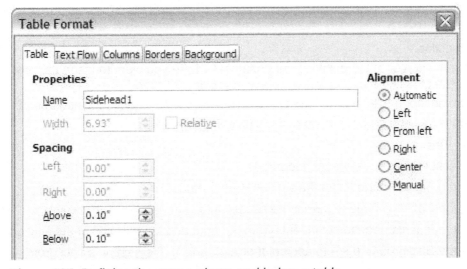

Figure 135: Defining the space above and below a table

You may also want to turn off number recognition so that Writer will not try to format numbers if you want them to be plain text. To turn number recognition off:

1) Right-click in the table and then click **Number Format** on the context menu.

2) On the Format Number dialog, make sure the *Category* is set to **Text**. Click **OK**.

Tip	If you use this table format often, you may want to save it as AutoText, as described in Chapter 3, Working with Text. Select the table (not just the contents) to assign the shortcut.

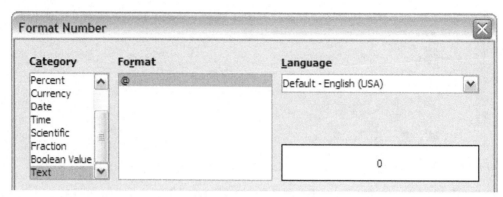

Figure 136: Setting number format to Text

Using sections for page layout

A section is a block of text that has special attributes and formatting. You can use sections to:

- Write-protect text
- Hide text
- Dynamically insert the contents of another document
- Add columns, margin indents, a background color, or a background graphic to a portion of your document
- Customize the footnotes and endnotes for a portion of your document

Creating sections

To create a section:

1) Place the cursor at the point in your document where you want to insert the new section. Or, select the text that you want to place in the new section.
2) From the Menu Bar, choose **Insert > Section**. The Insert Section dialog opens.
3) Choose settings for each page of the dialog as required.
4) Click **Insert**.

The Insert Section dialog has five tabbed pages.

- Use the *Section* page to set the section's attributes.
- Use the *Columns* page to format the section into columns.
- Use the *Indents* page to set indents from the right and left margins of the section.
- Use the *Background* page to add color or a graphic to the section's background.
- Use the *Footnotes/Endnotes* page to customize the section's footnotes and endnotes.

At any time before closing the dialog, you can reset a tabbed page to its default settings by clicking the **Reset** button. (Note, however, that you cannot reset the *Section* page. If you wish to undo changes to the *Section* page, you must do so manually).

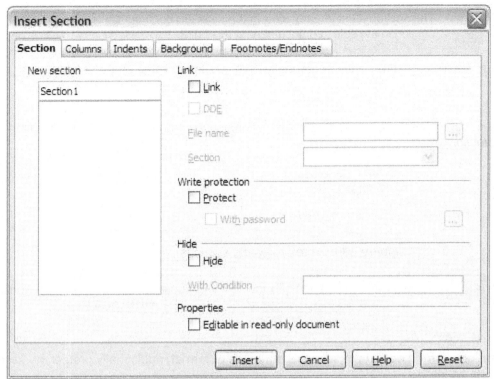

Figure 137: Inserting a section using the Insert Section dialog

Naming sections

Writer automatically enters a name for the section in the name box of the *New section* list box. To change the name, select it and type over it. The name is displayed in the *Sections* category of the Navigator window. If you give your sections meaningful names, you can navigate to them more easily.

Linking sections

You can insert the contents of another document into the section and then have Writer update it whenever the other document is updated. This is called *linking* the section to the other document.

To link the section to another document, follow these steps:

1) In the *Link* section of the dialog, select the **Link** option.

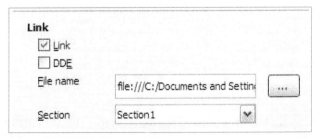

Figure 138: Linking sections

2) Click the (**...**) button to the right of the *File name* field. The Insert dialog opens.

3) Find and select the document you want to insert and then click the **Insert** button. The Insert dialog closes and the name of the selected document appears in the *File name* field.

4) If you want to insert only a section of the selected document, select the desired section from the *Section* drop-down list.

Note	The section must already exist in the selected document. You cannot create a section in the selected document at this point.

You can update links automatically or manually. See "Updating links" on page 144.

Write-protecting sections

To write-protect the section so that its contents cannot be edited, select the **Protect** option in the *Write protection* area.

Figure 139: Write-protecting sections

Note	Write-protection protects only the section's contents, not its attributes or format.

Password-protecting sections

To prevent others from editing the section's attributes or format, additionally protect the section with a password, as follows:

1) Select the **With password** option. The Enter Password dialog opens.

2) Type a password in the *Password* field and then confirm the password by typing it again in the *Confirm* field.

3) Click **OK**. The Enter Password dialog closes. Anyone who tries to edit the section's attributes or format will be prompted to enter the password.

Figure 140: Password-protecting a section

Hiding sections

You can hide the section so that it will not be displayed on the screen or printed. You can also specify conditions for hiding the section. For example, you can hide the section only from certain users.

Note	You cannot hide a section if it is the only content on the page or if the section is in a header, footer, footnote, endnote, frame, or table cell.

To hide a section, select the **Hide** option in the *Hide* section of the dialog.

Figure 141: Hiding sections

To hide the section only under certain conditions, enter the desired conditions in the *With Condition* field. The syntax and operators that you use to enter conditions are the same ones that you use to enter formulas. For syntax and a list of operators, see Writer's online help under **conditions**.

If the section is write-protected with a password, the password must be entered to hide or reveal the text.

Hiding text can be useful for printed documents, if for example you have an instruction manual for two widgets, Model A and Model B which are very similar. By setting a condition for, say, Model A widget, you can hide that text which only applies to Model B, before printing it.

Note	Hiding text is not a secure way to stop someone else reading it. It will stop the casual reader but will not prevent someone who actively wants to find out what you have hidden—even if it is password protected.

Formatting a section into columns

Use the *Columns* page of the Insert Section dialog to format the section into columns. This page is very similar to the Columns dialog shown in Figure 124 on page 129. Please refer to that topic for details.

Indenting the section from margins

Use the *Indents* page (Figure 142), to set indents from the right and left margins of the section.

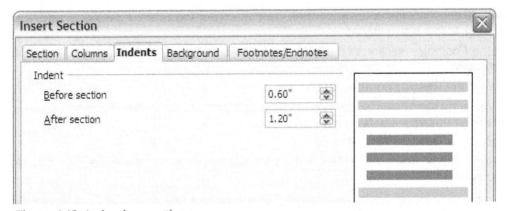

Figure 142: Indenting sections

Enter the desired left-margin indent in the *Before section* box. Enter the desired right-margin indent in the *After section* box. The preview box on the right-hand side of the page shows you how the section will look with the indents applied.

Changing the background of the section

Use the *Background* page to add color or a graphic to the background of the current section. This page is similar to the Background pages for paragraphs, frames, tables, and other objects in LibreOffice. For more information, refer to Chapter 7, Working with Styles.

Customizing footnotes and endnotes in a section

Use the *Footnotes/Endnotes* page to customize the current section's footnotes and endnotes.

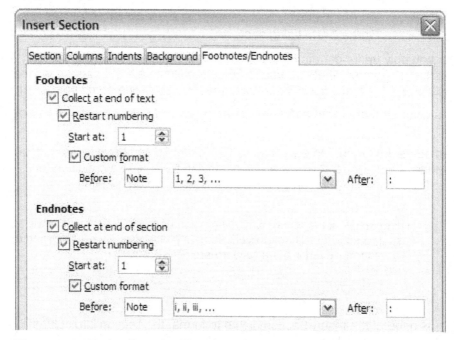

Figure 143: Setting footnotes and endnotes for sections

Customizing footnotes

If you want the section's footnotes to appear separately from the other footnotes in the document, select the **Collect at end of text** option in the *Footnotes* area.

To number the section's footnotes separately from the other footnotes in the document, and format the numbering, follow these steps:

1) In the *Footnotes* section of the page, make sure that the **Collect at end of text** option is selected.
2) Select the **Restart numbering** option.
3) If you want the section's footnotes to start at a number other than 1, enter the desired starting number in the *Start at* number box.
4) Select the **Custom format** option.
5) From the drop-down list of the **Custom format** option, select a numbering format for the footnotes.

To add text to the selected numbering format, use the *Before* and *After* text input boxes. For example, if you want the footnote numbers to be preceded by the word "Note" and followed by a colon, fill the *Before* and *After* fields as shown in Figure 143.

Customizing endnotes

If you want the section's endnotes to appear at the end of the section rather than at the end of the document, select the **Collect at end of section** option in the *Endnotes* area.

To number the current section's endnotes separately from the other endnotes in the document, and format the numbering, apply the procedures described above to the Endnotes settings.

Saving a new section

To save a new section so that it appears in your document, click the **Insert** button. The Insert Section dialog closes and the new section appears in your document.

Editing and deleting sections

To edit a section, follow these steps:

1) From the Menu Bar, choose **Format > Sections**. The Edit Sections dialog (Figure 144) opens.
2) Select the section you want to edit by clicking its name in the list box.

Editing section attributes

To rename the selected section, simply type over its name in the *Section* name box.

From the Edit Sections dialog, you can also edit the selected section's link, write-protect, and hide attributes. To learn how to edit these attributes, see:

"Linking sections" on page 139.

"Write-protecting sections" on page 140.

"Hiding sections" on page 140.

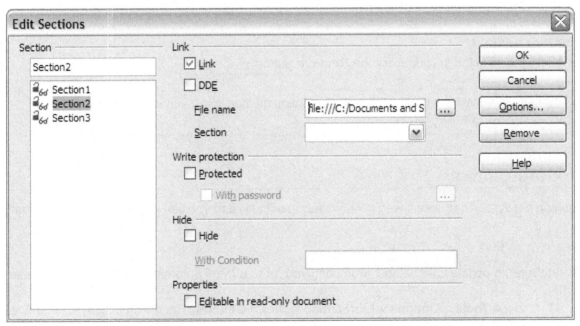

Figure 144: Edit Sections dialog

Editing the format of a section

To edit the format of the selected section, click the **Options** button.

The Options dialog has four tabbed pages: *Columns, Indents, Background,* and *Footnotes/Endnotes.* The use of these pages is described earlier in this topic.

To reset a page to the conditions in place when the dialog opened, click the **Reset** button.

To save your Options settings and return to the Edit Sections dialog, click **OK**.

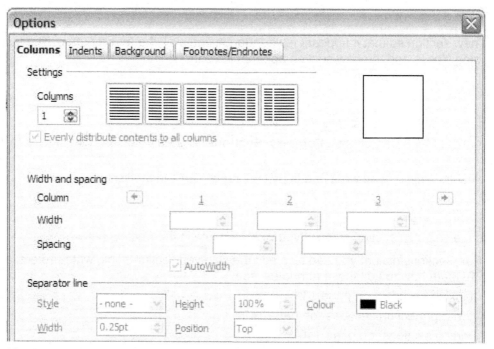

Figure 145: Options dialog for sections

Deleting sections

To delete the selected section, click the **Remove** button.

Note	Writer will not prompt you to confirm the deletion. To undo a deletion, click the **Cancel** button.

Updating links

You can set Writer to update linked sections automatically, and you can also update links manually.

Updating links automatically

To set Writer to update links without prompting you, or to turn off automatic updating, follow these steps:

1) Choose **Tools > Options > LibreOffice Writer > General**. The dialog displays general text document settings.

2) In the *Update* section of the dialog, under *Update links when loading*, select one of the following three options:

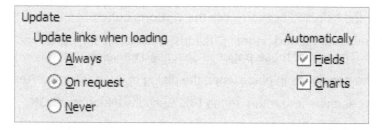

- Select **Always** if you want Writer to update links automatically, without prompting you, whenever you open a document that contains links.
- Select **On request** if you want Writer to prompt you before updating links.
- Select **Never** if you do not want Writer to update links.

3) Click **OK** to save your settings. The Options dialog closes.

Updating links manually

A protected section cannot be updated manually. It must first be unprotected.

To update a link manually:

1) Open the document that contains the link.
2) Choose **Edit > Links**. The Edit Links dialog opens.
3) The list in the Edit Links dialog displays the names of all the files that are linked to the current document. Click the file that corresponds to the link that you want to update.
4) Click the **Update** button. The most recently saved contents of the linked file appear in the current document.
5) To close the Edit Links dialog, click **Close**.

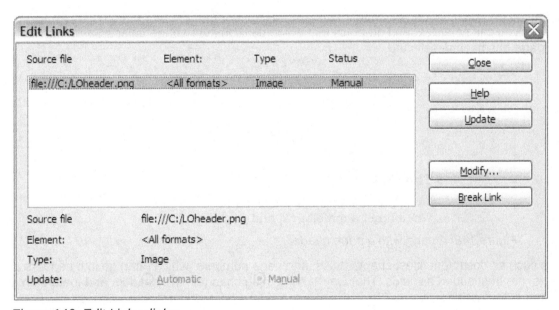

Figure 146: Edit Links dialog

Creating headers and footers

Headers are portions of a document that always appear at the top of a page; footers appear at the bottom of a page. Typically, headers display the title or chapter name of a document.

In LibreOffice, headers are specified by page styles; therefore, when inserted, all the pages with the same page style will display the same header. The option to make the header/footer on the first page of a document different is available (see "Defining a different first page for a document" on page 123). Chapter 7 describes how to format a header as part of the page style formatting. For the purpose of this example, we will insert a header in the *Default* pages using manual formatting.

There are two ways to insert a header. The simplest method is to click above the top of the text area, then when the Header marker appears (Figure 135), click on the **+**. (To insert a footer, click below the bottom of the text area to display the Footer marker, and then click on the **+**.)

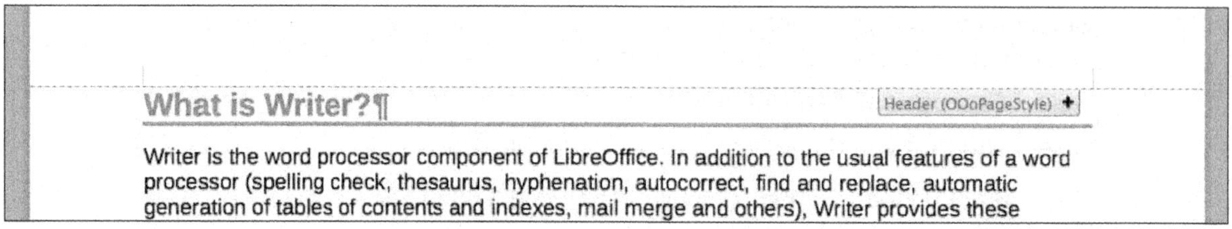

What is Writer?¶
Header (OOoPageStyle)
Writer is the word processor component of LibreOffice. In addition to the usual features of a word processor (spelling check, thesaurus, hyphenation, autocorrect, find and replace, automatic generation of tables of contents and indexes, mail merge and others), Writer provides these

Figure 147: Header marker at top of text area

Headers can also be inserted from the Menu Bar by selecting **Insert > Header > [Page Style]**. The submenu lists the page styles used in your document. In addition, the submenu includes the entry **All**, which activates headers on all the pages of the document regardless of their page style.

For our example, select the **Default** menu item to activate the headers only on the pages that use the *Default* page style. Similarly, to insert a footer, choose **Insert > Footer > [Page Style].**

Note	The **Insert** menu can also be used for *deleting* a preexisting header or footer for a page style. If that page style has a check mark in front of it, it contains a header/footer, and clicking on it opens a message box warning about deletion and asks whether you want to delete the header or footer for that particular page style.

Depending on which option you choose, an area will appear at the top or bottom of the page. In this area you can enter text and graphics that will appear on every page unless **Same content on first page** has been deselected..

Page Header
The Old Salt
I was walking through the Dockyard in a panic,
When I met a matelot old and grey.

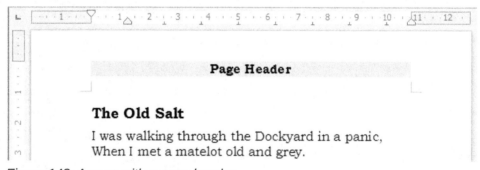

Figure 148: A page with a page header

Items such as document titles, chapter titles, and page numbers, which often go into headers and footers, are best added as fields. That way, if something changes, the headers and footers are all updated automatically.

Fields are covered in Chapter 14, Working with Fields, but one example here may be useful. To insert the document title into the header on a Default page style:

1) Select **File > Properties > Description**, enter a title for your document in the *Title* area, and click **OK** to close the dialog.
2) Add a header (**Insert > Header > Default**).
3) Place the cursor in the header part of the page.
4) Select **Insert > Fields > Title**. The title should appear on a gray background (which does not show when printed and can be turned off).
5) To change the title of the document, reselect **File > Properties > Description** and edit.

Formatting headers and footers

In Writer headers and footers are considered paragraphs and therefore you can format the header or footer text using the same techniques you use for formatting text in the main body of the document.

Tip	You can define styles for headers and footers so that you can quickly obtain a consistent formatting in case you use several page styles. Writer includes three named header and footer styles: header/footer, left header/footer styles, and right header/footer styles. All six are identical and are available for the user to modify.

You can format the layout of headers and footers using two different methods. The first method is to use the Header or Footer markers that appear within headers and footers.

For example, to use the Header marker:

1) Click the top of the page. The blue Header marker will appear.
2) Click the plus sign in the Header marker. The plus sign will change to a down arrow.
3) Click the down arrow.
4) Select **Format Header**. This opens the Page Style dialog where you can change the margins, spacing, and height.
5) Click **More** to open the Border/Background dialog where you can add borders, background colors, and background images to the header.

You can also format headers and footers by modifying the page style at **Format** > **Page** > **Header**.

Caution	Do not use the Background and Borders tabs on the Page Style dialog to format headers. Style choices selected from those tabs will apply to the entire page rather than to the header.

Portrait headers on landscape pages

When you define a header and footer on a landscape page, they will be aligned with the long side of the page. If your landscape pages are going to be inserted between portrait pages, you might want the headers and footers to be on the short sides of the landscape pages, so the final printed product looks like the contents of the landscape pages have been rotated 90 degrees on portrait pages.

You can set up portrait headers and footers on landscape pages by using a trick involving frames. These are a bit tedious to set up, but once you have done so, you can copy and paste them to other landscape pages. This cannot be made part of the landscape page style. In the following example we want to insert a landscape page into our printed document, to have the same header and footer, and margins, as our portrait pages. We will use an A4 page size here.

To set up portrait headers and footers on landscape pages:

1) Note the margin settings for the portrait page which is the same as the landscape page will be, that is to say, for a right landscape page, the settings from a right portrait page (see the table)

We now need to make the landscape right and left margins 1 cm larger than the portrait top and bottom margins, respectively. This difference allows for the extra space used by the portrait header and footer (0.5 cm for the height of the header or footer and a 0.5 cm gap between the header or footer and the main text).

Portrait page (right page)		Landscape page (right page)	
Top margin	1.5 cm	Right margin	2.5 cm
Bottom margin	1.5 cm	Left margin	2.5 cm
Left (inner) margin	2.8 cm	Top margin	2.8 cm
Right (outer) margin	1.8 cm	Bottom margin	1.8 cm

2) We will continue this example setting the frame for the footer. The procedure is the same for doing the header. Apply these margin settings in the *Landscape* page style.

3) Copy and paste the footer from the portrait page into a blank paragraph in the text. Paste or move it into the landscape page. This text will then have the *Footer* style so the typeface, font size, and tab settings will match.

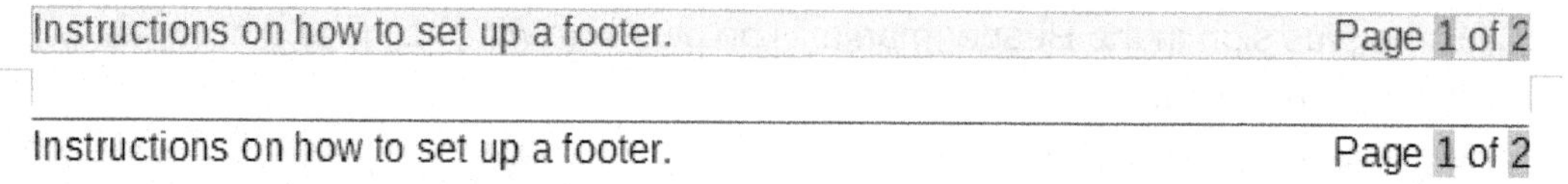

Instructions on how to set up a footer.	Page 1 of 2
Instructions on how to set up a footer.	Page 1 of 2

Figure 149: Copy the footer, paste, and select it.

4) Select the text (including the fields) you just entered. Choose **Format > Character**. On the Character dialog, choose the *Position* tab and set *Rotation / scaling* to **270 degrees** (counterclockwise). Note in the preview pane that the tabs are removed in this process. Click **OK**.

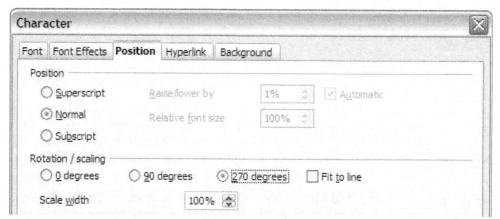

Figure 150: Rotating the footer text 270 degrees

5) With the text still selected, choose **Insert > Frame**. In the Frame dialog, select the *Type* tab and enter the width, height, and horizontal and vertical position for the footer. Deselect the Automatic options in Width and Height if they are selected.

- The width is the footer height taken from the Footer page of the portrait page style dialog.

- The frame height is obtained by simple arithmetic. The A4 page-width is 21cm, minus the sum of the top and bottom margins of 2.8cm and 1.8cm resulting in a frame height of 16.4cm.

- The horizontal position is the portrait page bottom margin.

- The vertical position is the landscape page top margin.

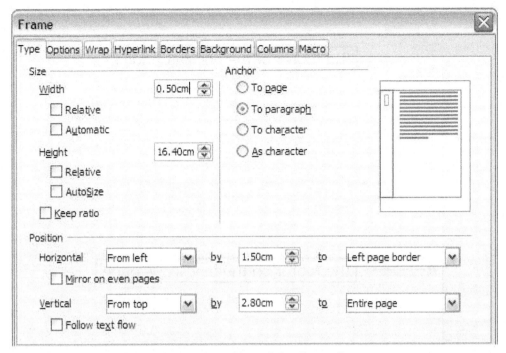

Figure 151: Defining the size and position of the footer frame

6) If your footer has a line above the text, as in this book, on the *Borders* page, select a right border and specify the line width and spacing to the frame's contents.

7) Click **OK** to save these settings. The footer will now appear in the required position and orientation. Any fields will update.

Because tabs have been removed, insert the cursor in the frame, at the end of the text where the tab was, and insert as many spaces using the keyboard space bar, as you require for the layout to match that on the portrait page.

Repeat these steps (using appropriate settings) to set up a portrait header on the landscape page.

Caution	Make sure to return to the paragraph in the document from which you rotated the text, and return it to **0 degrees,** or any text typed in this location will rotate.

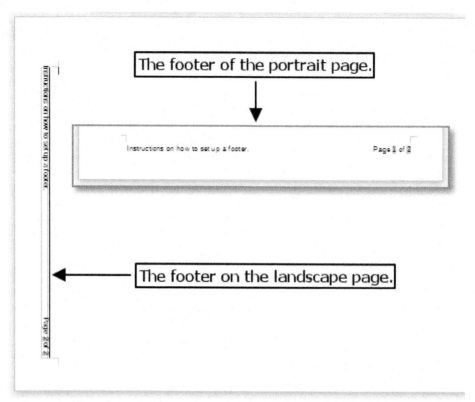

Figure 152: Footers in place for both page styles

Numbering pages

This section describes techniques to insert page numbers and related information in a document. Some basic knowledge of page styles, which are fully described in chapters 6 and 7, may be needed to follow some of the examples given.

Preliminaries: fields

LibreOffice uses *fields* to manage page numbers. To insert a page number field, position the cursor where you want to insert the number and choose **Insert > Fields > Page Number**. The page number appears with a gray background. The gray background denotes a field; although it is visible on screen, it is not printed.

Tip	If you wish to turn off the gray background, choose **View > Field Shadings** (or press *Ctrl+F8).*

The page number field always displays the page number for the page where it is placed. If you see the words "Page number" instead of a number, press *Ctrl+F9*. This shortcut key toggles LibreOffice between displaying the *Field Name* (the variable) and the field's *result* (the data in the variable).

Note	For a full introduction to fields, see Chapter 14, Working with Fields.

Preliminaries: insert and format a header

For the purpose of this example, we will insert a header in the Default page style pages using manual formatting. See "Creating headers and footers" on page 145.

Simple page numbering

The simplest case is to have the page number at the top of every page and nothing more. To do this, put the cursor on the header and select **Insert > Fields > Page Number**.

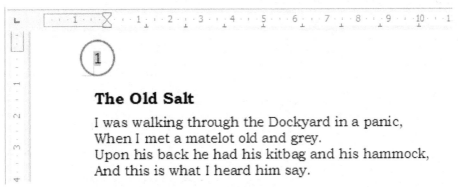

Figure 153: Page number inserted in the header

Now the correct page number appears on every page.

Combining header text and page number

There are a lot of interesting variations that you can apply without further knowledge of page styles. Here are some suggestions:

- Right-align the header to make the page number appear on the top-right.
- Type the word **page** before the page number field so the header reads **page 1, page 2**, and so on. This also requires using the *Page Number* field, discussed earlier (page 150).
- Add the document title so the header reads, for example: **Peter's Favourite Poems**, left justified, and **page x** with right justification, where x is the value of the *Page Number* field. Consider using a (right-aligned) tab to separate the title from the page number.
- LibreOffice also has a *Page Count* field (**Insert > Fields > Page Count**). Using it, you could, for example, have a header that reads **page 2 of 12**.

These variations are all illustrated in Figure 154.

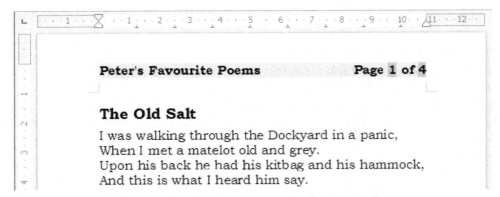

Figure 154: Variations on the simple page numbering method

Changing the number format

Many more variations are possible. For example, you can set the page number to display in Roman numerals. To do that, you can double-click on the page number and select the desired format; however, a better choice is to specify the format of numbers in the page style as explained here.

Right-click in the text area of the page and select Page from the context menu.

On the Page page of the Page Style dialog, in the *Layout settings* section, select **i, ii, iii, ...** from the *Format* drop-down list to use lowercase numerals.

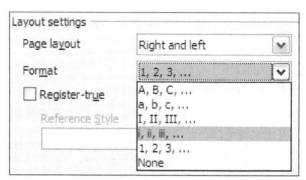

Figure 155: Changing format of page numbers

Numbering the first page something other than 1

Sometimes you may want to start a document with a page number greater than 1. For example, you may be writing a book, with each chapter in a separate file. Chapter 1 may start with page 1, but Chapter 2 could begin with page 25 and Chapter 3 with page 51.

Follow these instructions to start the page numbering in a document at a number greater than 1. (These instructions are for a page number in a footer, but you could use a header instead.)

Tip	Do not set a starting page number that is an even number because you will end up with a blank page before the first page when you print the file or export it as a PDF.

1) Choose **Insert > Footer > [page style]** to activate the footer. If the page style already has footers active, there will be a check mark against its name. In which case click in the footer area of the page without clicking on the page style. If you do click the checked page style name, select **No** in the warning dialog if you do not want to remove any footer text already in place, or **Yes** if you do. Click in the footer area.

2) The cursor is now in the footer. To insert the page number, choose **Insert > Fields > Page Number**. The page number will be **1**.

3) Click in the first paragraph in the text area.

4) Choose **Format > Paragraph** (or right-click and choose **Paragraph** from the context menu), to display the Paragraph dialog.

5) On the *Text Flow* page, in the *Breaks* section, select **Insert** and select **Page** in the *Type* drop-down list. Select **With Page Style** and the page style you are using for the first page of the document. Note that you are not inserting a page break, but a break in the page numbering.

6) The *Page number* field is now active. Type the page number you want to start with. Click **OK** to close the Paragraph dialog.

Numbering pages by chapter

Technical documents often include the chapter number with the page number in the header or footer. For example, 1-1, 1-2, 1-3, ...; 2-1, 2-2, 2-3, ...

To set up this type of page numbering in LibreOffice, you need to do three things:

1) Ensure that your chapter titles are all identified by the same paragraph style, for example, the Heading1 style.

2) Use **Tools > Outline Numbering** to tell LibreOffice what paragraph style you are using for Level 1 in your outline, and specify "1,2,3" in the Number box.

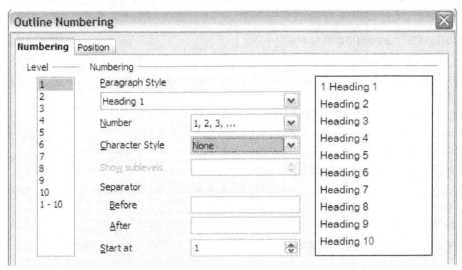

Figure 156: Specifying paragraph style and numbering for chapter titles

3) Insert the chapter number in your document. To do this:

   a) Place the cursor in the header or footer just before the page number you inserted earlier, and choose **Insert > Fields > Other** from the Menu Bar.

   b) On the Fields dialog (Figure 157), go to the *Document* page. Select **Chapter** in the *Type* list, **Chapter number** in the *Format* list, and **1** in the *Level* box. Click **Insert**.

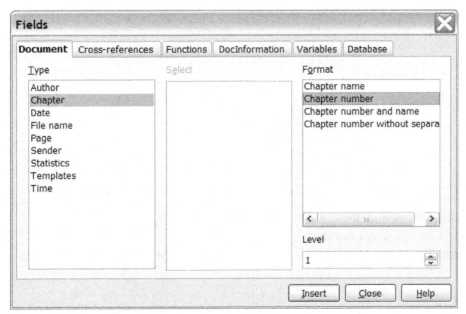

Figure 157: Inserting a chapter number field

c) Type a hyphen or other punctuation between the chapter number and the page number.

For more information, see "Choosing paragraph styles for outline levels" and "Including chapter or section information in page headers" in Chapter 7, Working with Styles.

Restarting page numbering

Often you will want to restart the page numbering at 1, for example, on the page following a title page or a table of contents. In addition, many documents have the *front matter* (such as the table of contents) numbered with Roman numerals and the main body of the document numbered in Arabic numerals, starting with 1.

You can restart page numbering in two ways.

Method 1:
1) Place the cursor in the first paragraph of the new page (be aware a heading is a paragraph).
2) Choose **Format > Paragraph.**
3) On the *Text Flow* page of the Paragraph dialog (Figure 119 on page 125), select **Insert** in the *Breaks* area.
4) In the *Type* drop-down list, select **Page**.
5) In the *Position* drop-down list, select **Before** or **After** to position where you want to insert the page numbering break.
6) Select **With Page Style** and specify the page style to use.
7) Specify the page number to start from and then click **OK**. This does not insert a new page.

Method 2:
1) Place the cursor in the first paragraph of the new page.
2) Choose **Insert > Manual break.**
3) **Page break** is the default selected on the Insert Break dialog.

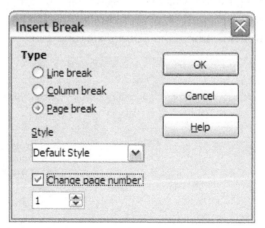

Figure 158: Restarting page numbering after a manual page break

4) Choose the required page in the *Style* drop-down list.
5) Select **Change page number**.
6) Specify the page number to start from and then click **OK**. This does insert a new page.

Example: Restart page numbering: a preface

A standard preface has the following properties:

- Page numbers are displayed in Roman numerals (i, ii, iii, iv, ...).
- After the preface, the document starts on a *Default* page.
- The page number resets to 1, and the number format becomes Arabic (1, 2, 3, 4, ...).

Resetting the page number requires page breaks.

First, do the preliminary work for the *Preface* style:

1) Create a new page style and name it **Preface**.
2) Set its *Next Style* to **Preface** because a preface could span multiple pages.
3) Add a header to *Preface* and insert the *Page Number* field. Make the page numbers display as Roman numerals (i, ii, iii, iv, ...):
4) Open the page style window for *Preface* (if not already open) and click the **Header** tab. Select **Header on** under *Header*.
5) Click the **Page** tab (Figure 159). Under *Layout settings,* in the *Format* drop-down list, set the format to **i, ii, iii, ...**. Click **OK** to close the dialog.

After the preface is written, we are ready to restart the page numbering in the main body of the document to Arabic numerals. Follow these steps:

1) Make an empty paragraph at the very end of the preface.
2) Put the cursor on the blank line.
3) Choose **Insert > Manual Break**.
4) Select **Page break** and choose the *Default Style*.
5) Select the **Change page number** option and set the new value to **1**. Click **OK** to close the dialog.

These settings are shown in Figure 158.

Note	You cannot assign an odd page number to a left page or an even page number to a right page. LibreOffice strongly adheres to the convention that odd page numbers go on right-hand pages and even page numbers on left-hand pages.

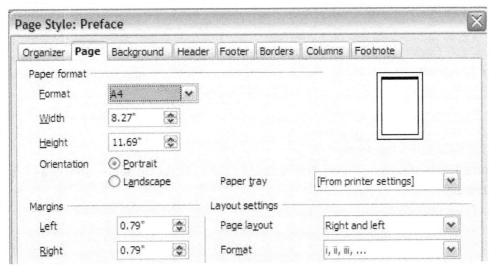

Figure 159: Set page number format to Roman numerals.

This change is also reflected on the Status Bar. The *Page* section of the status bar now shows the page number, the sequence number and the total page count (the graphic shows the cursor location is in Page 1, and that it is the forty-third page of forty-seven in the document).

| Page 1 43 / 47 | 11697 words, 65507 characters |

Figure 160: Page number in the status bar

Problems with restarting page numbering

Restarting page numbering may lead to two problems.

- The *Statistics* page in the document's properties (**File > Properties**) always displays the total number of pages in the document, which may not be what you want to appear in the *Page Count* field.

- When page numbering is restarted, LibreOffice always makes odd-numbered pages to be on the right and even-numbered pages to be on the left. It does this by inserting a blank page, if necessary. Sometimes this blank page is not desired, particularly when creating PDFs or when printing single sided.

Solving the page count problem

Suppose you know exactly how many pages are not to be included in the page count. (You want one page to be excluded in the page count for the following example.)

Instead of inserting a *Page Count* field, you can do the following:

1) Position the cursor where you want the page count to appear.
2) Press *F2* to open the formula bar, just above the horizontal ruler in the main Writer window (see Figure 161).
3) After the equal sign, type **page-1**. If you want to exclude several pages, substitute the number of excluded pages for 1 in the formula.
4) Press *Enter* to close the formula bar and insert the resulting field into the document.

Figure 161: Formula bar

If you do not know the total number of pages in advance, then one approach is to create a bookmark on the last page and then insert a cross reference to it.

To create a bookmark on the last page:

1) Go to the last page (*Ctrl+End*).
2) Choose **Insert > Bookmark**.
3) In the Insert Bookmark dialog, type a name for the bookmark, for example **LastPage**.
4) Click **OK**.

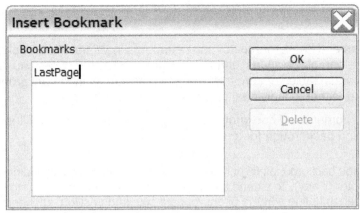

Figure 162: Inserting a bookmark

To insert a cross-reference to the last page in the header or footer where you want to refer to the total number of pages:

1) Position the cursor at the desired location—for example after the space added after **of** in the header or footer, as in **page xx of yy**.

2) Choose **Insert > Cross-reference**.

3) On the *Cross-references* page of the Fields dialog (Figure 163), select **Bookmarks** in the *Type* column and **LastPage** in the *Selection* column. **LastPage** now appears in the *Name* box.

4) In the *Insert Reference to* box, select **As page style**. Click **Insert**.

Note	Do not delete the bookmark at the end of the document. If you do, the cross-reference will not work.
	If a field, such as a cross-reference, does not automatically update, press *F9*.

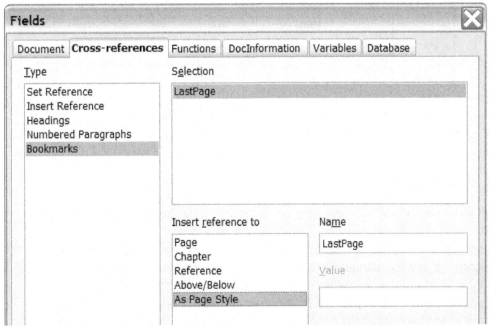

Figure 163: Inserting a cross-reference to a bookmark on the last page of a document

Defining borders and backgrounds

You can apply borders and backgrounds to many elements in Writer. Paragraphs, pages, frames, sections, page styles, paragraph styles, character styles, and frame styles can include both borders and backgrounds; tables of contents, and indexes can include backgrounds only. Text can have a border applied, either to individual characters or to selected text.

The dialog pages for borders and backgrounds are similar in each case. To illustrate their use, we will define a border and background for a text frame.

Tip	Page backgrounds fill only the area within the margins, including the header or footer (if any). To extend the background color or graphic into the margins, you need to define a frame of appropriate size and position, anchor it to the page or a paragraph, and send it to the background. For more about anchoring frames, see Chapter 8, Working with Graphics.

Adding a border

To begin, select the frame, right-click, and choose Frame from the context menu. Select the *Borders* tab.

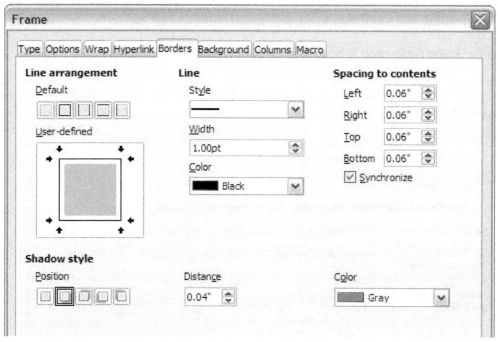

Figure 164: Frame dialog: Borders page

Borders have three components: where they go, what they look like, and how much space is left around them.

- *Line arrangement* specifies where the borders go. Writer provides five default arrangements but you can just as easily click on the line you want to customize in the *User-defined* area to get exactly what you want. Each line can be individually formatted.
- *Line* specifies what the border looks like: the style, width and color. There are a number of different styles and colors to choose from. The Line Style, Width and Color will apply to those borders highlighted by a pair of black arrows in the User-defined thumbnail on the left hand side of the dialog.

- *Spacing to contents* specifies how much space to leave between the border and the contents of the element. Spaces can be specified to the left, right, above, and below. Check **Synchronize** to have the same spacing for all four sides. This spacing is like a padding and it is not factored in when calculating the text measurements.

- *Shadow style* properties always apply to the whole element. A shadow has three components: where it is, how far from the element it is cast, and what color it is.

Adding color to the background

In the Frame dialog, choose the Background page (Figure 167). Here you can add color, a gradient or a graphic.

To add color to the background, select from the color grid. You can adjust the transparency of the color to make any text easier to read.

Adding a gradient to the background

To add a gradient to the background:

1) From the *As* drop-down list on the Background page, select **Gradient**. The page now displays the gradient options (Figure 165), with an example in the preview pane to the right.
2) Select the required gradient from the list.
3) Click **OK**.

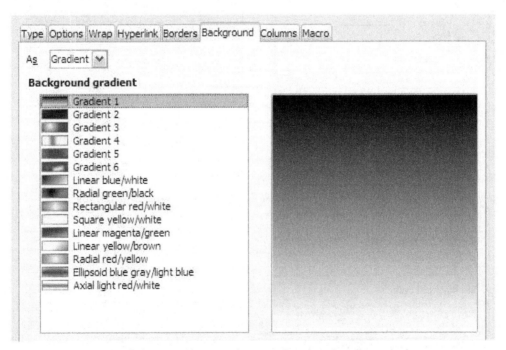

Figure 165: Frame dialog: Background page showing Gradient choices

Adding a graphic to the background

To add a graphic to the background:

1) From the *As* drop-down list on the Background page, select **Graphic**. The page now displays the graphics options, as shown in Figure 166.
2) Click the **Browse** button. The Find Graphics dialog opens.

3) Find the file you want and then click the **Open** button. The Find Graphics dialog closes and the selected graphic appears in the preview box on the right-hand side of the *Background* page. (If you do not see the graphic, select the **Preview** option.)

4) To embed the graphic in your document, deselect **Link**. To link the graphic to the document but not embed it, select **Link**. For more about linking graphics, see Chapter 8, Working with Graphics.

5) In the *Type* area, choose how you want the background graphic to appear:

   a) To position the graphic in a specific location, select **Position** and then click the desired location in the position grid.

   b) To stretch the graphic to fill the entire background area, select **Area**.

   c) To repeat the graphic across the entire background area, select **Tile**.

6) In the *Transparency* area, you can adjust the transparency of the graphic. This adjustment is often necessary to make any text easier to read.

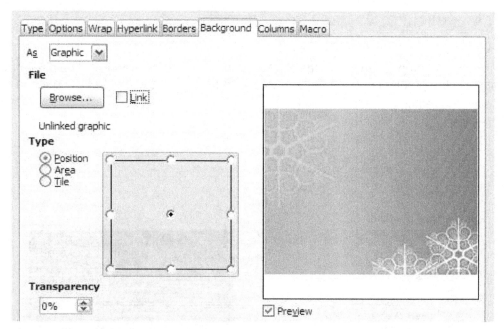

Figure 166: Graphic options on the Background page of the Frame dialog

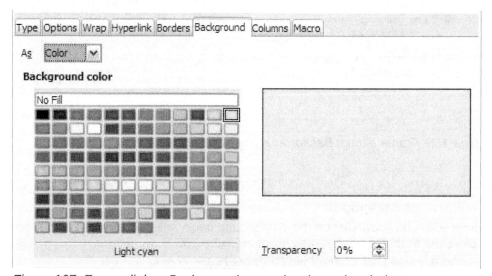

Figure 167: Frame dialog: Background page showing color choices

Deleting color, gradient or graphics from the background

To delete color, gradient or graphics from the background:

1) From the *As* drop-down list, select **Color**.
2) Click **No Fill** on the color grid.
3) Click **OK**.

Chapter 5
Printing, Exporting, Faxing, and E-Mailing

Quick printing

Click the **Print File Directly** icon 🖫 to send the entire document to the default printer defined for your computer.

Note	You can change the action of the **Print File Directly** icon to send the document to the printer defined for the document instead of the default printer for the computer. Go to **Tools > Options > Load/Save > General** and select the **Load printer settings with the document** option.

Controlling printing

For more control over printing, use the Print dialog (**File > Print** or *Ctrl+P*).

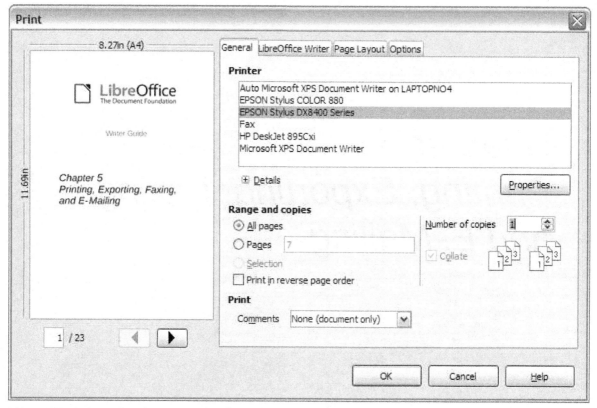

Figure 168: The Print dialog

Note	The options selected on the Print dialog apply to this printing of this document only. To specify default printing settings for LibreOffice, go to **Tools > Options > LibreOffice > Print** and **Tools > Options > LibreOffice Writer > Print**. See Chapter 2, Setting Up Writer, for more details.

The Print dialog has four tabs, from which you can choose a range of options, as described in the following sections.

Selecting general printing options for a document

On the *General* tab of the Print dialog, you can choose:

- The **printer** (from the printers available)
- Which **pages** to print (the current page number is displayed here), the number of copies to print, and whether to collate multiple copies (*Range and copies* section)
- Whether to print any **comments** that are in the document, and where to print the comments.

Some selections may not be available all the time. For example, if the document contains no comments, the Print – Comments drop-down list does not work.

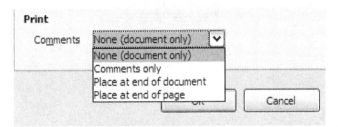

Figure 169: Choosing whether and where to print comments

Click the **Properties** button to display a dialog where you can choose portrait or landscape orientation, which paper tray to use, and the paper size to print on.

On the *Options* tab of the Print dialog, you can choose various other options for printing.

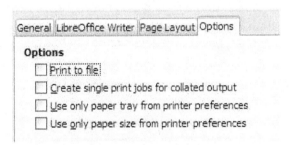

Figure 170: General print options

Printing multiple pages on a single sheet of paper

You can print multiple pages of a document on one sheet of paper. To do this:

1) In the Print dialog, select the *Page Layout* tab (Figure 171).

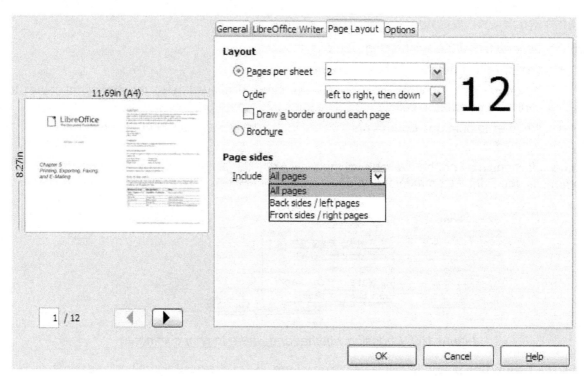

Figure 171: Printing multiple page per sheet of paper

2) In the *Layout* section, select from the drop-down list the number of pages to print per sheet. The preview panel on the left of the Print dialog shows how the printed document will look.

When printing more than 2 pages per sheet, you can choose the order in which they are printed across and down the paper. The two pictures below show the difference.

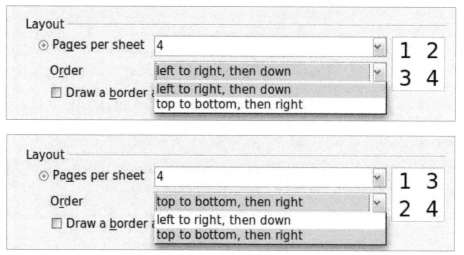

3) In the *Page sides* section, select whether to print all pages or only some pages.
4) Click the **OK** button.

Tip	To print two pages per sheet in "facing pages" (book layout) style, print from Print Preview instead. See page 169.

Selecting what to print

In addition to printing a full document, you can choose to print individual pages, ranges of pages, or a selection of a document, as described in this section.

Printing an individual page:
1) Choose **File > Print** from the Menu bar.
2) On the Print dialog, select the page to print.
3) In the *Range and copies* section of the General page, select the *Pages* option.
4) Enter the *sequence number* of the page you want to print. This may differ from the page number if you have restarted page numbering within the document. The preview box changes to show the selected page.
5) Click the **OK** button.

Printing a range of pages:
1) Choose **File > Print** from the Menu bar.
2) On the Print dialog, select the range of pages to print.
3) In the *Ranges and copies* section of the General page, select the *Pages* option.
4) Enter the sequence numbers of the pages to print (for example, 1–4 or 1,3,7,11).
5) Click the **OK** button.

Printing a selection of text:
1) In the document, select the material (text and graphics) to print.
2) Choose **File > Print** from the menu bar.
3) The *Ranges and copies* section of the Print dialog now includes a *Selection* option and the preview box shows the selected material. See Figure 172.
4) Click the **OK** button.

Printing a brochure

In Writer, Impress, and Draw, you can print a document with two pages on each side of a sheet of paper, arranged so that when the printed pages are folded in half, the pages are in the correct order to form a booklet or brochure.

Tip	Plan your document so it will look good when printed half size; choose appropriate margins, font sizes, and so on. You may need to experiment.

To print a brochure on a single-sided printer:
1) Choose **File > Print**.
2) On the *General* page of the Print dialog, click **Properties**.
3) Check the printer is set to the same orientation (portrait or landscape) as specified in the page setup for your document. Usually the orientation does not matter, but it does for brochures. Click **OK** to return to the Print dialog.
4) Select the *Page layout* tab in the Print dialog.
5) Select the **Brochure** option.
6) In the *Page sides* section, select *Back sides / left pages* option from the Include drop-down list. (See Figure 173.)
7) Click the **OK** button.

Selecting what to print

In addition to printing a full document, you can choose to print individual pages, ranges of pages, or a selection of a document, as described in this section.

Printing an individual page:

1) Choose **File > Print** from the Menu bar.
2) On the Print dialog box, select the page to print.
3) In the *Range and*
4) Enter the sequenc
   number if you hav
   changes to show t
5) Click the **OK** butto

Printing a range of pages

1) Choose **File > Pri**
2) On the Print dialo
3) In the *Ranges and*
4) Enter the sequenc
5) Click the **OK** butto

Printing a selection of tex

1) In the document,
2) Choose **File > Pri**
3) The *Ranges and*
   the preview box s
4) Click the **OK** butto

Printing a brochur

In Writer, Impress, and D
paper, arranged so that w
order to form a booklet or

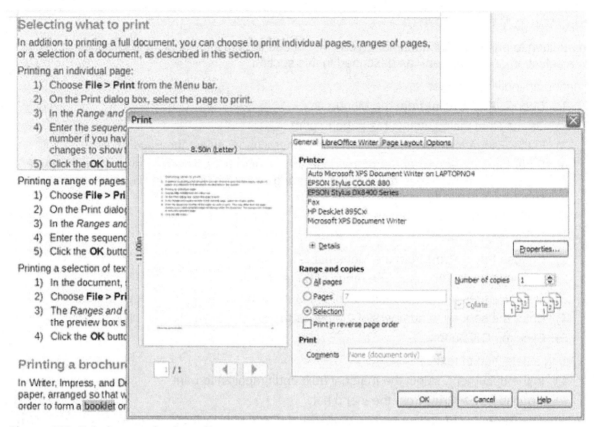

Figure 172: Printing a selection of text

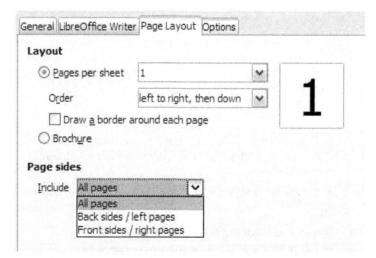

Figure 173: Selecting which pages to print

8) Take the printed pages out of the printer, turn the pages over, and put them back into the printer in the correct orientation to print on the blank side. You may need to experiment a bit to find out what the correct arrangement is for your printer.

9) On the Print dialog, in the *Page sides* section, select *Front sides / right pages* option from the Include drop-down box.

10) Click the **OK** button.

Tip	If your printer can print double-sided automatically, choose **All pages**.

Printing in black and white (on a color printer)

You may wish to print documents in black and white on a color printer. Several choices are available. Please note that some color printers may print in color regardless of the settings you choose.

Change the printer settings to print in black and white or grayscale:

1) Choose **File > Print** to open the Print dialog.

2) Click **Properties** to open the Properties dialog for the printer. The available choices vary from one printer to another, but you should find options for the Color settings. See your printer's help or user manual for more information.

3) The choices for color might include *black and white* or *grayscale*. Choose the required setting.

4) Click **OK** to confirm your choice and return to the Print dialog,

5) Click the **OK** button to print the document.

Tip	Grayscale is best if you have any graphics in the document.

Change the LibreOffice settings to print all color text and graphics as grayscale:

1) Choose **Tools > Options > LibreOffice > Print**.

2) Select the **Convert colors to grayscale** option. Click **OK** to save the change.

3) Open the Print dialog (**File > Print**).

4) Click the **OK** button to print the document.

Change the LibreOffice Writer settings to print all color text as black, and all graphics as grayscale:

1) Choose **Tools > Options > LibreOffice [Component] > Print**.

2) Under *Contents*, select the **Print text in black** option. Click **OK** to save the change.

3) Open the Print dialog (**File > Print**).

4) Click the **OK** button to print the document.

Previewing pages before printing

The normal page view in Writer shows you what each page will look like when printed and you can edit the pages in that view. If you are designing a document to be printed double-sided, you may want to see what facing pages look like. Writer provides two ways to do this:

- View Layout (editable view): use the Facing Pages (Book Preview) button on the status bar.

- Page Preview (read-only view).

To use Page Preview:

1) Choose **File > Page Preview** (or click the **Page Preview** button 🔲 on the Standard toolbar). Writer now displays the **Page Preview** toolbar instead of the Formatting toolbar.

Figure 174: Page Preview toolbar

2) Select the required preview button: **Two Pages** ⚌ , **Multiple Pages** ⊞ ▾ or **Book Preview** ⚌ .

3) To print the document from this view, click the **Print document** button 🖶 to open the Print dialog.

4) Choose the print options and click the **OK** button.

Printing envelopes

Printing envelopes involves two steps: setup and printing.

To set up an envelope to be printed by itself or with your document:

1) Click **Insert > Envelope** from the Menu bar.

2) In the Envelope dialog, start with the *Envelope* tab. Verify, add, or edit the information in the Addressee and Sender (the "from" on the envelope) boxes.

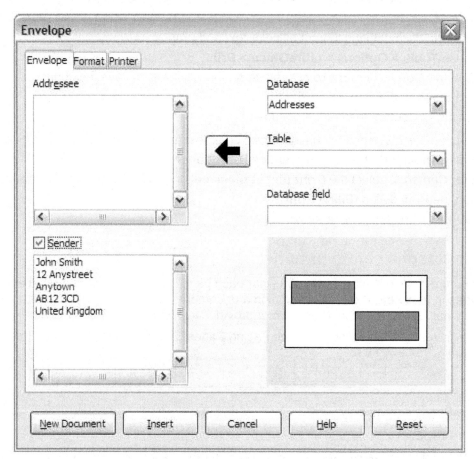

Figure 175: Choosing addressee and sender information for an envelope

You can type information directly into the Addressee and Sender boxes, or use the right-hand drop-down lists to select the database or table from which you can draw the envelope information, if desired. See Chapter 11, Using Mail Merge, for details on how to print envelopes from a database.

3) On the *Format* page, verify or edit the positioning of the addressee and the sender information. The preview area on the lower right shows the effect of your positioning choices.

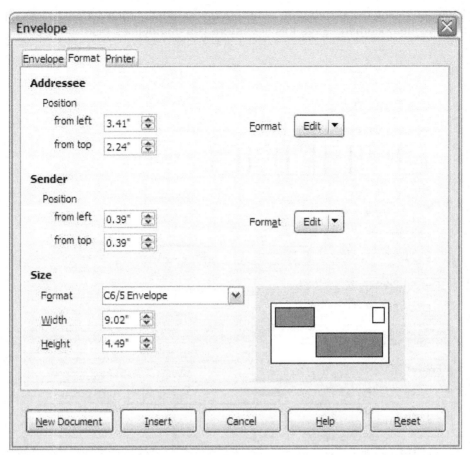

Figure 176: Choosing positioning and size of elements for an envelope

4) To format the text of these blocks, click the **Edit** buttons to the right. In the drop-down list you have two choices for each button: Character and Paragraph.

- Selecting Character opens a Character dialog, similar to the standard Character dialog, but omitting Borders, allowing you to set the formatting of the text's attributes.

- Selecting Paragraph opens a Paragraph dialog, similar to the standard Paragraph dialog, but omitting Outline & Numbering, allowing you to set the paragraph's attributes.

5) In the lower left of this page, the Size section, choose the envelope format from the drop-down list. The width and height of the selected envelope then show in the boxes below the selected format. If you chose a pre-existing format, just verify these sizes. If you chose *User defined* in the Format list, then you can edit the sizes.

6) After formatting, go to the *Printer* page to choose printer options such as envelope orientation and shifting. You may need to experiment a bit to see what works best for your printer.

You can also choose a different printer or alter printer setup (for example, specify the tray that holds envelopes) for this print job by clicking the **Setup** button and making selections on the Printer Setup dialog.

7) When you have finished formatting and are ready to print, click either the **New Document** or **Insert** button to finish. **New Document** makes only an envelope or starts a new document with the envelope. **Insert** puts the envelope into your existing document as page 1.

To not proceed with this envelope, click **Cancel** or press the *Esc* key. You can also click **Reset** to remove your changes and return to the original settings when the dialog opened.

When the Envelope dialog closes, you are returned to your document, which now has the envelope in the same file as the document. Save this file before you do anything else.

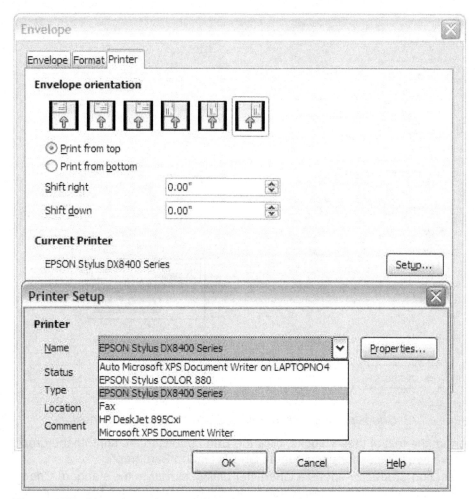

Figure 177: Choosing printer options for an envelope

To print the envelope:

1) Choose **File > Print** from the menu bar.

2) On the Print dialog, under **Print range**, choose **Pages** and type **1** in the box. Click **OK** to print.

Printing labels

Labels are commonly used for printing address lists (where each label shows a different address), but they can also be used for making multiple copies of one label only, for example return-address stickers. To print labels:

1) Choose **File > New > Labels** on the Menu bar. The Labels dialog opens.

2) On the *Labels* page, fill in your own label text in the Inscription box, or use the **Database** and **Table** drop-down lists to choose the required information, as described in Chapter 11, Using Mail Merge.

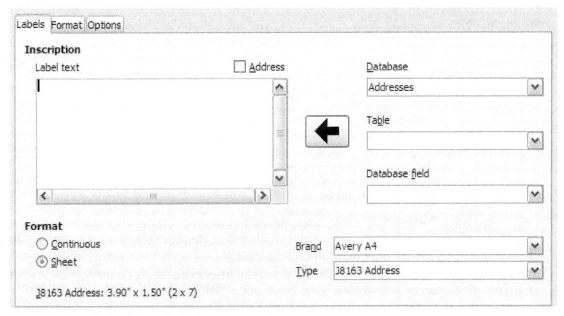

Figure 178: Labels dialog, Labels page

3) Select the label stock in the **Brand** drop-down list. The types for that brand then appear in the **Type** drop-down list. Select the size and type of labels required. You can also select **User** in the **Type** drop-down list and then make specific selections on the *Format* page.

4) On the *Format* page, choose the pitch, sizes, margins, columns and rows for user-defined labels, or just verify with a brand of label stock you have loaded into the printer.

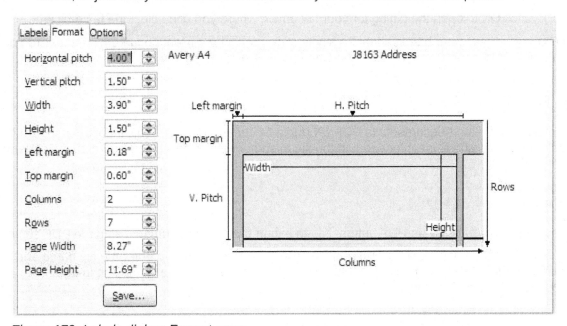

Figure 179: Labels dialog, Format page

5) Click **Save** to save your new format.

6) On the *Options* page, choose to print the entire page of labels or one single label, then select which one by the column and row. You can also change printer setup.

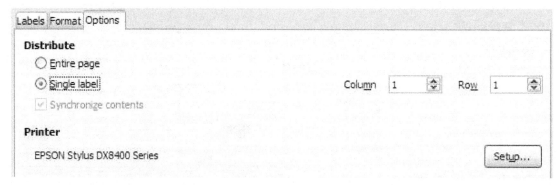

Figure 180: Labels dialog, Options page

7) When you have finished formatting, click **New Document** to create your sheet of labels or click **Cancel** (or press the *Esc* key). You can also click **Reset** to remove your changes and return to the original settings when the dialog opened.

8) You can print using the **Print File Directly** icon on the toolbar or by choosing **File > Print** from the Menu bar, or you can save the file to print later.

Sending a fax

To send a fax directly from LibreOffice, you need a fax modem and a fax driver that allows applications to communicate with the fax modem.

1) Open the Print dialog (Figure 168) by choosing **File > Print** and select the fax driver in the **Printer** list.

2) Click **OK** to open the dialog for your fax driver, where you can select the fax recipient.

You can set up a toolbar button so that a single click sends the current document as a fax. To add a button for this purpose to a toolbar, see Chapter 16, Customizing Writer.

Exporting to PDF

LibreOffice can export documents to PDF (Portable Document Format). This industry-standard file format for file viewing is ideal for sending the file to someone else to view using Acrobat Reader or other PDF viewer.

Quick export to PDF

Click the **Export Directly as PDF** button to export the entire document using the PDF settings you most recently selected in the PDF Options dialog. You are asked to enter the file name and location for the PDF file, but you do not get a chance to choose a page range, the image compression, or other options.

Controlling PDF content and quality

For more control over the content and quality of the resulting PDF, use **File > Export as PDF**. The PDF Options dialog opens. This dialog has five pages (General, Initial View, User Interface, Links, and Security). Select the appropriate settings, and then click **Export.** On the Export dialog, enter the location and file name of the PDF to be created, then click **Export** to export the file.

On the *General* page (Figure 181), you can choose which pages to include in the PDF, the type of compression to use for images (which affects the quality of images in the PDF), and other options.

Range section
- **All**: Exports the entire document.
- **Pages**: To export a range of pages, use the format **3-6** (pages 3 to 6). To export single pages, use the format **7;9;11** (pages 7, 9, and 11). You can also export a combination of page ranges and single pages, by using a format like **3-6;8;12**.
- **Selection**: Exports whatever material is selected.

Images section
- **Lossless compression**: Images are stored without any loss of quality. Tends to make large files when used with photographs. Recommended for other kinds of images or graphics.
- **JPEG compression**: Allows for varying degrees of quality. A setting of 90% works well with photographs (small file size, little perceptible loss of quality).
- **Reduce image resolution**: Lower-DPI (dots per inch) images have lower quality. For viewing on a computer screen generally a resolution of 72dpi (for Windows) or 96dpi (GNU/Linux) is sufficient, while for printing it is generally preferable to use at least 300 or 600 dpi, depending on the capability of the printer. Higher dpi settings greatly increase the size of the exported file.

Note	EPS (Encapsulated PostScript) images with embedded previews are exported only as previews. EPS images without embedded previews are exported as empty placeholders.

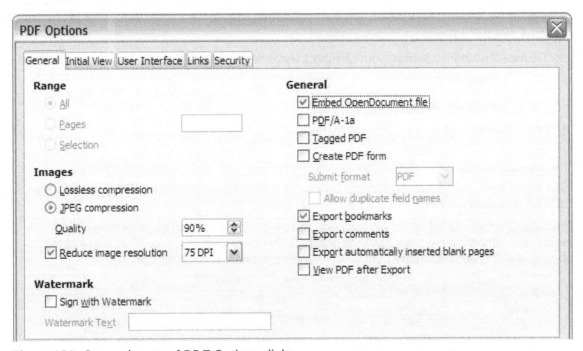

Figure 181: General page of PDF Options dialog

Watermark section

- **Sign with Watermark:** When this option is selected, a transparent overlay of the text you enter into the **Watermark Text** box will appear on each page of the PDF.

General section

- **Embed OpenDocument file:** Use this setting to export the document as a PDF file containing two file formats: PDF and ODF. In PDF viewers it behaves like a normal PDF file, and it remains fully editable in LibreOffice.

- **PDF/A-1a**: PDF/A-1a is an ISO standard for long-term preservation of documents, by embedding all the information necessary for faithful reproduction (such as fonts) while forbidding other elements (including forms, security, and encryption). PDF tags are written. If you select PDF/A-1a, the forbidden elements are grayed-out (not available).

- **Tagged PDF**: Tagged PDF contains information about the structure of the document's contents. This can help to display the document on devices with different screens, and when using screen reader software. Some tags that are exported are table of contents, hyperlinks, and controls. This option can increase file sizes significantly.

- **Create PDF form – Submit format**: Choose the format of submitting forms from within the PDF file. This setting overrides the control's URL property that you set in the document. There is only one common setting valid for the whole PDF document: PDF (sends the whole document), FDF (sends the control contents), HTML, and XML. Most often you will choose the PDF format.

- **Export bookmarks**: Creates PDF bookmarks (a table of contents list displayed by most PDF viewers, including Adobe Reader) for all headings in the document.

- **Export comments:** Exports comments as PDF notes. You may not want this!

- **Export automatically inserted blank pages**: If selected, automatically inserted blank pages are exported to the PDF. This is best if you are printing the PDF double-sided. For example, books usually have chapters set to always start on an odd-numbered (right-hand) page. When the previous chapter ends on an odd page, LibreOffice inserts a blank page between the two odd pages. This option controls whether to export that blank page.

Earlier versions of LibreOffice had the option:

- **Embed standard fonts:** Normally the 14 standard PostScript fonts were not embedded in a PDF file, because PDF reader software already contained these fonts. However, you could choose to embed these fonts in all PDF documents created by LibreOffice to enhance display accuracy in PDF viewers.

The PostScript fonts are now embedded by default.

Initial View page of PDF Options dialog

On the *Initial View* page, you can choose how the PDF opens by default in a PDF viewer. The selections should be self-explanatory.

If you have Complex Text Layout enabled (in **Tools > Options > Language settings > Languages**), an additional selection is available under *Continuous facing*: **First page is left** (normally, the first page is on the right when using the *Continuous facing* option).

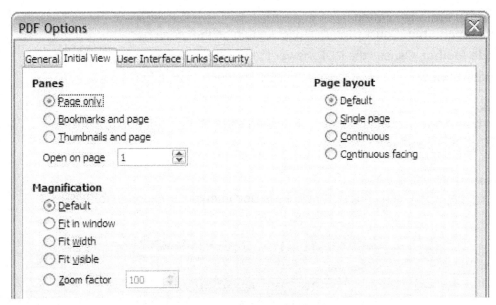

Figure 182: Initial View page of PDF Options dialog

User Interface page of PDF Options dialog

On the *User Interface* page, you can choose more settings to control how a PDF viewer displays the file. Some of these choices are particularly useful when you are creating a PDF to be used as a presentation or a kiosk-type display.

Window options section

- **Resize window to initial page.** Causes the PDF viewer window to resize to fit the first page of the PDF.
- **Center window on screen.** Causes the PDF viewer window to be centered on the computer screen.
- **Open in full screen mode.** Causes the PDF viewer to open full-screen instead of in a smaller window.
- **Display document title.** Causes the PDF viewer to display the document's title in the title bar.

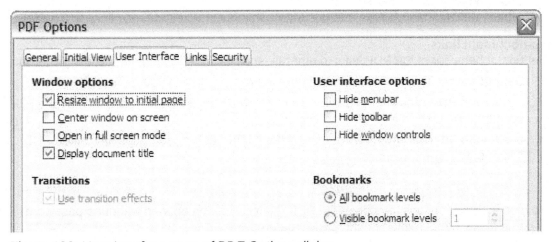

Figure 183: User Interface page of PDF Options dialog

User interface options section
- **Hide menu bar.** Causes the PDF viewer to hide the menu bar.
- **Hide toolbar.** Causes the PDF viewer to hide the toolbar.
- **Hide window controls.** Causes the PDF viewer to hide other window controls.

Bookmarks
Select how many heading levels are displayed as bookmarks, if *Export bookmarks* is selected on the General page.

Links page of PDF Options dialog

On the *Links* page, you can choose how links in documents are exported to PDF.

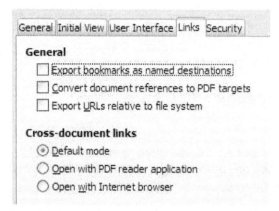

Figure 184: Links page of PDF Options dialog

Export bookmarks as named destinations
If you have defined Writer bookmarks, this option exports them as "named destinations" to which Web pages and PDF documents can link.

Convert document references to PDF targets
If you have defined links to other documents with OpenDocument extensions (such as .odt, .ods, and .odp), this option converts the files names to .pdf in the exported PDF document.

Export URLs relative to the file system
If you have defined relative links in a document, this option exports those links to the PDF.

Cross-document links
Set up the behavior of the PDF links to other files. Select one among the following alternatives:
- **Default mode**: The PDF links will be handled as specified in your operating system.
- **Open with PDF reader application**: Use the same application used to display the PDF document to open linked PDF documents.
- **Open with Internet browser**: Use the default Internet browser to display linked PDF documents.

Security page of PDF Options dialog

PDF export includes options to encrypt the PDF (so it cannot be opened without a password) and apply some digital rights management (DRM) features.

- With an *open password* set, the PDF can only be opened with the password. Once opened, there are no restrictions on what the user can do with the document (for example, print, copy, or change it).

- With a *permissions password set*, the PDF can be opened by anyone, but its permissions can be restricted. See Figure 185. After you set a password for permissions, the other choices on the Security page become available.

- With *both* the *open password* and *permission password* set, the PDF can only be opened with the correct password, and its permissions can be restricted.

Note	Permissions settings are effective only if the user's PDF viewer respects the settings.

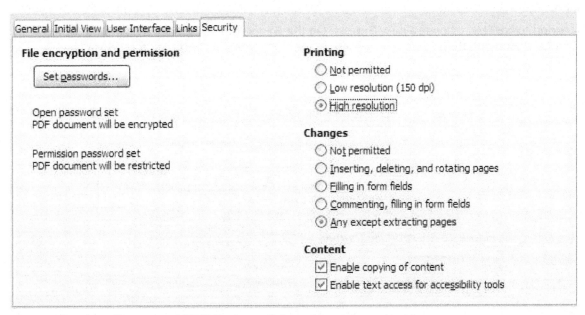

Figure 185: Security page of PDF Options dialog with passwords set

Figure 186 shows the pop-up dialog displayed when you click the **Set passwords** button on the Security page of the PDF Options dialog.

Once you have set all the options you require, click on **Export** to open the Export dialog, where you can set the file name and the save location.

Figure 186: Setting a password to encrypt a PDF

Note	Another choice is to use **File > Export**. This opens the Export dialog. Select the PDF file format, file name and location and click **Export**. This then opens the PDF Options dialog, as described above. Click **Export** when all the selections have been made.

Exporting to XHTML

LibreOffice uses the term "export" for some file operations involving a change of file type. LibreOffice can export files to XHTML. Other formats may be made available through extensions.

To export to XHTML, choose **File > Export**. On the Export dialog, specify a file name for the exported document, then select the XHTML in the *File format* list and click the **Export** button.

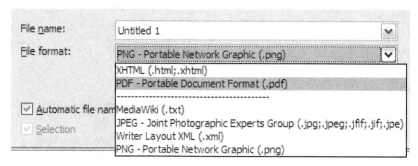

Figure 187: Export file formats

E-mailing Writer documents

LibreOffice provides several ways to quickly and easily send a Writer document as an e-mail attachment in one of three formats: ODT (OpenDocument Text, Writer's default format), DOC (Microsoft Word format), or PDF.

Note	Documents can only be sent from the LibreOffice mail merge wizard if a mail profile has been set up in **Tools > Option > LibreOffice Writer > Mail Merge E-mail**.

To send the current document in ODT format, choose:

1) **File > Send > Document as E-mail, or File > Send > E-mail as OpenDocument Text**. Writer opens your default e-mail program. The document is attached.

2) In your e-mail program, enter the recipient, subject, and any text you want to add, then send the e-mail.

If you choose **E-mail as Microsoft Word**, Writer first creates a DOC file and then opens your e-mail program with the DOC file attached. Similarly, if you choose **E-mail as PDF**, Writer opens the PDF Options dialog where you can select the settings you want, then creates a PDF and then opens your email program with the PDF file attached.

E-mailing a document to several recipients

To e-mail a document to several recipients, you can use the features in your e-mail program or you can use LibreOffice's mail merge facilities to extract email addresses from an address book.

You can use LibreOffice's mail merge to send e-mail in two ways:

- Use the Mail Merge Wizard to create the document and send it. See Chapter 11, Using Mail Merge, for details.

- Create the document in Writer without using the Wizard, then use the Wizard to send it. This method is described here.

To use the Mail Merge Wizard to send a previously-created Writer document:

1) Open the document in Writer. Click **Tools > Mail Merge Wizard**. On the first page of the wizard, select **Use the current document** and click **Next**.

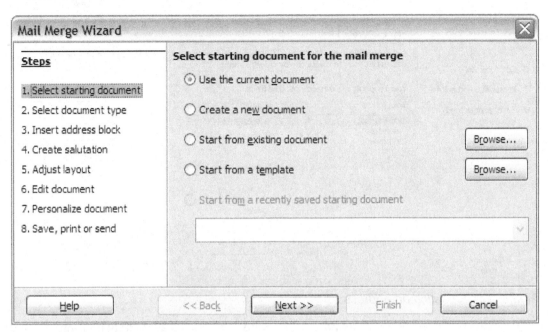

Figure 188: Select starting document

2) On the second page, select **E-mail message** for the type of document to create and click **Next**.

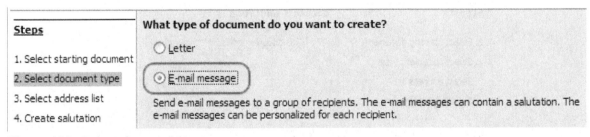

Figure 189: Select document type

3) On the third page, click the **Select Address List** button. Select the required address list (even if only one is shown) and then click **OK**. (If the address list you need is not shown here, you can click **Add** to find and add it to the list.)

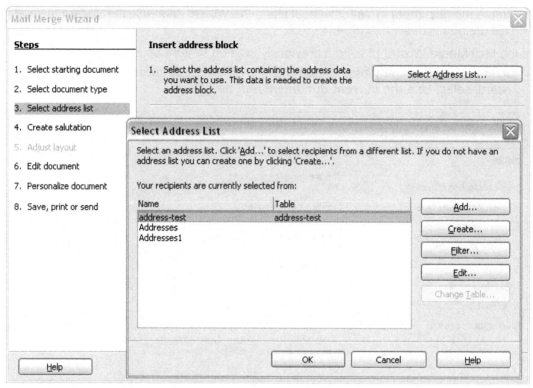

Figure 190: Selecting an address list

4) Back on the *Select address list* page, click **Next**. On the Create salutation page, deselect the checkbox by **This document should contain a salutation**.

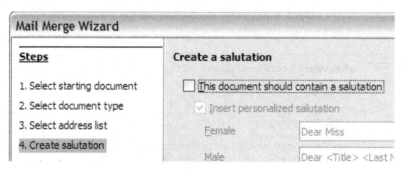

Figure 191: Deselecting a salutation

5) In the left-hand list, click **Step 8. Save, print or send**. LibreOffice displays a "Creating documents" message and then displays the *Save, print or send* page of the Wizard.

6) Select **Send merged document as E-Mail**. The lower part of the page changes to show e-mail settings choices.

7) Type a subject for your email and click **Send documents**. LibreOffice sends the e-mails.

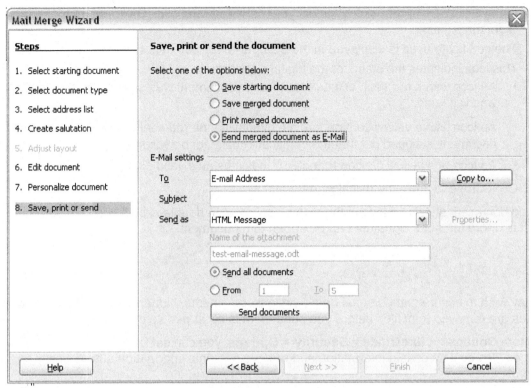

Figure 192: Sending a document as an email message

Digital signing of documents

To sign a document digitally, you need a personal key, also known as a certificate. A personal key is stored on your computer as a combination of a private key, which must be kept secret, and a public key, which you add to your documents when you sign them. You can get a certificate from a certification authority, which may be a private company or a governmental institution.

When you apply a digital signature to a document, a kind of checksum is computed from the document's content plus your personal key. The checksum and your public key are stored together with the document.

When someone later opens the document on any computer with a recent version of LibreOffice, the program will compute the checksum again and compare it with the stored checksum. If both are the same, the program will signal that you see the original, unchanged document. In addition, the program can show you the public key information from the certificate. You can compare the public key with the public key that is published on the web site of the certificate authority.

Whenever someone changes something in the document, this change breaks the digital signature.

On Windows operating systems, the Windows features of validating a signature are used. On Solaris and Linux systems, files that are supplied by Thunderbird, Mozilla or Firefox are used. For a more detailed description of how to get and manage a certificate, and signature validation, see "Digital Signatures" in the LibreOffice Help.

To sign a document:

1) Choose **File > Digital Signatures**.
2) If you have not saved the document since the last change, a message box appears. Click **Yes** to save the file.
3) The Digital Signatures dialog opens. Click **Sign Document** to add a public key to the document.

---

4) In the Select Certificate dialog, select your certificate and click **OK** to return to the Digital Signatures dialog.

5) The certificate used is displayed in the dialog with an icon next to its name.

    This icon indicates the status of the digital signature.

    - An icon with a red seal ⬚ indicates that the document was signed and the certificate was validated.

    - An icon with a yellow caution triangle overlaying the red seal ⬚ indicates that the document is signed but that the certificate could not be validated.

    - An icon of a yellow caution triangle ⚠ indicates an invalid digital signature.

6) Click **Close** to apply the digital signature.

A signed document shows an icon in the status bar. You can double-click the icon to view the certificate. More than one signature can be added to a document.

Removing personal data

You may wish to ensure that personal data, versions, comments, hidden information, or recorded changes are removed from files before you send them to other people or create PDFs from them.

In **Tools > Options > LibreOffice > Security > Options**, you can set LibreOffice to remind (warn) you when files contain certain information and remove personal information automatically on saving.

To remove personal and some other data from a file, go to **File > Properties**. On the *General* tab, uncheck **Apply user data** and then click the **Reset** button. This removes any names in the created and modified fields, deletes the modification and printing dates, and resets the editing time to zero, the creation date to the current date and time, and the version number to 1.

To remove version information, either (a) go to **File > Versions**, select the versions from the list and click **Delete**, or (b) use **Save As** and save the file with a different name.

Chapter 6
Introduction to Styles

Paragraph, Page, Character, and List Styles

What are styles?

Most people are used to writing documents according to *physical* attributes. For example, you might specify the font family, font size, and weight (for example: Helvetica 12pt, bold).

Styles are *logical* attributes. We use styles every day. For example, there are different styles of personal computer: desktop, tablet, netbook, laptop, and so on. Each has its own distinctive set of properties. You never say "my computer is a low-weight, one-piece unit with an LCD screen attached to a rectangular casing containing the computing components and the keyboard". Instead, you would probably say that you have a laptop.

LibreOffice styles are a way to do the same thing for your document. Using styles means that you could stop saying "font size 14pt, Times New Roman, bold, centered" and start saying "title" for describing that particular font usage. In other words, styles mean that you shift the emphasis from what the text *looks like* to what the text *is*.

Why use styles?

Styles help improve consistency in a document. They also make major formatting changes easy. For example, you might decide to change the indentation of all paragraphs or change the font of all titles. For a long document, this simple task could be prohibitive. Styles make the task easy.

The time is 9:50 AM, and Jane is finishing the 30-page paper for school that is due at 10:00 AM. She looks over the assignment one more time, and suddenly she realizes that:

- The text must use Arial font instead of Times New Roman.
- The headings must be dark blue and indented.
- The title must appear at the top-right of every page except the first.
- Even-numbered pages must have a wider right margin, and odd-numbered pages must have a wider left margin.

Thankfully, Jane used LibreOffice Writer and styles. She makes all the changes in only two minutes and hands in the paper on time.

Style categories

LibreOffice Writer has five style categories:

- *Paragraph* styles affect entire paragraphs represented with those styles.
- *Character* styles affect a block of text inside a paragraph.
- *Page* styles affect page formatting (page size, margin, and the like).
- *Frame* styles affect frames and graphics.
- *List* styles affect outlines, numbered lists, and bulleted lists.

In the same way that characters are the building blocks for creating words, paragraphs are the building blocks of every document. Headings (subheads) are paragraphs; headers, footers, and numbered lists are also paragraphs. Paragraph styles are, therefore, the most frequently used styles and are the ones treated in most detail in this and the next chapter.

The Styles and Formatting window

Styles are available through a floating or dockable window called *Styles and Formatting*, shown in Figure 193. This window is at the center of styles management. Do not worry if, at first, some contents of this section seem obscure while progressing through this or the next chapter. This guide describes how to use all these functions.

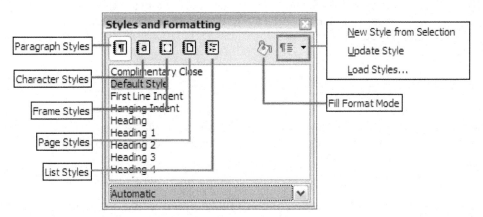

Figure 193: The Styles and Formatting window showing paragraph styles

To open the Styles and Formatting window, do *any one* of the following:

- Click on the ( ) icon located at the left-hand end of the Formatting toolbar.

- Select **Format > Styles and Formatting**.

- Press *F11*.

Tip	You can move the Styles and Formatting window to a convenient position on the screen or dock it to an edge.

Style selection basics

The first five buttons at the top of the Styles and Formatting window select the category of styles to work on. Click on one of these buttons to display a list of styles in that category, such as paragraph or character styles.

To apply a character style to existing text, select the text and then double-click on the name of the style in the *Character Styles* list. To apply any other style, put the cursor in the paragraph, frame, or page you want to modify and double-click on the name of the style in the corresponding section. You can select more than one paragraph or frame and apply the same style to all of them at the same time.

Using Fill Format mode

The sixth icon at the top of the Styles and Formatting window activates the *Fill Format* mode. You can use Fill Format to apply a style to many different areas quickly without having to go back to the Styles and Formatting window and double-click every time. This method is useful for formatting many scattered paragraphs, words, or other items with the same style, and it may be easier to use than making multiple selections first and then applying a style to all of them.

1) Open the Styles and Formatting window (Figure 193) and select a style.

2) Click the **Fill Format Mode** button ( ).

3) To apply a paragraph, page, or frame style, hover the mouse over the paragraph, page, or frame and click. To apply a character style, hold down the mouse button while selecting the characters. Clicking on a word applies the character style to that word.

4) Repeat step 3 until you have made all the changes for that style.

5) To quit the Fill Format mode, click the button again or press the *Esc* key.

Caution	When this mode is active, a right-click anywhere in the document undoes the last Fill Format action. Be careful not to accidentally right-click and mistakenly undo actions you want to keep.

Using New Style from Selection, Update Style, and Load Styles

Styles are part of the document properties, therefore changes made to a style or new styles you create are only available within the document they belong to. Styles always stay with a document. So, for example, if you e-mail a document to another person, the styles go with it.

If you want to reuse modified or new styles in other documents, you need to either save the styles in a template (see Chapter 10) or copy the styles into the document where you want to use them.

The last button in the toolbar of the Styles and Formatting window is a menu button that gives access to three submenu functions: *New Style from Selection*, *Update Style*, and *Load Styles*.

New Style from Selection

Use the first function of the button to create a new style from the formatting of an object in the current document. For instance, you can change the formatting of a paragraph or frame until it appears as you like, and then you can turn that object's formatting into a new style. This procedure can save time because you do not have to remember all the formatting settings you want, as is necessary when creating a new style with the Style dialog. In addition, unlike when setting the formatting parameters in the pages of dialogs, which you will learn to do later, you can immediately see how the objects will look when formatted with the style you are creating.

Follow these steps to create a new style from a selection:

1) Change the formatting of the object (paragraph, frame, etc.) to your liking.

2) From the buttons at the top of the window, choose the category of style to create (paragraph, character, and so on).

3) In the document, select the item to save as a style.

4) Go back to the Styles and Formatting window and click the **New Style from Selection** button, then select **New Style from Selection** from the menu.

In the Create Style dialog, type a name for the new style. The list shows the names of existing custom styles of the selected type, if any. Click **OK** to save the new style.

Update Style (from a selection)

Let's use paragraph styles as an example.

1) Create a new paragraph (or select an existing paragraph) and edit all the properties you want to alter in the style (such as indentation, font properties, alignment, and others).

Caution	Make sure that there are uniform properties in this paragraph. For example, if there are two different font sizes in the paragraph which is selected to be used to update the style, that particular property will not be updated.

2) Select the paragraph by clicking anywhere in the paragraph.

3) In the Styles and Formatting window, select the style you want to update (single-click, not double-click) and then click on the **New Style from Selection** button and select **Update Style**.

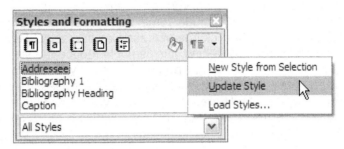

Figure 194: Updating a style from a selection

The procedure to update another category of style (character, page, or frame styles) is the same: select the item in question, modify it, select the style you want to update, and choose **Update Style**.

Load Styles (from a template or document)

The last option under the **New Style from Selection** icon is used to copy styles into the current document by loading them from a template or another document. Using this method, you can copy all styles, or groups of styles, at one time.

1) Open the document to copy styles into.

2) In the Styles and Formatting window, click on the **New Style from Selection icon** and then on **Load Styles** (see Figure 194).

3) In the Load Styles dialog (Figure 195), find and select the template to copy styles from.

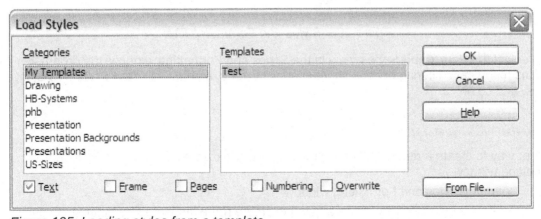

Figure 195: Loading styles from a template

4) Click on the **From File** button if the styles you want are contained in a text document rather than a template. In this case, a standard file selection dialog opens up, where you can select the desired document.

5) Select the options for the types of styles to be copied: Text (Paragraph and Character styles), Frame, Pages, Numbering (List styles). If you select **Overwrite,** the styles being copied will replace any styles of the same names in the target document.

6) Click **OK** to copy the styles.

Using the visible styles filters

At the bottom of the Styles and Formatting window (Figure 196), use the drop-down menu to select a filtering criterion for the contents of the main body of the window. Normally, you will find that only a handful of styles are needed in any given document, and it makes sense to have only these styles shown.

So, at the beginning of the writing process, you may want to have access to all the available styles (by selecting **All Styles**), and to then exclude some of them from use (Ctrl+click to select each style to be excluded and finally right-click one of these files and select **Hide** from the context menu). However, as the document develops, it is useful to reduce the size of the list displayed to only the styles already in use (by selecting **Applied Styles**). If you work on a document where you want to apply special-purpose styles only (such as those styles used in writing this user guide), select instead **Custom Styles**. The **Hierarchical Styles** view is most useful when modifying styles as it reveals which styles are linked together. This topic is discussed in more detail in Chapter 7, Working with Styles.

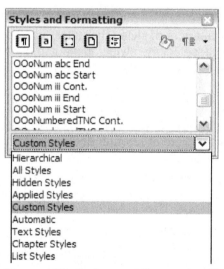

Figure 196: Styles and Formatting filter

If you select the **Paragraph Styles** view in the Styles and Formatting window, the drop-down menu contains many more filtering options so you can view, for example, only **Text Styles**, **Special Styles**, and so on.

Drag-and-drop a selection to create a style

Another way to create a new style is to drag-and-drop a text selection into the Styles and Formatting window.

1) Open the Styles and Formatting window.

2) Select the style category you are going to create (for example a character style) using one of the five icons in the top left part of the window.

3) Select the object on which you want to base the style and drag it to the Styles and Formatting window. The cursor changes to indicate whether the operation is possible or not.

4) In the Create Style dialog which opens, type a name for the new style and click **OK** to save the style.

Note	You cannot use the drag-and-drop method to create a custom page style.

Applying styles

Styles can be applied easily by means of the Styles and Formatting window. However, alternative ways exist to apply certain styles, as explained in this section.

Applying paragraph styles

When drafting a document, the most used style is the paragraph style. LibreOffice offers two quick alternatives to the Styles and Formatting window to apply this category of style: the *Apply Style* list and the *Format Paintbrush* button.

Using the Apply Style list

When a paragraph style is in use in a document, the style name appears on the *Apply Style* list near the left end of the formatting bar, to the right of the *Styles and Formatting* button. You can select styles from this menu, just as you can from the Styles and Formatting window.

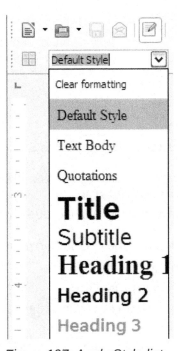

Figure 197: Apply Style list

To apply a style from this menu, place the cursor in the paragraph to change, click on the desired style or use the up or down arrow keys to move through the list, then press *Enter* to apply the highlighted style.

Tip	Select **More** at the bottom of the list to open the Styles and Formatting window.

You can use the Format Paintbrush to apply a certain paragraph style to another paragraph or to a group of paragraphs. Start by placing the cursor inside the paragraph you want to copy. Table 6 shows the formatting copied as a result of a particular cursor position. Table 7 shows the formatting painted as a result of the format copied and the cursor position when painting. Cases A, B, and C refer to the example shown in Figure 198.

Table 6: Cursor positioning

Case	Type of selection	Action
A	No selection. Cursor in the space between two words.	Copies the formatting of the paragraph and the character formatting of the next character in the text flow direction.
B	No selection, cursor in any word.	As above.
C	Text selected.	Copies the formatting of the last selected character and the paragraph.

Table 7: Format Paintbrush click position

Case selection	Paint position	Result
A, or B, or C	In a space between words.	Paragraph formatting only.
A	In a word or selection.	As above.
B, or C	In a word or a selection.	Paragraph formatting applied. Word or selection formatted with character format from original paragraph.

Now do one of the following:

1) To format a single paragraph:

   a) Click the **Format Paintbrush** icon (🖌) in the Standard Toolbar.

   b) The cursor changes into an ink bottle (🖋). Now click the paragraph (see Table 7) to which you want to apply the copied style.

      If you press *Shift+Ctrl* while clicking, you exclude any character formatting wherever you select to click.

   c) The paragraph is formatted and the cursor then returns to normal

2) To format more than one paragraph:

   a) *Double-click* the **Format Paintbrush** icon.

   b) The cursor changes shape. Now click each of the paragraphs (see Table 7) to which you want to apply the copied style.

      If you press *Shift+Ctrl* while clicking, you exclude any character formatting wherever you select to click.

   c) The paragraphs are formatted. Click the **Format Paintbrush** icon once more, or press the Esc key to revert to normal.

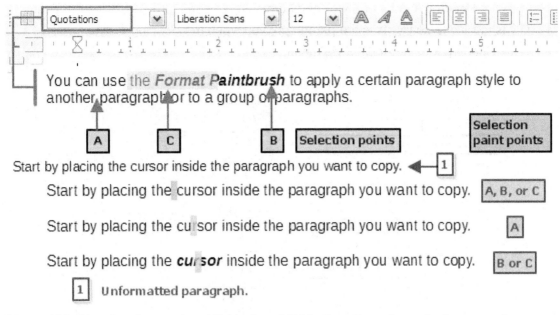

Start by placing the cursor inside the paragraph you want to copy. ◀	1
Start by placing the cursor inside the paragraph you want to copy.	A, B, or C
Start by placing the cursor inside the paragraph you want to copy.	A
Start by placing the **cursor** inside the paragraph you want to copy.	B or C

1 Unformatted paragraph.

Figure 198: Showing the results of Table 6 and Table 7 on the unformatted paragraph

Example: Applying a paragraph style

Let's see the three methods described above in action with an example.

To use the *Styles and Formatting* method:

1) Create a new document (choose **File > New > Text Document** or press *Ctrl+N*).

2) Type the words **Heading 1** in the new document, but do not press *Enter* so that the cursor remains in that same line where you typed.

3) Click the **Styles and Formatting** button (⊞) located on the Formatting Bar or press the *F11* key. This opens the Styles and Formatting window.

4) Make sure the window is showing the *Paragraph Styles* section: click on the top-left button (¶) of the Styles and Formatting window if it's not.

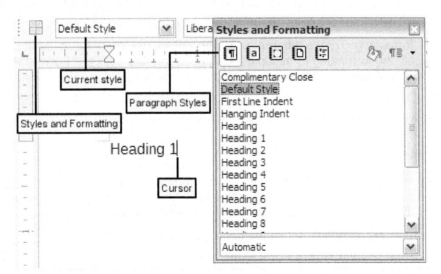

Figure 199: Click on the Styles and Formatting button to bring up the window

Double-click the **Heading 1** entry of Styles and Formatting (Figure 200). This does two things:

- Gives the line (actually, its entire paragraph) you typed the *Heading 1* style.
- Adds **Heading 1** to the *Apply Style* menu.

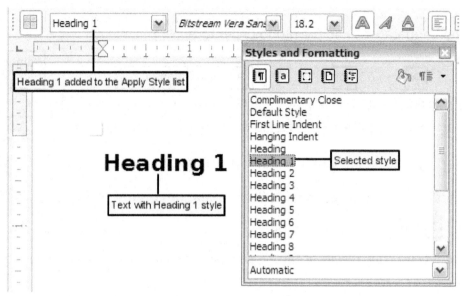

Figure 200: Applying paragraph styles

To use the *Apply Styles* list (Figure 200):

1) Repeat steps 1 and 2 from the previous example.
2) Select **Heading 1** in the *Apply Styles* list.

The text acquires the properties of the *Heading 1* style. If the paragraph style you want is not in the *Apply Style* list, select **More** to bring up the Styles and Formatting window. If the Styles and Formatting window is still open, you may notice that the *Heading 1* style is also highlighted in the main window, as shown in Figure 200.

Finally, try the *Format Paintbrush*.

Recreate the text in Figure 198 and add extra formatting to some of the text; bold and italic was used in the example. Place the cursor at a point in the text and click the **Format Paintbrush** icon ( ) to activate it. The cursor changes shape. Move the cursor to one of the new paragraphs and left-click to apply formatting. Try the different selection points and the different paint points to see the effects. To apply the formatting to multiple paragraphs, double-click the **Format Paintbrush** icon before clicking at a paint point. Clicking back on the icon, or pressing the *Esc* key, cancels the format painting.

The cursor shape changes back to the normal one on completion.

Applying character styles

You may have a document that contains character formatting applied directly using the Formatting toolbar or shortcut keys, and you decide to replace this with character styles formatting. The direct formatting should be removed before applying new character styles.

To remove the formatting manually, select the characters or words to be altered:

- Select **Format > Clear Direct Formatting**
- Alternatively, press *Ctrl+M*.

You can now proceed to apply character styles.

	Select all the formatting of one type at a time. Manually removing this formatting leaves the text elements selected so you can then apply the new character style immediately.
Tip	For example, to remove a number of manually italicized elements: 1) Select each instance (press *Ctrl* when selecting each subsequent element). 2) Use one of the methods above to remove the formatting (the text remains selected after removal). 3) In this example, pressing *Ctrl+I* will also toggle off italics. 4) Apply the character style (for example, Emphasis). Repeat for each formatted style you wish to replace.

Using the Styles and Formatting window

Open the Styles and Formatting window (press *F11*) and click the second button in the top bar. The list of available character styles is displayed. To apply a character style, follow these steps:

1) Select the block of text, or put the cursor into the single word, where you wish to apply the style.
2) Double-click the appropriate character style in the Styles and Formatting window.

Some character styles supplied in LibreOffice include:

> *Emphasis* character style.
>
> **Strong Emphasis** character style.
>
> `Teletype` character style.

	One difference between character styles and paragraph styles is the need for selecting text (highlighting). To apply a character style to more than a single word, you need to select all of the text to be changed. To apply the style to a single word, you only have to place the cursor in the word. Paragraph styles are applied to the whole of the paragraph in which the cursor is placed.
Note	

Using the Format Paintbrush

The Format Paintbrush can be used to apply character styles in much the same way as for paragraphs (see "Using the Format Paintbrush" on page 192).

The difference is that you must select a word that has the required formatting, and that to paint only the character style, without the underlying paragraph style, you must hold down the *Ctrl* key when applying the style.

Unset/undo character styles

Sometimes, you will want to remove the character style formatting from a block of text. *You must resist the temptation to do this manually using the Formatting toolbar*. This will only cause trouble down the road. To remove character style formatting from selected text:

1) Open the Styles and Formatting window (press *F11*) and click the second button (Character Styles) in the top bar.
2) With the Styles and Formatting window open, double-click the *Default* character style.

Applying frame styles

Whenever you insert an object (such as a graphic) into a document, it will automatically have an invisible frame around it. Some designers like to add frame styles to introduce variety. For example, you could have one frame style for photographs and a different frame style for other graphics such as line drawings. The one for photographs might have a border with a drop shadow, while the one for drawings might have only a border.

To apply a style to a frame:

1) Select the frame.
2) Bring up the Styles and Formatting window (for example, by pressing *F11*).
3) Click the **Frame Styles** icon (the third one from the left).
4) Double-click the frame style you want.

Having applied a style to a frame, you can now modify the frame to be just how you want it. Most of a frame's design can be set in a style, but the following options must be set manually:

- Anchoring: how the frame is positioned in relation to the rest of the page's contents (**Format > Anchor**).

- Arrangement: the frame's position in a stack of objects (**Format > Arrange**).

- Adding a hyperlink: so that a click on the frame opens a Web page or another document in an HTML file (**Insert > Hyperlink**).

When a frame is selected, the Frame toolbar replaces the Formatting toolbar, allowing you to modify the settings. The right-click (context) menu also has items for anchoring and arrangement, as well as for wrap and alignment.

Applying page styles

To apply a page style, place the cursor anywhere on the page to which the style should be applied. You can easily check which page style is applied because it is shown on the status bar.

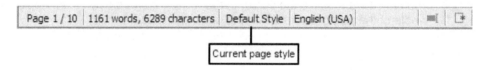

Figure 201: The current page style is displayed on the status bar

If you want to apply a different style, you can either right-click on the style in the status bar and select a new style from the context menu, or you can open the Styles and Formatting window (press *F11)*, select the page style icon at the top of the window (fourth icon), and then double-click on the desired style.

Caution	Changing a page style may cause the style of subsequent pages to change as well. The results may not be what you want. To change the style of only one page, you may need to insert a manual page break, as described below.

As discussed in Chapter 7, Working with Styles, a correctly set up page style will, in most cases, contain information on what the page style of the next page should be. For example, when you apply a *Left* page style to a page, you can indicate in the style settings that the next page has to apply a *Right* page style, a *First* page style could be followed by either a *Left* page style or a *Default* page style, and so on.

Another very useful mechanism to change the page style is to insert a manual page break and specify the style of the subsequent page. The idea is simple: you break a sequence of page styles and start a new sequence. To insert a page break, choose **Insert > Manual Break** and choose **Page break**. This section illustrates two common scenarios where page breaks are useful.

Example: Chapters

A possible scenario: You are writing a book that is divided into chapters. Each chapter starts with a page style called *New Chapter*. The following pages use the *Default* page style. At the end of each (except the last) chapter, we return to the *New Chapter* page style for the first page of the next chapter.

Figure 202 illustrates the flow of page styles when using page breaks.

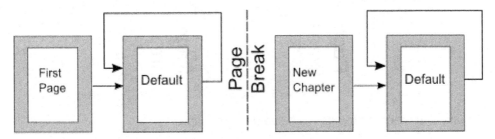

Figure 202: Page style flow using a page break

Writer doesn't have a predefined *New Chapter* page style, so you must create a custom style (see Chapter 7). (You could also use the First Page style for this purpose, but in our examples we use that style for the title page of the book.) Let's suppose that you already have the page styles with the following properties:

Page style	Next Style
New Chapter	Default
Default	Default

At some point, you will want to start a new chapter. Follow these steps:

1) Put the cursor at the end of the chapter, on a blank line (empty paragraph) of its own.

2) Choose **Insert > Manual Break**. The Insert Break dialog (Figure 203) appears.

3) Under *Type*, choose **Page break** and under *Style*, select **New Chapter**.

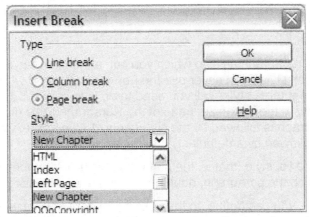

Figure 203: Choose Page break and select the New Chapter page style

Sometimes you may need to insert a page with special formatting, for example a landscape page or a page with more columns. This can also be done with page breaks. Suppose that the current page has the *Default Style* page style.

1) Choose **Insert > Manual Break**.
2) Select the desired page style (say, *Special Page*) in the Insert Break dialog.
3) Fill in the contents for this page. Then insert another page break.
4) Then select *Default Style* again. The pagination continues on as normal, except that one page has been replaced by a different page style.

This concept is illustrated in Figure 204.

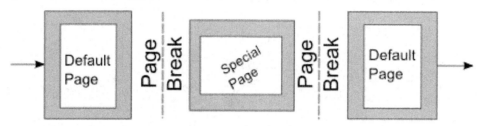

Figure 204: Inserting a page with special formatting

Applying list styles

List styles define properties such as indentation, numbering style (for example, *1,2,3*; *a,b,c*; or bullets), and punctuation after the number, but they do not by themselves define properties such as font, borders, text flow, and so on. The latter are properties of paragraph styles.

If you need your list to have specific paragraph-style properties, you should embed the list style into paragraph styles, as explained in Chapter 7. You can then create a numbered list by applying paragraph styles alone.

Writer has two series of predefined list styles, named *List* and *Numbering*. Each series contains five list styles, intended for the different levels of a nested list. As with any style, you can redefine the properties of these styles, for example the numbering or bullet symbol and the indentation. You can also define other list styles in these series or create your own series.

Each of the list styles predefined in Writer has four associated paragraph styles. For example, the *Numbering 1* **list** style is associated with four **paragraph** styles:

- Numbering 1
- Numbering 1 Cont.
- Numbering 1 End
- Numbering 1 Start

Numbering 1 is a default paragraph style to which you can attach a list style. If you want to make exclusive use of paragraph styles and never use the Formatting toolbar when creating a numbered list, you could use the other three styles. All you need to do is to create a suitable list style and set up the *Next Style* property in the Organizer page of the Paragraph Style dialog so that the *Numbering 1 Start* paragraph is followed by the *Numbering 1 Cont.* style, while the *Numbering 1 End* paragraph style is followed by a default style paragraph.

If you only want to apply a list style (that is, the numbering or bullet symbol and the indentation) then, when the cursor is on the paragraph, double-click on the desired list style.

When creating a list style, you can define up to ten levels of depth for nested lists. Switch from one level to the other with either the **Promote One Level** (⇐) or the **Demote One Level** (⇒) buttons on the Bullets and Numbering toolbar or by pressing the *Tab* key (one level down) or

Shift+Tab key combination (one level up) or by right-clicking on the list element and select **Up One Level** or **Down One Level** from the context menu.

Restarting or continuing the numbering

When creating more than one numbered list of the same type within the same chapter, Writer applies sequential numbering to all the lists. Sometimes this is what you want (for example, when placing illustrations between the numbered paragraphs), while at other times you want to restart the numbering.

To restart numbering from 1, you can do any of the following:

- Click on the **Restart numbering** icon ( ) on the Bullets and Numbering toolbar.

- Right-click on the first element of the list and choose **Restart numbering** from the context menu.

- Right-click on the first element of the list, choose **Paragraph** from the context menu, and go to the Outline & Numbering tab of the Paragraph dialog. In the *Numbering* section, select the options **Restart at this paragraph** and **Start with**, and set the number (see Figure 205).

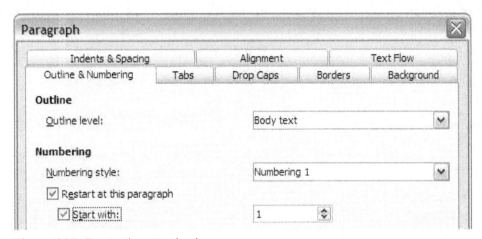

Figure 205: Restarting numbering

If you find that the numbering does not restart as intended using the first or second method, or if you want to restart from a number greater than 1, use the third method.

When editing a document, you may want to change from restarting numbering to continuing the numbering from a previous list. To do so, right-click on the list element and choose **Continue previous numbering** from the context menu.

Modifying styles

Writer provides several predefined styles, but you may find that they do not fit your preferences. You can build your own library of custom styles to use in place of the predefined ones, or you can modify the existing styles. LibreOffice offers four mechanisms to modify both both predefined and custom (user-created) styles:

- Update a style from a selection.
- Load or copy styles from another document or template.
- Change a style using the Style dialog.
- Use AutoUpdate (paragraph and frame styles only).

The first two methods are discussed in "Update Style (from a selection)" and "Load Styles (from a template or document)" on page 189, while Chapter 7, Working with Styles, discusses at length the process of creating a new style.

This section shows how you can quickly make simple modifications to existing paragraph styles using the same tools you would use for applying formatting manually.

Tip	Any changes made to a style are effective only in the current document. If you want to reuse modified or new styles in other documents, you need to either save the styles in a template (see Chapter 10, Working with Templates) or copy the styles into the other documents, as described in "Load Styles (from a template or document)" on page 189.

Changing a style using the Style dialog

To change an existing style using the Style dialog, right-click on the style in the Styles and Formatting window and select **Modify** from the pop-up menu.

The dialog displayed depends on the type of style selected. Figure 206 shows an example of the dialog for a paragraph style. Each style's dialog has several tabs. The various properties on these dialogs are described in the next chapter.

Move to the page where the setting you want to modify is specified and input the new value. You can click the **Help** button at any time to bring up the online help where all the options of the current page are briefly described. When you are done, click **OK** to close the dialog.

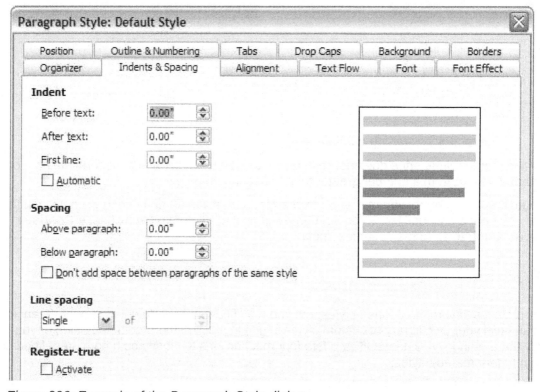

Figure 206: Example of the Paragraph Style dialog

Examples: Modifying paragraph styles

For this example, we need five lines of text with three LibreOffice-supplied paragraph styles: *Heading 1*, *Heading 2*, and *Heading 3*. These paragraph styles could be used in formatting headings (subheads) in the framework for a document that will be "fleshed out" afterwards.

Open a new text document for this exercise and type `Title` on the first line, click the **Paragraph Styles** icon on the Styles and Formatting window, and double-click **Heading 1** in the drop-down list. Press *Enter* to start a new line and type **First section heading**, applying the *Heading 2* style. Repeat this procedure for the other headings shown in Figure 207, using the proper paragraph style for each: Heading 3 for **Subsection heading**, and so on.

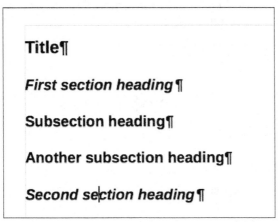

Figure 207: Headings 1–3 with default styles

Now, suppose you decide to make the following changes to these styles:

- *Heading 1* should be centered.
- *Heading 3* should be indented.

Center Heading 1

On the Styles and Formatting window, select the **Paragraph Styles** icon (if it isn't already chosen), right-click on **Heading 1**, and choose **Modify**.

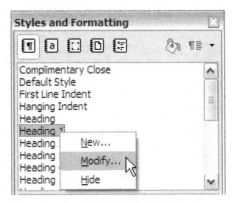

Figure 208: Modifying a style

After the Paragraph Style window opens, choose the **Alignment** tab, select **Center** (as shown below), and click **OK**.

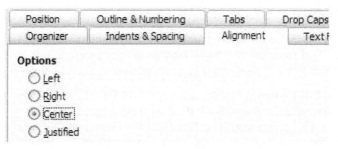

Figure 209: Center Heading 1

Now, every paragraph marked as *Heading 1* will be centered (as shown below). If you make another *Heading 1* entry, it will be centered as well.

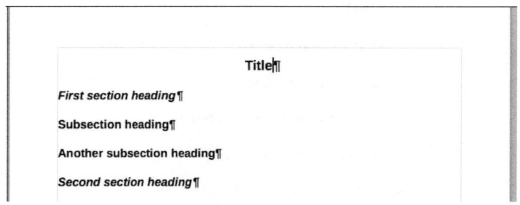

Figure 210: The text Title, which is formatted as a centered Heading 1 style

Indent Heading 3

On the Styles and Formatting window, right-click on the **Heading 3** paragraph style and choose **Modify** (as before). After the Paragraph Style dialog opens, follow the steps below:

1) Click the **Indents & Spacing** tab.
2) Under the *Indent* section, set the indentation before the text to **0.60"**, as shown below. Your display might be different, depending upon what measurement unit was set in the options (**Tools > Options > LibreOffice Writer > General > Settings**).

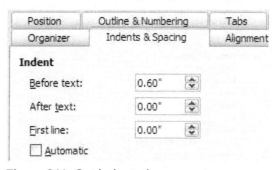

Figure 211: Set indentation

The result should resemble the illustration below.

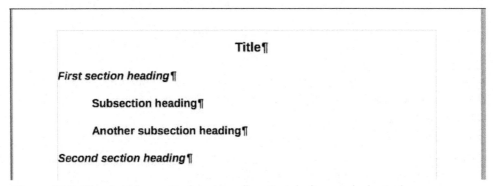

Figure 212: The text formatted as Heading 3 style is now indented

Using AutoUpdate

On the Organizer page of the Paragraph Style dialog is a check box named AutoUpdate. It is present only for paragraph and frame styles. If this check box is selected, then LibreOffice itself will apply to the style, any modification made manually to a paragraph formatted with that style.

Caution

If you are in the habit of manually overriding styles in your document, be sure that AutoUpdate is **not** enabled, or you will suddenly find whole sections of your document reformatting unexpectedly.

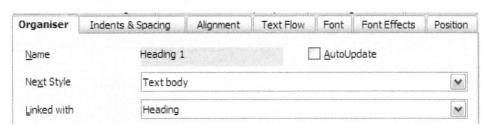

Figure 213: The Organizer page of the Paragraph Style dialog

Creating custom paragraph styles: examples

You have seen that the Styles and Formatting window provides several predefined styles, such as *Heading 1* and *Text body*. But what if you need something different, like a poem style, that is not in Styles and Formatting? With Writer you can make your own styles to suit your needs.

Chapter 7, Working with Styles, describes in detail the options on the various pages of the Paragraph Style dialog. This section provides an example of a typical use of custom paragraph styles.

We will create a *Poem* paragraph style and a *Poem Header* paragraph style, with the following properties:

- *Poem*: Centered, with a font size of 10pt.
- *PoemHeading*: Centered, bold, with a 12pt font size.

In addition, a *PoemHeading* style is to be followed by a *Poem* style. In other words, when you press *Enter*, the next paragraph style in the document changes to *Poem*.

Note	You may have noticed this behavior already. After you enter a heading using a *Heading* paragraph style and press *Enter*, the next style switches to *Text body*.

Creating the *Poem* paragraph style

Our next example creates the *Poem* style. We will use the *Default* style as a starting point.

1) Click the **Styles and Formatting** button, or press *F11*.
2) Click the **Paragraph Styles** button.
3) Right-click **Default Style** and choose **New**.

The Paragraph Style dialog opens, with the **Organizer** page selected. To create a *custom style*, you have to understand and configure the top three entries.

Style fields	Description
Name	This is the name of the style itself, like *Heading 1* or *Text body*. Set (type in the text box) the name to **Poem**.
Next Style	This is the style of a paragraph that follows the paragraph that is in *Poem* style. When you press *Enter* while typing text in the *Poem* style, this style is applied to the new paragraph. Set this value to **Poem**. When you press *Enter*, the text of the new paragraph will remain in the *Poem* style.
Linked with	If the *Poem* style is linked with another style, say *Default Style*, then any change in *Default* will affect *Poem*, just as you saw with *Heading* in the previous section. For our example, this is not the behavior we want. Set this entry to **– None –**. This means that **Poem** is not linked with any other style.

Select the Custom Styles category for new styles. After making these changes, your dialog should look like Figure 217.

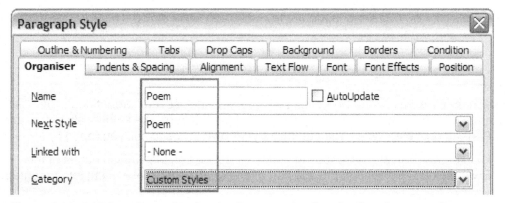

Figure 214: Initial configuration for the Poem style. Set the first three entries as shown.

The next step is to configure the alignment and font properties of this style.

- On the *Alignment* page, select the **Center** option.
- On the *Font* page, select the **12pt** font size.

Click **OK** to save the new *Poem* style.

Creating the PoemHeading style

Create a new *PoemHeading* style. Use the same procedure as before, using with these changes:

- *Next Style*: Select **Poem**, not **PoemHeading**.
- *Linked with*: **Heading**.

The dialog should look like Figure 215.

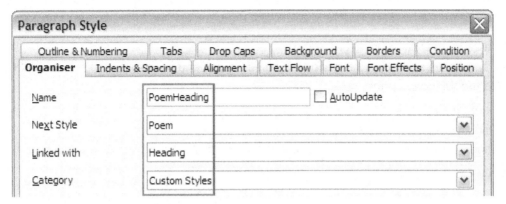

Figure 215: Settings for the PoemHeading style

Now set the settings of the new style:

1) On the *Alignment* page, select **Center**.
2) On the *Font* page, choose **Bold** and size **14pt**.

Click **OK** to save the new *PoemHeading* style.

Sample poem

It is a good idea to test out your new styles and see if you are happy with them. Typing a poem using the styles we have just defined should produce the results in Figure 216.

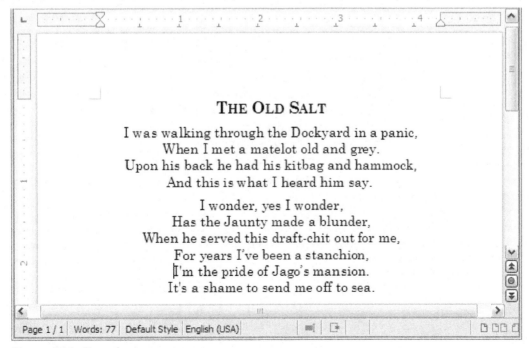

Figure 216: Sample poem

Changing the formatting of your styles

One of the main advantages of styles is that they allow the document formatting to be changed after the content has been written. For example, suppose you have written a 100-page book of poetry. Then you decide you don't like the way the poems look after all. Or, perhaps, your publisher doesn't like it.

To learn about reconfiguring styles, we add an indentation to the *Poem* style instead of centering it.

Indent Poem

First, set the *Poem* style to left alignment:

1) In the Styles and Formatting window, select **Poem** and right-click and select **Modify**.
2) On the *Alignment* page, select **Left**.

Set the indentation:

1) Click the **Indents & Spacing** tab.
2) Under *Indent*, set the indentation before the text to **0.5in**.

Done! Click **OK**, and you should see the text change.

Final result

After all these changes, the poem should look similar to Figure 217. Note in the figure that a third style has been created for the author of the poem.

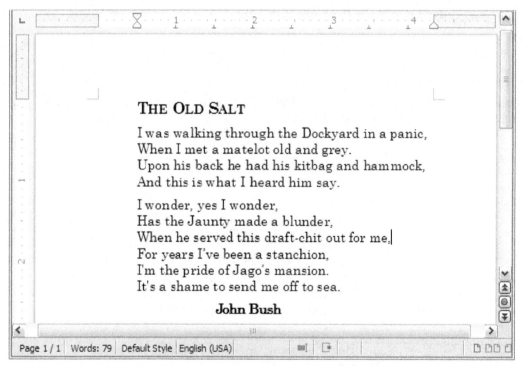

Figure 217: Final result, using three custom styles

Deleting styles

It is not possible to delete LibreOffice's predefined styles from a document or template, even if they are not in use. However, custom styles can be deleted.

To delete any unwanted styles, in the Styles and Formatting window select each one to be deleted (hold *Ctrl* while selecting multiple styles), and then right-click on a selected style and select **Delete** in the context menu. If the style is in use, a message appears, warning you that the style is in use and asking you to verify that you really want to delete the style.

If the style is not in use it is deleted immediately without confirmation.

Caution	If you delete a style that is in use, all objects with that style will return to the style it was based on (linked with) but retain some of the deleted style's formatting as manual formatting.

Tip	If an unwanted paragraph style is in use, you can use **Find & Replace** to replace it with a substitute style before deleting it. See Chapter 3, Working with Text, for more information.

Assigning styles to shortcut keys

You can configure shortcut keys to quickly assign styles in your document. Some shortcuts are predefined, such as *Ctrl+1* for the *Heading 1* paragraph style and *Ctrl+2* for *Heading 2*. You can modify these shortcuts and create your own. See Chapter 16, Customizing Writer, for details.

Defining a hierarchy of headings

Tools > Outline Numbering defines the hierarchy of headings in a document. Headings can be numbered or not; typically the first-level headings in a book-length document are the next level of headings after the chapter titles, which may be numbered, but lower-level headings are not numbered. Some chapter title and heading styles (such as those commonly used in engineering documents) number each chapter and heading level, for example 1, 1.1, 1.2, 2, 2.1, and so on. When chapters or sections are added or deleted, the numbering is automatically changed.

Paragraph styles are the key to LibreOffice's outline numbering feature. The default paragraph styles assigned to outline levels are the heading styles supplied with LibreOffice: *Heading 1*, *Heading 2*, and so on. However, you can substitute any styles you wish, including custom (user-defined) styles.

The headings defined using the outline numbering feature can be used for more than the table of contents (described in Chapter 12). For example, fields are commonly used to display headings in headers and footers of pages (see Chapter 14, Working with Fields), and Writer can send the outline to Impress to use as the basis for a presentation (see the *Impress Guide* for details).

Choosing paragraph styles for outline levels

If you are using the default heading styles for the headings in your outline, and you do not want to use heading numbering, you do not need to do anything on the Outline Numbering dialog. The default outline numbering scheme uses the default heading styles (Heading 1, Heading 2, and so on).

To use custom styles in place of one or more of the default heading styles:

1) Choose **Tools > Outline Numbering** to open the Outline Numbering dialog.
2) Click the number in the *Level* box corresponding to the heading for which you want to change the paragraph style.

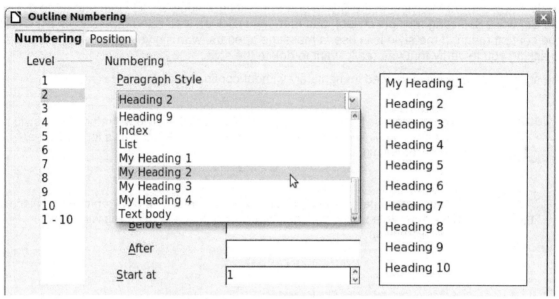

Figure 218: Choosing paragraph styles for outline levels

3) In the *Numbering: Paragraph Style* section, choose from the drop-down list the paragraph style you want to assign to that heading level. In this example, you might choose **My Heading 1** to replace **Heading 1** and for **Level 2**, **My Heading 2** to replace **Heading 2**.
4) Repeat for each outline level that you want to change. Click **OK** when done.

Assigning outline levels to other styles

In Writer, you can assign an outline level to any paragraph style. This feature enables you to create a table of contents that includes those headings along with the headings using styles listed in the Outline Numbering dialog. For example, you might use a different sequence of styles for annexes (appendixes), but you want the annex headings and subheadings to appear in the TOC at the same levels as the chapter headings and subheadings.

To assign an outline level to a paragraph style, go to the Outline & Numbering page for the style, and select the required outline level. Click **OK** to save this change.

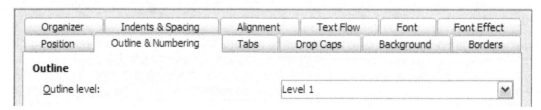

Figure 219: Specifying an outline level for a paragraph style

Setting up heading numbering

If you want one or more heading levels to be numbered, many choices are available; this example defines a scheme to create headings that look like those in the illustration below.

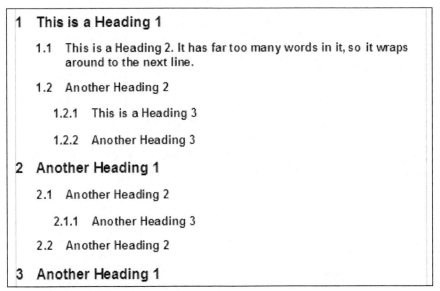

Figure 220: The numbering scheme to be set up

Use the Numbering page of the Outline Numbering dialog to define the numbering scheme and its appearance. Figure 221 shows the default settings.

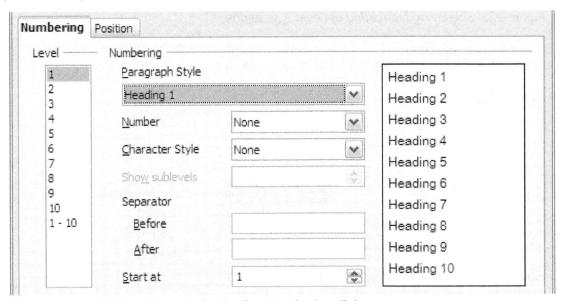

Figure 221: Default settings on the Outline Numbering dialog

1) In the *Level* list, choose **1**. In the *Number* list, choose **1, 2, 3, ...**. The result is shown in the preview box on the right in Figure 222.

Figure 222: Specifying numbering of Level 1 headings

2) In the *Level* list, choose **2**. In the *Number* list, choose **1, 2, 3, ...**. The *Show sublevels* list is now active; it should show **2** (if not, choose **2**). The result is shown in Figure 223.

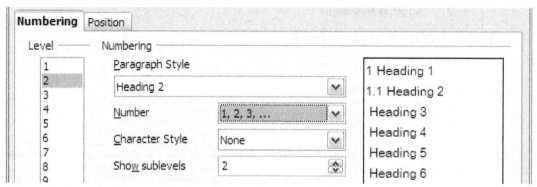

Figure 223: Specifying numbering of Level 2 headings

3) In the *Level* list, choose **3**. In the *Number* list, choose **1, 2, 3, ...**. The *Show sublevels* list should show **3** (if not, choose **3**). The result is shown in Figure 224.

Figure 224: Specifying numbering of Level 3 headings

These choices produce the layout shown in Figure 225.

```
1   This·is·a·Heading·1¶
¶
1.1    This·is·a·Heading·2.·It·has·far·too·many·words·in·it,·so·it·wraps
around·to·the·next·line.¶
¶
1.1.1    This·is·a·Heading·3¶
```

Figure 225: Results of numbering choices for headings

Setting up the indentation of headings

Whether or not the headings are numbered, you may want to change some of their formatting. For example, you may want the second-level and third-level headings to be indented from the margin. For numbered headings, you may also want the second line of long headings to line up with the first word of the heading, not the number. For these changes, use the **Position** page of the Outline Numbering dialog.

Note	The Position page for documents created in LibreOffice is slightly different from the Position page for documents created in earlier versions of similar programs that are opened in LibreOffice. This difference is provided for backwards compatibility. For more information, refer to "Position page for older documents opened in LibreOffice" (under "Creating a new list style") in Chapter 7, Working with Styles.

Positioning in new LibreOffice documents

Figure 226 shows the Position page as it appears for documents created in LibreOffice.

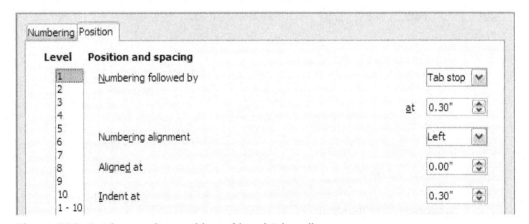

Figure 226: Setting up the position of level 1 headings

1) In the *Level* list on the left, choose 2. Change the values for *Numbering followed by, at* and *Aligned at*, as shown in Figure 227. You may want to use a different value. This indents the entire heading but does not affect the way long headings wrap around (see Figure 228).

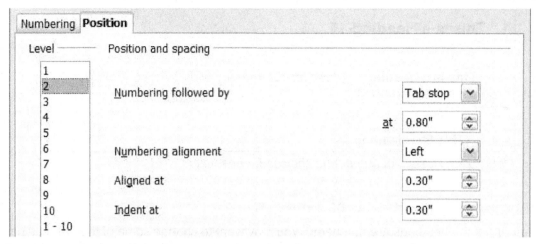

Figure 227: Indenting Level 2 headings

Figure 228: Result of changes to indentation of Level 2 headings

2) To change the wrapping behavior of long headings, change *Indent at* to a larger value, as shown in Figure 229. The result is shown in Figure 230.

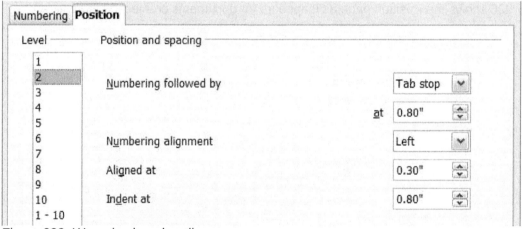

Figure 229: Wrapping long headings

Figure 230: Result of changing Indent at value

3) In the *Level* list, choose 3. Change the values for *Numbering followed by, at, Aligned at,* and *Indent at,* as shown in Figure 231. The final result is shown in Figure 232.

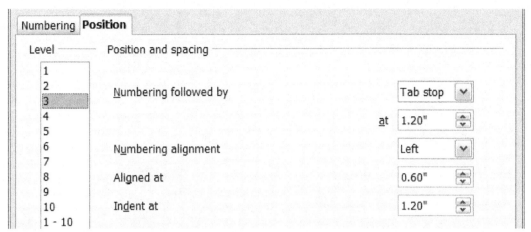

Figure 231: Indenting level 3 headings

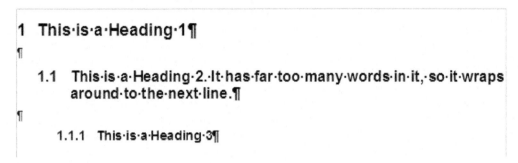

Figure 232: The results of Level 3 settings

Chapter 7
Working with Styles

Introduction

Chapter 6, Introduction to Styles, describes the basics of how to use, apply, and manage styles. This chapter gives a more detailed description of how to create or modify a style, using the many options available on the various pages of the Style dialog. You will learn how these options affect the appearance of the style and how to use them efficiently. Examples and hints are also provided.

The Style dialogs share many of the same pages as the manual formatting dialogs, so you can also use this chapter to help you apply manual formatting (though you do not need that if you use styles).

Creating custom (new) styles

In addition to using the predefined styles provided by LibreOffice, you can add new custom (user-defined) styles. In Chapter 6, two methods are given for creating a new style: the drag-and-drop approach and the **New Style from Selection** icon in the Styles and Formatting window.

These methods are very convenient because it is possible to immediately check the visual effects that the style produces before creating it. However, they may require you to access several different menus, and you have a somewhat reduced amount of control on style (particularly when it comes to organizing them). The method described in this chapter, therefore, concerns only the use of the Style dialog.

The Style dialog

Open the Styles and Formatting window. Select the category of style you want to create by clicking on the appropriate button in the top part of the Styles and Formatting window. For example, select the third button from the left if you want to create a new frame style.

Right-click in the window and select **New** from the context menu. Except for the *Page* and *List* styles, the style dialog which opens will be linked to one of the existing styles. You can choose a different style from the *Linked with* drop-down list, or choose **None**.

The dialog that is displayed depends on the type of style you selected. Many of the pages are the same as those that are displayed when manual formatting is applied. Therefore, if you are familiar with manual formatting, you will find that you already know how to use most of the options.

Tip	The dialogs used to create a new style and to modify an existing style are mostly the same, but with one exception: conditional styles have a different dialog. See "Working with conditional paragraph styles" on page 228.

The Organizer page

When creating a new style, the first page you need to set up is the *Organizer,* which is shown in Figure 233. This page is common to all style categories, with only small differences between them. Therefore, it is described only once.

Depending on the style you are creating, you will find the following information on this page:

- **Name**: present on all the categories. Use this field to give a name to the style you are creating.
- **AutoUpdate**: only present for paragraph and frame styles. If it is checked, then Writer will apply any modification made manually to a paragraph formatted with that style to the style itself.

Caution

If you are in the habit of manually overriding styles in your document, be sure that AutoUpdate is **not** enabled, or you will suddenly find whole sections of your document reformatted unexpectedly.

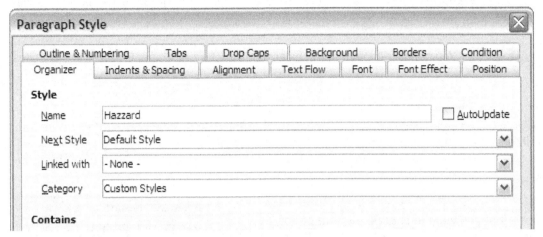

Figure 233: The Organizer page displayed when a new Paragraph style is created.

- **Next Style**: only available for paragraph and page styles. Use it to specify which style will be applied to the next element. It is customary, for example, to have a left page style followed by a right page, a first page followed by a left page, a heading followed by body text, and so on. You will see in the example later how this property is used. Predefined paragraph styles for lists or bullets also make large use of the *Next Style* property.

- **Linked with**: available for paragraph, character, and frame styles; it determines the position of the style in the hierarchy. When creating a new style and linking it to an existing style, all the starting properties of the style are copied from the linked style.

- **Category**: available for all styles; use it to associate the new style with one of the categories. Note that you cannot change the category of the predefined styles. Setting this field is useful when filtering the contents of the Styles and Formatting window.

- **Contains**: shows a summary of the properties of the style.

Understanding linked styles

When creating a new paragraph or a new character style, you may use an existing style as a starting point for its settings. In this sense, LibreOffice *links* the styles together.

When styles are linked, a change in the *parent* style affects every style linked to it. You can easily visualize the connections between styles by switching to the **Hierarchical** view in the Styles and Formatting window filter. For example, every *Heading* style (such as *Heading 1*, *Heading 2*) is linked with a style called *Heading*. This relationship is illustrated in Figure 234.

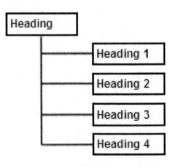

Figure 234: Hierarchical view of linked styles.

Linking styles is a very powerful method to create "families" of styles and allows you to change their properties simultaneously. For example, if you decide that all the headings should be green (such as in this guide), you only need to change the font color of the parent style to achieve the desired result. Note however, that changes made to a parameter of the parent style do not override changes previously made to the same parameter in the child styles. For example, if you changed the *Heading 2* font color to green, a change of the font color of the *Heading* style (the parent style) to red will not affect the *Heading 2* font color.

You can easily check which properties are specific to a style by looking at the *Contains* section of the *Organizer* page. In case you want to reset the properties of a child style to that of the parent style, click the **Standard** button located at the bottom of each Paragraph and Character style dialog page.

Note	You cannot define a hierarchical style structure for Page, Frame and List styles.

Creating a linked style

To create a linked style, you can either specify the parent style (the "linked with" style) in the **Organizer** page of the Style dialog, or you can start creating a new style by right-clicking in the Styles and Formatting window on the style to be linked with and selecting **New** from the drop-down menu.

Example: Changing a property of a parent style

Suppose that you want to change the font of not only *Heading 1* or *Heading 2*, but *all* headings. The easiest way to do that is to take advantage of *linking*.

Open the Styles and Formatting window (press *F11*), select the Paragraph Styles category, *right-click* on **Heading**, then select **Modify** to open the Paragraph Style dialog for the *Heading* style.

Select the **Font** tab, then select a font and click **OK**.

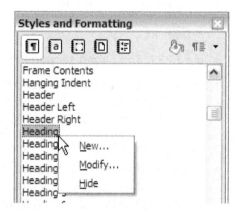

Figure 235: Select Heading style.

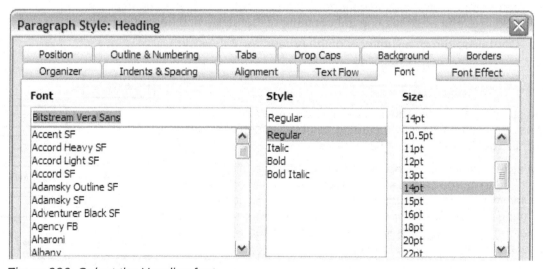

Figure 236: Select the Heading font.

Now, the fonts of all the heading styles (*Heading 1* through *Heading 10*) are changed in a single operation. Figure 237 shows on the left a document using the headings 1, 2 and 3 and on the right the same document after changes have been made to the *Heading* style.

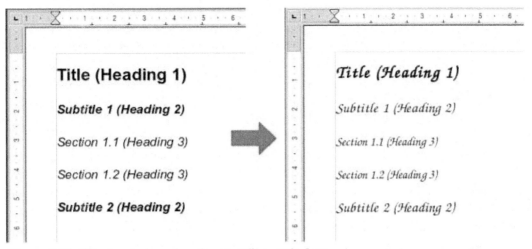

Figure 237: Effects of changing the Heading style font.

Working with paragraph styles

Although this section describes most of the parameters scattered over the twelve tabbed pages shown in Figure 236, you do not need to configure them all. In fact, in the vast majority of cases it is sufficient to modify only a few attributes, particularly if you make use of the linking properties of styles or when basing the new style on one which is already similar.

Settings on the Indents & Spacing page

On the Indents & Spacing page, you can set up the parameters that affect the position of the paragraph on the page and the spacing between lines and between this paragraph and the paragraphs nearby. The right hand side of the page shows a preview of the applied settings.

Use the *Indent* section of the page to set up the indentation, using these parameters:

- **Before text**: controls the space in the selected unit of measurement between the left margin of the page and the leftmost part of the paragraph area. Entering a negative value results in the text starting on the left of the margin. This may be useful in situations where your left margin is quite wide, but you want the headings to be centered in the page.
- **After text**: controls the space in the selected unit of measurement between the right margin of the page and the rightmost part of the paragraph area. Entering a negative value results in the text extending into the right margin of the page.
- **First line**: enter the offset in this box (either positive or negative) of the first line of the paragraph relative to the paragraph area. A positive value increases the indentation of the first line, while a negative value makes the first line start to the left of the paragraph area.
- **Automatic**: check this box to allow Writer to automatically control the indentation of the first line. The value is calculated by Writer on the basis of the font size and other parameters.

Use the *Spacing* section of the page to determine the amount of vertical space above and below the paragraph. It is customary to include some "space above" in heading styles so that they are separated from the text body of the previous section without the need to insert empty paragraphs. Spacing between paragraphs is also normal in certain types of documents. The body text style of this guide is configured to leave some space between consecutive paragraphs.

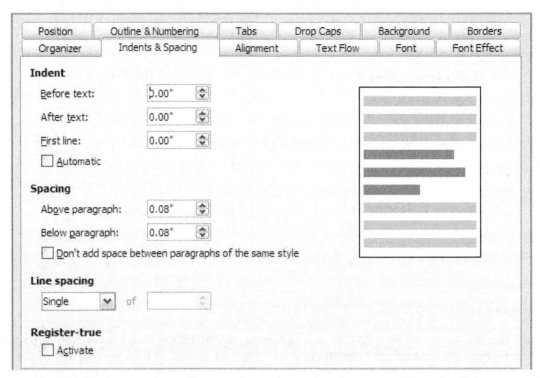

Figure 238: Settings on the Indents and Spacing page of a paragraph style dialog

The option to remove space between paragraphs of the same style is available by selecting the check box.

The spacing between paragraphs does not affect the spacing between lines, which is controlled using the drop-down box in the *Line spacing* section. You can select one of the following values:

- **Single**: the default setting—applies a single line spacing to the paragraph. This is calculated automatically based on the font size.

- **1.5 lines**: sets the line spacing to 1.5 lines.

- **Double**: sets the line spacing to 2 lines.

- **Proportional**: this value activates the edit box next to the drop-down list where you can enter a percentage value. 100% means a single line spacing, 200% double line spacing and so on.

- **At least**: this choice activates the edit box next to the drop-down list, where you can enter the minimum value (in your selected unit of measurement) to be used for the line spacing.

- **Leading**: if this is selected, you can control the height of the vertical space between the base lines of two successive lines of text, by entering a value, which is summed with the value of single line spacing, into the edit box.

- **Fixed**: this choice activates the edit box next to the drop-down list, where you can enter the exact value of the line spacing.

Tip	When using different font sizes in the same paragraph, the line spacing will be uneven, as Writer automatically calculates the optimal value. To obtain evenly spaced lines, select **Fixed** or **At least** in the drop-down list and a value that is large enough to create a spacing between the lines sufficient to account for the largest font size used.

The last parameter that can be set in this page is *Register-true*. This is a typography term that is used in printing. This term refers to the congruent imprint of the lines within a type area on the front and the back side of book pages, newspaper pages, and magazine pages. The register-true feature make these pages easier to read by preventing gray shadows from shining through between the lines of text. The register-true term also refers to lines in adjacent text columns that are of the same height.

When you define a paragraph, Paragraph Style, or Page Style as register-true, the base lines of the affected characters are aligned to a vertical page grid, regardless of font size or of the presence of graphics. This aligns the baseline of each line of text to a vertical document grid, so that each line is the same height.

To use this feature, you must first activate the *Register-true* option for the current page style. If you have activated the Register-true for the page style in use (refer to "General settings for the page style" on page 235) then the *Reference style* and all the styles hierarchically dependent on it will have the **Activate Register-True** box selected. You may also, however, want to activate the vertical grid for other styles (or not apply it to styles dependent on the reference style) and this is where this can be done.

Settings on the Alignment page

Use the Alignment page to modify the horizontal alignment of the text, choosing between **Left**, **Right**, **Center**, and **Justified**. The results of the selection are shown in a preview window on the right-hand side of the page.

When selecting the *Justified* alignment, you can also decide how Writer should treat the last line of the paragraph. By default, Writer aligns the last line to the left, but you can choose to align it to the center or to justify it (meaning that the words on the last line will be spaced in order to occupy it fully). If you have selected to justify the last line and select the **Expand single word** option, then whenever the last line of a justified paragraph consists of a single word, this word is stretched by inserting spaces between characters so that it occupies the full length of the line.

The alignment page is also used to control the *Text to Text* vertical alignment—useful when you have mixed font sizes on the same row. Choose the element of the fonts on the line that will be aligned between *Automatic*, *Baseline*, *Top*, *Middle*, *Bottom*. Refer to Figure 239 for a visual representation of these reference points.

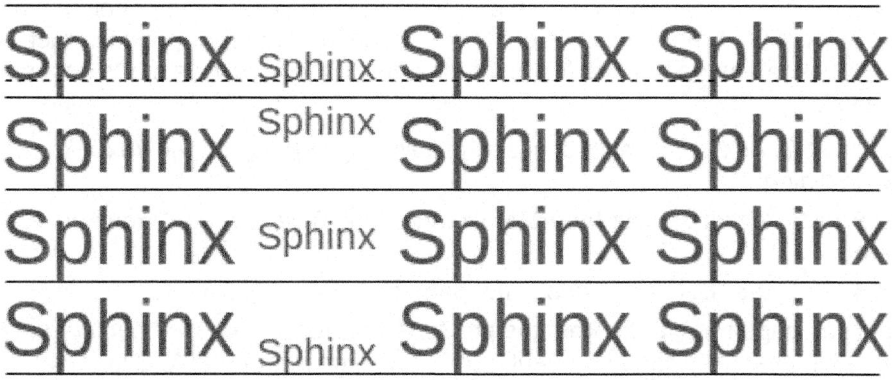

Figure 239: Text to text vertical alignment: Baseline, Top, Middle, Bottom

Text flow options for paragraph styles

The page of the dialog controlling the text flow options is shown in Figure 240. This page is divided into three parts: *Hyphenation*, *Breaks*, and *Options*.

With *Hyphenation* selected, three parameters are settable:

- *Characters at line end*: controls the minimum number of characters to be left on a line before inserting a hyphen.
- *Characters at line begin*: controls the minimum number of characters that can be placed at the beginning of a new line following a hyphen.
- *Maximum number of consecutive hyphens*: controls the number of consecutive lines that terminate with a hyphen.

If you prefer Writer to automatically control the hyphenation, select the **Automatically** option.

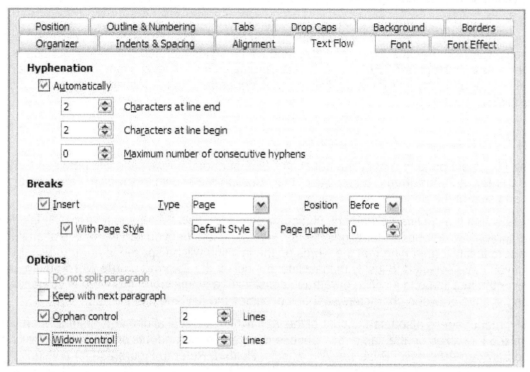

Figure 240: The options on the Text Flow page of the Paragraph dialog

In the *Breaks* section, you can require a paragraph to start on a new page or column, as well as specify the position of the break, the style of the new page, and the new page number. A typical use for this option is to ensure that the first page of a new chapter always starts on a new (usually right-hand) page.

To always start a style on a new page, choose the following settings on the *Text Flow* page of the Paragraph Style dialog:

1) In the *Breaks* section, select **Insert**. Make sure that *Type* is set to **Page** and *Position* is set to **Before**.
2) Select **With Page Style** and choose the page style from the list.
3) To continue page numbering from the previous chapter, leave *Page number* set at **0**. To restart each chapter's page numbering at 1, set *Page number* to **1**. Click **OK**.

Note	If you want the first page of a new chapter to always start on a right (recto) page, make sure that the page style for the first chapter page is set for the *right page only* by making this selection in the *Layout settings* field on the **Page** tab of the Page Style dialog.

The *Options* section of the *Text Flow* page provides settings to control what happens when a paragraph does not fit on the bottom of a page:

- **Do not split paragraph** means that the paragraph is never split across two pages. If it does not fit on the bottom of one page, the entire paragraph moves to the top of the next page.

- **Keep with next paragraph** is appropriate for headings or the lead-in sentence to a list, to ensure that it is not the last paragraph on a page.

- **Orphan control** and **Widow control**. Widows and orphans are typographic terms. An *orphan* is the first line of a paragraph alone at the bottom of a page or column. A *widow* is the last line of a paragraph that appears alone at the top of the next page or column. Use these options to allow paragraphs to split across pages or columns but require at least two or more lines to remain together at the bottom or top of a page or column. You can specify how many lines must remain together.

Font options for the paragraph style

Three pages of the Paragraph Style dialog are dedicated to settings controlling the appearance of the font, namely, the *Font*, *Font Effects*, and *Position* pages. The use of the first two pages is straightforward. Many of the options used when creating a character style are discussed in "Creating a new character style" on page 231. Options that can be used when creating a paragraph style are described here.

Specifying a relative font size

If you are creating a style based on another style (linked style), you can specify a font size *relative* to that other style—either as a percentage or as a plus or minus point value (–2pt or +5pt). Relative font sizes are commonly used for Web pages.

For example, the paragraph style *Heading 1* is based on the paragraph style *Heading*. The font size of the paragraph style *Heading* is 14pt, and the font size of paragraph style *Heading 1* is specified as 130%. Thus, the resultant font size of text in a paragraph formatted with the *Heading 1* paragraph style is 14pt times 130% = 18.2pt.

To specify a percentage font size: in the Paragraph Style dialog, select the **Font** tab. In the *Size* box, enter the percentage amount followed by the symbol % (see Figure 241). Similarly, you can enter a plus or minus sign followed by the number of points to be added or subtracted from the base font size.

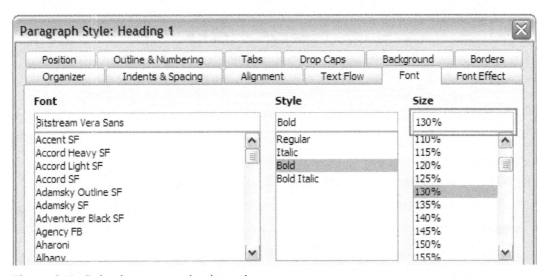

Figure 241: Selecting a type size based on a percentage

To change from a relative font size back to an absolute font size, enter the desired font size in points followed by the letters **pt**.

It is also possible to use a Percentage Font size for character styles.

Selecting a language for a paragraph style

The language you select for a document (on **Tools > Options > Language Settings > Languages**) determines the dictionary used for spell checking, thesaurus, hyphenation, the decimal and thousands delimiter used, and the default currency format.

Within the document, you can apply a separate language to any paragraph style. This setting has priority over the language of the whole document. On the *Font* page of the Paragraph Style dialog, languages with installed dictionaries are marked in the *Language* list by a small **ABC** icon (Figure 242). When checking spelling, Writer will use the correct dictionary for paragraphs with this style. If you write documents in multiple languages, you can use the linked styles to create two paragraph styles that differ only in the language option. If you then want to change some of the other properties of the paragraph style, all you need do is to change the parent style.

To insert occasional words in a different language and avoid their being picked by mistake with the check-spelling function, it is more convenient to use a character style, as discussed in "Creating a new character style" on page 231.

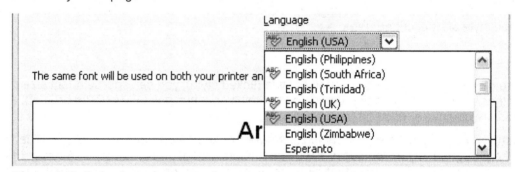

Figure 242: Selecting a language for a paragraph style

Options for positioning text

The Position page of the Paragraph Style dialog collects all the options that affect the position of the text on the screen or printed page. This page is divided into three sections, plus a preview area. They are: *Position*, *Rotation/Scaling*, and *Spacing*.

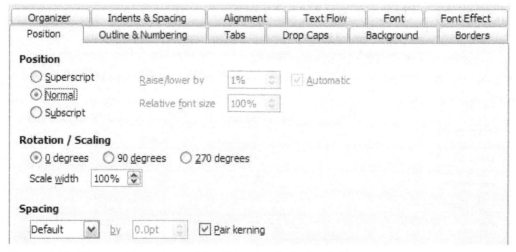

Figure 243: The position page of the Paragraph Style dialog

Use the *Position* section to control the appearance of superscripts and subscripts. However, you will normally apply superscript and subscripts to groups of characters rather than to entire paragraphs. Therefore, it is strongly recommended to change these parameters only when defining a character style and, instead, leave the default settings for the paragraph styles.

The second section of the Position page controls the rotation of the paragraph area. Two common uses for rotated paragraphs are:

- To put portrait headers and footers on a landscape page
- To fit headings above narrow table columns (as shown in Figure 244)

This is long	Another long heading	A rotated heading	Another heading	Another heading	Another heading	Another heading

Figure 244: A table with rotated headings

The **Scale width** box controls the percentage of the font width by which to compress or stretch the rotated text *horizontally*. That is, from the first character to the last.

Chapter 4, Formatting Pages, describes how to create portrait headers and footers on landscape pages by rotating *characters*. You can achieve the same effect by defining a separate header or footer paragraph style specifically for landscape pages.

Example: Rotating the text in a paragraph style

As an example, we will apply rotated table headings to a pre-existing table.

1) Create a new paragraph style. Name it **`Table Heading Rotated`**.
2) On the *Position* page of the Paragraph Style dialog, in the *Rotation / scaling* section, select **90 degrees**. Click **OK** to save the new style.

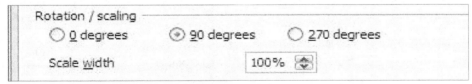

Figure 245: Rotating a paragraph 90 degrees

3) Select the heading row of the table and apply the new style. Any text in the cells of the heading row is now rotated.
4) If the headings are aligned to the top of the cells, you may want to change the alignment to the bottom of the cells, as shown in Figure 244. To do this, click the **Bottom** button on the Table toolbar or select **Format > Alignment > Bottom** from the main menu.

Use the *Spacing* section of the Position page to control the spacing between individual characters in the paragraph. When selecting an option other than default in the drop-down menu, use the edit box to enter the value in points by which you want to expand or condense the text.

The **Pair Kerning** option (selected by default) increases or decreases the amount of space between certain pairs of letters to improve the overall appearance of the text. Kerning automatically adjusts the character spacing for specific letter combinations. Kerning is only available for certain font types and, for printed documents, only works if your printer supports it.

Figure 246: Kerning disabled (left) and enabled (right).

Controlling tab stops

Although borderless tables are generally considered a much better solution to space out material across a page, in many situations tabs are sufficient to do what you need, with the added advantages of being simpler to manage and quicker to apply.

Caution	If you need to use tabs, and you will be sending a document to other people, *do not* use the default tab stops. If the recipients of the document have defined default tab stops that are different from the ones you are using, the paragraph may look very different on their machines. Instead, define the tab stops explicitly in the paragraph or the paragraph style; then you can be sure that everyone will see the same layout.

To define tab stops in your paragraph style, use the Tabs page, shown in Figure 247. Here you can choose the *type* of tab: left, right, centered, or decimal; the character to be used as a decimal point; and the *fill character*—the characters that appear between the end of the text before the tab and the beginning of the text after the tab. You can also create a custom fill character by entering it in the corresponding box. Common use of a fill character is adding dots between a heading and a page number in a table of contents or underscore character when creating a form to fill in.

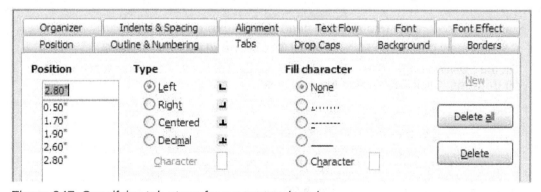

Figure 247: Specifying tab stops for a paragraph style

Creating a new tab stop, therefore, is just a matter of deciding its position relative to the left margin, the type, the fill character and clicking the **New** button. The tab stop will be entered in the *Position* list on the left hand side. Unfortunately, the only way to modify the position of a tab stop is to create a new one in the desired position and delete the old one using the buttons on the right-hand side of the page.

Note that it is not possible to define tabs that exceed the page margin. In the rare cases where that may be needed, use a borderless table instead.

Using the Outline & Numbering page

Use the Outline & Numbering page if you want to number the paragraph, if for example this style is to be used for a heading or list item.

You can assign an outline level to any paragraph style. This feature enables you to create a table of contents that includes those headings along with the headings using styles listed in **Tools > Outline Numbering**. For example, you might use a different sequence of styles for annexes (appendixes), but you want the annex headings and subheadings to appear in the TOC at the same levels as the chapter headings and subheadings.

To assign an outline level to a paragraph style, go to the Outline & Numbering page for the style, and select the required outline level. Click **OK** to save this change.

This page should be used in combination with list styles when you need to associate a certain paragraph style with a list style. Refer to "Combining list and paragraph styles" on page 245 for additional information on how to use this page, as well as an example.

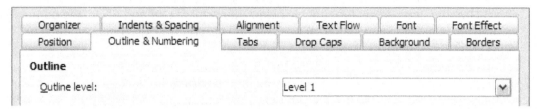

Figure 248: Setting the outline level on the Outline & Numbering page

Setting up a drop cap

If you want your paragraph to use drop caps (usually this is suitable for a first paragraph style), then you can predefine the properties in the Drop Caps page of the paragraph style dialog. Selecting the option to display drop caps enables the subsequent options where you can fine tune the appearance: the number of lines occupied, the number of characters to enlarge (if you want the whole first word, check the corresponding box), and the space between the drop caps and the text.

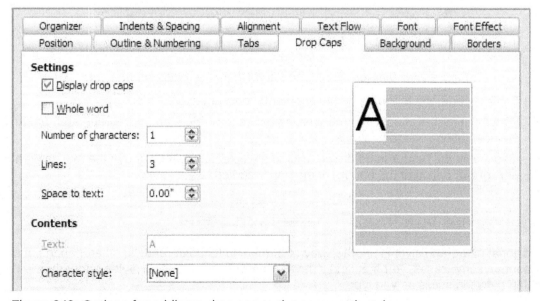

Figure 249: Options for adding a drop cap to the paragraph style

Drop caps use the same font and have the same properties as the rest of the paragraph; however, you can easily modify their appearance by creating a specific character style and using it. For example, you may want the drop caps to be of a different color or apply an outline effect. Select the character style you want to use in the corresponding drop-down menu.

Setting up paragraph background and borders

Adding a background color and a border to a paragraph is a good way to make it stand out without having to insert a frame. You can customize the background and border of the paragraph areas using the corresponding pages of the Paragraph Style dialog. In addition to highlighting, borders are also often used to separate header and footer areas from the main text area (such as in this guide) as well as to provide decorative elements in some heading styles.

The two pages are fairly intuitive. You may want to pay attention to the following points when working with the *Background* page:

- In case you do not find the desired color in the list of predefined ones, you can define your own by selecting **Tools > Options > LibreOffice > Colors**.

- You can use a graphic instead of a solid color as background. In the **As** drop-down list, select **Graphic**, then select the graphic object you want to use and adjust the parameters, as required. Detailed instructions on working with graphic backgrounds can be found in the *Impress Guide*.

- Different backgrounds can be selected for the paragraph area and for the characters in the paragraph. Select **Paragraph** in the **For** box for the paragraph background, and **Character** for the background of the text. View your choices in action by clicking **Apply**. To accept your choices click **OK**. Click **Standard** to return **all** the settings to defaults for a modified style.

- The background is only applied to the paragraph area. If you have defined an indented paragraph, the space between the paragraph and the margin does not have the paragraph's background color.

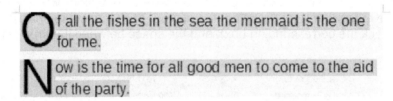

Figure 250: Different Paragraph and Character backgrounds set

On the *Borders* page, the following points are worth considering:

- Watch out for the effects that the spacing between borders and paragraph area produces on indentations and tabulations.

- If you want the border to be drawn around multiple paragraphs, leave the **Merge with next paragraph** option at the bottom of the page marked.

Working with conditional paragraph styles

A conditional paragraph style is another way of formatting text differently in different parts of a document. In some cases, you may find it saves time to use conditional styles rather than switching between styles as you type.

Making a paragraph style conditional means it changes its formatting depending on where it is used. For example, you may want the style *MyTextBody* to be black by default but turn white when inside a frame with a blue background.

Probably the most common use for conditional formatting is with single-style outlining. Single-style outlining is a type of outline numbering designed with a *Numbering* style, rather than with **Tools > Outline Numbering**. Instead of using different styles, it changes the number formatting whenever you press the *Tab* key to create a subordinate heading.

The only trouble with single-style outlining is that all levels look the same. This is where a conditional paragraph style comes in handy. Assign the paragraph style to an outline numbering style in the **Outline & Numbering** page and then open the **Condition** page. There, you can assign the levels of the outline numbering style to other paragraph styles. Then, when you press the *Tab* key while using the paragraph style, each level of the outline takes on different formatting, making single-style outlining even more convenient than it is on its own.

Note	Predefined styles (other than *Text body*) such as *Default*, *Heading 1*, and *Heading 2* cannot be set to be conditional.

Caution	If you want to make a style conditional, you have to do it while the style window is still open for the first time. After the window closes, the *Condition* tab no longer appears in the window.

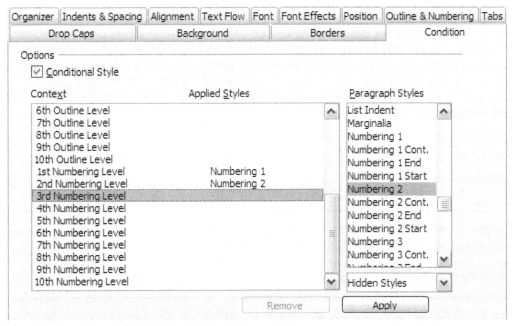

Figure 251: Condition page for paragraph styles

When you create a conditional style, you are saying "in this condition make this style look like that other style". For example, "When typing into a footer, make this style look like the *my_footer* paragraph style; when typing into a table, make this style look like the *table_text* paragraph style".

In addition to setting the normal (unconditional) properties of the style, you need to define which other style it will look like in different situations. You do this on the *Condition* page.

To set up a conditional paragraph style:

1) Define a new paragraph style.
2) Select all the paragraph properties for the style. Do not click OK!
3) Click the **Condition** tab.
4) Select the **Conditional Style** option.

5) Select the first condition in the *Context* list (left side of the dialog) and select the style you want for this condition in the *Paragraph Styles* list on the right-hand side.

6) Click **Apply**. The name of the paragraph style appears in the middle list.

7) Repeat steps 5 and 6 for each condition you want to have linked to a different style.

8) Click **OK**.

When the style is selected, you will see that the formatting of your text depends on the context.

Working with character styles

Character styles complement paragraph styles and are applied to groups of characters, rather than whole paragraphs. They are mainly used when you want to change the appearance or attributes of parts of a paragraph without affecting other parts. Examples of effects that can be obtained by means of character styles are **bold** or *italic* typeface or colored words.

Two of the character styles used in this document are:

- Keystroke uses a custom *KeyStroke* style. For example:

  "To set Writer to full screen, press *Control+Shift+J*".

- Menu paths use a custom *MenuPath* style. For example:

  "To turn field shadings on or off, choose **View > Field Shadings**".

Other ways of using character styles are described elsewhere in the *Writer Guide*. These uses include making chapter numbers, page numbers, or list numbers larger than the surrounding text and formatting hyperlinks. When inserting words in different language or words you do not want the spell checker to detect as mistakes (for example procedure names in some programming language), character styles are quite useful because you can define the language to be applied in the character-style properties.

Why use character styles?

New Writer users often wonder, "*Why use character styles?*" or "*How is this different from clicking the bold icon to change the font typeface?*" The following real-life event illustrates the difference.

Jean is a technical writer from Australia. She learned the value of character styles after her publisher told her to unbold menu paths in her 200-page book. Jean had *not* used character styles. She had to edit all 200 pages by hand, with some help from **Find & Replace**. This was the last time Jean failed to used character styles.

Character styles do not have as many options as paragraph styles or page styles. Their benefits are of a different nature.

- **Formatting changes**

  As Jean's story illustrates, the ability to make formatting changes throughout a document can be important. Character styles provide this.

- **Consistency**

  Character styles help ensure that typesetting guidelines are applied consistently.

- **Focus on content**

  "*Was I supposed to bold keystrokes? How about menus?*"
  A writer should not have to remember the answers to these questions. Typesetting details distract you from the real content of your work. A properly named custom character style (such as *KeyStroke* or *MenuPath*) will remove this burden from you.

Creating a new character style

This section illustrates the use of the Character Styles dialog for creating a new character style.

The pages used to configure the character style have already been seen in the previous section on paragraph styles. Therefore, once you are familiar with creating paragraph styles, it will only take a few minutes to create a character style.

- Use the *Organizer* to set up the hierarchical level of the new character style (if needed) and to give it a name.

- Use the *Font* page to determine the font, style, and size for your character style. As with paragraph styles, you can specify the size as a percentage rather than providing the absolute value. For example, 150% means that when the character style is applied to a 10pt font size, the new font size will be 15pt, while if applied to a 14pt font size, the new size will be 21pt. You can also specify the **Language** of the text to which a certain character style is applied, so you can insert words in a different language and have them spell checked using the correct dictionary.

- In the *Font Effects* page, you can set up attributes such as font color, underlining, relief, or other effects. If you frequently use hidden text, for example, it is very convenient to define a character style where the **Hidden** option is marked. This way you only need a few mouse clicks to hide text. **Relief** effects may be appropriate for a drop cap or to give more emphasis to the chapter number or other parts of the title (as it is the case of this guide).

- You can use the **Position** page to create a subscript in case you are not satisfied with the default one or even a sub-subscript which may be useful for certain scientific publications. In the same page, you can create rotated, condensed, or expanded text.

Note	When rotating a group of characters, you also need to specify whether the rotated text should fit in the line or if, instead, it is allowed to expand above and below the line. This property only becomes active for character styles.

- Use the Background page to apply a colored background to the text. Applying a background to a character style yields the same effect as using the Highlighting tool on the Standard Toolbar.

- Finish creating a character style by assigning a border and a shadow to the text, if so desired.

Migrating to character styles

For people accustomed to formatting text manually, character styles can take some getting used to. Here are some suggestions for making the transition easier:

- *Never* mix character styles and manual formatting. Manual formatting supersedes character styles. If you combine them, you may end up wasting hours in frustration trying to figure out why your character styles don't work.

- Right-clicking and choosing **Clear Direct Formatting** removes manual formatting but not character styles. To remove a character style, select the characters, then select the **Default** character style.

- Realize that clicking the **Bold** icon in the toolbar is not easier than double-clicking on a character style that is preset for bolding the font typeface.

- Leave the Styles and Formatting window open to make character styles easy to access.

Working with frame styles

Frames are often used as containers for text or graphics. To provide consistency in the appearance of frames used for similar purposes, it is a good idea to define styles for frames. For example, you might want photographs to be enclosed in a frame with a drop-shadowed border, line drawings in a frame with a plain border, marginal notes in a frame without a border but with a shaded background, and so on.

Writer provides several predefined frame styles, which you can modify as needed, and you can define new frame styles. The technique for defining and applying frame styles is similar to that for other styles.

Tip	There is considerable overlap between the uses of frames and of sections for some page layout purposes. You may find it useful to take a look at Chapter 4, Formatting Pages, for information about the use of frames and sections.

How frame styles work

When an object is added to Writer, it is automatically enclosed in a frame of a predetermined type. The frame sets how the object is placed on the page, as well as how it interacts with other elements in the document. You can edit the frame by modifying the frame style it uses or by using a manual override when a frame is added to the document.

Because frames and objects are used together, it is sometimes easy to forget they are separate elements. In some cases, such as charts, you can edit the frame and object separately, so the distinction is worth remembering.

Unlike other elements that use styles, frames can be defined only partly by their style because their use can vary so much. Several elements of frames, such as the anchor and protected elements, need to be defined manually for individual frames.

You can format a frame manually when you select **Insert > Frame**. The dialog that opens contains all the settings available when frame styles are set up, as well as some only available when the frame is inserted. As with other styles, the most efficient way to format frames is in the Styles and Formatting window.

Planning the styles

If you are using a mix of graphics, you may want to define two related styles, one with a border line for graphics with white backgrounds and one without a border for all other backgrounds. You also may want to design one or more frames for text only.

Otherwise, the default frame styles (listed in Table 8) cover most users' needs. The only significant addition that many users might need is one or more styles for text frames.

Table 8: Various frame styles and their uses

Style	Comments and Use
Formula	The frame style used for formulas. The default includes **AutoSize**, which adjusts the size of the frame to the formula.
Frame	The default frame style.

Style	Comments and Use
Graphics	The default style for graphics. The defaults include autosizing to fit the graphic, no text wrap, and a thin border around the frame. These are reasonable defaults, except for the border. Unless the background of the graphic is white and the document's background also is white, the border usually is unnecessary.
Labels	The default style for use with **File > New > Labels**. It seems to be used by LibreOffice automatically and is not intended for users at all.
Marginalia	A style for placing a frame beside the left margin. As the name suggests, the *Marginalia* style is intended for comments added in the margin of text. The style also is useful for creating sideheads—headings against the left margin, which often are used in technical documentation. To set up sideheads, create body-text paragraph styles with two inches or more indentation from the left. Then, place the cursor at the start of a body-text paragraph, add the frame, and apply the *Marginalia* style.
OLE	The default style for OLE objects and floating frames. The default places the frame at the top and center of a body of text.
Watermark	The default style for a watermark, a graphic placed as the background to a body of text. The default is a Through wrap, with text passing over the frame and anything in it. The graphic should be faint enough that text still is readable over top of it.

Creating new frame styles

You can access frame settings by selecting **New** or **Modify** in the Styles and Formatting window for a frame style.

- *Type* page: sets the size and position of the frame. One of the most useful options here is **AutoSize**, which automatically adjusts the frame to the object it contains. If the frame style is one used automatically, then this option should be selected.

- *Options* page: sets whether the contents of the frame are printed and able to be edited in a read-only document. This page also sets the text direction, which is useful if you are using the frame for contents in a language that uses right-to-left text direction.

- *Wrap* page: sets how text is positioned in relation to the frame and how close text comes to a frame. If you want the frame contents to stand out from the paragraphs around it, set the wrap to **None**. This probably is the single most important page for frames.

- *Background* page: sets the background color or graphic. This page is useful mostly for text frames in complex page layouts, in which a text frame has an appearance different from the general background of the page.

- *Borders* page: sets the line around the frame, if any. Many new designers make the mistake of adding a border to every frame. However, when a colored background distinctly marks the division between the frame's contents and the rest of the page, borders are unnecessary.

- *Columns* page: this page can be ignored unless the frame is being used for text. The page is the same as is used to set up a page style, and its parameters are described in the section "Columns page" on page 237.

- *Macro* page: sets a macro to use with the frame in order to trigger an action when the user interacts with the frame. These options are useful only in an on-line Writer or HTML document.

Working with page styles

Page styles control page properties (margins, page size, header and footer, among others). However, unlike paragraphs, which can have directly applied properties, pages only have a page style and no directly applied properties.

> Christian is a lawyer from California, USA. For his letters, the first page has his letterhead, and subsequent pages only identify the recipient, the date, and the page number. Christian does this using page styles. He also uses page styles to comply with the spacing requirements (such as margins) for legal briefs in California State courts.

This section describes how to create a new page style, explains the meaning of some of the options in the Page style dialog, and illustrates their usage.

Creating a new page style

Unlike other styles, page styles can be created or modified only by using the Styles and Formatting window. Open the Styles and Formatting window and click the Page Styles icon (![icon]). Right-click anywhere in the window and select **New**. It does not matter if you right-click a style or right-click in blank space.

The Page Style dialog contains eight pages.

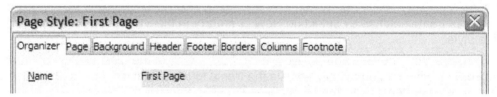

Figure 252: The tabbed pages for the Page Style dialog

The Organizer page

The Organizer page is described in "The Organizer page" on page 216.

The next style property

Use the **Next style** property to specify the style for the subsequent page style element. This property is particularly important for a page style, as the following example demonstrates.

Setting up a title page

Consider a common scenario: you want the document to have a title page that is different from the rest of the document:

- It should not have a header or page number.
- The left and right margins should be the same.

For the title page, we can use the predefined *First Page* page style that comes with LibreOffice, and for the rest of the document, we can use the *Default* page style.

Figure 253 shows the required flow of page styles. On the **Organizer** page of the *Default* page style, leave the *Next Style* property set to **Default**. On the **Organizer** page of the *First Page* style, make sure that the *Next Style* property is set to **Default**.

LibreOffice 4.2 Writer Guide

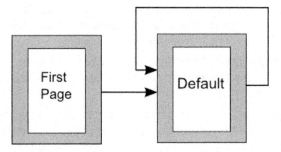

Figure 253: Flow of page styles

Note	Depending on your requirement, it may be possible to achieve this just by using the Default page style. On the document's first page, deselect the *Same content on first page* option with **Header on** selected. The header can thus be omitted from the first page.

General settings for the page style

The **Page** page of the Page Style dialog is where you can control the general settings of the page. The page consists of three sections, plus a preview area in the top right corner.

Figure 254: The Page page for the Page Style dialog

In the *Paper format* section, you can specify the size of the paper choosing from one of the many predefined formats. Selecting "user", you can use the *Width* and *Height* fields to define your own paper size. If using a predefined format, select the orientation of the paper between portrait and landscape. If your printer has more than one tray, you can specify the tray from which to print pages in the new page style.

In the *Margins* section, specify the size of the margins in your preferred unit of measurement. If you select **Mirrored** for *Page layout* in the *Layout settings* section, then the names of the margins change from **Left** and **Right** to **Inner** and **Outer**.

In the *Layout settings* section, choose the desired *Page layout* from the four available options. Decide whether the page style being defined applies to both left and right pages (default), or applies to right or left only. Some considerations:

- If you plan to bind the printed pages using this style like a book, select a mirrored layout. Use the **Format** drop-down menu to determine the page numbering style to apply to this page style.

- A common practice in page layouts is to have asymmetrical page margins—both for left and right margins and for top and bottom margins. There are various schemes for accomplishing this. The most common of them follow these two general rules for printed page layouts: (a) The outer margin (right margin on a right-hand page) would have a wider margin than an inner margin (left margin on a right-hand page); (b) The bottom margin would be larger than a top margin. The rationale for an asymmetrical page layout is allowing more space for readers to place their hands while holding the books or other printed documents. About.com describes some page layouts on their Web site: Perfect Proportions Using Page Margins in Desktop Publishing.

- If you want the first page of a new chapter to always start on a right (recto) page, make sure that the page style for the first chapter page is set for the right page only by making this selection in the *Layout settings* field. The typical procedure for the rest of a chapter is to define a single "mirrored" page style for both left and right pages. A mirrored page can have different headers and footers. If done this way, every chapter will use two page styles.

- You can choose to define separate page styles for left and right pages, if you want the pages to be very different in appearance (for example, different margins or headers and footers only on right pages but not on left pages; imagine a book with a full-page photograph on the left pages and text on the right pages). In that case, make sure that the *Next Style* field for the first page style is then set for a left-only page, which, in turn, is then set to be followed by a right-only page style. If done this way, every chapter will use three page styles. A hypothetical case might have these page-style names: *First page*, *Left*, and *Right*.

If you check the **Register-true** box, Writer will create a vertical grid on the page with a spacing between grid points that depends on the selected **Reference Style**. The vertical grid makes sure that text printed on adjacent columns, opposite pages, or even both sides of the same sheet of paper, is aligned—making it easier to read as well as being more pleasant to see.

Background and Border pages

Use the **Background** page to apply a background or the **Border** page to draw a border around the text area of the page (the margins). You can also add a shadow to the text area. You can choose between a solid color or a graphic image for the background and several styles of line for the borders. Note that the page area affected by these changes does **not** include the area outside the margins. If you plan to print on colored paper and want to have a feel of the final result you will obtain or want to use a light color for the font, rather than changing the background, then go to **Tools > Options > LibreOffice** and in the *Appearance* section, change the *Document background* color.

Header and Footer pages

You can associate a different header or footer to each page style. This property makes it very easy to have different headers on left and right pages, to avoid headers on pages at the start of a new chapter, and so on. You can also have a different header or footer on the same page style where it is used for the first page of a document.

Setting up the header and footer pages is straightforward. The instructions here refer to the header, but the footer page has the same options. Activate the input boxes by selecting **Header on**, then specify the left margin, right margin, and spacing to the main text area. For the height of the header area, you can either select the **AutoFit height** box, which will make Writer adapt the size to the contents, or specify the height manually. Clicking **More** opens a new dialog, where you can set the borders and background of the header area.

If you deselect the **Same content left/right** box, you can specify a different header for left or right pages, even if you use a single style for both as shown here. This option is not available on the predefined *Left* and *Right* page styles or on any other page style defined to be a left or right page only.

Deselecting **Same content on first page** allows you to set a different header on a first page when using the same style for the Next Style.

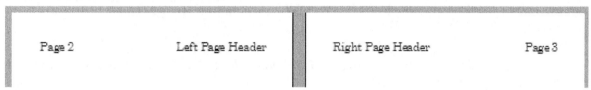

| Page 2 | Left Page Header | | Right Page Header | Page 3 |

Figure 255: Different content on left and right pages

Columns page

Use this page to create the desired column layout for the page style. The page is subdivided into three sections: *Settings*, *Width and Spacing* and *Separator Line*. The *Settings* section contains thumbnails of predefined columns settings you can select, as well as a text box where you can enter the desired number of columns if you need to create a customized one.

After you select more than one column, the *Width and Spacing* section becomes active. If you are not satisfied with the predefined settings (equally spaced columns), deselect the **AutoWidth** option and enter the parameters manually. When you work with multiple columns per page, you can also fine tune the position and size of a separator line between the columns.

Footnote page

Use this page to adjust the appearance of the footnotes. Keeping the default setting **Not larger than page area**, the footnotes area is calculated automatically on the basis of the number of footnotes. If you prefer to control manually the maximum space that footnotes can take, select the **Maximum footnote height** option and enter the value in the preferred unit of measurement. Use the second section of the page to customize the separator between the footnotes and the main area.

Example: A book chapter sequence of pages

Book chapters typically start on a right-hand page, with the first page of the chapter having a different layout from the rest of the pages. The other pages in the chapter are "mirrored" for double-sided printing. For example, page numbers in the header or footer may be positioned on the outside edge of pages and in this instance a wider margin (allowing for binding) is placed on the inside edge.

Table 9 shows the properties of two page styles (*Right Page* and *Default*) set up for a typical book chapter's sequence of pages.

Table 9: Properties of customized page styles for book chapter

Page Style	Desired effect	Property: setting
Right Page	First page always on the right (an odd-numbered page)	**Page > Page layout > Only right**
	No header or footer	**Header > Header on: Not selected**
	Top margin of page larger than on other pages	**Page > Margins > Top: 6.00cm**
Default	Mirrored margins	**Page > Page layout: Mirrored**
	Header with page number on the top outside of the page and chapter title in the top middle center of the page	**Header > Header on: Selected** **Header > Header > Same content left/right: Not selected**

Figure 256 illustrates the transitions from the *Right Page* to *Default* page styles, with the change of header between left and right pages shown by the # symbol.

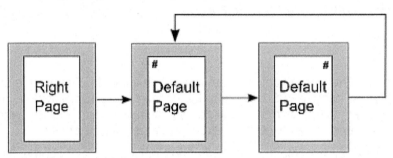

Figure 256: Right Page and then the Default page style with different headers for alternate pages.

Step 1. Set up the Right Page style.

1) On the Styles and Formatting window, click the Page Styles icon ( ) to display a list of page styles.
2) Right-click on *Right Page* and select **Modify** from the pop-up menu.
3) On the *Organizer* page of the Page Style: Right Page dialog, change *Next Style* to **Default**.

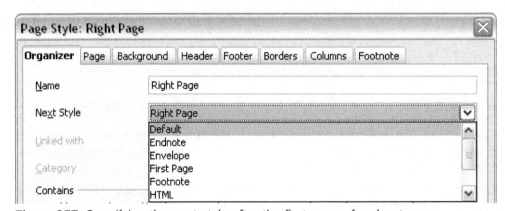

Figure 257: Specifying the next style after the first page of a chapter

4) On the *Page* tab, specify a larger left margin for binding, and a larger top margin to move the chapter title down the page.

|

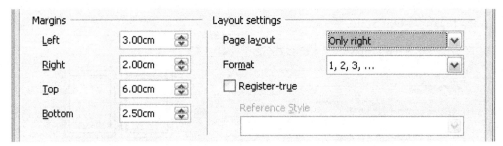

Figure 258: Setting page margins and layout for the Right Page style

5) On the *Header* and *Footer* pages, be sure the **Header on** and **Footer on** options are not selected. Click **OK** to save your changes.

Step 2. Set up the Default page style.

1) On the Styles and Formatting window, in the list of page styles, right-click on *Default* and select **Modify** from the pop-up menu.

2) On the *Organizer* page of the Page Style: Default dialog, be sure **Next Style** is set to **Default**.

3) On the *Page* tab of the Page Style: Default dialog, select **Mirrored** for *Page layout* and set the *Inner* and *Outer* margins to the same width as the *Left* and *Right* margins, respectively, on the *Right Page* style.

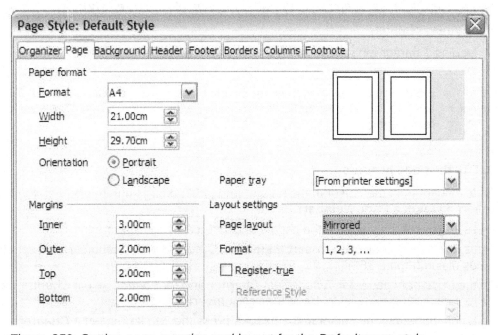

Figure 259: Setting page margins and layout for the Default page style

4) On the *Header* page of the Page Style: Default dialog, select the **Header on** option and deselect the **Same content left/right** option. Click **OK** to save your changes.

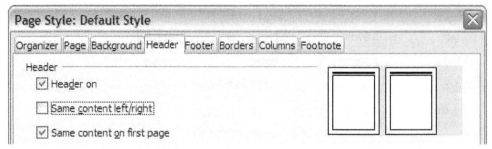

Figure 260: Setting up the header properties for the Default page style

Step 3. Set up the Heading 1 paragraph style to start on a new right-hand page.

1) In the Styles and Formatting window, on the Paragraph Styles page, right-click on *Heading 1* and select **Modify**.

2) On the *Text Flow* page of the Paragraph Style dialog, in the *Breaks* section, select **Insert**, **With Page Style**, and **Right Page**. Click **OK** to save your changes.

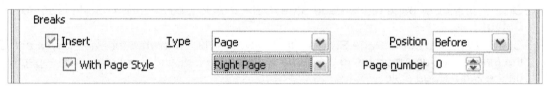

Figure 261: Setting a paragraph style to start on a page of a selected style

Step 4. Start a new chapter.

Apply the *Heading 1* paragraph style to the first paragraph, which is the title of the chapter.

Note	By default, the *Heading 1* paragraph style is assigned to *Outline Level 1*. The assignment of paragraph styles to outline levels is done through **Tools > Outline Numbering**.

Step 5. Set up the page headers.

1) On a left page, put the cursor in the header and insert a page number field on the left (**Insert > Fields > Page Number**).

2) Press *Tab* to put the cursor in the middle and insert a Chapter reference:

   Press *Control+F2* (or choose **Insert > Fields > Other** from the menu bar) to display the Fields dialog (Figure 262).

   On the *Document* page, for *Type*, select **Chapter** and for *Format*, select **Chapter name**. Make sure that *Level* is set to **1** and then click **Insert**.

3) On a right page, put the cursor in the header, press the *Tab* key, insert a **Chapter** reference, press *Tab* again, and insert a page number field.

4) If you need to adjust the tab stops for the header, modify the *Header* paragraph style. Do not manually adjust the tab stops.

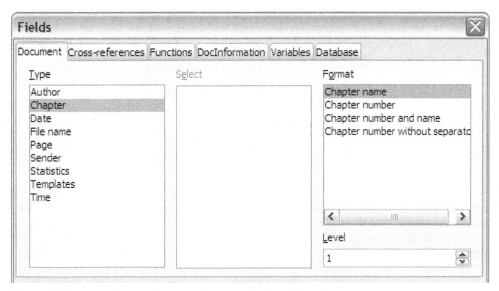

Figure 262: Inserting a chapter title into the header of a page

Working with list styles

List styles (also called numbering styles) work together with paragraph styles. They define indentation, alignment, and the numbering or bullet characters used for list items. You can define many list styles, from simple bulleted lists to complex multi-level (nested) lists.

As with other styles, the main reasons for using list styles are consistency and speeding up your work. Although you can create simple lists quickly by clicking the **Numbering On/Off** or **Bullets On/Off** icons on the Formatting toolbar, and create quite complex nested lists using the buttons on the Bullets and Numbering toolbar, the appearance of the resulting lists may not be what you want —and you might want to have more than one style of list. You can use the Bullets and Numbering choice on the Format menu to manually format the appearance of some or all of the lists, but if you later need to change their appearance, you will have a lot of manual work to do.

Note	LibreOffice uses the terms "numbering style" and "list style" inconsistently, but they are the same thing. For example, the tooltip in the Styles and Formatting window says "List Styles", but its style dialog says "Numbering Style".

Defining the appearance of a nested list

A nested list is a numbered or bulleted list with subordinate (usually indented) numbered or bulleted lists. Rather than just a list of numbered items (*1, 2, 3...*), a nested list may have item 1, then indented items numbered *a, b, c* or *i, ii, iii* or some other numbering method before the main number 2. With numbering styles, you can achieve any combination of numbering formats you want. A nested list may even combine numbered items with bulleted items.

There is no difference between defining a nested list style or a simple list, although nested lists require more work. An example of a nested list is given in Chapter 3, Working with Text. In that case, the list was built using one of the predefined outline schemes as a starting point, while in this section we follow a more general approach so that the list can more fully suit your needs.

Creating a new list style

The dialog to create a new list style consists of six pages in addition to the usual *Organizer* page discussed in "The Organizer page" on page 216.

Bullets, Numbering Styles, and Image pages

The *Bullets*, *Numbering Style*, and *Image* pages contain predefined formatting for list item symbols (bullets or numbers). To use one of them for your style, click on the image. A thick border indicates the selection. The bullets on the Bullets tab are font characters; those on the Image tab are graphics.

If you choose a graphics bullet, on the *Options* page you can select the **Link Graphics option** to create a link to the graphic object rather than embedding it in the document. If you decide to link the graphic, keep in mind that the bullet will not be displayed when the document is opened on a different computer (unless the same graphic file is located in the same location on both computers) or if the graphic file used is moved to a different location on the computer.

Outline page

Use the *Outline* page to select from eight predefined nested lists. You can also select one and use it as a starting point for your own style, customizing the list using the *Position* page and the *Options* page, as described below.

Position page

Use the *Position* page to fine tune the indentation and spacing of the list item symbol and the text of the list item. This page is particularly effective when used in combination with the *Options* page.

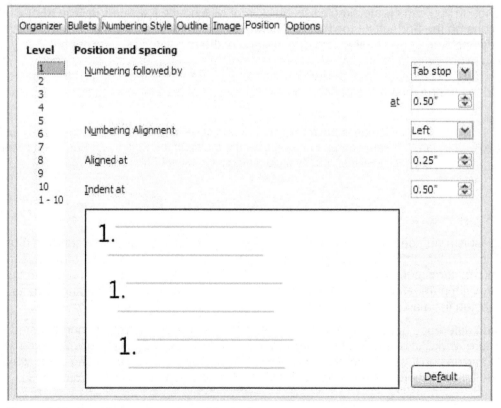

Figure 263: Position settings for a List style

LibreOffice 4.2 Writer Guide

You can adjust the following settings for each individual level or all levels at once (to make them all the same). It is generally easier to adjust the settings in the order given below, instead of the order on the dialog. That is, start from the overall indentation for the list elements, then fix the position of the symbols, and finally adjust the alignment of the symbols.

- **Numbering followed by**: the character to follow the numbering symbol (plus any characters—for example a punctuation mark—chosen on the Options page to appear after the number). Choose between a tab stop, a space, or nothing. If you select the tab stop, you can specify the position of the tab.

- **Indent at**: how much space is reserved for the numbering symbol, measured from the left page margin. The alignment of the first line of the list is also affected by any tab you may have set to follow the numbering.

- **Aligned at**: the position of the numbering symbol, measured from the left margin of the page.

- **Numbering alignment**: how the numbering (including any text before or after as set in the *Options* page) will be aligned. The **Aligned at** value determines the symbol alignment.

Note	When defining an indentation different from 0, the position of the tabulation is not considered.

Tip	In normal circumstances, setting the *Numbering followed by* distance to be equal to the *Indent at* distance works well. See Figure 264 for a graphic representation of the effects of the above parameters.

Figure 264: A numbered list of CD tracks highlighting the various elements

Position page for older documents opened in LibreOffice

If your document was created with an earlier version of a similar program such as OpenOffice.org, or if the document was saved for compatibility reasons using the ODF file format version 1.1 or earlier, the *Position* page will appear as in Figure 265.

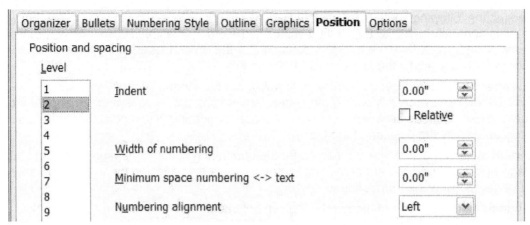

Figure 265: The Position page for older documents

In this case you can adjust the following settings:

- **Indent**: the indentation of the number or bullet area, measured from the left margin of the paragraph linked to the numbering style. In other words, if the paragraph style already has an indentation, when the list style is applied the indentations are added together.

  For any level other than Level 1, the **Relative** option causes the indentation to be measured from the start of the previous level rather than from the page margin.

- **Width of numbering**: how much space is used by the numbering symbol. Writer reserves this space, even if only part of it is used.

- **Minimum spacing numbering <-> text**: the spacing between the right edge of the numbering symbol and the text. If the spacing to text is not sufficient, Writer will honor this setting by expanding the numbering area. Setting the minimum spacing between numbering and text is very useful when right-aligning the numbering or when there is much text before or after the numbering.

- **Numbering alignment**: how the numbering (including any text before or after) will be aligned.

Tip	To fully appreciate how the Numbering alignment works, try to create a numbered list with more than ten elements and make sure that enough room has been made for numbers with two or more digits. You may also wish to right-align numbers 10 or greater, as in Figure 264 on page 243.

Options page

Use the *Options* page (Figure 266) to define the style of the outline levels. The options available on this page depend on the type of marker selected for the list. First, on the left side, select the level you want to modify. To modify all ten levels at once, select **1 – 10** as the level. If you started from a predefined outline, some of the levels will already have settings.

Depending on the numbering style selected in the *Number* box (bullet, graphic, numbering), some of the following options become available on the page:

- **Before**: any text to appear before the number (for example, `Step`).

- **After**: any text to appear after the number (for example, a punctuation mark).

- **Start at**: the first value of the list (for example, you might want the list to start at 4 instead of 1).

- **Character Style**: the style to be used for the number or bullet.

- **Character** button: click to select the character for the bullet.

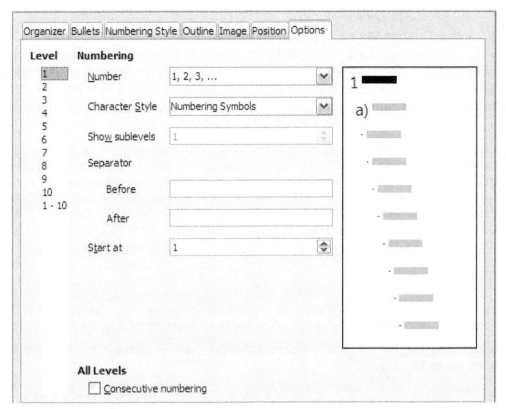

Figure 266: The Options page for a list style

- **Graphics** selection button: opens a list of available graphics (Gallery) or allows the selection of a file on the hard disk to be used as the list marker.
- **Width and Height**: the dimensions of the graphic marker.
- **Alignment**: the alignment of the graphic object.
- **Keep ratio** option: fixes the ratio between the width and the height of the graphic marker.

The right-hand side of the dialog shows a preview of the modifications made.

To revert to the default values, click the **Reset** button in the bottom right corner. Finally, if you wish to use consecutive numbers regardless of the outline level, check the **Consecutive numbering** box at the bottom of the page.

Combining list and paragraph styles

When applying a list style, the underlying paragraph style remains unchanged. If your list must also have a certain font size, indentations, and so on, you might expect to first apply a paragraph style and then a list style (or the other way around). However, you can embed a list style in a paragraph style using the Numbering page of the Paragraph Style dialog, and then apply only the paragraph style to the list.

This section gives an example of combining list and paragraph styles.

1) Create a list style you want to use for the paragraph. For example: *MyNumberedList*.
2) Create a new paragraph style.
3) On the **Organizer** page of the Paragraph Style dialog:
   a) Give the new paragraph style a name, say **NumberedParagraph**.
   b) For the *Next Style*, choose **NumberedParagraph** (this will make the following paragraph also be in this style, until you choose a different style).

    c) In *Linked with*, choose **None**.

    d) Leave **Custom Styles**, in the *Category* field.

4) Set up this paragraph style to your liking. Because the indentation is controlled by the *List* style, to avoid undesired interactions do not change the indent settings on the Indents & Spacing page. (You might want to change the spacing above and below the paragraph.)

5) On the **Outline & Numbering** page, choose the *MyNumberedList* style created in step 1.

6) Click **OK** to save this style.

To have full control, it is common practice to define three base paragraph styles for lists: *List Start* for the first element of the list, *List Continue* for the subsequent elements of the list, and *List End* for the last element of the list. You should also define a paragraph style to be used for unnumbered list items (one for each nested level you intend to use) as well as an introductory style for the paragraph preceding the start of the list (to allow for keeping the introductory paragraph with the first list item, or for specifying spacing before the first list item that is different from the spacing between other paragraphs).

Example: Creating a simple list style

In this example, we will create a numbered list that is used to number the songs on a CD. The numbers are right aligned, and some space is left between the number and the title of the track.

As we want to reuse the same numbered list for other CDs, we will define a new list style and then apply it to the tracks list.

Creating the CDTracks numbered list

As for the previous example, start by clicking the **List Styles** icon (fifth from the left) in the Styles and Formatting window. Then right-click anywhere in the list box and choose **New**.

The Numbering style dialog is displayed. For the *CDTracks* style, we need to customize fields in the *Organizer*, the *Options*, and the *Position* pages.

Style fields	Description
Name	Enter **CDTrack**
Category	Custom styles will be OK for us.

Modify the options of the *Options* page as follows:

1) In the *Level* box, choose **1**.

2) In the *Numbering* list, choose **1, 2, 3,...**.

3) Leave the *Before* and *After* boxes empty.

4) Leave the *Character Style* field as **None**.

5) *Show sublevels* should be grayed out.

6) Make sure *Start at* is set to **1**.

7) Do **not** select **Consecutive numbering**.

As discussed above, the numbered list will adopt the settings of the underlying paragraph style. If you want to use a special font, size or color for the numbering, you can create a character style and apply it in the Options page.

If you want the word *Track* to appear before the number, add it to the *Before* field in the Options dialog. Do not forget to add a space character to separate the word from the number.

LibreOffice 4.2 Writer Guide

Set up the final parameters of the *CDTracks* list style in the *Position* page.

1) In the *Level* box, choose **1**.
2) For *Numbering followed by*, choose tab stop and set it at **4.0cm**.
3) For *Numbering* alignment, choose **Right.**
4) For *Aligned at* choose **1.5cm**. (this refers to the alignment of the numbers)
5) For *Indent at* choose **4.0cm**. (This sets the indentation of the whole list.) Click **OK** to finish.

Applying the list style

Now that the list style is available, it can be quickly applied to any list in the document:

1) If starting a new list, before pressing *Enter* to start a new line, double-click on the desired list style name in the Styles and Formatting window.
2) If you already have a list, select it and then double-click on the desired list style name in the Styles and Formatting window.

Note	Remember that applying a list style does not affect the characteristics of the underlying paragraph; therefore you may want to check if you are satisfied with the paragraph style before applying the list style.

If you have more than one list in a document, the second and subsequent lists with the same style continue their numbering from the previous list. To restart at 1, place the cursor anywhere in the paragraph you want numbered 1, right-click, and choose **Restart numbering**.

To stop using numbering, press the **Numbering On/Off** button on the Standard Toolbar. The final result is illustrated in Figure 264.

Chapter 8
Working with Images

Images (graphics) in Writer

When you create a text document using LibreOffice Writer, you may want to include some illustrations. Illustrations (images or graphics) are added to documents for a variety of reasons: from supporting the description provided in the text—as used in this Guide—to providing an immediate visual representation of the contents, as is often found in a newspaper.

Images in Writer are of three basic types:

- Image files, such as photos, drawings, and scanned images
- Diagrams created using LibreOffice's drawing tools
- Charts created using LibreOffice's Chart facility

This chapter covers images and diagrams.

More detailed descriptions on working with drawing tools can be found in the *Draw Guide* and *Impress Guide*. Instructions on how to create charts are given in the *Calc Guide*.

Creating and editing images

You might create images (also called 'pictures' in LibreOffice) using a graphics program, scan them, or download them from the Internet (make sure you have permission to use them), or use photos taken with a digital camera. Writer can import various vector (line drawing) images, and can rotate and flip such images. Writer also supports raster (bitmap) file formats, the most common of which are GIF, JPG, PNG, and BMP. See the Help for a full list.

Writer can import SmartArt images from Microsoft Office files. For example, Writer can open a Microsoft Word file that contains SmartArt, and you can use Writer to edit the images.

Some things to consider when choosing or creating pictures include image quality and whether the picture will be printed in color or black and white (grayscale).

To edit photos and other bitmap images, use a bitmap editor. To edit line drawings, use a vector drawing program. You do not need to buy expensive programs. Open-source (and usually no-cost) tools such as Gimp (bitmap editor) and Inkscape (vector drawing program) are excellent. For many graphics, LibreOffice Draw is sufficient. These and many other programs work on Windows, Macintosh OS X, and Linux.

For best results:

- Create images that have the exact dimensions required for the document, or use an appropriate graphics package to scale photographs and large drawings to the required dimensions. Do not scale images with Writer, even though Writer has tools for doing this, because the results might not be as clear as you would like.

- Do any other required image manipulation (brightness and contrast, color balance, cropping, conversion to grayscale, and so on) in a graphics package, not in Writer, even though Writer has the tools to do a lot of these things too.

- If the document is meant for screen use only, there is no need to use high resolution images of 300 or more dpi (dots per inch). Most computer monitors work at between 72 and 96 dpi; reducing the resolution (and the file size) has no negative impact on what is displayed but does make Writer more responsive.

Preparing images for black-and-white printing

If color images are to be printed in grayscale, check that any adjacent colors have good contrast and print dark enough. Test by printing on a black-and-white printer using a grayscale setting. Better still: change the "mode" of the image to grayscale, either in a photo editor or in Writer itself (see "Graphics mode" on page 256).

For example, the following diagram looks good in color. The circle is dark red and the square is dark blue. In grayscale, the difference between the two is not so clear. A third element in the diagram is a yellow arrow, which is almost invisible in grayscale.

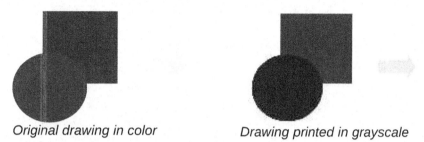

Original drawing in color   *Drawing printed in grayscale*

Changing the colors of the circle and the arrow improves the contrast and visibility of the resulting grayscale image.

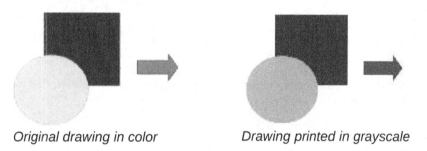

Original drawing in color   *Drawing printed in grayscale*

If the document will be available in black-and-white print only, a better result can often be obtained by choosing grayscale fills, not color fills—and you don't have to guess and test to see if you've made good choices.

Adding images to a document

Images can be added to a document in several ways: by inserting an image file, directly from a graphics program or a scanner, from a file stored on your computer, or by copying and pasting from a source being viewed on your computer.

Inserting an image file

When the image is in a file stored on the computer, you can insert it into a LibreOffice document using either of the following methods.

Drag and drop

1) Open a file browser window and locate the image you want to insert.
2) Drag the image into the Writer document and drop it where you want it to appear. A faint vertical line marks where the image will be dropped.

This method embeds (saves a copy of) the image file in the Writer document. To link the file instead of embedding it, hold down the *Control+Shift* keys while dragging the image.

Insert Image dialog

1) Click in the LibreOffice document where you want the image to appear.
2) Choose **Insert > Image > From File** from the Menu bar.
3) On the Insert Image dialog, navigate to the file to be inserted, and select it.

   At the bottom of the dialog are two options, **Preview** and **Link**. Select **Preview** to view a thumbnail of the selected image on the right (as shown in the example), so you can verify that you have the correct file. See "Inserting an image file" below for the use of **Link**.
4) Click **Open**.

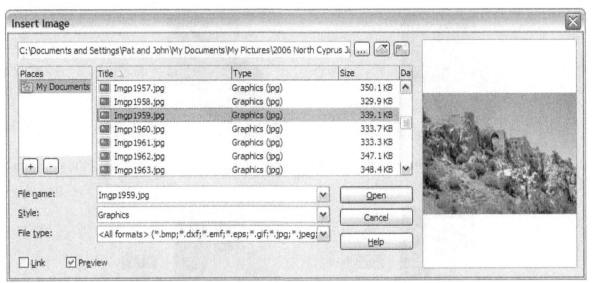

Figure 267: Insert Image dialog

Linking an image file

If the **Link** option in the Insert picture dialog is selected, LibreOffice creates a link to the file containing the image instead of saving a copy of the image in the document. The result is that the image is displayed in the document, but when the document is saved, it contains only a reference to the image file—not the image itself. The document and the image remain as two separate files, and they are merged together only when you open the document again.

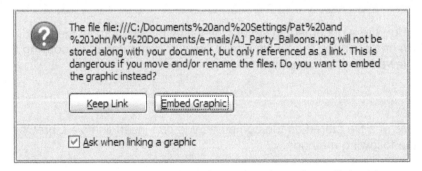

Figure 268: Cautionary message box when inserting a linked image

Linking an image has two advantages and one disadvantage:

* Advantage – Linking can reduce the size of the document when it is saved, because the image file itself is not included. File size is usually not a problem on a modern computer with a reasonable amount of memory, unless the document includes many large images files; LibreOffice can handle quite large files.

- Advantage – You can modify the image file separately without changing the document because the link to the file remains valid, and the modified image will appear when you next open the document. This can be a big advantage if you (or someone else, perhaps a graphic artist) is updating images.

- Disadvantage – If you send the document to someone else, or move it to a different computer, you must also send the image files, or the recipient will not be able to see the linked images. You need to keep track of the location of the images and make sure the recipient knows where to put them on another machine, so the document can find them. For example, you might keep images in a subfolder named Images (under the folder containing the document); the recipient of the file needs to put the images in a subfolder with the same name (under the folder containing the document).

Note	When inserting the same image several times in the document it would appear beneficial to create links; however, this is not necessary as LibreOffice embeds in the document only one copy of the image file.

Embedding linked images

If you originally linked the images, you can easily embed one or more of them later if you wish. To do so:

1) Open the document in LibreOffice and choose **Edit > Links**.
2) The Edit Links dialog shows all the linked files. In the *Source file* list, select the files you want to change from linked to embedded. Click **Update** to ensure you have the latest image where changes may have taken place.
3) Click the **Break Link** button.
4) Click **Yes** in the confirmation message box.
5) Save the document.

Note	Going the other way, from embedded to linked, is not so easy—you must delete and reinsert each image, one at a time, selecting the **Link** option when you do so.

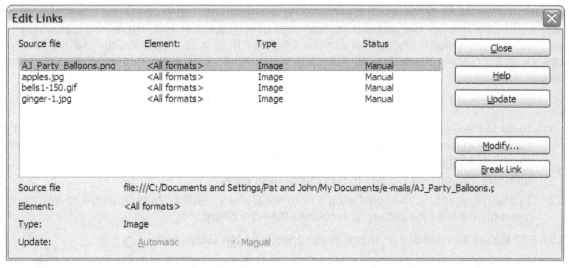

Figure 269: The Edit Links dialog

Inserting an image from the clipboard

Using the clipboard, you can copy images into a LibreOffice document from another LibreOffice document and from other programs. To do this:

1) Open both the source document and the target document.
2) In the source document, select the image to be copied.
3) Move the mouse pointer over the selected image and press *Control+C* (or right-click and select **Copy** from the context menu) to copy the image to the clipboard.
4) Switch to the target document.
5) Click to place the cursor where the image is to be inserted.
6) Press *Control+V* (or right-click and select **Paste** from the context menu) to insert the image.

Caution	If the application from which the image was copied is closed before the image is pasted into the target, the image stored on the clipboard could be lost.

Inserting an image using a scanner

If a scanner is connected to your computer, LibreOffice can call the scanning application and insert the scanned item into the LibreOffice document as an image. To start this procedure, click where you want the image to be inserted and select **Insert > Image > Scan > Select Source**.

Select the scan source from the list. This list will contain available devices and, on Windows systems the Windows Imaging Acquisition (WIA) platform to these devices. After choosing the device, select **Insert > Image > Scan > Request**. This will open the imaging software to permit you to adjust settings for picture quality, size, and other settable attributes. This practice is quick and easy, but may not result in a high-quality image of the correct size. You may get better results by scanning material into a graphics program and cleaning it up there before inserting the resulting image into LibreOffice.

Inserting an image from the Gallery

The Gallery provides a convenient way to group reusable objects such as images and sounds that you can insert into your documents. The Gallery is available in all components of LibreOffice. It comes with many images, but you can still add your own pictures or find extensions containing more images. The Gallery is explained in more detail in Chapter 11, Graphics, the Gallery, and Fontwork, in the *Getting Started* guide. For more about extensions, see Chapter 16, Customizing Writer, in this book.

This section explains the basics of inserting a Gallery image into a Writer document.

1) To open the Gallery, click on the **Gallery** icon () (located in the Standard toolbar and in the Drawing toolbar) or choose **Tools > Gallery** from the Menu bar. The Gallery can also be accessed through the Gallery tab on the Sidebar (**View > Sidebar > Gallery**).
2) Navigate through the Gallery to find the desired picture.
3) To insert the picture, click and drag it from the Gallery into the Writer document. You can also right-click on the picture and choose **Insert > Copy**.

Figure 270 shows an example of an image dragged from the Gallery.

By default, the Gallery is docked above the Writer workspace unless accessed from the Sidebar, in which case it is docked on the right hand side in a vertical orientation. To expand the Gallery opened from other than the Sidebar, position the pointer over the line that divides it from the top of the workspace. When the pointer changes to parallel lines with arrows, click and drag downward. The workspace re-sizes in response.

To expand the Gallery without affecting the workspace, undock it so it floats over the workspace. To do so, hold down the *Control* key and double-click on the upper part of the Gallery next to the View icons. Double-click in the same area while holding down the *Control* key to dock it again (restore it to its position over the workspace).

When the Gallery is docked, to hide it and view the full Writer workspace, click the **Hide/Show** button in the middle of the thin bar separating the Gallery from the workspace (circled in Figure 270).

The vertically oriented Gallery of the Sidebar can be manipulated by similar cursor placements and control selection.

To close the Gallery, choose **Tools > Gallery** to toggle the Gallery entry, or click on the Gallery icon again. The Sidebar can be closed by deselecting **View > Sidebar** from the Menu bar.

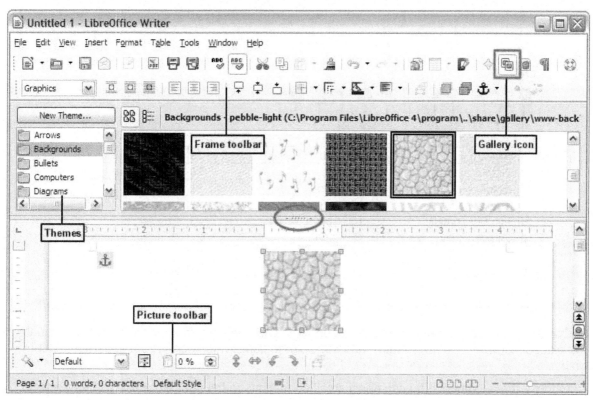

Figure 270: Inserting an image from the Gallery

Modifying an image

When you insert a new image, you may need to modify it to suit the document. The placement of the picture relative to the text is discussed in "Positioning images within the text" on page 263. This section describes the use of the Picture toolbar, resizing, cropping, and a workaround to rotate a picture.

Writer provides many tools for working with images. These tools are sufficient for most people's everyday requirements. However, for professional results it is generally better to use an image manipulation program such as GIMP to modify images (for example, to crop, resize, rotate, and change color values) and then insert the result into Writer. GIMP is an open-source graphics program that can be downloaded from http://www.gimp.org/downloads/.

Using the Picture toolbar

When you insert an image or select one already present in the document, the Picture toolbar appears. You can set it to always be present (**View > Toolbars > Picture**). Picture control buttons from the Picture toolbar can also be added to the Standard Toolbar. See Chapter 16, Customizing Writer, for more information.

This toolbar can be either floating or docked. Figure 271 shows what the Picture toolbar looks like when it is floating.

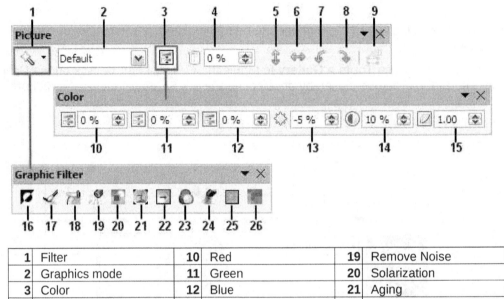

1	Filter	10	Red	19	Remove Noise
2	Graphics mode	11	Green	20	Solarization
3	Color	12	Blue	21	Aging
4	Transparency	13	Brightness	22	Posterize
5	Flip Horizontally	14	Contrast	23	Pop Art
6	Flip Vertically	15	Gamma	24	Charcoal Sketch
7	Rotate 90° Left	16	Invert	25	Relief
8	Rotate 90° Right	17	Smooth	26	Mosaic
9	Frame Properties	18	Sharpen		

Figure 271: Picture toolbar plus tear-off Graphic Filter toolbar and floating Color toolbar

Two other toolbars can be opened from this one: the Graphic Filter toolbar, which can be torn off and placed elsewhere on the window, and the Color toolbar, which opens as a separate floating toolbar.

From these three toolbars, you can apply small corrections to the image or obtain special effects.

Graphics mode

You can change color images to grayscale, to black and white, or to a watermark by selecting the image and then selecting the relevant menu item from the Graphics mode list.

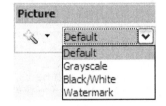

Flip vertically, horizontally or in 90° rotations

To flip an image vertically horizontally or rotate it by ninety degrees, select the image, and then click the relevant button.

Filters

Table 10 provides a short description of the available filters, however the best way to understand them is to see them in action. Experiment with the different filters and filter settings, remembering that you can undo all the changes by pressing *Ctrl+Z* or *Alt+Backspace* or by selecting **Edit > Undo**.

Table 10: Graphic filters and their effects

Icon	Name	Effect
	Invert	Inverts the color values of a color image or the brightness values of a grayscale image.
	Smooth	Softens the contrast of an image.
	Sharpen	Increases the contrast of an image.
	Remove noise	Removes single pixels from an image.
	Solarization	Mimics the effects of too much light in a picture. A further dialog opens to adjust the parameters.
	Aging	Simulates the effects of time on a picture. Can be applied several times. A further dialog opens to adjust the aging level.
	Posterize	Makes a picture appear like a painting by reducing the number of colors used.
	Pop Art	Modifies the picture dramatically.
	Charcoal	Displays the image as a charcoal sketch.
	Relief	A dialog is displayed to adjust the light source that will create the shadow and, hence, the relief effect.
	Mosaic	Joins groups of pixels into a single area of one color.

Color

Use this toolbar to modify the individual RGB color components of the image (red, green, blue) as well as the brightness, contrast, and gamma of the image. If the result is not satisfactory, you can press *Control+Z* to restore the default values.

Transparency

Modify the percentage value in the *Transparency* box on the Picture toolbar to make the image more transparent. This is particularly useful when creating a watermark or when wrapping the image in the background.

Using the Formatting toolbar and Picture dialog

When an image is selected, you can customize some aspects of its appearance using the tools available on the Formatting toolbar (shown in Figure 277) as well as in the dialog that is shown by right-clicking on the image and selecting **Picture**. You can, for example, create a border around the image, selecting style and color; or you can (in the **Borders** page of the Picture dialog) add a shadow to the image.

Cropping images

When you are only interested in a section of the image for the purpose of your document, you may wish to crop (cut off) parts of it.

Note	If you crop an image in Writer, the image itself is not changed. Writer hides, not cuts off, part of the image. If you export the document to HTML, the original image is exported, not the cropped image.

To start cropping the image, right-click on it and select **Picture** from the context menu. In the Picture dialog, select the **Crop** page.

The units of measurement shown on the Crop page are those set in **Tools > Options > LibreOffice Writer > General**.

Two options are available in the crop section for cropping an image.

The first option is the default; **Keep scale**. You can visualize this as using scissors on a paper picture. As you cut parts off, the image gets smaller.

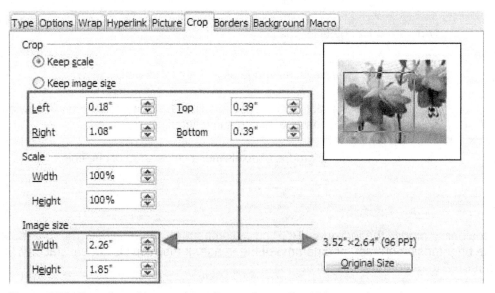

Figure 272: Result on image size of cropping using Keep scale option

The second option is **Keep image size**. You can visualize this as having a picture frame and the image is zoomed in as much as required to fill the fixed-size frame.

You can see in Figure 272 that as the values in Left, Right, Top, and Bottom are altered, the boundaries of the image in the preview box alter to show the crop area on the image. This results in either an image size change, or a scale change for a fixed image size (Figure 273).

The *Width* and *Height* fields under either *Scale* or *Image size* change as you enter values in the Left, Right, Top, and Bottom fields, depending on which option, Keep scale, or Keep image size, is selected.

The original image size is indicated above the **Original Size** button. The bitmap image density is shown alongside this dimension.

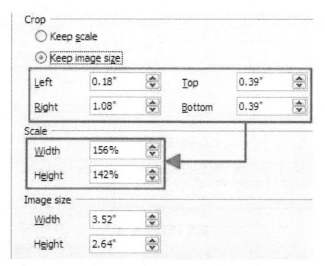

Figure 273: Result using Keep image scale option

Resizing an image

To perfectly fit the image into your document, you may have to resize it. There are a number of options available in Writer to do this.

A quick and easy way to resize is by dragging the image's sizing handles:

1) Click the image, if necessary, to show the green sizing handles.
2) Position the pointer over one of the green sizing handles. The pointer changes shape giving a graphical representation of the direction of the resizing.
3) Click and drag to resize the image.
4) Release the mouse button when satisfied with the new size.

The corner handles resize both the width and the height of the image simultaneously, while the other four handles only resize one dimension at a time.

Tip	To retain the original proportions of the image, *Shift+click* one of the corner handles, then drag.

Figure 274 shows three examples of an image inserted into a document and resized.

For more accurate resizing of images, use either the **Crop** page of the Picture dialog (Figure 272) or, the **Type** page of the Picture dialog.

On the **Crop** page you can adjust the following settings:

- **Scale Width** and **Height**: specify in percentages the scaling of the image. The size of the image changes accordingly. For a symmetrical resizing, both values need to be identical.

- **Image size**: specify the size of the image in your preferred unit of measurement. The image enlarges or shrinks accordingly.

- **Original size** button: when clicked, restores the image to its original size. This will be the size resulting **after** any cropping was carried out.

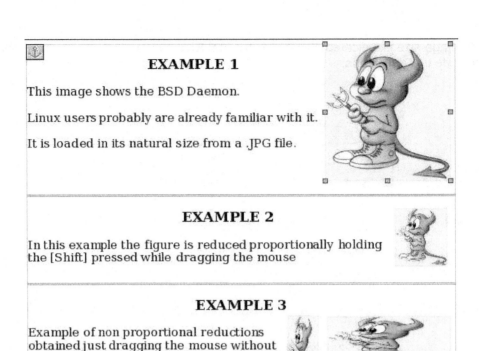

Figure 274: Three examples of resized images, plus the original image

On the **Type** page of the Picture dialog, select the **Relative** option to toggle between percentage and actual dimension. For a symmetrical resizing, select the **Keep ratio** option. Clicking on the **Original Size** button restores the original image size, the scale dimensions are altered if the image has been cropped.

Rotating an image

Writer does not provide a tool for rotating an image in other than 90° increments; however, there is a simple workaround:

1) Open a new *Draw* or *Impress* document (**File > New > Drawing** or **File > New > Presentation**).

2) Insert the image you want to rotate. You can use any of the mechanisms described in "Adding images to a document" on page 251, although there are some slight variations in the position of the menu entries and icons.

3) Select the image, then in the Drawing toolbar (shown by default at the bottom of the window in Impress and Draw), select the **Rotate** icon (   ) from the **Effects** tear-off toolbar (   ).

4) Rotate the image as desired. Use the red handles at the corners of the image and move the mouse in the direction you wish to rotate. By default the image rotates around its center (indicated by a black cross-hair), but you can change the pivot point by moving the black cross-hair to the desired rotation center.

Tip	To restrict the rotation angle to multiples of 15 degrees keep the *Shift* key pressed while rotating the image.

5) Select the rotated image by pressing *Ctrl+A*, then copy the image to the clipboard with *Ctrl+C*.

6) Finish by going back to the location of the Writer document where the image is to be inserted and pressing *Ctrl+V*.

Other settings

The Picture dialog (Figure 272) consists of nine pages. The Crop page was described on page 258, while the use of the Type and the Wrap pages is explained in "Positioning images within the text" on page 263. The other pages serve the following purposes:

- **Options**: use this page to give the image a descriptive name (as you want it to appear in the Navigator), display alternative text when the mouse hovers over the image in a web browser when the image is not available, and protect some of the image settings from accidental changes. You can also prevent the image from being printed by deselecting the corresponding option.

- **Borders**: use this page to create borders around the image. The Borders dialog is the same as the one used for defining table or paragraph borders. You can also add a shadow to the image if so desired.

- **Background**: use this page to change the background color of the image. This setting produces the desired results only for images with a transparent color.

- **Hyperlink**: use this page to associate a hyperlink to the image. You can also create an image map so that only certain areas of the image respond to a mouse click by opening the associated URI (Uniform Resource Identifier) in the default browser. More information on image maps can be found in the *Impress Guide*.

- **Picture**: use this page to flip the image as well as to display the original location of the file in case the image is linked rather than embedded.

- **Macro**: allows you to associate a macro to the image. You can choose among the predefined macros or write your own.

Deleting an image

To delete an image:

1) Click on the image to show the green resizing handles.
2) Press **Delete**.

Using Writer's drawing tools

You can use Writer's drawing tools to create graphics, such as simple diagrams using rectangles, circles, lines, text, and other predefined shapes. You can also group several drawing objects to make sure they maintain their relative position and proportion.

You can place the drawing objects directly on a page in your document, or you can insert them into a frame.

You can also use the drawing tools to annotate photographs, screen captures, or other illustrations produced by other programs, but this is not recommended because:

- You cannot include images in a group with drawing objects, so they may get out of alignment in your document.

- If you convert a Writer document to another format, such as HTML, the drawing objects and the images will not remain associated; they are saved separately.

In general, if you need to create complex drawings, it is recommended you use LibreOffice Draw, which includes many more features such as layers, styles, and so on.

Creating drawing objects

To begin using the drawing tools, display the Drawing toolbar (Figure 275), by clicking **View > Toolbars > Drawing**.

If you are planning to use the drawing tools repeatedly, you can tear off this toolbar and move it to a convenient place on the window.

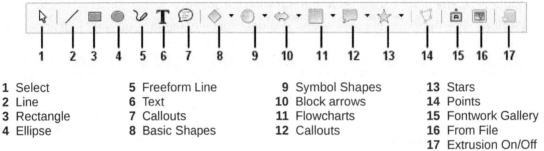

1 Select	5 Freeform Line	9 Symbol Shapes	13 Stars
2 Line	6 Text	10 Block arrows	14 Points
3 Rectangle	7 Callouts	11 Flowcharts	15 Fontwork Gallery
4 Ellipse	8 Basic Shapes	12 Callouts	16 From File
			17 Extrusion On/Off

Figure 275: The Drawing toolbar

To use a drawing tool:

1) Click in the document where you want the drawing to be anchored. You can change the anchor later, if necessary.

2) Select the tool from the Drawing toolbar (Figure 275). The mouse pointer changes to a drawing-functions pointer similar to this one for a rectangle shape (⌐).

3) Move the cross-hair pointer to the place in the document where you want the image to appear and then click-and-drag to create the drawing object. Release the mouse button. The selected drawing function remains active, so you can draw another object of the same type.

4) To cancel the selected drawing function, press the *Esc* key or click on the **Select** icon (the arrow) on the Drawing toolbar.

5) You can now change the properties (fill color, line type and weight, anchoring, and others) of the drawing object using either the Drawing Object Properties toolbar (Figure 276) or the choices and dialog reached by right-clicking on the drawing object.

Set or change properties for drawing objects

To set the properties for a drawing object before you draw it:

1) On the Drawing toolbar (Figure 275), click the **Select** tool.

2) On the Drawing Object Properties toolbar (Figure 276), click on the icon for each property and select the value you want for that property.

3) For more control, or to define new attributes, you can click on the **Area** or **Line** icons on the toolbar to display detailed dialogs.

The default you set applies to the current document and session. It is not retained when you close the document or close Writer, and it does not apply to any other document you open. The defaults apply to all the drawing objects except text objects.

To change the properties for an existing drawing object, select the object, then continue as described above.

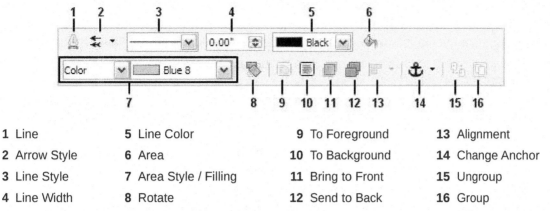

1 Line	**5** Line Color	**9** To Foreground	**13** Alignment
2 Arrow Style	**6** Area	**10** To Background	**14** Change Anchor
3 Line Style	**7** Area Style / Filling	**11** Bring to Front	**15** Ungroup
4 Line Width	**8** Rotate	**12** Send to Back	**16** Group

Figure 276: Drawing Object Properties toolbar

You can also specify the position and size, rotation, and slant and corner radius properties of the drawing object:

1) Right-click on the drawing object and then click **Position and Size** from the context menu. The *Position and Size* dialog is displayed.

2) Choose any properties, as required.

Resizing a drawing object

The same considerations for resizing an image apply also to resizing an object. Select the object, click on one of the eight handles around it and drag it to its new position. For a scaled resizing, select one of the corner handles and keep the *Shift* key pressed while dragging the handle to its new position.

For more sophisticated control of the size of the object, select **Format > Object > Position and Size** from the Menu bar. Use the Position and Size dialog to set the width and height independently. If the **Keep ratio** option is selected, then the two dimensions change so that the proportion is maintained, allowing for a scaled resizing.

Grouping drawing objects

To group drawing objects:

1) Select one object, then hold down the *Shift* key and select the others you want to include in the group. The bounding box expands to include all the selected objects.

2) With the objects selected, hover the mouse pointer over one of the objects and choose **Format > Group > Group** from the Menu bar or right-click and choose **Group > Group** from the context menu.

Note	You cannot include an embedded or linked image in a group with drawing objects.

Positioning images within the text

When you add an image to a text document, you need to choose how to position it with respect to the text and other images. The positioning of images is often rather time-consuming and may be very frustrating for both inexperienced and experienced users. As Writer is a word processor rather than a desktop publishing program, there are some limitations to the flexibility in positioning images and it takes time to get things exactly as you would like them.

Positioning of an image is controlled by four settings:

- *Arrangement* refers to the placement of an image on an imaginary vertical axis. Arrangement controls how images are stacked upon each other or relative to the text.
- *Alignment* refers to the vertical or horizontal placement of an image in relation to the chosen anchor point.
- *Anchoring* refers to the reference point for the images. This point could be the page, or frame where the object is, a paragraph, or even a character. An image always has an anchor point.
- *Text wrapping* refers to the relation of images to the surrounding text, which may wrap around the graphic on one or both sides, be overprinted behind or in front of the graphic, or treat the graphic as a separate paragraph or character.

The settings can be accessed in a number of ways, depending on the nature of the images:

1) From the **Format** menu, where you can find **Alignment**, **Arrange**, **Wrap, and Anchor** (both for images and drawing objects).
2) From the context menu displayed when you right-click on the graphic.
3) From the OLE-Object toolbar (default setting shown in Figure 277).
4) For images, from the *Type* and *Wrapping* pages of the Picture dialog. Note that you cannot control the arrangement using the dialog. To open the Picture dialog, click on the image to select it and then choose **Format > Picture** or right-click on the graphic and choose **Picture** on the context menu.
5) For drawing objects, from the *Position and Size* page of the Position and Size dialog. To open the Position and Size dialog, click on the drawing object to select it and then choose **Format > Object > Position and Size** or right-click on the graphic and choose **Position and Size** on the context menu. Note that you can only control the alignment and anchoring.

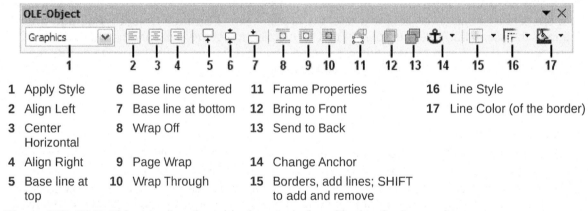

1	Apply Style	6	Base line centered	11	Frame Properties	16	Line Style
2	Align Left	7	Base line at bottom	12	Bring to Front	17	Line Color (of the border)
3	Center Horizontal	8	Wrap Off	13	Send to Back		
4	Align Right	9	Page Wrap	14	Change Anchor		
5	Base line at top	10	Wrap Through	15	Borders, add lines; SHIFT to add and remove		

Figure 277: OLE-Object toolbar (graphical control of positioning for images)

Arranging images

Arranging an image means to determine its vertical position relative to other images or text. Arranging is only relevant when objects are overlapping. You can choose between four common settings, plus a fifth special setting for drawing objects:

Bring to Front

Places the image on top of any other images or text.

Bring Forward

Brings the image one level up in the stack (z-axis). Depending on the number of overlapping objects, you may need to apply this option several times to obtain the desired result.

Send Backward

The opposite of Bring Forward; sends the selected graphic one level down in the object stack.

Send to Back

Sends the selected graphic to the bottom of the stack, so that other images and text cover it.

To Background / To Foreground

Only available for drawing objects; moves the drawing object behind or in front of the text respectively.

Anchoring images

You can anchor images as a character or to a page, paragraph, or character. You can also place images in a frame and anchor the frame to a page, paragraph, or character. Which method you choose depends on what you are trying to achieve.

Here are the ways you can anchor images or drawing objects:

To Page

The graphic keeps the same position in relation to the page margins. It does not move as you add or delete text or other images. This method is useful when the graphic does not need to be visually associated with a particular piece of text. It is often used when producing newsletters or other documents that are very layout intensive, or for placing logos in letterheads.

Caution	If you plan to use a document within a master document, do not anchor images **To Page** because the images will disappear from the master document. See Chapter 13, Working with Master Documents, for more information.

To Paragraph

The graphic is associated with a paragraph and moves with the paragraph. It may be placed in the margin or another location. This method is useful as an alternative to a table for placing icons beside paragraphs.

To Character

The graphic is associated with a character but is not in the text sequence. It moves with the paragraph but may be placed in the margin or another location. This method is similar to anchoring to a paragraph but cannot be used with drawing objects.

As Character

The graphic is placed in the document like any other character and, therefore, affects the height of the text line and the line break. The graphic moves with the paragraph as you add or delete text before the paragraph. This method is useful for keeping screen-shots in sequence in a procedure (by anchoring them as a character in a blank paragraph) or for adding a small (inline) icon in sequence in a sentence.

To Frame

If the graphic has been placed in a frame, you can anchor the graphic in a fixed position inside the frame. The frame can then be anchored to the page, a paragraph, or a character, as required.

Aligning images

Once you have established the anchor point of the graphic, you can decide the position of the graphic relative to this anchor: this is called aligning the images. Choose from six options: three for aligning the graphic horizontally (left, center, right) and three for aligning the graphic vertically (top, center, bottom). Horizontal alignment is not available for images anchored As Character.

For finer control of the alignment, use the Position options on the Type page of the Picture dialog, shown in Figure 278.

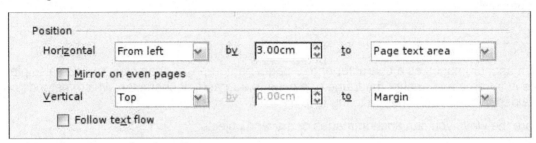

Figure 278: Fine tuning the alignment

For both the horizontal and vertical position, start by picking the reference point in the right hand side drop-down menu, then select in the first drop-down menu among **Left**, **Right** or **Center**. If you select the value **From left** (or **From top** for the vertical positioning) you can specify the amount in your selected unit of measurement. In the example in Figure 278, the upper-left corner of the image will be placed at 3 cm from the left margin of the page horizontally and on the top margin vertically.

A visual representation of the area to which the image is anchored is shown in the preview pane to the right of the page, indicated by a red bordered area. The graphic position is indicated by a green bordered area.

Wrapping text around images

The Wrap setting determines the relation between the text and the graphic. Several choices are available from the context menu:

No Wrap
> With this option the text is placed above and below the image but not to either side of it. This is the wrapping type used for most of the figures in this guide.

Page Wrap or Optimal Page Wrap
> The text flows around the image. Moving the image around the page causes the text to be rearranged to fill the space to the left and right of it. **Optimal Page Wrap** prevents text from being placed to the side of the image if the spacing between the image and the margin is less than 2 cm.

Wrap Through
> Superimposes the image on the text. That is, the image is *in front of* the text. This option must be used in conjunction with the image-transparency setting in order to make the text under the picture visible.

In Background
> Similar to **Wrap Through**, but the image is placed *behind* the text so there may be no need to change the transparency to make the text visible.

Note	The **No Wrap** option found in the context menu of a picture is equivalent to the **Wrap Off** menu item in the **Format > Wrap** menu.

The wrap format is normally selected after the anchoring and the alignment of the picture have been decided. To set the position of an image to the desired wrap format, follow these steps:

1) Select an image by clicking on it.
2) Right-click to display the context menu and move the mouse pointer to **Wrap** to display the available wrap formats. Alternatively you can select **Format > Wrap** from the Menu bar.
3) Select the desired wrap format.

Note	When anchoring an image as character, you can only adjust the distance between the image and the text, but no wrapping option is displayed.

To fine-tune the wrapping options, open the Picture dialog and select the Wrap page, shown in Figure 279.

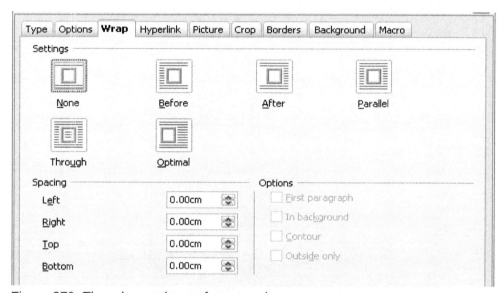

Figure 279: The advanced wrap format options

For images, you can open this dialog by selecting **Format > Picture** from the Menu bar or right-click and select **Picture** from the context menu. For drawing objects, you can access the **Wrap** page by selecting **Format > Wrap > Edit** in the Menu bar or right-click and select **Wrap > Edit** from the context menu.

This page is divided into three sections. In the top part you can select from the wrap types mentioned above, plus two additional wrap formats that prevent the text from filling the area to the left (**After**) or to the right (**Before**) of the picture. Use the *Spacing* section of the page to adjust the spacing between the image and the text. The contents of the *Options* section of the page may change depending on the selected wrap format.

First paragraph
Check this box if you want LibreOffice to start a new paragraph after the image even if it could still wrap around the image.

In background
This option becomes available if **Through Wrap** is selected; it moves the image to the background.

Contour
Wraps the text around a custom contour rather than around the edge of the picture. This option is only available for Page or Optimal Page Wrap.

Outside only

Forces the text to wrap on the outside of the image, even if the contour contains open areas within the shape.

Editing the contour

If you select wrapping around a drawing object, LibreOffice automatically creates a contour. The Edit Contour option is only available for image wrapping. You can automatically create a contour from the context menu after right-clicking the image, by selecting **Contour**. You can access the Contour Editor by selecting **Format > Wrap > Edit Contour** or from the right-click menu.

The dialog shown in Figure 280 opens with the image loaded in the main window. Use the tools to draw the region of the image you do **not** want to be covered by the text—this area will be shaded.

Figure 280: The Contour Editor in action with AutoContour

There are four tools available to create a contour in the Contour Editor window: **Rectangle**, **Ellipse**, **Polygon**, and **AutoContour**. Some familiarity with drawing tools is required to create complex contours; however, in most circumstances there is no need for high accuracy. Figure 280 shows the actual contour used for "Example 2: Simple contour wrapping in action" when using AutoContour, and as you can see the shape of the line around the edge of the apple is quite acceptable.

When you are done, click on the **Apply** button to save the contour. If you are not satisfied with the result, you can select the contour line and press the *Delete* key to restart, or click the Workspace icon and then click inside the contour. You can also undo the previous steps or you can select the **Edit Points** button and adjust the contour shape point by point. Be aware that any of the graphic outside the contour line is not shown in the document.

For simple images, the **AutoContour** button does a decent job. If the contour has to be drawn around an area with the same or a similar color, you can select this region using the eyedropper. Select this tool, then click on a point in the image having the desired color. LibreOffice automatically selects all the points which have the same or a similar color. The similarity level can be changed by modifying the value in the tolerance box (100% = perfect match).

Note	While all the positioning techniques discussed in this section apply equally to frames, contour wrapping is not possible.

Example 1: Page wrapping

Figure 281 shows an example of page wrapping in action.

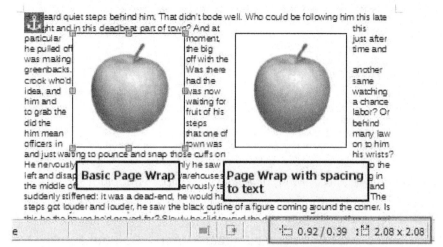

Figure 281: Example of image with Page Wrap formatting

To achieve this:

1) Insert the image into the document, then anchor it to the paragraph of your choice. To move the anchor, select the image or the anchor, and move it until the anchor symbol is at the beginning of the chosen paragraph.

2) Align the image so that the left margin of the image is where you want it to be. This can be done with the mouse or using the advanced settings. The taskbar shows the location of the upper left corner and the image size.

3) Change the wrap to Page Wrap. We now wish to increase the space between the image and the text. To do this, access the Wrap page of the Picture dialog and set the gap between the image and text to 0.1" in all the boxes.

4) The last touch is to change the position so that the image has our chosen number of lines of the paragraph above it. Again, you can use the mouse to drag the image or use the advanced settings, which require a bit of trial and error. Moving with the mouse is the simplest method.

Example 2: Simple contour wrapping in action

In this example we again apply page wrapping as in Example 1, enabling this time the contour option. We will work on an image and on a drawing object as the contour option works slightly differently in each case.

The example of Figure 282 was created following the steps below, which you can use to practice.

1) Create some text (a very quick way to do that is to use the dummy text available in AutoText. Type **DT** and then press the *F3* key).

2) Insert an image of your choice and anchor it to the first paragraph. Adjust the alignment as desired then change the wrap type to Page Wrap.

3) Right-click on the picture to select the option **Wrap > Contour**, then right-click again and select **Wrap > Edit Contour** from the context menu.

4) Use the technique discussed in "Editing the contour" on page 268 to create a custom contour and click **Apply**. If needed, adjust the spacing between the edge of the image and the text using the Wrap page of the Picture dialog.

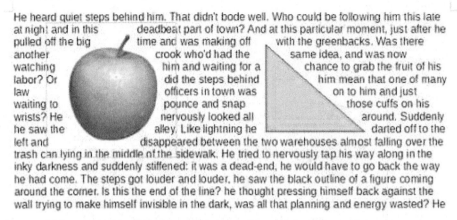

He heard quiet steps behind him. That didn't bode well. Who could be following him this late at night and in this deadbeat part of town? And at this particular moment, just after he pulled off the big time and was making off with the greenbacks. Was there another crook who'd had the same idea, and was now watching him and waiting for a chance to grab the fruit of his labor? Or did the steps behind him mean that one of many law officers in town was waiting to pounce and snap those cuffs on his wrists? He nervously looked all around. Suddenly he saw the alley. Like lightning he darted off to the left and disappeared between the two warehouses almost falling over the trash can lying in the middle of the sidewalk. He tried to nervously tap his way along in the inky darkness and suddenly stiffened: it was a dead-end, he would have to go back the way he had come. The steps got louder and louder, he saw the black outline of a figure coming around the corner. Is this the end of the line? he thought pressing himself back against the wall trying to make himself invisible in the dark, was all that planning and energy wasted? He

Figure 282: Image and drawing objects with contour wrapping

5) Insert an AutoShape of your choice (a triangle in the example) and proceed as in step 2 above.

6) Enable the contour wrap by selecting **Format > Wrap > Contour** from the Menu bar. As discussed previously, LibreOffice automatically generates the contour. You may need to adjust the distance between the drawing object and the text using **Format > Wrap > Edit**.

Example 3: Wrap Through and In Background

This example shows how to use an image as a watermark by wrapping the text through it and adjusting the transparency. This is not the best way to create watermarks and it is presented here only for illustration purposes. If you need to create a watermark, it is best to use a Fontworks object wrapped in the background.

Selecting the Wrap Through option for an inserted image causes the image to overlap the text, which as a result will be hidden. To make the text appear, change the transparency of the picture; although the words under the image become visible, they may be difficult to read and will appear lighter than the rest of the text.

To reproduce the example of Figure 283 create some dummy text, then insert the image of your choice. Anchor the image (to the page in the example) and select the wrap through option from the **Format > Wrap** menu or right-clicking on the image and selecting **Wrap > Wrap Through** from the context menu. Move the image into the desired position. The Picture toolbar should be displayed when the image is selected. Change the transparency to a suitable value (in the example this is 40%) so that the text can be read.

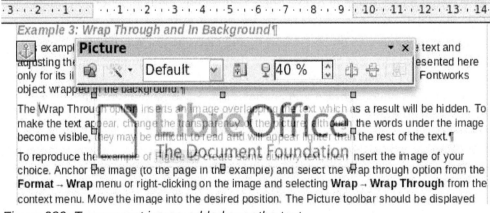

Figure 283: Transparent image added over the text

You can obtain a better result if you set an image's wrap to *In Background*. With this selection all the text will be clearly readable, with all characters having the same intensity, as long as the background is not too dark. You may still need to adjust the transparency of the image.

Adding captions to images

You can add captions to images in three ways: automatically, by using the Caption dialog, or manually.

Adding captions automatically

You can set up LibreOffice to add captions automatically whenever you insert an image, a table, or other objects into a document. You can choose which objects are captioned automatically, what the sequence name is for each caption (for example, "Table" or "Illustration"), and the position of the caption.

To set up automatic captions:

1) Click **Tools > Options**. On the *Options* dialog, click on the + sign next to LibreOffice Writer to show a list of options.

2) Select **AutoCaption**. Several choices are available at the right of the dialog for adding captions automatically.

3) Choose which objects you want to be automatically captioned and specify the characteristics of the captions.

For more information, see "AutoCaption options" in Chapter 2, Setting up Writer.

When you insert an image, if automatic captioning is enabled, the graphic is placed in a frame along with a caption containing the default sequence name for images—Illustration. Position the cursor in the caption area and type the text for the caption. You can change the sequence name by selecting one from the drop-down Category list or typing in your own.

Note	You can specify where to place an automatic caption for any object except a picture; picture captions can only be automatically placed below the picture. If you need a caption above the picture (for example, for data plots in scientific publications), you must add the captions manually, as described in "Adding captions manually" on page 273.

Tip	A common sequence name—Figure—is not one of the names provided: **<None>**, **Drawing**, **Illustration**, **Table**, and **Text**. If you want the name "Figure" or any other custom name for your images, do the following: 1) Open the **Options – LibreOffice Writer – AutoCaption** dialog, as described above. 2) In the *Add captions automatically when inserting* section, select **LibreOffice Writer Picture**. This activates the Caption area in the dialog for pictures (images). 3) Under the *Category* drop-down list, enter the name that you want added (say, `Figure`), by overwriting any sequence name in the list. (Overwriting a term does not delete it from the drop-down list.) You can also set some options for the number style and for a separator between the name and the number, if desired. Click **OK** to save the changes.

Adding captions using the Caption dialog

To add captions using the Caption dialog:

1) Insert the graphic, then either right-click it and select **Caption** from the context menu, or select it and choose **Insert > Caption** from the Menu bar.

2) Under *Properties* on the Caption dialog (Figure 284), make your selections for the *Category*, *Numbering*, and *Separator* fields (**Illustration**, **Arabic (1 2 3)**, and a colon (**:**), respectively, for the example in Figure 284 and type your caption text in the *Caption* text box at the top. Whatever text you enter for the caption appears in the box at the bottom, after the sequence name, number, and separator.

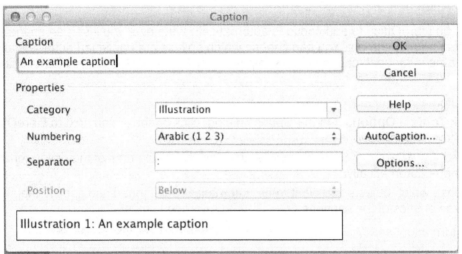

Figure 284: Defining the caption for an illustration

3) Click **OK**. The graphic and its caption are placed in a frame, as shown in Figure 285.

Tip	In the Category box, you can type any name you want, for example *Figure*. LibreOffice will create a numbering sequence using that name.

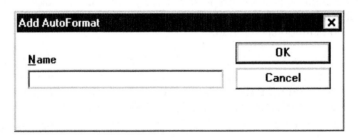

Illustration 1. An example

Figure 285: An example of an image and its caption contained in a frame. The outer box shows the edge of the frame; this border is normally set to be invisible.

Overriding the default positioning of captions

The default positioning for picture captions is *Below*, and that position cannot be changed using the Caption dialog. However, you can override the positioning manually, as follows:

1) Follow the instructions in "Adding captions using the Caption dialog" on page 272 to create the caption.

2) Right-click on the picture (not the frame surrounding picture and caption) and make sure that **Anchor > As Character** is selected.

3) Left-click on the picture and drag and drop it after the caption.

Tip	You may wish to adjust the spacing above and below the caption text to fine-tune the appearance of the picture and its caption.

Adding captions manually

If you need to save as *.doc files or export in other formats, you may find that captions applied as described above (either automatically or using the Caption dialog) are lost during the export.

To avoid export problems, or as another way to put captions above pictures or below them (the usual case), you can add a caption manually, in either of two ways:

- Place the graphic and its caption in separate paragraphs.
- Use a table.

Place the graphic and its caption in separate paragraphs

Insert the graphic and anchor it to its paragraph as a character. Press *Enter* to create a new paragraph for the caption.

1) In the caption paragraph, type, for example, **Figure** and add a space.

2) To insert the figure number automatically, click **Insert > Fields > Other** (*Control + F2*) and select the Variables tab.

3) Select **Number range** in the *Type* list. Select **Figure** in the Selection list and choose, for example, **Arabic (1 2 3)** in the Format drop-down list. Click the **Insert** button.

4) A number will appear after the word "Figure" in the caption. Now, type the text of the caption.

Tips	If you are manually adding captions to a lot of figures using this method, you might want to make an AutoText entry containing, for example, **Figure** and a space, the figure-number field, and an optional separator and a space after it.
	To ensure the picture and its caption stay together on the page, create a new paragraph style, for example Figure: if the picture is going above the caption, define the text flow of the Figure paragraph style as **Keep with next paragraph** and the next style as **Caption**. Conversely, if the caption is going above, define the Caption paragraph style as **Keep with next paragraph** and the next style as **Figure**.

Use a table

Create a one-column, two-row table. Place the picture in one row and type the caption in the other row—or use two or more rows for the caption and other text. This method can be especially useful for pictures with numbered legends, such as Figure 277 in this chapter.

Creating an image map

An image map defines areas of an image (called *hotspots*) with hyperlinks to web addresses, other files on the computer, or parts of the same document. Hotspots are the graphic equivalent of text hyperlinks (described in Chapter 12). Clicking on a hotspot causes LibreOffice to open the linked page in the appropriate program (for example, the default browser for an HTML page; LibreOffice Calc for a ODS file; a PDF viewer for a PDF file). You can create hotspots of various shapes and include several hotspots in the same image.

Figure 286: The dialog to create or edit an image map

To use the image map editor:

1) In your LibreOffice document, select the image where you want to define the hotspots.

2) Choose **Edit > ImageMap** from the Menu bar. The ImageMap Editor (Figure 286) opens.

3) Use the tools and fields in the dialog (described on the next page) to define the hotspots and links necessary.

4) Click the **Apply** icon (✓) to apply the settings.

5) When done, click the **Save** icon (🖫) to save the image map to a file, then click the **X** in the upper right corner to close the dialog.

The main part of the dialog shows the image on which the hotspots are defined. A hotspot is identified by a line indicating its shape.

The toolbar at the top of the dialog contains the following tools:

- **Apply** button: click this button to apply the changes.

- **Open, Save,** and **Select** icons.

- Tools for drawing a hotspot shape: these tools work in exactly the same way as the corresponding tools in the Drawing toolbar.

- **Edit**, **Move**, **Insert**, **Delete Points**: advanced editing tools to manipulate the shape of a polygon hotspot. Select the Edit Points tool to activate the other tools.
- **Active** icon: toggles the status of a selected hotspot between active and inactive.
- **Macro**: associates a macro with the hotspot instead of just associating a hyperlink.
- **Properties**: sets the hyperlink properties and adds the Name attribute to the hyperlink.

Below the toolbar, specify for the selected hotspot:

- **Address:** the address pointed by the hyperlink. You can also point to an anchor in a document; to do this, write the address in this format:
  file:///<path>/document_name#anchor_name
- **Text**: type the text that you want to be displayed when the mouse pointer is moved over the hotspot.
- **Frame:** where the target of the hyperlink will open: pick among _blank (opens in a new browser window), _self (opens in the active browser window), _top or _parent.

Tip	The value _self for the target frame will work just fine in the vast majority of occasions. It is therefore not recommended to use the other choices unless absolutely necessary.

Managing the Gallery

Note	In a default installation, only the *My themes* theme is customizable, although new themes can be added as explained in "Adding a new theme to the Gallery" on page 276. The locked themes are easily recognizable by right-clicking on them; the only available option in the context menu is **Properties**. In some installations, or when you are running LibreOffice as an Administrator, all themes are customizable.

Adding an image to the Gallery

You may wish to add to the Gallery any images that you use frequently, for example, a company logo. You can then very easily insert these images into a document later.

Method 1 (selecting a file)

1) Open the Gallery and select the theme where you want to add images. (You can also create a new theme for your images; see page 276.)
2) Right-click on the desired theme and select **Properties** in the context menu. This displays a dialog, into which the files from which the selection will be made, are added.

Figure 287: Properties of My Theme in the Gallery

Either:

a)   On the *Files* page, click the **Find Files** button. The Select path dialog (not shown) opens which allows you to navigate to the folder containing the files of interest.

b)   You can enter the path for the folder's directory in the *Path* text box, or you can navigate to locate the folder's directory.

c)   Click the **Select** button to start the search. Subfolders are included in the search. A list of graphic files is then displayed in the Properties window. You can use the *File type* filter to limit the files displayed.

d)   To add all of the files shown in the list, click **Add All.** Otherwise, select the files to add and then click **Add**. (Hold down either the *Shift* key or the *Control* key when you click on multiple files.)

Or, to add a single file:

a)   Click the **Add** button to open the Gallery dialog.

b)   Use the navigation controls to locate the image to add to the theme. Select it and then click **Open** to add it to the theme.

c)   Click the **OK** button of the Properties dialog to close it.

Note	You may need to import some images or create your own on your computer if the existing files are insufficient for your needs.

Method 2 (drag and drop)

You can drag and drop an image into the Gallery from a document.

1)   Open the document containing an image you want to add to the Gallery, and display the Gallery theme to which you want to add it.

2)   Position the mouse pointer above the image, without clicking.

3)   If the mouse pointer changes to a hand symbol, the image refers to a hyperlink. In this case, press the *Alt* key while you click the image, to select it without activating the link. If the mouse pointer does not change to a hand symbol, you can simply click the image to select it.

4)   Once the image is selected, evident from the colored selection handles around it, release the mouse button. Click again on the image, keeping the mouse button pressed for more than two seconds before moving the mouse. Without releasing the mouse button, drag the image into the Gallery.

5)   Release the mouse button.

Deleting images from the Gallery

To delete an image from a theme:

1)   Right-click on the name of the image file or its thumbnail in the Gallery.

2)   Click **Delete** on the context menu. A message appears, asking if you want to delete this object. Click **Yes.**

Note	Deleting the name of a file from the list in the Gallery does not delete the file from the hard disk or other location. This includes the dragdrop folder in the Gallery.

Adding a new theme to the Gallery

To add a new theme to the Gallery:

1)   Click the **New Theme** button above the list of themes (see Figure 287).

2) In the *Properties of New Theme* dialog, click the *General* tab and type a name for the new theme.

3) Click the *Files* tab and add images to the theme, as described earlier.

Deleting a theme from the Gallery

To delete a theme from the Gallery:

1) Go to **Tools > Gallery.**

2) Select from the list of themes the theme you wish to delete.

3) Right-click on the theme, then click **Delete** on the context menu.

Location of the Gallery and the objects in it

Images and other objects shown in the Gallery can be located anywhere on your computer's hard disk, on a network drive, or on a CD-ROM. Listings in the Gallery refer to the location of each object. When you add images to the Gallery using method 1, the files are not moved or copied; only the location of each new object is added as a reference. When files are added using drag and drop, they are copied into a folder (dragdrop) in the Gallery, and allocated a file name.

Figure 288 shows in *Detailed View*, two files in the *My Theme* in the Gallery, one is contained in the dragdrop folder, and the other is a reference path to its actual location.

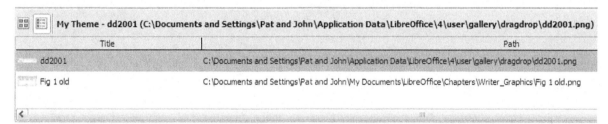

Figure 288: Theme showing files inserted with drag-and-drop and by reference

In a workgroup situation, you may have access to a shared Gallery (where you cannot change the contents unless authorized to do so) and a user Gallery, where you can add, change, or delete objects.

The location of the user Gallery is specified in **Tools > Options > LibreOffice > Paths**. You can change this location, and you can copy your gallery files (SDV) to other computers.

Gallery contents provided with LibreOffice are stored in a different location. You cannot change this location.

LibreLogo scripting

LibreLogo is an embedded vector graphics language that provides a simple, native, Logo-like programming environment with turtle vector graphics for the teaching of computing (programming and word processing), desktop publishing (DTP), and graphic design.

Logo toolbar

Display the Logo toolbar by selecting **View > Toolbars > Logo** from the Menu bar.

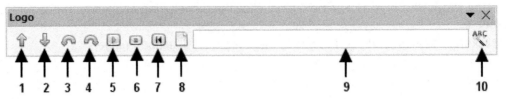

The undocked Logo toolbar

1 Forward (10 pt)
2 Back (10 pt)
3 Left (15 degrees)
4 Right (15 degrees)
5 Start Logo program (text or selected text of document)

6 Stop
7 Home
8 Clear screen
9 Logo command line (press *Enter* for execution)
10 Uppercase commands, also translate them to the language of the document

To start using the program, open a new blank document and click the **Start** button (5) on the toolbar. This sets the turtle, Figure 289, to the center of the page. You may find it useful to adjust the page zoom level so you can view the whole page.

Figure 289: The graphical turtle

The turtle has three attributes:

1) A location
2) An orientation
3) A pen, itself having attributes such as color, width, and up and down.

The turtle moves with commands that are relative to its own position, such as "move forward 10 spaces" and "turn left 90 degrees". The pen carried by the turtle can also be controlled, by enabling it, setting its color, or setting its width.

The basics

Click on the buttons 1 – 4 to see the effects of these controls on the turtle. Click the **Home** button (7) to return the turtle to its default settings and position in the center of the page. The **Clear screen** button (8) deletes all drawings from the page.

The command text input box allows you to enter command strings before pressing the *Enter* key so that a sequence of commands can be executed at the same time.

For example, entering the sequence `circle 10cm fillcolor 'blue' pencolor 'red' pensize 2 circle 5cm forward 200 right 89 circle 50` into the command line and then pressing *Enter* results in the following graphic:

Note that the graphic is anchored *To Page*, and that the turtle attributes follow the setting for the line, in this instance fillcolor 'blue'; pencolor 'red'; linesize 2.

You can also write your program on the page instead of entering it into the command line, allowing a larger and more complex set of instructions to be built. In this case, clicking the Start Logo program button runs the script on the page. The text can be deleted from the page after completing the program to just leave the graphic.

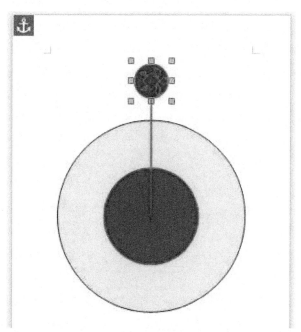

Figure 290: Sample graphic from command line

The distance units are typographic points unless expressly defined as standard units such as inch or centimeters (72 pt = 1 in = 2.54 cm).

See the **Help** for comprehensive information about LibreLogo.

LibreLogo examples can be found on http://extensions.libreoffice.org/extension-center/librelogo

Chapter 9
Working with Tables

Introduction

Tables are a useful way to organize and present large amounts of information, for example:

- Technical, financial, or statistical reports.
- Product catalogs showing descriptions, prices, characteristics, and photographs of products.
- Bills or invoices.
- Lists of names with address, age, profession, and other information.

Tables can often be used as an alternative to spreadsheets to organize materials. A well-designed table can help readers understand better what you are saying. While you would normally use tables for text or numbers, you could put other objects, such as pictures, in cells.

Tables can also be used as a page-layout tool to position text in areas of a document instead of using several *Tab* characters. For example, the descriptions under Figure 303 were created in a table with invisible borders. Another, perhaps better, example would be in headers and footers to support independent positioning of different elements, such as page number, document title etc. This use of tables is described in Chapter 4, Formatting Pages.

Creating a table

Before you insert a table into a document, it helps to have an idea of the visual result you want to obtain as well as an estimate of the number of rows and columns required. Every parameter can be changed at a later stage; however, thinking ahead can save a large amount of time as changes to fully formatted tables often require a significant effort.

Inserting a new table

To insert a new table, position the cursor where you want the table to appear, then use any of the following methods to open the Insert Table dialog (Figure 291):

- From the Menu bar, choose **Insert > Table**.
- From the Menu bar, choose **Table > Insert > Table**.
- Press *Ctrl+F12*.
- On the Standard toolbar, click the left side of the split **Table** button

Tip	To directly insert a table with the default properties, click on the arrow button next to the Table icon on the Standard toolbar. A graphic appears where you can choose the size of the table (up to fifteen rows and up to ten columns). To create the table, click on the cell that you want to be on the last row of the last column. Holding down the mouse button over the Table icon will also display the graphic.

In the Insert Table dialog, you can specify the properties for the new table.

General settings: In the *Name* box, you can enter a different name from the LibreOffice-generated default for the table. This might come in handy when using the Navigator to quickly jump to a table.

In the *Columns* and *Rows* boxes, specify the number of columns and rows for the new table. You can change the size of the table later, if necessary.

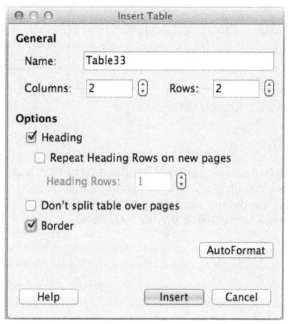

Figure 291: Inserting a new table using the Insert Table dialog

Under *Options*, set up the initial table characteristics. Selecting the options in this section of the dialog produces the following results:

- **Heading** — Selecting this enables a heading to be used in the table and enables further options for the heading. Defines the number of rows in the table to be used as headings.

  The default *Table Heading* paragraph style is applied to the heading rows. You can edit the *Table Heading* paragraph style in the Styles and Formatting window to change these default settings (centered, bold, and italic text). When splitting a table into two tables, the Heading rows can be copied into the second table.

  Repeat Heading Rows on new pages — Selection enables the heading rows of the table to be repeated at the top of subsequent pages if the table spans more than one page.

  Heading Rows —Specifies the number of rows to be used for the heading. Default is 1.

- **Don't split table over pages** — Prevents the table from spanning more than one page. This can be useful if the table starts near the end of a page, and would look better if it were completely located on the following page. If the table becomes longer than would fit on one page, you will need to either deselect this option or manually split the table.

- **Border** — Surrounds each cell of the table with a border. This border can be modified or deleted later.

The **AutoFormat** button opens a dialog from which you can select one of the many predefined table layouts. See "Automatic formatting of tables" on page 300 for more information. Click **OK** after selecting your table layout.

After making your choices, click **Insert**. Writer creates a table as wide as the text area (from the left page margin to the right page margin), with all columns the same width and all rows the same height. You can adjust the columns and rows later to suit your needs.

Creating nested tables

You can create tables within tables, nested to a depth only limited by imagination and practicality. Figure 292 demonstrates a simple, two-level example. The shaded table is inside a cell of the larger table. To achieve this, simply click in a cell of an existing table and use any of the methods mentioned in "Inserting a new table" above.

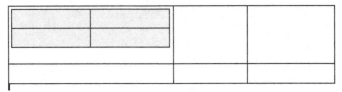

Figure 292: Nested table example

Using AutoCorrect to create a table

You can also create a table by typing a series of hyphens (-) or tabs separated by plus signs. Use the plus signs to indicate column dividers, while hyphens and tabs are used to indicate the width of a column. When using tabs, the default tab setting determines the width; this setting can be changed in **Tools > Options > LibreOffice Writer > General**.

For example, this character sequence:

+-----------------+---------------+------+

creates a table like this:

Note	This function can be disabled or enabled in **Tools > AutoCorrect Options**. On the *Options* tab, deselect or select **Create table**.

Create a table from formatted text

You can create a table from plain text by using the **Table > Convert > Text to Table** menu item. The text to be converted must contain characters to indicate column separators. Paragraph marks indicate an end of a table row.

To convert text to a table, start by editing the text to ensure the column separator character is in place where you want it. Select the text you want to convert and choose **Table > Convert > Text to Table** to open the dialog shown in Figure 293.

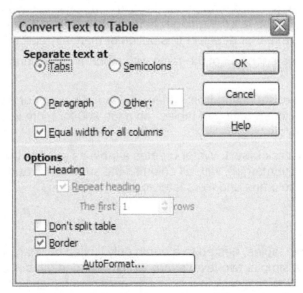

Figure 293: Dialog for the text to table conversion

LibreOffice 4.2 Writer Guide

The *Separate text at* part of the dialog has four options for the separator for the columns of text. Select **Other** to choose the default comma (useful if you are importing a CSV file) or type any character in the box. The other options in this dialog are the same as those in the dialog used to insert a table shown in Figure 291.

Click **OK** when all your choices have been made.

Example

In this example we will convert the following text into a table.

Row 1 Column 1; Row 1 Column 2; Row 1 Column 3

Row 2 Column 1; Row 2 Column 2; Row 2 Column 3

Choose **Table > Convert > Text to Table**

In this case, the separator between elements is a semicolon. By selecting the text and applying the conversion, we obtain the following result.

Row 1 Column 1	Row 1 Column 2	Row 1 Column 3
Row 2 Column 1	Row 2 Column 2	Row 2 Column 3

Note that, unlike when creating a table with other mechanisms, the conversion from text to table preserves the paragraph style and character style applied to the original text.

You can also use the **Convert** menu to perform the opposite operation; that is, to transform a table into plain text. This may be useful when you want to export the table contents into a different program.

To transform a table into text, place the cursor anywhere in the table, choose **Table > Convert > Table to Text** in the Menu bar, pick the preferred row separator, and click **OK** to finish.

Formatting the table layout

Formatting a table is, generally speaking, a two-step process: formatting of the table layout (the subject of this section) and formatting of the table text (the subject of the next section).

Formatting the layout normally involves one or more of the following operations: adjusting the size of the table and its position on the page, adjusting sizes of rows and columns, adding or removing rows or columns, merging and splitting individual cells, changing borders and background.

Default parameters

If you create a table using the Insert Table dialog or the **Table** button on the Standard toolbar, the following defaults are set:

- The cells use the *Table Contents* paragraph style, which, in the default template, is identical to the *Default Style* paragraph style.
- The default table occupies all the space from margin to margin (text area).
- The default table has thin black borders around each cell (grid).

Additionally, if you activate the **Heading** option, the cells in the heading row (or rows) use the *Table Heading* paragraph style. In the default template, the text is centered and set with a bold font.

Resizing and positioning the table

Using the default settings, any newly created table will occupy the entire width of the text area. This is sometimes what you want, or you may prefer a smaller table. To quickly resize a table, first move the mouse to either the left or right edge. When the cursor changes shape into a double arrow, drag the border to the new position. This operation only changes the size of the first or last column; it does not change the alignment of the table on the page.

If you need more precise control over the size and position of the table on the page, open the Table Format dialog by choosing **Table > Table Properties** or by right-clicking anywhere in the table and choosing **Table** from the context menu. Select the Table page of the dialog.

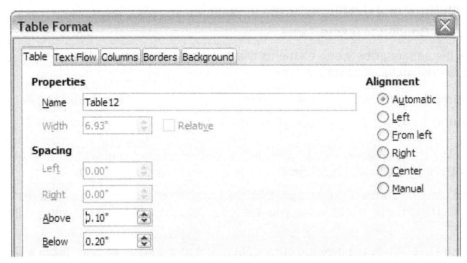

Figure 294: The Table page of the Table Format dialog

On this page you can set the alignment of the table, choosing among the following options:

- **Automatic**: the default setting for a table, fills the width of the text area.
- **Left**: aligns the table with the left margin.
- **Right**: aligns the table with the right margin.
- **From Left**: lets you specify under *Spacing* exactly how far from the left margin the table is placed.
- **Center**: aligns the table in the middle between the left and right margins. If the table width is greater than the margin, the table will extend outside of the margins.
- **Manual**: lets you specify the distances from both left and right margins under *Spacing*.

Selecting an alignment option other than **Automatic** activates the **Width** field in the *Properties* section, where you can enter the desired size of the table. Select **Relative** to see the width as percentage of the text area.

In the *Spacing* section, use the **Above** and **Below** boxes to modify the separation between the text and the table. When the size of the table is less than the size of the text area, LibreOffice will insert some values in the **Left** and **Right** boxes. You can enter values in both the **Left** and **Right** boxes if you select **Manual** alignment. You can enter values in the **Left** box when you select the **From Left, Right** or **Center** alignment. You can enter values in the **Right** box if you select **Left** alignment. Otherwise these values are not available. Note that the sum of the table width, and the values in the **Left** and **Right** boxes, should not be greater than the width of the text area.

Resizing rows and columns

You can adjust the height of rows and the width of columns in a table in several ways.

- Move the mouse next to the edge of the cell and when a double-headed arrow appears, click and hold the left mouse button, drag the border to the desired position, and release the mouse button.

- On the horizontal ruler, column dividers are marked by a pair of thin gray lines; the vertical ruler indicates row dividers in the same way. You can resize a row or column by holding the mouse button down on the appropriate divider and dragging it to the desired location.

- Use the keyboard as described below.

Selecting **Table > Autofit** from the Menu bar also offers some resizing options:

- Select **Column Width** or **Row Height** to enter a dimension into the size box for each selectable column or row of the table.

- The **Optimal Column Width** or **Optimal Row Height** options make the selected columns or rows as narrow as possible while still fitting their contents. This option is only available if the table is selected and has content.

- **Distribute Columns/Rows Evenly** to quickly bring them back to all being the same width or height. This option is only available if the table is selected.

For greater control over the width of each column, use the *Columns* page of the Table Format dialog.

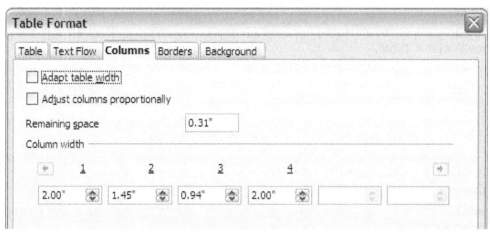

Figure 295: Table Format dialog: Columns page

Right-click on the table and choose **Table** from the context menu or choose **Table > Table Properties** from the Menu bar. On the Table Format dialog, select the *Columns* tab.

- **Adapt table width**: If a table already stretches to the page margins, it cannot stretch any wider and the *Adapt table width* option can only be used to reduce the column width. If the table is narrower, increasing the width of a column will increase the width of the whole table. This option is not available if Automatic has been selected in the Alignment area of the Table page.

  If the table width already extends past the margins, with the *Adapt table width* option checked, attempting to change a column width will automatically decrease that column's size so that the table will now shrink to the page margins while keeping the size of any other column intact.

- **Adjust columns proportionally** results in all columns changing their widths by the same percentage when one is changed. For example, if you reduce by half the size of a column, the sizes of all the other columns will be halved. This option is not available if Automatic has been selected in the Alignment area of the Table page.

- **Remaining space** shows how much further the table can expand before hitting the limit of the margins. This value cannot be edited and will not be negative in the event that the table width is already larger than the space between the left and right margins.

- Under **Column width**, each individual column can be adjusted. If you have more than six columns, use the arrows at the right and left to view them all. With no options selected, the column to the right of the one being adjusted will automatically adjust to keep the table width constant. Adjusting the most right hand column causes the first column to adjust.

Rather than start from the *Table Format* dialog, it is often more efficient to make rough adjustments to a new table using the mouse, and then fine tune the layout using the *Columns* page in conjunction with the *Table* page of the Table Format dialog.

It is also possible to resize a table using only the keyboard. This is sometimes easier than using the mouse.

1) Place the cursor in the cell where you want to make changes.

2) Press and hold the *Alt* key while using the arrow keys.

   a) The left and right arrow keys adjust the column width by moving the border on the right edge of the cell, but not past the margin.

   b) The up and down arrows adjust the row height (when possible) by moving the border on the lower edge of the cell.

3) Press and hold the *Shift+Alt* key while using the left/right arrow keys.

   Adjusts the column width by moving the border on the left edge of the cell, but not past the margin.

To adjust the resizing parameters and behavior for keyboard handling, choose **Tools > Options > LibreOffice Writer > Table**.

Use the *Row* and *Column* values in the *Move cells* section to determine the amount of change produced by a single keystroke while resizing. In the *Behavior of rows/columns* section you can choose one of the following three strategies when resizing:

- **Fixed**: select this if you want the resizing to affect only the adjacent cell and not the entire table. The width of the table does not change when resizing its cells.

- **Fixed, proportional**: when resizing a cell with this option selected, all the other cells are also resized proportionally, but in the opposite direction so as to maintain the width of the table.

- **Variable**: this is the default option. Resizing a cell affects the table size. For example, when you widen a cell, the width of the table increases.

Resizing individual cells

Place the cursor in the cell you wish to change.

1) Press and hold the *Ctrl+Alt* key while using the left/right arrow keys.

   Re-sizes the current cell on its right edge, but not past the margin.

2) Press and hold the *Ctrl+Shift+Alt* key while using the left/right arrow keys.

   Re-sizes the current cell on its left edge, but not past the margin.

Inserting rows and columns

To insert any number of rows or columns:

1) Place the cursor in the row or column where you want to add new rows or columns and right-click.

2) In the context menu, choose **Row > Insert** or **Column > Insert**. This will display a dialog where you can select the number of rows or columns to add, and whether they appear before or after the one selected.

3) Set *Amount* to the number of rows or columns to insert, and *Position* to **Before** or **After**.

4) Click **OK** to close the dialog.

The **Table > Insert > Row** and **Table > Insert > Column** choices from the Menu bar provide the same options.

Note	Clicking on the **Insert Row** icon on the Table toolbar inserts one row *below* the selected one. Clicking on the **Insert Column** icon on the Table toolbar inserts a column *after* (*to the right of*) the selected one.
	Regardless of how they are inserted, new rows or columns have the same formatting as the row or column where the cursor was when the insert command was issued.

You can also quickly insert a row or a column using the keyboard:

1) Place the cursor in the row or column next to the row or column you want to insert.

2) Press *Alt+Insert* to activate keyboard handling.

3) Use the arrow keys as desired to add a row or column:

Left to insert a new column to the left of the cell where the cursor is located.
Right to insert a new column to the right of the cell where the cursor is.
Down to insert a new row below the cell where the cursor is.
Up to insert a new row above the cell where the cursor is.

The above keyboard technique can also be used to delete rows or columns by replacing the *Alt+Insert* keystroke combination in Step 2 with *Alt+Delete*.

Merging and splitting cells

To merge a cell or group of cells into one cell:

1) Select the cells to merge.

2) Right-click and choose **Cell > Merge** in the context menu, or choose **Table > Merge Cells** from the Menu bar. Any content of the cells appears in the merged cell.

To merge a single cell into an adjacent cell, you can also place the cursor in the cell (origin), press *Alt+Delete*, release, then hold down *Ctrl*, and then press the left or the right arrow key. Any contents in the origin cell are lost.

To split a cell into multiple cells:

1) Position the cursor inside the cell.

2) Right-click and choose **Cell > Split** in the context menu, or choose **Table > Split Cells** from the Menu bar.

3) Select how to split the cell. A cell can be split either horizontally (create more rows) or vertically (create more columns), and you can specify the total number of cells to create.

To split a single cell, you can also place the cursor in an adjacent cell, press *Alt+Ins*, release, then hold down *Ctrl*, and then press the left or the right arrow key to split the cell to the left/right.

It is generally a good rule to merge and split cells after completing other layout formatting. This is because some operations such as deleting a column or a row may produce a result difficult to predict when applied to a table with merged or split cells.

Specifying table borders

On the Table Format dialog, select the *Borders* tab. Here you can set borders for a whole table or groups of cells within a table. In addition, a shadow can be set for the whole table.

Borders have three components: where they go, what they look like, and how much space is left around them.

*   *Line arrangement* specifies where the borders go. If a group of cells is selected, the border will be applied only to those cells. You can specify individually the style of the border for the outside edges of the selected cells as well as for the cell divisions. Writer provides five default arrangements but you can just as easily click on the line you want to customize in the *User-defined* area to get exactly what you want. When multiple cells are selected, the User-defined area allows you to select the edges of the selection as well as the cell dividers. By clicking at the intersection of the lines, you can modify multiple borders simultaneously. For example, in Figure 296 the right edge and horizontal separators are modified with a single operation.

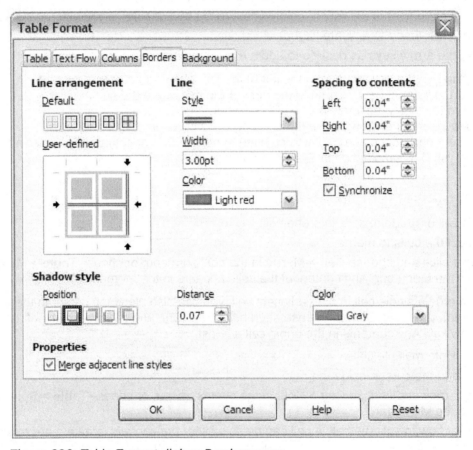

Figure 296: Table Format dialog: Borders page

Note	When the selected cells have different styles of border the User-defined area shows the border as a gray line. You can click on the gray line to choose a new border style (first click), leave the border as it is (second click) or delete the border (third click).

*   *Line* specifies what the border looks like: the style, width, and color. There are a number of different styles and colors to choose from. Style, Width, and Color selections apply to those borders highlighted by a pair of black arrows in the User-defined map on the left-hand side of the dialog.

- *Spacing to contents* specifies how much space to leave between the border and the cell contents. Spaces can be specified to the left, right, above, and below. Check **Synchronize** to have the same spacing for all four sides. This spacing is like a padding and it is not factored in when calculating the text measurements.

- *Shadow style* properties always apply to the whole table. A shadow has three components: where it is, how far from the table it is cast, and what color it is.

- If **Merge adjacent line styles** is checked, two cells sharing a common border will have their borders merged, rather than being side by side.

Tip	To reset everything if you are having problems with borders, right-click in the table and choose **Table** or choose **Table > Table Properties** from the Menu bar. On the *Borders* tab, select the **Set No Borders** icon under *Line arrangement: Default* (the box on the left).

Selecting background colors and graphics

A table background can greatly improve the readability of the data, visually highlight important parts of the table (such as the heading or a specific cell), or just make the table more appealing. You can choose between two types of background when formatting the table: solid color or graphic. The background can be applied to the whole table, to a single cell, or to a row. The background selected for a cell will be in front of the row background which in turn will hide the table background.

The row background option is quite handy when you want to create alternate color rows or assign a different background to the heading of the table. The tables in this guide adopt this technique.

To set the background for a cell, row, or table:

1) Place the cursor anywhere inside the cell, row or table you want to work with. If you want to apply a background to a group of cells, select the group.

2) Right-click and choose **Table** from the context menu, or choose **Table > Table Properties** from the Menu bar.

3) In the Table Format dialog, select the *Background* tab (see Figure 297).

4) In the *For* section, chose whether to apply the settings to cell, row, or table.

    - If you choose **Cell**, changes apply only to the selected cells, or the cell where the cursor currently resides. Even when selecting a group of cells, the background settings are applied to each cell individually.

    - If you choose **Row**, changes affect the entire row where the cursor resides.

    - If you choose **Table**, changes will set the background for the entire table, regardless of the cursor position or selected cells.

5) In the *As* selection box, choose whether the background is a color or a graphic.

    To apply a color, select the color and click **OK**. Remember that you can add custom colors by choosing **Tools > Options > LibreOffice > Colors**.

    To apply a graphic:

    a) First select the graphic from your computer's file system with the **Browse** button. (Writer supports a large number of graphics formats.)

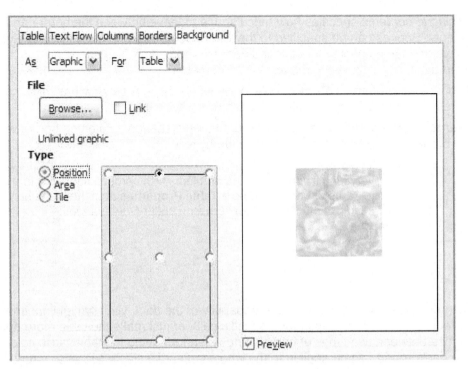

Figure 297: Table Format dialog: inserting a graphic background

b) You can use the **Link** option to link the graphic file. If it is linked, changes to the graphic (for example, if you edit it in a different software package) are reflected in your document. However, you also need to keep the linked graphic file with the document file. If, for example, you email the document without the graphic file, the graphic will no longer be visible.

c) Under *Type*, select the type of placement for the graphic.

- If you choose **Position**, you can select in the position map where the graphic will be displayed in the selected area.

- If you choose **Area**, the graphic is stretched to fill the whole area.

- If you choose **Tile**, the graphic is tiled (repeated horizontally and vertically) to fill the area.

d) If the **Preview** option is checked, the graphic displays in the pane on the right.

e) To apply the graphic, click **OK**.

Figure 298 shows an example of a table set with a background image, and the first row background colored. As you can see, the row background covers the table background.

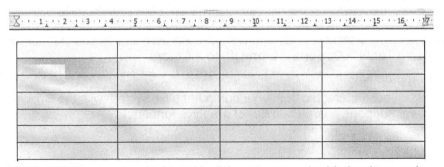

Figure 298: Example of table with different row and table backgrounds

Displaying or hiding table boundaries

A *table boundary* is a set of pale (usually gray) lines around the cells when viewed on-screen in LibreOffice with no borders enabled. These boundaries are not printed; their only function is to help you see where the table cells are.

To display the table the same way on the screen as on the printed page, with no boundary lines, right-click on the table and choose **Table Boundaries** from the context menu. Repeat this to have the boundaries appear again.

Note	Turning boundaries off does not hide any borders that the table may have.

Tip	You can also turn table boundaries on and off through **Tools > Options > LibreOffice > Appearance**. On that page, you can display or hide boundaries around text, pages headers and footers, figures, and other parts of a document.

Formatting the table text

Once the table layout is satisfactory, you can move on to formatting the text in the individual cells. You can apply manual formatting as with any other paragraph in the text, but it is highly recommended, for the sake of consistency and ease of maintenance, that you define your own paragraph and character styles.

Besides the paragraph and character styles, there are other aspects to consider when placing text in a table cell, such as text flow, alignment and orientation.

You can format each cell independently of other cells, or you can simultaneously format a group of cells by selecting them before applying the desired formatting.

Specifying text flow

On the *Text Flow* page of the Table Format dialog (Figure 299), you can:

*   Insert a page or column break either before or after the table. Use the *Text Flow*: **Break** option, combined with the **Page** or **Column** and the **Before** or **After** buttons.
    If you insert a page break before the table (that is, start the table on a new page), you can also change the page style that will go with it by checking the **With Page Style** box and selecting a new page style. As with any page break, you can also reset the page numbers using the *Page number* box.

*   Keep a table on one page by deselecting the **Allow table to split across pages and columns** option. If this item is deselected, the next item is not active.

*   Keep each row on one page by deselecting the **Allow row to break across pages and columns** option.

*   Use the **Keep with next paragraph** option to keep the table and an immediately following paragraph together if you insert a page break.

*   Use the **Repeat heading** option, and its associated numbers box, to select the number of table heading rows that will be repeated on each page. A complicated table may need two or three heading rows to be easily read and understood.

*   Use the *Text orientation* list to select the direction for the text in the cells. Select either **Horizontal**, **Vertical**, or **Use superordinate object settings**.

Note	The term **Use superordinate object settings** means "use the default text flow settings for the page".

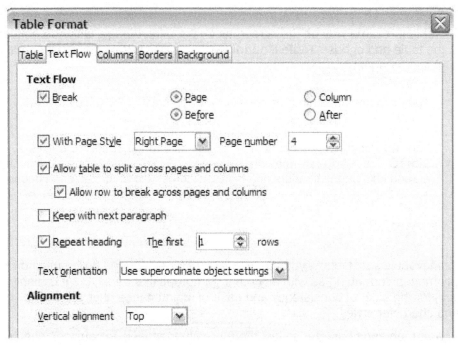

Figure 299: Table Format dialog: Text Flow page

- Select the vertical alignment of the text in the table or the selected cells; the choices are to align with the top of the cell, the center of the cell, or the bottom of the cell. This alignment is in addition to the Left-Right alignment options available on the Table page of the Table Format dialog.

Note	A table heading row can not span two pages, but any other row can. A one-row table (often used for page layout purposes), if set up with the default of including a heading, will not break across pages. The cure is to make sure the table is defined without a heading row.

Vertical alignment

By default, text entered into a table is aligned to the top-left of the cell. You can change the default for the entire table, as described above, or for individually selected cells.

To vertically align the text in specific cells:

- Place the cursor in the cell you wish to change, or click and drag to select multiple cells.
- Right-click in the selected area and choose **Cell > Center**, **Top**, or **Bottom** from the context menu to vertically align the text as desired.

Number formats

The number format can be set for a whole table or group of cells. For example, cells can be set to display in a particular currency, to four decimal places, or in a particular date format.

The Number recognition option can be enabled under **Tools > Options > LibreOffice Writer > Table** within the *Input in Tables* section.

LibreOffice 4.2 Writer Guide

Number recognition specifies that numbers in a text table are recognized and formatted as numbers. If Number recognition is not selected, numbers are saved in text format and are automatically left-aligned.

If **Number format recognition** is not selected, only input in the format that has been set for the cell is accepted. Any other input resets the format to *Text*.

Select the cells to format, then right-click and choose **Number Format** from the context menu. The Number Format dialog opens for you to set options for various categories of numerical data.

- In the *Category* list, select the category you want, such as currency, date, or text.
- In the *Format* list, choose a format for the category you just selected.
- For some categories, such as date, you may wish to change the language using the *Language* list, while for other numerical categories you can use the *Options* section of the dialog to customize the appearance.

Tip	You will notice that LibreOffice displays the formatting code for the category and format selected in Format Code section at the bottom of the dialog. For example, if you select a date format such as 31 Dec 1999 the corresponding code is `D MMM YYYY`. Advanced users can easily customize this formatting code as well as create new user-defined codes.

Alignment specifies that numbers are always bottom right aligned in the cell. If this field is not selected numbers are always top left aligned in the cell.

Note	Direct formatting is not influenced by the **Alignment** field. If you center align the cell content directly, it remains centered irrespective of whether text or numbers are involved.

Rotating text in a table cell

You can rotate text in a table cell by 90 or 270 degrees. Text rotation is useful when you have long headings for narrow columns.

- Select the text to be rotated and then choose **Format > Character**, or right-click and select **Character** from the context menu.
- On the *Position* page, in the *Rotation / scaling* section, choose the rotation angle and click **OK**.

Figure 300 shows a sample table with rotated headings.

This is long	*Another long heading*	*A rotated heading*	*Another heading*	*Another heading*	*Another heading*	*Another heading*

Figure 300: A table with rotated headings

Note	Text rotation within table cells can also be achieved with the use of paragraph styles, discussed in greater detail in Chapter 7, Working with Styles.

Data entry and manipulation in tables

Moving between cells

Within a table, you can use the mouse, the cursor keys, or the *Tab* key to move between cells.

The cursor keys move the cursor one text character left or right at a time. With an empty cell, pressing the cursor key will move the cursor to the adjacent cell.

The *Tab* key moves directly to the next cell and, if the cursor is in the last cell in the table, creates a new row. Pressing *Shift+Tab* moves the cursor back a cell.

Tip	To enter a *Tab* character as part of the text of the cell, press the *Ctrl* and *Tab* keys at the same time.

To move to the beginning of the table, press *Ctrl+Home*. If the active cell is empty, the move is to the beginning of the table. If the cell has content, the first press goes to the beginning of the cell and the next press goes to the beginning of the table (pressing again takes you to the beginning of the document).

To move to the end of the table, press *Ctrl+End*. If the active cell is empty, the move is to the end of the table. If the cell has content, the first press goes to the end of the cell and the next press goes to the end of the table (pressing again takes you to the end of the document).

Sorting data in a table

Just as in a spreadsheet, Writer allows data in a table to be sorted. Up to three levels of sorting can be specified (for example, sort first by age numerically, then alphabetically by name within each age).

To sort data in a table:

1) Select the table (or part of the table) to be sorted.
2) From the Menu bar, choose **Table > Sort**, or select the **Sort** icon from the *Table* toolbar.
3) In the Sort dialog:

   a) Decide whether you want to sort in the direction of rows or columns. The default sorting direction is by rows, which results in sorting the data in a column.
   b) Select up to three keys to sort on, in the correct order.
   c) For each key, select which column or row to sort on, whether the sort is **Numeric** or **Alphanumeric** and whether it is **Ascending** or **Descending**.
   d) Click **OK** to perform the sort.

Note	You have to select all cells that might be affected by the sorting. For example, if you select only the cells of one column, the sort affects that column only, while the others remain unchanged. In such a case, you risk mixing the data of the rows.

Using spreadsheet functions in a table

In a table in a Writer document, you can use some of the mathematical functions that are normally implemented by LibreOffice Calc. For many simple functions, Writer tables can be used as basic spreadsheets.

Just as in a spreadsheet, each table cell is identified by a letter (for the column) and a number (for the row). For example, cell C4 is the cell in the third column from the left and fourth row from the top. When the cursor is in a cell, the table name and this cell reference is displayed on the status bar.

Tip	Basic spreadsheet functions in tables are much the same as in LibreOffice Calc. The main difference is that cell references are formatted differently. Cell A2 (first column, second row) is referred to in Calc as A2 (or A2 for an absolute reference). In Writer tables, it is referred to as <A2>.

For example, suppose you had two numbers in cells <B1> and <C2> and wanted to display the sum of the two in cell <A1>, as shown in Figure 301.

Do the following:

1) Click in cell <A1> and press the = key, or choose **Table > Formula** from the Menu bar, or press *F2*. The Formula bar appears automatically, near the top of the screen. In the leftmost side of the bar, you can see the coordinates of the selected cell.

2) Click in cell <B1>. The identifiers of this cell are automatically displayed in the Formula bar and inserted into cell <A1>.

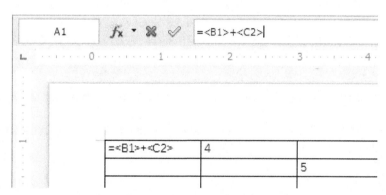

Figure 301: Using spreadsheet functions in a table

3) Press the + key.

4) Click on cell <C2>. You can see the final formula **= <B1>+<C2>** displayed both in the selected cell and in the Object bar.

5) Press the *Enter* key, or click the green tick (check mark) on the Formula Bar, to replace the formula in the cell with the result of the calculation.

Tip	To display a cell's formula and make it available for editing, choose **Table > Formula** from the Menu bar, or press *F2*.

Tip	To display the list of the mathematical functions that you can use in a table: 1) Display the Formula toolbar by pressing *F2* or by selecting a blank cell and pressing the = *key*. 2) Click the **Formula f(x)** icon.

In our example, this gives the result **9** in the top left cell. For summing contiguous cells, you can simply select the cells in the row, column, or the rectangle of rows and columns. Thus, for example, to add a column of numbers, do this:

1) Type an equals sign = in an empty cell.
2) Select the cells to be added together—in this case the cells from A2 to A5. The formula should be something like **=<A2:A5>**.
3) Press the *Enter* key or click the green tick (check mark) on the Formula Bar.
4) The result appears in the cell you have selected.

When using a function, you can enter the cells manually or by selecting them. Thus, to add up the four numbers that we added above (A2, A3, A4, A5), do this:

1) Type an equals sign = in an empty cell.
2) Type **sum** or select it from the function list **f(x)**.
3) Select the contiguous cells to be added together. The formula should be something like **=sum<A2:A5>**.
4) Press the *Enter* key or click the green tick (check mark) on the Formula Bar.
5) The answer appears in the cell you have selected.

Caution	Unlike in Calc, when inserting or deleting rows or columns of the table, formulas are not updated automatically. If you plan to use complex formulas you should consider embedding a Calc spreadsheet in your Writer document.

Additional table operations

Protecting cells in a table

You can protect the contents of individual cells of a text table from changes.

Note	This protection is not intended for secure protection. It is just a switch to protect the cells against accidental changes.

To turn on cell protection:

Place the cursor in a cell or select cells. Right-click to open the context menu, then choose **Cell > Protect**.

To tun off cell protection, do one of the following:

• Place the cursor in the cell or select the cells. First, if necessary, choose **Tools > Options > LibreOffice Writer > Formatting Aids** and mark **Cursor in protected areas > Enable**. Then right-click the cell to open the context menu and choose **Cell > Unprotect**.

• Select the table in the Navigator, open the context menu and select **Table > Unprotect**.

• Use *Shift+Ctrl+T* to remove protection for the entire current table or all selected tables.

Adding a caption

You can easily add a caption to any table. Writer will keep track of all your captioned tables, automatically number them, and update any links to them.

To add a caption to a table:

1) Place the cursor in the table.

2) Right-click and choose **Caption** from the pop-up menu. Alternatively, the **Insert > Caption** menu option becomes available whenever your cursor is inside a table cell.

3) Enter the text for your caption, your category selection, the numbering style, separator, and position (above or below the table).

4) Click **OK**.

Note	Once the category, numbering style, and separator are established in the Caption dialog, you can edit them in the document if you choose. However, doing so may damage the automatic numbering and reference links. If you need to establish the numbering and reference link for the caption, you can choose to leave your caption blank in the Caption dialog and add it later.

Writer supplies five category labels for captions: <None>, Drawing, Table, Illustration, and Text.

You can also create your own category labels, formatting, and separators. For example, you might want your tables to be labeled as **Fantasia**, formatted with roman numerals, and using a period (*.*) as a separator, as follows:

Fantasia I. *Interesting data*

Fantasia II. *More interesting data*

Fantasia III. *Yet more interesting data*

To accomplish this:

1) Open the Caption dialog following the instructions above.

2) In the *Category* field, select the text and type the word `Fantasia`.

3) In the *Numbering* drop-down list, select the **Roman (I II III)** option.

4) In the *Separator* field, select the text and type a period (.) followed by a space.

Note	Writer will use exactly what you type into the Category and Separator fields, so be sure to include any additional spaces or punctuation you want to see in your caption.

Additional options for numbering captions by chapter are available under the *Options* button in the Captions dialog. Some of these settings which refer to the outline level will only have an effect if you are using outline level paragraph styles on the chapter headings within your document. See Chapter 7. Working With Styles, for information.

By adding chapter numbers to your captions, LibreOffice will restart the caption numbering for each chapter it encounters. For example, if the last figure caption you create in chapter 1 is Figure 1.15, and the next figure caption you create is in chapter 2, the numbering will start over at Figure 2.1.

Options available to chapter numbering for captions include the following:

- Use **Level** to specify the outline levels that triggers a restart of the numbering as well as how many levels of outline numbering are shown before the table number. An example may be useful. Suppose your document uses Heading 1 style for chapters and Heading 2 style for sub-headings, and that this is how you set up your outline numbering. If you want all the tables in a chapter (that is, between two Heading 1 paragraphs) to be numbered sequentially independently of the sub-heading they are under, select 1 as Level. If instead you want to restart the numbering at each sub-heading select level 2.

- Use the **Separator** field to establish the separator between the chapter number and figure number.

- Use **Character style** to set a character style for the caption. This is useful if the separator of your choice is not a symbol included in the default font type of your document or if you want the caption to have a special color, size and so on.

- The **Apply border and shadow** option does not apply to table captions. LibreOffice normally wraps the objects you can add a caption to in a frame, but not for tables.

- Use **Caption order** to specify whether you want the category or numbering to appear first in the caption.

All of the features described above can also be set up to automatically apply to any new tables you create in your document.

To automatically caption all your tables:

1) Place the cursor in a table.

2) Right-click and choose **Caption > AutoCaption** from the pop-up menu.

3) Select **LibreOffice Writer Table** and select the settings you want and click **OK**. This dialog is covered in more detail in Chapter 2, Setting up Writer.

When AutoCaption is enabled for tables, any new tables will be captioned according to your selections in the AutoCaption dialog; however, you will need to add the specific text for each caption onto the table manually.

Cross-referencing a table

You can insert a cross-reference to a captioned table. Clicking on the cross-reference takes the reader directly to the table.

1) Position the cursor where you want the cross reference.

2) Choose **Insert > Cross-reference** from the Menu bar.

3) Set the *Type* to Table (or whatever you chose as the category). A list of captioned tables will be shown in the *Selection* panel; select the one you want to reference.

4) In the *Format* pane, choose how the cross reference will appear.

    Page creates a reference of the page number that the caption appears on.

    Chapter places a reference to the chapter number in which the caption appears. This will only produce an empty space unless you have set up your chapter headings with outline level paragraph styles.

    Reference inserts the entire caption's category, number and caption text as a reference.

    Above/Below inserts "above" or "below" depending on whether the table appears above or below the cross-reference.

    As Page Style creates a reference to the page number that the caption appears on using the page style format.

    Category and Number creates a cross-reference with only the caption's category and number; for example, **Table 1** for the first table.

    Caption Text creates the reference using the caption text, leaving off the category and number.

    Numbering inserts only the number of the caption.

5) Click **Insert** to add the cross-reference and click **Close** to exit the dialog.

Automatic formatting of tables

Using AutoFormat, you can apply an elaborate format to your table with just a few clicks. AutoFormat is somewhat similar to paragraph styles and will enable you to obtain consistent looking tables across your document. You can also create your own table formats and save them as another AutoFormat option.

To apply an AutoFormat, place the cursor anywhere in the table and choose **Table > AutoFormat**. This opens the dialog shown in Figure 302.

Select from the list on the left the Format most suitable for your table and click **OK** to apply it. You can rename the selected table format scheme as well as decide which parts of the predefined formatting you want to apply to your table. You can selectively apply the number format, the font, the alignment, the border, or the pattern.

Note	You cannot rename or delete the **Default** format. Figure 302 shows that with **Default** selected, the **Rename** and **Delete** buttons are not available.

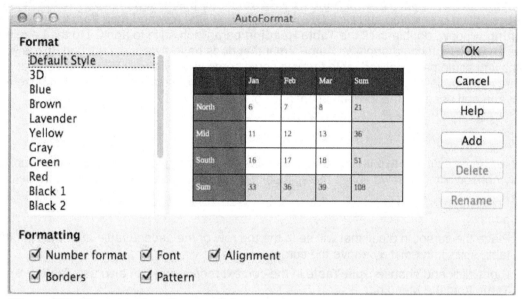

Figure 302: The table AutoFormat dialog

To create your own AutoFormat, proceed as follows:

1) Create a table and manually format it as you wish, including borders, spacing of text from the top and bottom borders, fonts to be used in the table heading and data cells, and background colors.
2) Position the cursor anywhere in the table and then click **Table > AutoFormat**.
3) On the AutoFormat dialog, click **Add** and give the table format a name in the Add AutoFormat dialog and click **OK**.
4) The newly named AutoFormat now appears as an available format. Click **OK** to close the AutoFormat dialog.

Table AutoFormats record the following table-level properties:

- Break
- Keep with next paragraph
- Repeat heading
- Allow table to split across pages
- Allow rows to break across pages
- Merge adjacent line styles
- Table shadow

Tip	This technique does not include table and column widths in the table format. To insert a table with predefined full formatting, save it as AutoText. See "Using AutoText" in Chapter 3, Working with Text, for instructions.

Caution	Autoformats are not easily removed. You can change to a different autoformat, but it takes **Undo** to get back to the original table.

Creating a heading row in an existing table

To create a heading row in an existing table that does not have one, select the first row in the table and from the Menu bar select **Table > Insert > Rows**. In the Insert Rows dialog that opens, ensure the **Before** option is selected and click **OK**. Select the new first row and then from the **Styles and Formatting** window, double-click the **Table Heading** paragraph style to apply it to the heading row. As an alternative, you could apply an AutoFormat that does have a heading defined. (Here is where having some personalized table formats could come in very handy.) Place the cursor anywhere in the table and then click **Table > AutoFormat**. Choose a format. Click **OK**. Use the **More** button and deselect the formatting options you do not want to apply to your table.

Merging and splitting tables

One table can be split into two tables, and two tables can be merged into a single table. Tables are split only horizontally (the rows above the split point are put into one table, and the rows below into another).

To split a table:

1) Place the cursor in a cell that will be in the top row of the second table after the split (the table splits immediately above the cursor).

2) Right-click and choose **Split Table** in the context menu. You can also use **Table > Split Table** from the Menu bar.

3) A Split Table dialog opens. You can select **No heading** or an alternative formatting for the heading—the top row(s) of the new table.

4) Click **OK**. The table is then split into two tables separated by a blank paragraph.

Note	If cells in one table include formulas using data from the other table, those cells will contain an error message: **Expression is faulty**.

To merge two tables:

1) Delete the blank paragraph between the tables. You must use the *Delete* key (not the *Backspace* key) to do this.

2) Select any cell in one of the tables.

3) Right-click and choose **Merge Tables** in the pop-up menu. You can also use **Table > Merge Table** from the Menu bar.

Tip	To see clearly where the paragraphs are and to delete them easily, choose **View > Nonprinting Characters** *(Ctrl+F10)* or click the ¶ button in the Standard toolbar.

Deleting a table

To delete a table:

1) Click anywhere in the table.

2) Choose **Table > Delete > Table** from the Menu bar.

Or:

   1) Select from the end of the paragraph before the table to the start of the paragraph after the table.

   2) Press the *Delete* key or the *Backspace* key.

Note	The second method also merges the paragraph after the table with the paragraph before the table, which may not be what you want.

Copying a table

To copy a table from one part of the document and paste it into another part:

   1) Click anywhere in the table.

   2) From the Menu bar choose **Table > Select > Table**.

   3) Press *Ctrl+C* or click the **Copy** icon on the Standard toolbar.

   4) Move the cursor to the target position and click on it to fix the insertion point.

   5) Press *Ctrl+V* or click the **Paste** icon in the Standard toolbar.

Moving a table

To move a table from one part of a document to another part:

   1) Click anywhere in the table.

   2) From the Menu bar, choose **Table > Select > Table**.

   3) Press *Ctrl+X* or click the **Cut** icon in the Standard toolbar. (This step removes the contents of the cells but leaves the empty cells, which must be removed in step 6.)

   4) Move the cursor to the target position and click on it to fix the insertion point.

   5) Press *Ctrl+V* or click the **Paste** icon in the Standard toolbar. (This pastes the cells and their contents and formatting.)

   6) Return to the original table, click somewhere in it and then choose **Table > Delete > Table** from the Menu bar.

Inserting a paragraph before or after a table

To insert a paragraph before a table, position the cursor before any text or other contents in the first (upper left-hand) cell and press *Enter* or *Alt+Enter*. To insert a paragraph after a table, position the cursor after any text in the last (lower right-hand) cell and press *Alt+Enter*.

Note	Captions are considered as paragraphs separate from the table itself. If there is a caption below a table, for example, just position the cursor at the end of the caption and press *Enter*.

Using tables as a page layout tool

Tables may be used as a page layout tool to position text in a document instead of using tabs or spaces. For example, the Tip below is formatted as a table.

For more information and tips about using tables in page layout, see Chapter 4. Formatting Pages.

Tip	When inserting a table used for layout, you may wish to deselect the **Heading** and **Border** options (see Inserting a new table on page 282). To remove the borders from an existing table, right-click on the table, choose **Table** from the context menu, select the **Borders** tab (see Figure 296 on page 290), and select the icon for no borders.

The Table menu and toolbar

All of the table commands described in this chapter are conveniently located in the Menu bar under the **Table** item and on the Table toolbar, shown in Figure 303.

Table 11 describes the effects of using these icons. When you create a table or select an existing table, the Table toolbar will be displayed automatically. You can manually display it at any time by clicking **View > Toolbars > Table**. The toolbar can float over the main Writer window (as shown in Figure 303), or it can be docked along any edge of the main window. See Chapter 1, Introducing Writer, for more about docking and floating toolbars, and how to hide and display specific tools on a toolbar.

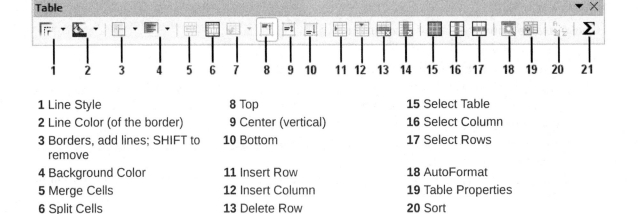

1 Line Style	**8** Top	**15** Select Table
2 Line Color (of the border)	**9** Center (vertical)	**16** Select Column
3 Borders, add lines; SHIFT to remove	**10** Bottom	**17** Select Rows
4 Background Color	**11** Insert Row	**18** AutoFormat
5 Merge Cells	**12** Insert Column	**19** Table Properties
6 Split Cells	**13** Delete Row	**20** Sort
7 Optimize	**14** Delete Column	**21** Sum

Figure 303: Table toolbar

Table 11: Functions of the icons on the Table toolbar

Name	Description
Line Style	Opens the Border Style window where you can modify the border line style. This can be torn off and floated separately.
Line Color (of the border)	A split button. You can apply the color with a single click on the icon, or by selecting the triangle button, open the *Border Color* window where you can modify the border color. This can be torn off and floated separately.
Borders, add lines; SHIFT to remove	Opens the *Borders* window where you can select which sides of the table or of the selected cells will have a border. This can be torn off and floated separately.
Background Color	A split button. You can apply the color with a single click on the icon, or by selecting the triangle button, open the *Background* color window where you can select the background color of the table or of the selected cells. This can be torn off and floated separately.

Name	Description
Merge Cells	Combines the selected cells into a single cell. Refer to Merging and splitting cells on page 289 for a description of the effect of this button.
Split Cells	Opens the *Split Cells* dialog where you can define how to split a cell. Refer to Merging and splitting cells on page 289 for a description of the effect of this button.
Optimize	Opens a window with four options you can use to let Writer optimize the distribution of the columns or rows or optimize the row height or column width. This can be torn off and floated separately.
Top	Press this button to align the contents of the selected cells to the top of the cell.
Center (vertical)	Press this button to align the contents of the selected cells to the vertical center of the cell.
Bottom	Press this button to align the contents of the selected cells to the bottom of the cell.
Insert Row	Inserts a row below the selected row.
Insert Column	Inserts a column after the selected column.
Delete Row	Deletes the selected rows from the table.
Delete Column	Deletes the selected columns from the table.
Select Table	Selects the entire table.
Select Column	Selects the column in which the cursor is positioned.
Select Row	Selects the row in which the cursor is positioned.
AutoFormat	Opens the *AutoFormat* dialog where you can select from several predefined formatting sets. Each set is characterized by its own fonts, shading, and border styles. You can also select **AutoFormat** from the *Insert Table* dialog.
Table Properties	Opens the T*able Format* dialog where you can control all the properties of the table, for example name, alignment, spacing, column width, borders, and background.
Sort	Opens the *Sort* dialog where you can specify the sort criteria for the selected cells.
Sum	Activates the *Sum* function. Refer to "Using spreadsheet functions in a table" on page 297 for an example of using this function.

Chapter 10
Working with Templates

Introduction

A template is a document model that you use to create other documents. For example, you can create a template for business reports that has your company's logo on the first page. New documents created from this template will all have your company's logo on the first page.

Templates can contain anything that regular documents can contain, such as text, graphics, a set of styles, and user-specific setup information such as measurement units, language, the default printer, and toolbar and menu customization.

All documents in LibreOffice are based on templates. If you do not specify a template when you start a new Writer document, then the document is based on the default template for text documents. If you have not specified a default template, Writer uses the blank template for text documents that is installed with LibreOffice. See "Setting a default template" on page 313 for more information.

LibreOffice 4.0 supplies one user-selectable text template, MediaWiki, as an alternative to the default in documents (Writer). Note that German is the default document language in the MediaWiki template. This can be changed on the **Languages** page in **Tools > Options > Language Settings.**

Ten colored backgrounds are supplied for presentations (Impress). No alternative templates are supplied for drawings (Draw) or spreadsheets (Calc).

Using a template to create a document

To use a template to create a document:

1) From the Menu bar, choose **File > New > Templates** to open the Template Manager dialog.

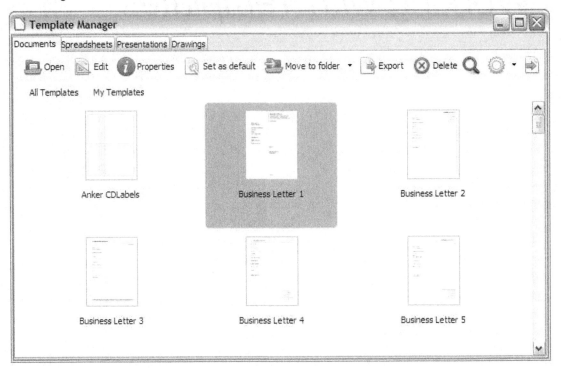

Figure 304: Template Manager

2) From the tabs at the top of the dialog, select the Documents category (type) of template. Folders containing templates are listed in the category page of the dialog. If no other folders than MediaWiki are visible, there are no templates available.

3) Double-click the folder that contains the template that you want to use, typically this will be My Templates. All the templates contained in that folder are then listed on the page, as shown in Figure 304.

4) Select the template that you want to use. If you wish to view the template's properties, click the **Properties** button above the list of templates. The template's properties appear in a pop-up window. Click **Close** to close this pop-up window.

5) Double-click on the required template. A new document based on the selected template opens in Writer. You can then edit and save the new document just as you would any other document.

Creating a template

You can create your own templates in two ways: from a document or using a wizard.

Creating a template from a document

To create a template from a document and save it to My Templates:

1) Open a new or existing document that you want to make into a template.

2) Add or modify the content and styles that you want.

3) From the Menu bar, choose **File > Templates > Save as Template.** The Template Manager dialog opens displaying the default folders (and any user created folders).

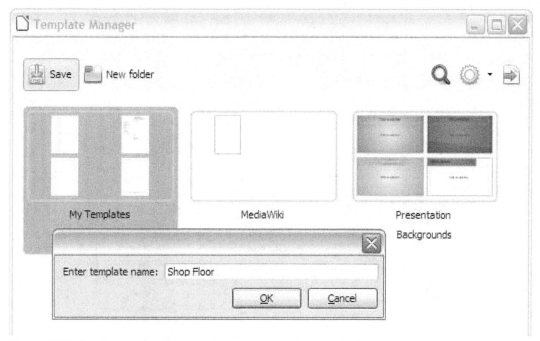

Figure 305: Saving a template

4) Select the My Templates folder.

5) Click the **Save** icon.

6) Enter a name for the template in the text input box that opens, and click **OK** (see Figure 305).

7) Close the Template Manager dialog.

Any settings that can be added to or modified in a document can be saved in a template. For example, below are some of the settings (although not a full list) that can be included in a Writer document and then saved as a template for later use:

- Printer settings: which printer, single-sided or double-sided printing, paper size, and so on
- Styles to be used, including character, page, frame, numbering, and paragraph styles
- Format and settings regarding indexes, tables, bibliographies, table of contents

Templates can also contain predefined text, saving you from having to type it every time you create a new document. For example, a letter template may contain your name, address, and salutation.

You can also save menu and toolbar customizations in templates; see Chapter 16, Customizing Writer, for more information.

Creating a template using a wizard

You can use wizards to create Writer templates for letters, faxes, and agendas.

For example, the Fax Wizard guides you through the following choices:

- Type of fax (business or personal)
- Document elements like the date, subject line (business fax), salutation, and complimentary close
- Options for sender and recipient information (business fax)
- Text to include in the footer (business fax)

To create a template using a wizard:

1) From the Menu bar, choose **File > Wizards >** [type of template required].

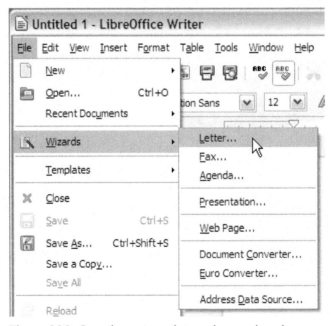

Figure 306: Creating a template using a wizard

2) Follow the instructions on the pages of the wizard. This process is slightly different for each type of template, but the format is similar for all of them.

3) In the last section of the wizard, you can specify the template name which will show in the Template Manager, and also the name and location for saving the template. The two names can be different but may cause you confusion if you choose two different names. The

default location is your user templates folder, but you can choose a different location if you prefer.

4) Selecting the **Path** button to set the file name, and perhaps change the directory, causes the **Save As** dialog to open. Setting the file name and clicking **Save** closes the dialog.

5) Finally, you have the option of creating a new document from your template immediately, or manually changing the template, by clicking **Finish**. For future documents, you can re-use the template created by the wizard, just as you would use any other template.

You may have to open the Template Manager and click **Refresh** on the **Action** menu to have any new templates appear in the listings.

Note	In this release of LibreOffice, clicking **Finish** reopens the Save As dialog in which you set the file name at Step 4. Clicking **Save** now, in the reopened dialog, causes the file to be saved to the hard drive, and the template to open. Clicking **Save** in Step 4 only saved the dialog in memory and not to the hard drive.

Editing a template

You can edit a template's styles and content, and then, if you wish, you can reapply the template's styles to documents that were created from that template. Note that you can only reapply styles. You cannot reapply content.

To edit a template:

1) From the Menu bar, choose **File > New > Templates.** The Template Manager dialog opens.

2) Navigate to the template that you want to edit. Click once on it to activate the file handling controls (see Figure 304). Click **Edit**. The template opens in LibreOffice.

3) Edit the template just as you would any other document. To save your changes, choose **File > Save** from the Menu bar.

Updating a document from a changed template

The next time you open a document that was created from the changed template, the following message appears.

Figure 307: Update styles message

Click **Update Styles** to apply the template's changed styles to the document. Click **Keep Old Styles** if you do not want to apply the template's changed styles to the document (but see the Caution notice below).

Note	To re-enable updating from a template:
	
	1) Use **Tools > Macros > Organize Macros > LibreOffice Basic**. Select the document from the list, click the expansion symbol (+ or triangle), and select Standard. If Standard has an expansion symbol beside it, click that and select a module.
	2) If the **Edit** button is active, click it. If the Edit button is not active, click **New**.
	3) In the Basic window, enter the following:
	`Sub FixDocV3`
	`' set UpdateFromTemplate`
	`oDocSettings = ThisComponent.createInstance( _`
	`"com.sun.star.document.Settings" )`
	`oDocSettings.UpdateFromTemplate = True`
	`End Sub 'FixDocV3`
	4) Click the **Run BASIC** icon, then close the Basic window.
	5) Save the document.
	
	Next time when you open this document you will have the update from template feature back.

Adding templates obtained from other sources

You can download templates for LibreOffice from many sources, including the official template repository at http://templates.libreoffice.org/, and install them on your computer. On other websites you may find collections of templates that have been packaged into extension (OXT) files. These are installed a little differently, as described below.

Installing individual templates

To install individual templates:

1) Download the template and save it anywhere on your computer.

2) Import the template into a template folder by following the instructions in "Importing a template" on page 316.

Tip	You can manually copy new templates into the template folders. The location varies with your computer's operating system. To learn where the template folders are stored on your computer, go to **Tools > Options > LibreOffice > Paths**.

Installing collections of templates

The Extension Manager provides an easy way to install collections of templates that have been packaged as extensions. Follow these steps:

1) Download the extension package (OXT file) and save it anywhere on your computer.

2) In Writer, select **Tools > Extension Manager** from the Menu bar. In the Extension Manager dialog (Figure 308), click **Add** to open a file browser window.

3) Find and select the package of templates you want to install and click **Open**. The package begins installing. You may be asked to accept a license agreement.

4) When the package installation is complete, the templates are available for use through **File > New > Templates** and the extension is listed in the Extension Manager.

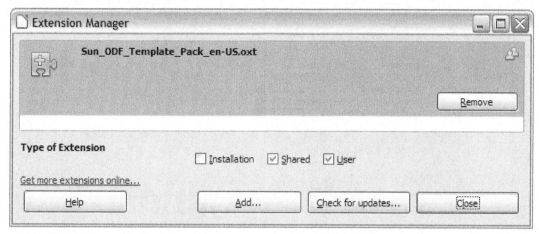

Figure 308: Newly-added package of templates

Extension packages may also be installed by double-clicking the file, and then accepting the installation and any license agreement which is requested.

See Chapter 16, Customizing Writer, for more about the Extension Manager.

Setting a default template

If you create a document by choosing **File > New > Text Document** from the Menu bar, Writer creates the document from the default template for text documents. You can, however, set a custom template to be the default. You can reset the default later, if you choose.

| **Note for Windows users** | You may know that Microsoft Word employs a normal.dot or normal.dotx file for its default template and how to regenerate it. |
| | LibreOffice does not have a similar default template file; the "factory defaults" are embedded within the software. |

Setting a custom template as the default

You can set any template to be the default, as long as it is in one of the folders displayed in the Template Manager dialog. If necessary, you can add the template to a folder as described in "Importing a template" on page 316.

To set a custom template as the default:

1) From the Menu bar, choose **File > New > Templates** to open the Template Manager dialog.

2) In the Template Manager dialog, open the folder containing the template that you want to set as the default, then select the template.

3) Click the **Set As Default** icon above the list of templates (see Figure 309).

The next time that you create a document by choosing **File > New > Text Document**, the document will be created from this template.

Although many important settings can be changed in the **Tools > Options** dialog (see Chapter 2, Setting up Writer), for example default fonts and page size, more advanced settings (such as page margins) can only be changed by replacing the default template with a new one.

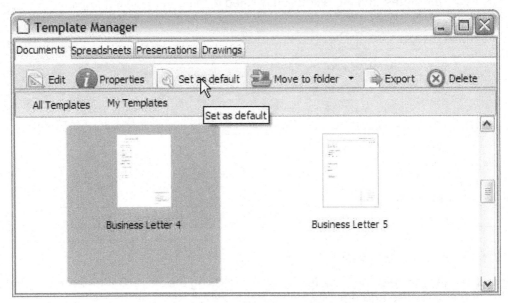

Figure 309: Setting a default template using the Template Manager dialog

Resetting Writer's default template as the default

To re-enable Writer's default template as the default:

1) In the Template Manager dialog (Figure 310), click the **Action Menu** icon on the right.
2) Point to **Reset Default Template** on the drop-down menu, and click **Text Document.**

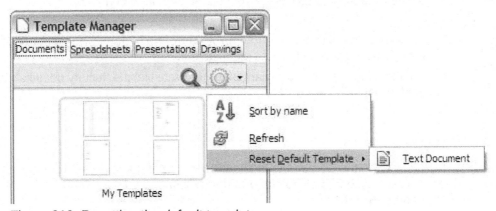

Figure 310: Resetting the default template

This choice does not appear unless a custom template had been set as the default, as described in the previous section.

The next time that you create a document by choosing **File > New > Text Document**, the document will be created from Writer's default template.

Associating a document with a different template

At times you might want to associate a document with a different template, or perhaps you're working with a document that did not start from a template.

One of the major advantages of using templates is the ease of updating styles in more than one document, as described in Chapter 7, Working with Styles. If you update styles in a document by loading a new set of styles from a different template (as described in Chapter 7), the document has no association with the template from which the styles were loaded—so you cannot use this method. What you need to do is associate the document with the different template.

Note	In LibreOffice 3.x, you could use the Template Changer extension to simplify this process. Unfortunately, this extension does not work in LibreOffice 4.x.

For best results, the names of styles should be the same in the existing document and the new template. If they are not, you will need to use **Edit > Find & Replace** to replace old styles with new ones. See Chapter 3, Working with Text, for more about replacing styles using Find & Replace.

1) Use **File > New > Templates**. In the Template Manager dialog, double-click the template you want to use. A new document opens, containing any text or graphics that were in the template. Delete any unwanted text or graphics from this new document.

2) Open the document you want to change. (It opens in a new window.) Press *Ctrl+A* to select everything in the document. Click in the blank document created in step 1. Press *Ctrl+V* to paste the content from the old document into the new one.

3) Update the table of contents, if there is one. Close the old file without saving. Use **Save As** to save this new file with the name of the file from which content was taken. Confirm you wish to overwrite the old file when asked.

Organizing templates

Writer can only use templates that are in LibreOffice template folders. You can, however, create new LibreOffice template folders and use them to organize your templates. For example, you might have one template folder for report templates and another for letter templates. You can also import and export templates.

To begin, choose **File > New > Templates** from the Menu bar to open the Template Manager dialog.

Creating a template folder

To create a template folder:

1) Click the **New folder** button.

2) In the pop-up dialog (see Figure 311), type a name for the new folder and click **OK**.

Deleting a template folder

To delete a template folder:

1) In the Template Manager dialog, select the folder that you want to delete.

2) In the row of icons above the list of folders, click the **Delete** button. A message box appears, asking you to confirm the deletion. Click **Yes**.

Figure 311: Create a new folder

Moving a template

To move a template from one template folder to another template folder:

1) In the Template Manager dialog, double-click the folder that contains the template that you want to move. A list of all the templates contained in that folder appears underneath the folder name.

2) Click the template that you want to move and click the **Move to folder** button above the list of templates (see Figure 309).

Deleting a template

To delete a template:

1) In the Template Manager dialog, double-click the folder that contains the template that you want to delete. A list of all the templates contained in that folder appears underneath the folder name.

2) Click the template that you want to delete.

3) Click the **Delete** button above the list of templates. A message box appears and asks you to confirm the deletion. Click **Yes**.

Importing a template

If the template that you want to use is in a different location, you must import it into a LibreOffice template folder.

To import a template into a template folder:

1) In the Template Manager dialog, select the folder into which you want to import the template.

2) Click the **Import** button above the list of template folders. A standard file browser window opens.

3) Find and select the template that you want to import, and then click **Open**. The file browser window closes and the template appears in the selected folder.

Exporting a template

To export a template from a template folder to another location:

1) In the Template Manager dialog, double-click the folder that contains the template that you want to export. A list of all the templates contained in that folder appears underneath the folder name.

2) Select the template that you want to export.

3) Click the **Export** button above the list of template folders. The **Select path** window opens.

4) Find the folder into which you want to export the template and click **Select**. A copy is placed into the selected folder.

Chapter 11
Using Mail Merge

Form Letters, Mailing Labels, and Envelopes

What is mail merge?

LibreOffice Writer provides very useful features to create and print:

- Multiple copies of a document to send to a list of different recipients (form letters)
- Mailing labels
- Envelopes

All these facilities, though different in application, are based around the concept of a registered data source, from which is derived the variable address information necessary to their function.

This chapter describes the entire process. The steps include:

1) How to create and register a data source.
2) How to create and print form letters, mailing labels, and envelopes.
3) Optionally, how to save the output in an editable file instead of printing it directly.

Creating and registering the data source

A *data source* is a database containing the name and address records (and optionally other information) from which a mailing list may be derived. Although you can create and print mailing labels and envelopes without using a data source, in most cases using one is the best approach. This chapter assumes that you are using a data source.

LibreOffice can access a wide variety of sources of data to create the database, including spreadsheets, text files and databases such as MySQL, Adabas, and ODBC. If the information to be used in the mail merge is currently in a format that LibreOffice cannot access directly, you need to convert it, for example by exporting it to a comma-separated values (CSV) file.

For the following example we start with a spreadsheet with the following column (field) headers: *Title, First Name, Last Name, Address, State/County, Country, Post Code, Sex,* and *Points.* A sample of data is shown in Figure 312.

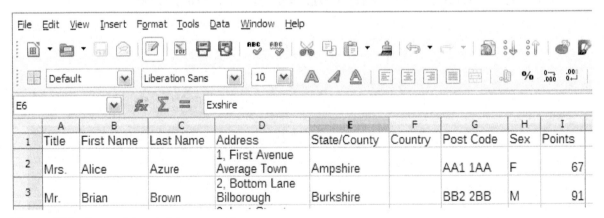

Figure 312: Spreadsheet data example

After being created as described below, for a data source to be directly accessible from within a Writer document, it must be registered. You only need to do this once; after that, the data source is available to all components of LibreOffice.

1) From within any Writer document, or from the LibreOffice Start Center, choose **File > Wizards > Address Data Source**.

2) The choices on the first page of the wizard vary with your operating system. Select the appropriate type of external address book. In this example, it is **Other external data source**. Click **Next**.

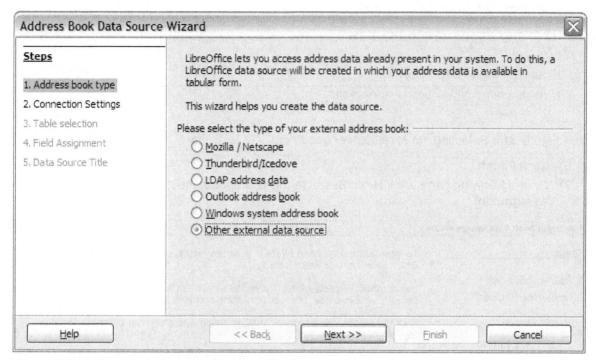

Figure 313: Select type of external address book

3) On the next page of the Wizard, click the **Settings** button.

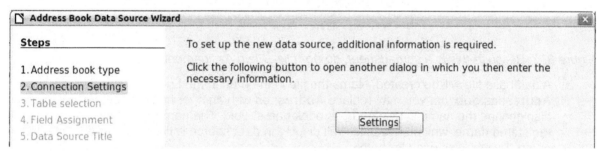

Figure 314: Starting the Settings part of the Wizard

4) In the Data Source Properties page, select the Database type. In our example, it is **Spreadsheet**. Click **Next**.

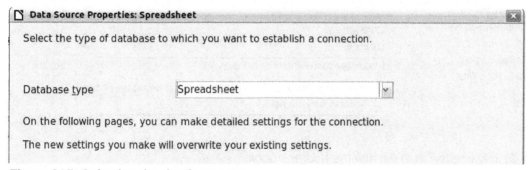

Figure 315: Selecting the database type

---

5) In the next dialog, click **Browse** and navigate to the spreadsheet that contains the address information. Select the spreadsheet and click **Open** to return to this dialog. At this time you may wish to test that the connection has been correctly established by clicking on the **Test Connection** button (not shown in illustration).

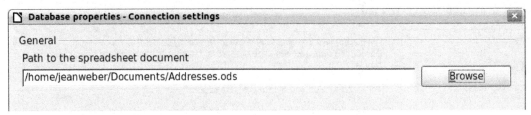

Figure 316: Selecting the spreadsheet document

6) Click **Finish**.

7) On the following page, click **Next**. Because this is a spreadsheet, *do not* click **Field Assignment**.

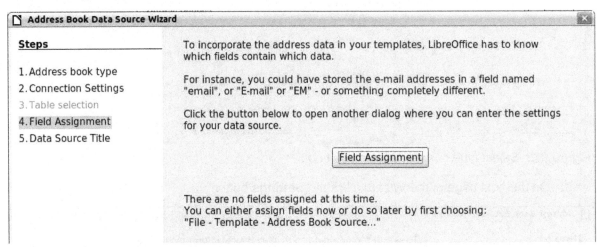

*Figure 317: Because this is a spreadsheet, do **not** click Field Assignment*

8) A database file will be created. Name the file in the path in the Location field. The default is **Addresses.odb**; but you may replace **Addresses** with another name if you wish. You may also change the name in the "Address book name" field. The name in this field is the registered name, which LibreOffice will display in data source listings. In our example, the name "Points" was used for both.

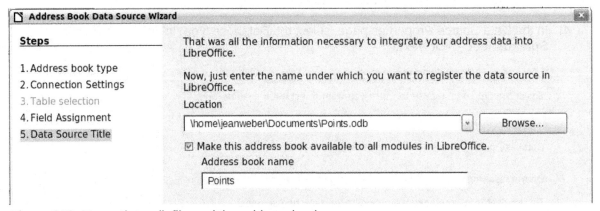

Figure 318: Name the .odb file and the address book

9) Click **Finish**. The data source is now registered.

Deregistering a data source

To remove a registered data source from LibreOffice so it is no longer available for use, as for example an obsolete address list, do the following:

1) Open the *Data sources* window (by selecting **View > Data Sources** from the Menu bar, or by pressing *F4*, or by selecting the Data Sources icon on the Standard toolbar).
2) In the left pane, the *Data source explorer*, right-click a data source.
3) Select **Registered databases** from the context menu.
4) In the *Registered databases* dialog which opens, select the data source to be removed.
5) Click **Delete**, then click **Yes** in the confirmation box which opens.
6) Repeat steps 4) and 5) as required.
7) Click **OK** to close the *Registered databases* dialog.

This does not delete the database from your system. It can be registered again using the methods outlined below.

Re-registering an existing data source

To re-register an existing database file of addresses do the following:

1) Open the *Data sources* window (by selecting **View > Data Sources** from the Menu bar, or by pressing *F4*, or by selecting the Data Sources icon on the Standard toolbar).
2) In the left pane, the *Data source explorer*, right-click a data source.
3) Select **Registered databases** from the context menu.
4) In the *Registered databases* dialog which opens, click the **New** button
5) In the *Create Database Link* dialog which opens, click the **Browse** button and navigate to the database file location and select it. Click the **Open** button to return to the *Create Database Link* dialog.
6) Change the **Registered name** if required.
7) Click the **OK** button to exit this dialog.
8) Click the **OK** button to exit the *Registered databases* dialog.

Creating a form letter

> ### Example: Sending a letter to your customer base
>
> A mail order company organized a campaign to assign credit points to their customers according to the quantity of goods they buy during one year.
> At the end of the year, they want to send a letter to each customer to show the total of credit points collected.

You can create a form letter manually, which is the simplest and most comprehensive method and is described here, or you can use the Mail Merge wizard as described in "Using the Mail Merge Wizard to create a form letter" starting on page 336. If you elect to use the wizard, pay close attention to its current limitations, as identified within its description.

1) Create a new text document: **File > New > Text Document**, or open a pre-existing form letter with **File > Open**.
2) Display the registered data sources: **View > Data sources** (or press *F4*).

3) Find the data source that you wish to use for the form letter, in this case **Points**. Expand the **Points** and **Tables** folders, and select **Sheet1**. The address data file is displayed.

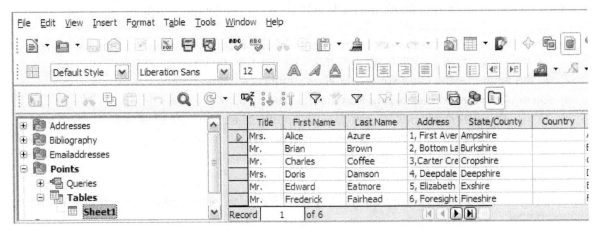

Figure 319: Selecting the data source

4) Now create or modify the form letter by typing in the text, punctuation, line breaks, and so on that will be present in all of the letters.

To add the mail-merge fields where needed (such as names and addresses), click in the field heading and drag it to the appropriate point in the letter.

Note that address lines should be in individual paragraphs, not separated by line breaks as might seem preferable. The reason for this will be made clear in the next step.

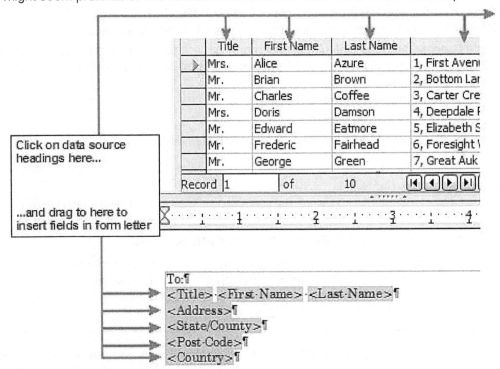

Figure 320: Dragging fields to the body of the form letter

5) Continue until you have composed the entire document. At this time you may wish to consider suppressing any blank lines that may appear in the resulting letters. If not, skip ahead to Step 7.

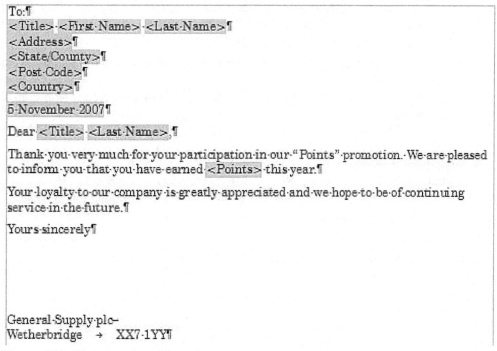

To:¶
<Title> <First·Name> <Last·Name>¶
<Address>¶
<State/County>¶
<Post·Code>¶
<Country>¶

5·November·2007¶

Dear <Title> <Last·Name>,¶

Thank·you·very·much·for·your·participation·in·our·"Points"·promotion.·We·are·pleased
to·inform·you·that·you·have·earned <Points>·this·year.¶

Your·loyalty·to·our·company·is·greatly·appreciated·and·we·hope·to·be·of·continuing
service·in·the·future.¶

Yours·sincerely¶

General·Supply·plc–
Wetherbridge   →   XX7·1YY¶

Figure 321: The completed form letter

6) To suppress blank lines:

    a)   Click at the end of the first paragraph to be suppressed if empty, and then choose **Insert > Fields > Other** to display the Fields dialog.

    b)   Select the *Functions* tab and then click on **Hidden Paragraph** in the *Type* column.

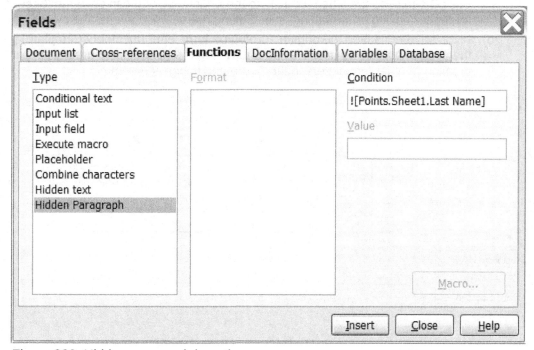

Figure 322: Hidden paragraph insertion

c)   Now click in the **Condition** box and enter the details of the condition that defines a blank address field. It has the general form of:

```
![Database.Table.Database field]
```

where the '!' (NOT) character indicates the negative case and the square brackets indicate the condition.

For example, in our Points database the condition to test if the *Last Name* field is empty would be:

```
![Points.Sheet1.Last Name]
```
as illustrated in Figure 322.

To test for multiple conditions use the operators *AND* and/or *OR* between the conditional statements, for example:

```
![Points.Sheet1.Title]AND![Points.Sheet1.Last Name]
```

d)   Click **Insert**, but do not close the dialog until you have amended all the lines that should be suppressed.

7) The document is now ready to be printed.

a)   Choose **File > Print** and respond with **Yes** in the message box.

Figure 323: Mail merge confirmation message

b)   In the Mail Merge dialog (Figure 324), you can choose to print all records or selected records. To select records to be printed, use *Ctrl+click* to select individual records. To select a block of records, select the first record in the block, scroll to the last record in the block, and *Shift+click* on the last record.

c)   Click **OK** to send the letters directly to the printer. Or, you can save the letters to a file for further editing or formatting; see "Editing merged documents" below.

d)   If you have not saved the original, prototype form letter document (template) previously, then you should do so now. Having a form letter template could greatly simplify the creation of other form letters in the future and is highly recommended.

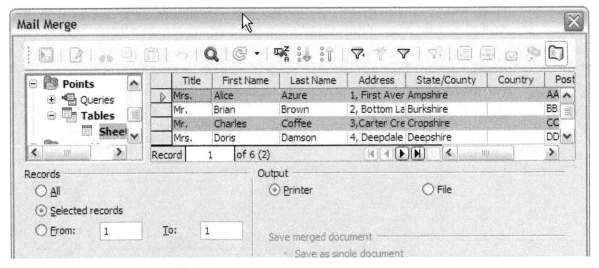

Figure 324: The Mail Merge dialog

Editing merged documents

You may prefer to save the letters to a file, to allow for proofreading or some later formatting. To do this:

1) In the Mail Merge dialog (Figure 324), select **File** in the output section, instead of using the default **Printer** selection.

2) This changes the dialog to display the *Save merged document* section, where **Save as single document** is preselected. You can choose to save each letter as an individual document instead.

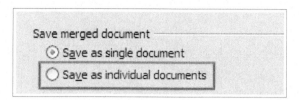

3) Click **OK**. In the Save as dialog, enter a file name for the saved letters and choose a folder in which to save them. The letters will be saved consecutively as separate pages in the single document, or numbered consecutively in individual files if saved as individual documents.

You can now open the letters and edit them individually as you would edit any other document.

Printing mailing labels

Before beginning this process, note the brand and type of labels you intend to use.

Preparing for printing

To prepare mailing labels for printing:

1) Choose **File > New > Labels**.

2) On the **Options** tab, ensure that the **Synchronize contents** option is selected.

3) On the **Labels** tab (Figure 326), select the **Database** and **Table**. Select the **Brand** of labels to be used, and then select the **Type** of label.

4) If you are unable to identify your label product in the list, then you can define the labels you have. Select the **User** setting in the *Type* selection box. Click on the **Format** tab of the Labels dialog. The default settings are shown in Figure 327. Take a ruler and measure on your labels those dimensions illustrated in Figure 325, and enter them into the respective boxes on the left side.

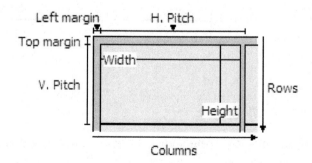

Figure 325: Required information for label set-up

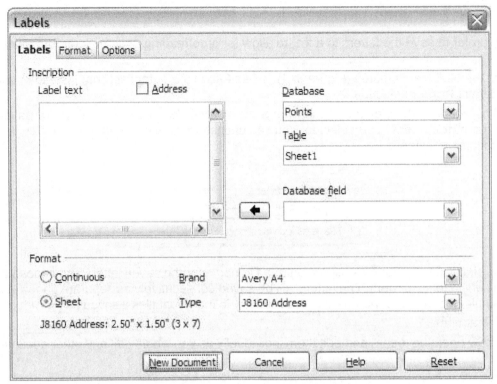

Figure 326: Select Database, Table, label Brand, and label Type

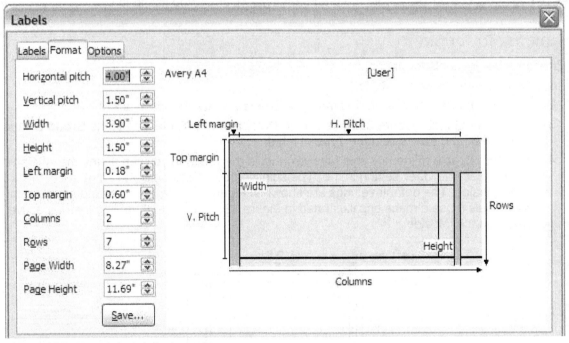

Figure 327: User label default settings

5) You can now save your label template if you are likely to use it again. Click **Save**.

6) In the Save Label Format dialog that opens (Figure 328), enter names for your label **Brand** and **Type**. Click **OK**.

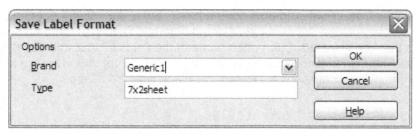

Figure 328: Name and save the label.

7) Click the **Labels** tab. Click the drop-down arrow under **Database field.** Select the first field to be used in the label (in this example, **Title**). Click the left arrow button to move this field to the **Label text** area, as shown in Figure 329.

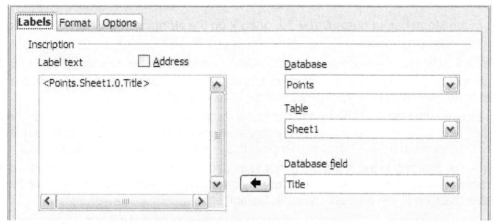

Figure 329: Move fields from Database field list to Label text area

8) Continue adding fields and inserting desired punctuation, spaces, and line breaks until the label is composed. Figure 330 shows the completed label.

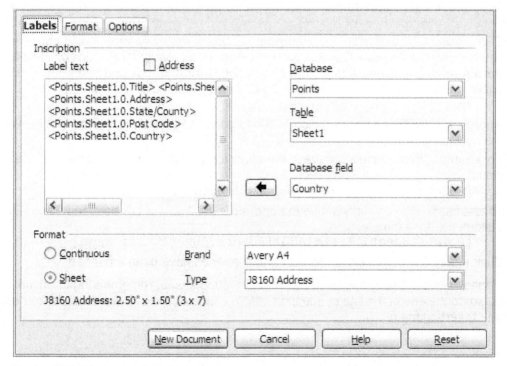

Figure 330: The completed label

9) Click **New Document**. You now have a new, single-page document containing a series of frames, one for each label of the selected type and filled with the data source address fields that you selected. Quite often some of the fields in your address data source will be unused, leading to blank lines in your labels. If this is not important, go to "Printing" on page 331; otherwise, continue with "Removing blank lines from labels".

Removing blank lines from labels

1) First ensure that the label frames are showing the field contents (data source headings), rather than their underlying field names. If this is not the case, then either press *Ctrl+F9* or choose **View > Field Names** to toggle the view.

2) Next, ensure that you can see non-printing characters, such as paragraph marks, line breaks and so on. If these are not already visible, choose **View > Nonprinting Characters** from the Menu bar, or press *Ctrl+F10*, or click on the **Nonprinting Characters** icon ( ) on the Standard toolbar.

   You will now see that address field separation is created by line breaks (⏎), rather than paragraphs (¶). As the suppression of blank address fields depends on hiding paragraphs, not lines, you need to replace line breaks with paragraphs as follows.

3) Click in the first label, at the end of the last data source address field in the first line of the label. Press *Delete* to remove the new line character and then press *Return* (or the *Enter* key) to insert a paragraph marker. Repeat this action for each line in the address.

   If the line spacing in the first label is not satisfactory, you may wish to correct this before proceeding, by modifying the paragraph style associated with the address. Unless you have changed it, the address uses the Default style.

Caution	The objective of step 3) is to replace all line breaks at the end of data source address fields with paragraphs. Sometimes the address data field may be longer than the width of the label and will wrap to the next physical line: make sure that you are not misled by this into deleting and replacing anything other than line break characters.

4) Click again at the end of the first paragraph to be conditionally suppressed and then choose **Insert > Fields > Other**. Select the **Functions** tab and then click on **Hidden Paragraph** in the *Type* column. Now click in the **Condition** box and enter the details of the condition that defines a blank address field. It has the general form of:

   `![Database.Table.Database field]`
   where the '!' (NOT) character indicates the negative case and the square brackets indicate the condition.

   For example, in our Points database the condition to test if the *Last Name* field is empty would be

   `![Points.Sheet1.Last Name]` as illustrated in Figure 322.

   To test for multiple conditions, use the operators *AND* and/or *OR* between the conditional statements, for example:

   `![Points.Sheet1.Title]AND![Points.Sheet1.Last Name]`

   Click **Insert,** but do not close the dialog until all lines have been amended.

5) Repeat for each paragraph to be conditionally suppressed, remembering to advance the cursor to the end of the line in question before changing the last element of the condition and **Insert**ing the result.

Caution

The last paragraph of the label address block ends with a special field, `Next record:Database.Table` (`Next record:Points.Sheet1` in our example), and the Hidden paragraph field **must** be inserted before this field. This can generally be accomplished by clicking at the end of the paragraph and then using the *Left Arrow* key once to skip back over it.

A clue that you omitted this action is the observation that some records have been skipped and are missing from the final output.

6) Remembering that we selected **Synchronize contents** earlier, you should now be able to see a small window containing a **Synchronize Labels** button. Click on this button and the hidden paragraph fields are propagated to all the labels in your document.

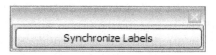

You now have a template suitable for future use with the same data source and type of label. If you wish to save it, use **File > Templates > Save as Template** to save it as an Open Document Text Template (.ott) into the My Templates folder in the Templates Manager dialog.

Printing

1) Choose **File > Print.** The message shown in Figure 323 appears. Click **Yes** to print.

2) In the Mail Merge dialog (Figure 324), you can choose to print all records or selected records. To select records to be printed, use *Ctrl+click* to select individual records. To select a block of records, select the first record in the block, scroll to the last record in the block, and *Shift+click* on the last record.

3) Click **OK** to send the labels directly to the printer.

If you prefer to save the labels to a file, perhaps to allow some later editing such as changing the typeface or paragraph format, then you should select **File** in the output section of the Mail Merge dialog, rather than using the default **Printer** selection. This changes the dialog to highlight the *Save merged document* section, where **Save as single document** is preselected.

In this case, clicking **OK** brings up the *Save as* dialog, where a file name can be entered for the saved labels.

If you did not save the prototype label fields document (template) in Step 6 of the *Removing blank lines from documents* paragraph, then you are prompted to do so now by another *Save as* dialog.

In either case, whether printing or saving to file, despite there apparently being only one page of labels, the printed or saved output will be expanded to include all of the selected records from the data source.

Editing a saved file of mailing labels

To edit a saved file of mailing labels, open the saved label file in the normal way. You will be prompted to update all links. Choose **No** for the following reason: The first label on the page is termed the "Master Label" and all other labels are linked to it. If you update the links, then all labels will end up containing the same data, which may not be what you want.

You can edit individual records in the normal way, by highlighting and changing the font name, for example.

However, you cannot edit all labels globally (for example, to change the font name for all records) by the technique of selecting the entire document. To achieve this result you have to edit the paragraph style associated with the label records as follows.

1) Right-click any correctly spelled word in a label record. Select **Edit Paragraph Style** from the context menu. (Note: If you click on a misspelled word, a different menu appears.)

2) Then from the Paragraph Style dialog, you can make changes to the font name, the font size, the indents, and other attributes.

Printing envelopes

Instead of printing mailing labels, you may wish to print directly onto envelopes. By selecting **Insert > Envelope** from the Menu bar, you may select one of two methods for their production. The first is where the envelope is embedded within a letter, generally as the first page (**Insert** in the Envelope dialog), and the second is where the envelope is an independent document (**New Document** in the dialog). In each case the addressing data may be manually entered, for example by copying and pasting from the letter with which it is associated, or it may originate within an address data source.

This section assumes the use of an address data source and, for convenience, a free-standing envelope. The production of envelopes involves two steps, setup and printing.

Setting up envelopes for printing

1) Choose **Insert > Envelope** from the Menu bar.

2) In the Envelope dialog, select the **Format** tab (Figure 331), where you can select the envelope format to use. You can then arrange the layout of the envelope to suit your requirements, together with the character and paragraph attributes to be used in the *Sender* and *Addressee* areas. These attributes are accessed using the **Edit** buttons to the right of the dialog, next to the word *Format*.

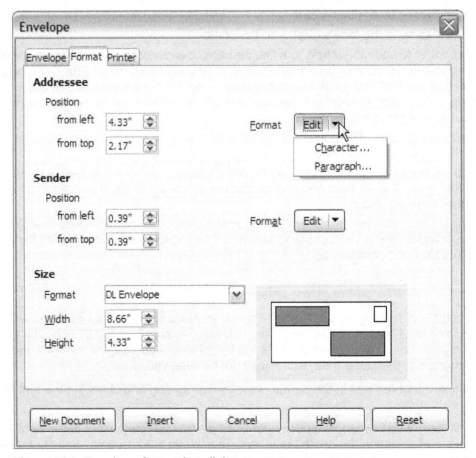

Figure 331: Envelope formatting dialog

Note	If the list of envelope formats in the *Size* section of this dialog does not include the size you need, choose **User Defined** (at the bottom of the list) and specify the envelope size using the **Width** and **Height** boxes.

Tip	At this stage it is only possible to vary the position of the origin points (upper left corners) of the frames that will hold the Sender and Addressee information, but once the envelope has been created, full adjustment of size and position will become possible and you may wish to make some cosmetic adjustments.

3) The next step is to select the **Printer** tab (Figure 332), from where you may choose the printer you intend to use, its setup—for example, specification of the tray holding envelopes —and other printer-related options such as envelope orientation and shifting. You may need to experiment with these settings to achieve the best results with your printer.

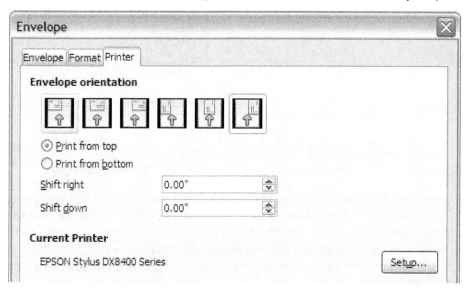

Figure 332: Choosing printer options for an envelope

4) Select the **Envelope** tab (Figure 333).

5) Choose whether or not to add *Sender* information to the envelope by selecting or deselecting the **Sender** option. If wanted, edit the information in the *Sender* box (Sender is the "from" on the envelope).

6) You now have the choice of creating the Addressee fields by dragging and dropping from the data source headings (as described in "Creating a form letter" on page 323, and in particular in Figure 320) or using the facilities of the **Envelope** tab.

7) If you prefer dragging and dropping, then click **New Document**, drag your data source headings into the *Addressee* area on your new envelope and skip to step 10), otherwise continue with the next step.

8) Verify, add, or edit the information in the *Addressee* box. You can use the right-hand drop-down lists to select the database and table from which you can access the Addressee information, in a similar fashion to that described for "Printing mailing labels", paragraphs 3, 4 and 5. The similarity of the method with Figure 329 and Figure 330 will be clear.

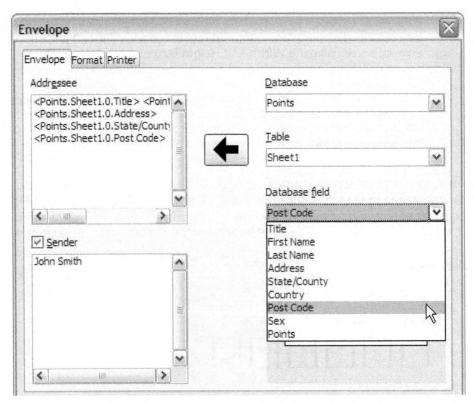

Figure 333: Choosing addressee and sender information for envelopes

9) When you have finished formatting, click either the **New Document** or **Insert** button to finish. As might be expected, **New Document** creates only the envelope template in a new document, whereas **Insert** inserts the envelope into your current document as page 1.

If you don't want to proceed with this envelope, click **Cancel** or press the *Esc* key. You can also click **Reset** to remove your changes and return to the original settings extant when the dialog opened.

You can now modify the placement of the frames containing the sender and addressee information, or make further changes to the character and paragraph attributes (for example, the font) or add a logo or other graphic to the envelope.

Tip	If you frequently print envelopes from the same database onto the same size envelopes, at this point you may wish to create a template from this setup. See "Creating an envelope template" on page 335.

10) Quite often some of the fields in your address data source will be unused, leading to blank lines in your envelope Addressee area. If this is not important, you can skip the next few paragraphs and go straight to "Merging and printing the envelopes" on page 335, otherwise continue as described here.

Tip	The following procedure is very similar to that used for a similar purpose in the section on printing mailing labels. It is reproduced here for ease of reference.

a) First ensure that the envelope is showing the field contents (data source headings), rather than their underlying field names. If this is not the case, then either press *Ctrl+F9* or choose **View > Field Names** to toggle the view.

b) Next, ensure that you can see non-printing characters, such as paragraph marks, line breaks and so on. If these are not already visible, choose **View > Nonprinting Characters** from the menu bar, or press *Ctrl+F10*, or click on the **Nonprinting Characters** icon (¶) on the Standard toolbar.

You will now see that address field separation is created by line breaks (↵), rather than paragraphs (¶). As the suppression of blank address fields depends on hiding paragraphs, not lines, you need to replace line breaks with paragraphs as follows.

c) Click at the end of the last data source address field in the first line of the envelope. Press *Delete* to remove the new line character and then press *Return* (or the *Enter* key) to insert a paragraph. Repeat this action for each line of the envelope.

If the line spacing in the Addressee area is not satisfactory, you may wish to correct this before proceeding, by modifying the paragraph style associated with the address. Unless you have changed it, the address uses the Default style.

d) Click again at the end of the first paragraph to be conditionally suppressed and then choose **Insert > Fields > Other**. Select the **Functions** tab and then click on **Hidden Paragraph** in the *Type* column. Now click in the **Condition** box and enter the details of the condition that defines a blank address field. It has the general form of:

`![Database.Table.Database field]`

where the '!' (NOT) character indicates the negative case and the square brackets indicate the condition.

For example, in our Points database the condition to test if the *Last Name* field is empty would be:

`![Points.Sheet1.Last Name]` as illustrated in Figure 322.

To test for multiple conditions, use the operators *AND* and/or *OR* between the conditional statements, for example:

`![Points.Sheet1.Title]AND![Points.Sheet1.Last Name]`

Click **Insert,** but do not close the dialog until all lines have been amended.

e) Repeat for each paragraph to be conditionally suppressed, remembering to advance the cursor to the end of the line in question before changing the last element of the condition and Inserting the result.

Merging and printing the envelopes

To merge addresses and print the envelopes:

1) Choose **File > Print**. A message box (Figure 323) appears. Click **Yes** to print.
2) The Mail Merge dialog (Figure 324) appears. As with form letters and mailing labels, you can choose to print envelopes for one, several or all address records in the database.
3) Make your selections and then click **OK** to print direct to the printer. To check the envelopes before printing them, see "Editing merged documents" on page 327 for instructions.

Creating an envelope template

When your envelope layout and fields are complete to your satisfaction, you can save the result as a template.

1) Choose **File > Templates > Save As Template**.
2) In the Template Manager dialog, select **My Templates** and click on **Save**.
3) Enter a name in the text input box and click **OK** to save the template.

Using the Mail Merge Wizard to create a form letter

The manual method of creating a form letter described in "Creating a form letter" on page 323 provides the most control over the result and is therefore recommended. If you prefer to use the Mail Merge wizard, the technique is described below.

Open a new document with **File > New > Text Document** and start the Mail Merge wizard using **Tools > Mail Merge Wizard**. The wizard opens, as shown in Figure 334.

Step 1: Select starting document

The wizard gives various options to select your starting document:

- Use the current document.
- Create a new document.
- Start with an existing document.
- Start from a template.

For the purposes of this description, we assume that you opened a new text document. This will ensure that all the steps in the wizard are fully explored, although with experience you may find it more practical to use a draft you prepared earlier, which will allow for the skipping of some steps.

Select **Use the current document** and click **Next**.

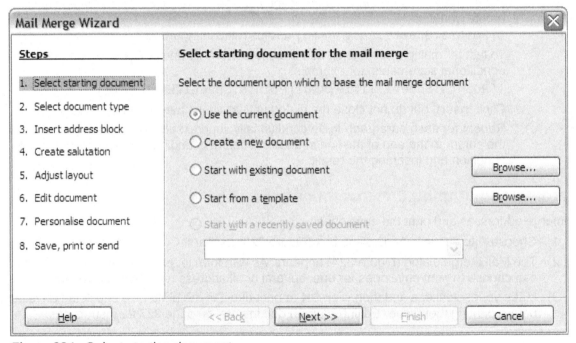

Figure 334: Select starting document

Step 2: Select document type

The wizard can produce letters or, if a Java Mail connection exists, email messages. In this example, we are producing a letter. Select **Letter** and click **Next**.

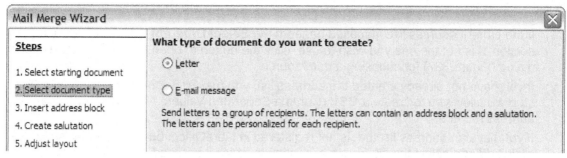

Figure 335: Choose document type

Step 3: Insert address block

This is the most complex step in the wizard. In this step (Figure 336) you will do three things:

1) Tell the wizard which data source to use. The data source must be an existing file; in this example it is the "Points" spreadsheet created earlier.

2) Select the address block to use in the document. This means choosing which fields appear (for example, whether the country is included) and how they look.

3) Make sure that the fields all match correctly. This is very important. For example, the UK English version of the wizard has a field called <Surname>. If your spreadsheet has a column called "Last Name", you need to tell the wizard that <Surname> and "Last Name" are equivalent. This is described in "Matching the fields" on page 339.

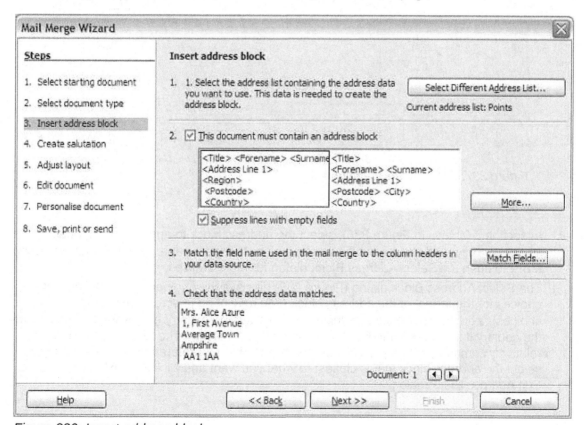

Figure 336: Insert address block

Selecting the data source (address list)

1) If the current address list, identified beneath the **Select Different Address List** button in section 1, is not the one you wish to use, click the button to open the Select Address List dialog (Figure 337) for choosing a data source.

2) If you have not already created the address list, you may click **Create** to do so now. This step will allow you to create a CSV (Comma Separated Values) file with a new list of address records.

   If you have an address list that is not registered in LibreOffice, but which you wish to use, click **Add** and select the file from the location in which it is saved.

   In each of the above cases a new data source (ODB file) will be created and registered.

3) Select the address list and click **OK** to return to step 3 of the wizard. We retain "Points" as our address book for this example. The wizard can also exclude certain records; click **Filter** to choose them.

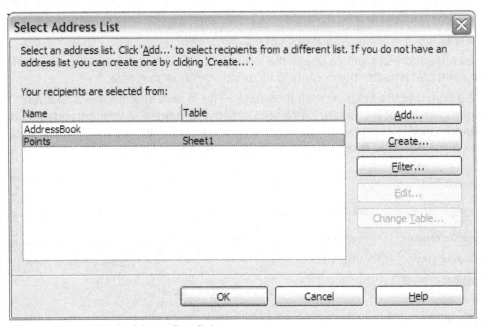

Figure 337: Select address list dialog

Selecting the address block

1) In section 2 (shown in Figure 336), select the address block to appear on the letter, define its appearance, and choose the fields it contains. The main page gives two choices. Click **More** to open the Select Address Block dialog for more choices.

2) The Select Address Block dialog (Figure 338) displays the original two blocks plus other choices for the format of the address block (you may need to scroll down to see all of the choices). You can also optionally include or exclude the country (for example, only include the country if it is not England) in the *Address block settings*. The formats provided are relatively common, but they might not exactly match your preference. If this is the case, select the address block that is closest to what you want and click **Edit**, which opens the Edit Address Block dialog.

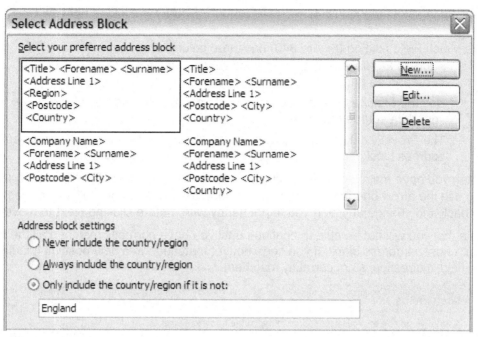

Figure 338: Select address block

3) In the Edit Address Block dialog, you can add or delete address elements using the arrow buttons on the left. To move elements around, use the arrow buttons on the right. For example, to add an extra space between forename and surname in Figure 339, click <Surname> and then click the **right arrow** button.

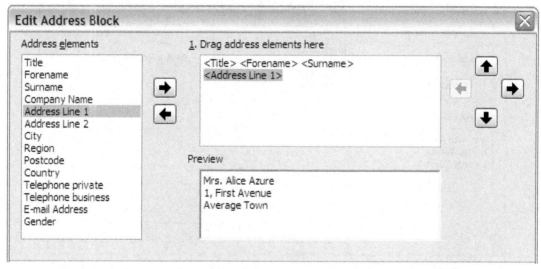

Figure 339: Edit address block

Matching the fields

Finally, it is time to match the wizard's fields with the spreadsheet fields, so that items like <Surname> and "Last Name" match correctly.

1) Look at section 3 of the wizard (shown in Figure 336 on page 337). The box at the bottom displays one record at a time, using the address block format you specified. Use the right and left arrow buttons below that address box to step through the addresses, checking that they display correctly. Do not assume that all the records display correctly, just because one or two do. Check them all if you can, or at least a good proportion.

2) If the addresses do not display correctly (and they probably will not right away), click **Match Fields**.

3) The Match Fields dialog (Figure 340) has three columns:

   - *Address Elements* are the terms the wizard uses for each field, such as <Forename> and <Surname>.

   - Use the *Matches to Field* column to select, for each address element, the field from your data source that matches it.

   - The *Preview* column shows what will be shown for this field from the selected address block, so you can double-check that the match is correct.

4) When you have matched all the fields, click **OK** to return to step 3 of the wizard. Now, when you use the arrow buttons to look at all the addresses, they should all look correct. If not, go back and change anything you're not happy with, before clicking **Next** to move to step 4.

   Note that you will not be able to continue until you have correctly matched all the fields in your chosen address block. If you see <not yet matched> in a field position it indicates that the field in question is not correctly matched.

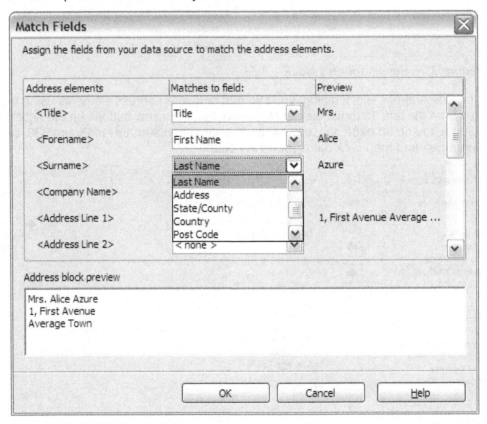

Figure 340: Match fields dialog

5) Notice the option for **Suppress lines with empty fields** in section 2 of Figure 336. Using the Wizard, you do not have to create your own conditional suppression fields.

Step 4: Create salutation

It is possible to create just about any salutation you want in this step.

By selecting the **This document should contain a salutation** option, the *General salutation* list box is enabled. Some general texts are available in the list box, or you can enter your own text, such as *Hello club member*. A preview pane displays your choice.

By also selecting the **Insert personalized salutation** option, further salutation constructs become available.

You can, for example, use a different greeting for men and women. To do this, Writer must have some way of knowing whether a person is male or female. In our spreadsheet (see Figure 312) we had a column called *Sex*. In the section **Address list field indicating a female recipient**, set the **Field name** to *Sex* and the **Field value** to *F*. The Male salutation is then printed for all men and the Female salutation for all women.

Note	You do not need to tell LibreOffice who is a male, because it assumes that all non-female records are males.

If you do not have such a column in your spreadsheet, then you can leave the **Field name** and **Field value** boxes empty and use the customized content of the **Male** list box for the salutation.

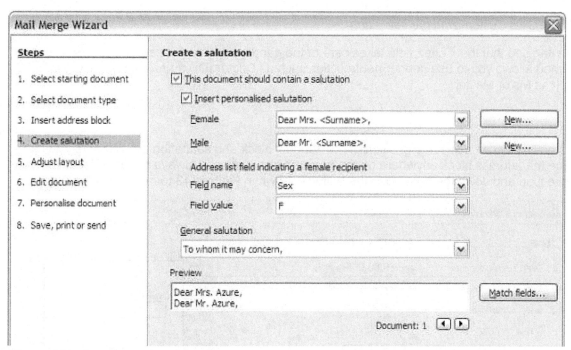

Figure 341: Create a salutation

As an example:

1) Click the New button alongside the Male list box. The *Custom Salutation (Male Recipients)* dialog opens (see Figure 342).

2) Select **Salutation** in the *Salutation elements* listings.

3) Click the **Add to salutation** arrow button to add it to box 1.

4) Open the list box choices for box 2, select an appropriate greeting or type your own text into the list box. Edit it as needed.

5) Select and move across **Title** from the *Salutation elements* listings into box 1.

6) Add a space and then move **Last Name** across.

7) Finally, move **Punctuation Mark** across and select the comma from the choices in box 2.

8) The construct is shown in the **Preview** box.

9) Carry out any final editing. Click **OK**.

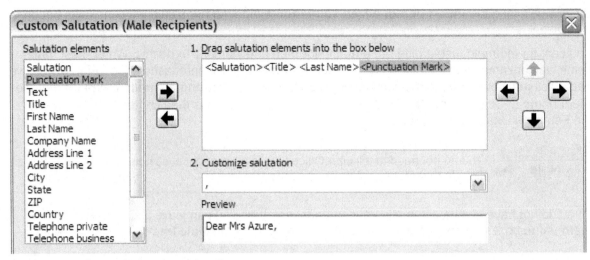

Figure 342: Customizing the salutation

You can see that the <Title> field takes care of the gender aspect of the salutation. Using this method allows you to use gender neutral titles such as Doctor (Dr) and Reverend (Rev), or titles such as Ms or Master.

Step 5: Adjust layout

In step 5, you can adjust the position of the address block and salutation on the page. You can place the address block anywhere on the page. The salutation is always on the left, but you can move it up and down the page. Use the buttons shown in Figure 343 to move the elements.

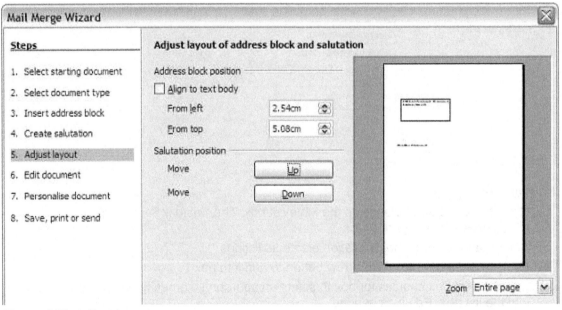

Figure 343: Adjust layout

Step 6: Edit document and insert extra fields

In step 6 you have another opportunity to exclude particular recipients from the mail merge, as shown in Figure 344.

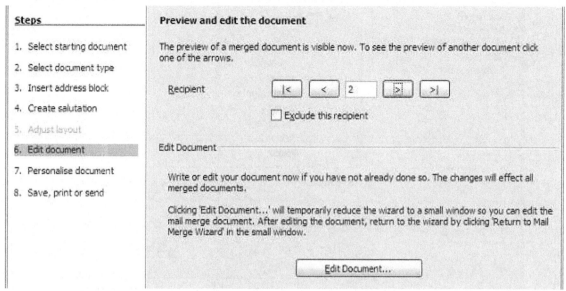

Figure 344: Edit document

You can also edit the body of the document. If you started with a blank document, you can write the whole letter in this step. Click **Edit Document** to shrink the wizard to a small window (Figure 345) so you can easily edit the letter.

Figure 345: Minimized mail merge wizard

You need to perform another important task in this step. The wizard only inserts information from the name and address fields, but you may wish to add additional data. In our example, we want to tell each person how many points they had accumulated during the year; that information is in the database. To do this:

1) Click **Edit Document** in step 6 of the wizard.
2) Choose **Insert > Fields > Other**. The Fields dialog opens.
3) Click the *Database* tab.
4) On the left hand side, select **Mail merge fields**.
5) Under *Database selection* find your data source (in this example, it is *Points*). Expand it to see the fields.
6) Click the field you want to insert (Points), then click **Insert** to insert the field.

   You can insert any number of fields any number of times into your mail merge document.
7) Click **Close** when you are done.

Note	The **Database selection** lists the data source you selected in step 3. All the information you need for the letter must be contained in that data source.

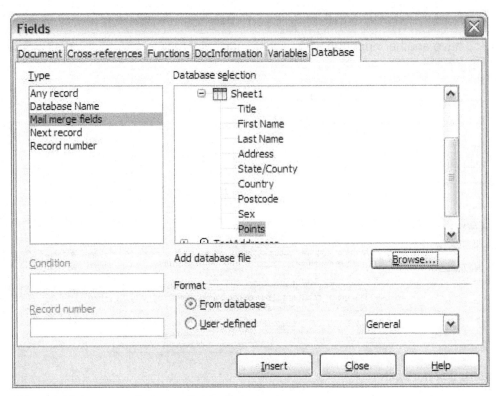

Figure 346: Insert mail merge fields dialog

Step 7: Personalize documents

This step creates all your letters, one per recipient.

Clicking the **Edit individual Document** button here is similar to step 6. The difference is that you now edit a long file containing all of the letters, so you can make changes to a particular letter to one person. In this step of the Mail Merge wizard, click **Find** to open a dialog that allows searches within the document, perhaps for an individual addressee.

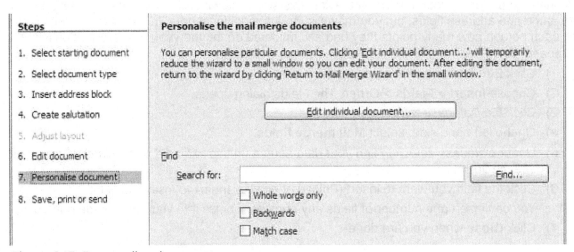

Figure 347: Personalize document

As with step 6, when editing the document, the wizard shrinks to a small window (Figure 345). Click on this window to expand the wizard to its full size.

Step 8: Save, print or send

You have now completed the mail merge process. The last step is to do something with it. In step 8, you can save the original sample letter, save the merged document, print the letters right away or, if you created email messages, send them.

You probably want to save the starting (prototype) document and the merged document. To do this, select **Save starting document** to reveal the **Save starting document** section containing the **Save starting document** button. This button will be active only if the document has not already been saved. Clicking on this button brings up the standard Save as dialog. Once you have named and saved the document you return to the Step 8 dialog as shown in Figure 349.

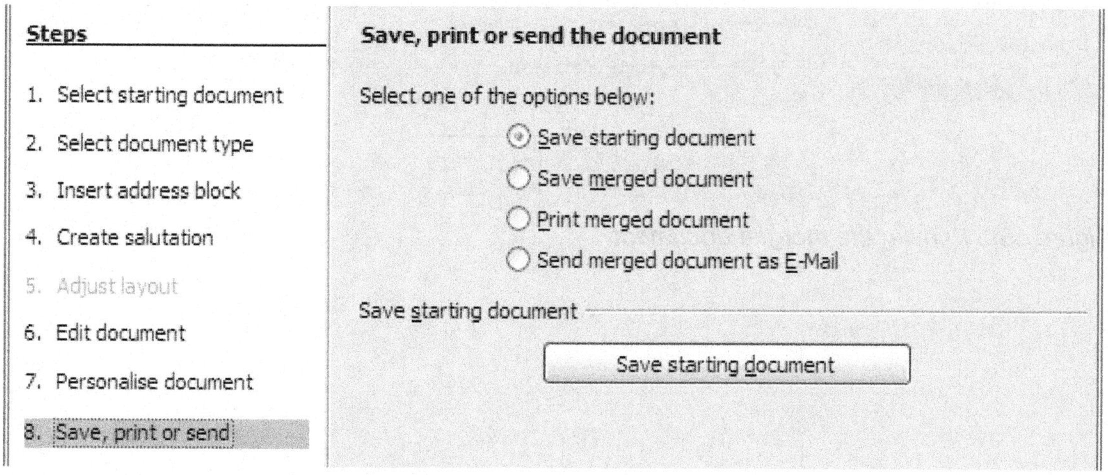

Figure 348: Step 8: Save, print or send

The merged document can now be saved by selecting **Save merged document**. This will reveal the **Save merged document settings** section, from which you can select to save either as one large file containing all the individual, generated letters or as a separate file for each letter.

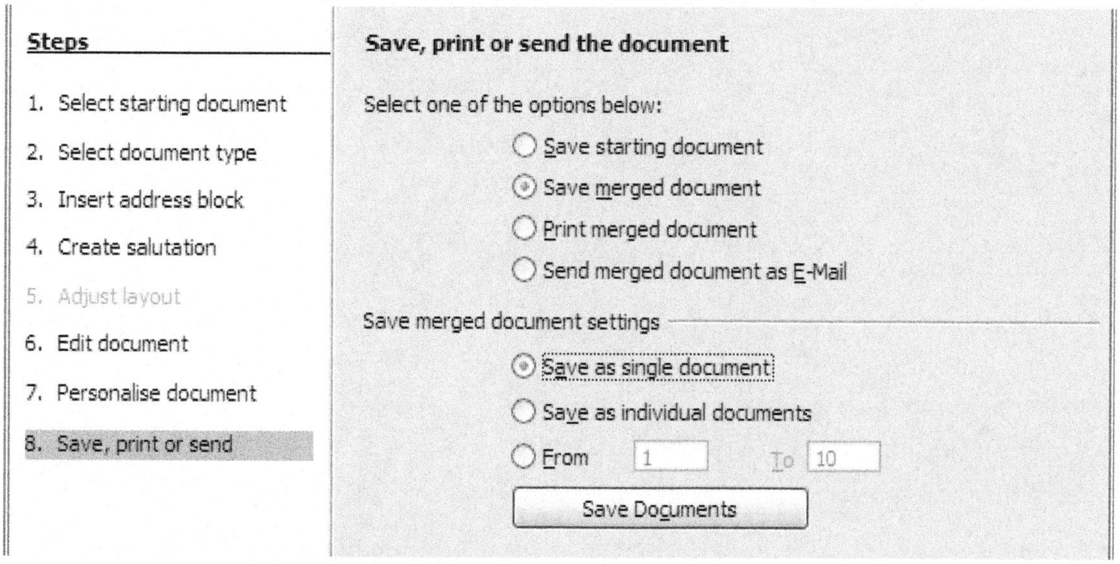

Figure 349: Saving a merged document

When you have saved the merged document, you can print the final letters now or later; and you can still manually check and edit the letters if necessary. If you elect to print at this stage, the dialog shown in Figure 350 appears; it should be self-explanatory.

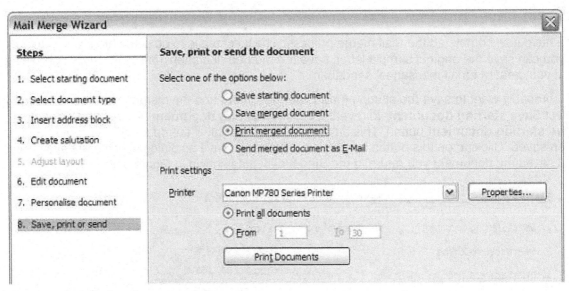

Figure 350: Printing the merged document

Chapter 12
Tables of Contents, Indexes,
and Bibliographies

Introduction

This chapter describes how to create and maintain a table of contents (TOC), an index, and a bibliography for a text document using LibreOffice Writer. To understand the instructions, you need to have a basic familiarity with Writer and styles (see Chapters 6 and 7).

This chapter does not cover all the possible ways to use the features available through the TOC/Index dialog in Writer. Some common usage examples are given.

Tables of contents

Writer's table of contents feature lets you build an automated table of contents from the headings in your document. These entries are automatically generated as hyperlinks in the table. Whenever changes are made to the text of a heading in the body of the document or the page on which the heading appears, those changes automatically appear in the table of contents when it is next updated.

Before you start, make sure that the headings are styled consistently. For example, you can use the *Heading 1* style for chapter titles and the *Heading 2* and *Heading 3* styles for chapter subheadings.

This section shows you how to:

- Create a table of contents quickly, using the defaults.
- Customize a table of contents.

Note	You can use any style you want for the different levels to appear in the table of contents; however, for simplicity, most of this chapter uses the default *Heading [x]* styles.

Creating a table of contents quickly

Most of the time you will probably find the default table of contents (TOC) to be what you need. Inserting a default TOC is simple:

1) When you create your document, use the following paragraph styles for different heading levels (such as chapter and section headings): *Heading 1*, *Heading 2*, and *Heading 3*. These are what will appear in your TOC. Writer can evaluate up to ten levels of headings.
2) Click in the document where you want the TOC to appear.
3) Choose **Insert > Indexes and Tables > Indexes and Tables**.
4) Click **OK**. The result will be a typical table of contents with the entries generated as hyperlinks.

Some tips you may find useful:

- If some of your headings do not show up in the table of contents, check that the headings have been tagged with the correct paragraph style. If a whole level of headings does not show up, check the settings in **Tools > Outline Numbering**. See "Defining a hierarchy of headings" in Chapter 6, Introduction to Styles, for more information.
- The TOC appears with a gray background. This background is there to remind you that the text is generated automatically. It is not printed and does not appear if the document is converted to a PDF. To turn off this gray background, go to **Tools > Options > LibreOffice > Appearance**, then scroll down to the *Text Document* section and deselect the option for **Index and table shadings**.

This change may leave a gray background showing behind the dots between the headings and the page numbers, because the dots are part of a tab. To turn that shading off, go to **Tools > Options > LibreOffice Writer > Formatting Aids** and deselect the option for **Tabs**.

- If you cannot place the cursor in the TOC, choose **Tools > Options > LibreOffice Writer > Formatting Aids**, and then select **Enable** in the *Cursor in protected areas* section.

If you add or delete text (so that headings move to different pages) or you add, delete, or change headings, you need to update the table of contents. To do this: Right-click anywhere in the TOC and select **Update Index/Table** from the pop-up menu.

Caution	If you have **Edit > Changes > Show** enabled when editing your document and you update the TOC, then errors may occur, as the TOC will still include any deleted headings and you may find that deleted text causes page numbering in the TOC to be wrong too. Simply ensure this option is deselected before updating a TOC.

Customizing a table of contents

Almost every aspect of the table of contents can be customized to suit the style and requirements of your document. However, with this flexibility also comes some complexity and it is good to have in mind the desired end result.

Start by clicking in the document where you want the table of contents to appear and choose **Insert > Indexes and Tables > Indexes and Tables** to open the Insert Index/Table dialog shown in Figure 351.

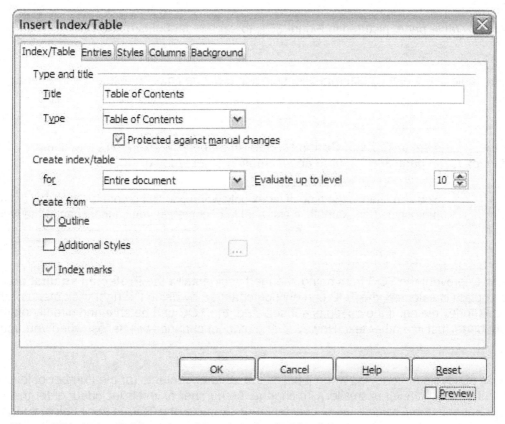

Figure 351: Index/Table page of Insert Index/Table dialog

You can also access this dialog at any time by right-clicking anywhere in an existing table of contents and choosing **Edit Index/Table** from the pop-up menu.

The Insert Index/Table dialog has five pages. Each of them covers a different aspect of the TOC structure and appearance:

- Use the *Index/Table* page to set the attributes of the TOC.
- Use the *Entries* and *Styles* pages to format the entries in the TOC.
- Use the *Columns* page to put the TOC into more than one column.
- Use the *Background* page to add color or a graphic to the background of the TOC.

You can display a preview box, located on the left-hand side of each page, to show as you work how the TOC will look. (If you do not see the preview box, select the **Preview** option in the lower right-hand corner of the dialog). The illustrations in this chapter show the dialog as it appears with the preview box hidden.

Note	The preview box only shows the appearance from settings made on the *Index/Table*, *Entries* and *Styles* pages. The *Columns* and *Background* pages each have their own preview panes.

After making all your changes, click **OK** to apply them. Before clicking **OK**, If you choose to revert to the default settings for the *Columns* and *Background* pages, select each page in turn and click the **Reset** button. The settings on the *Entries* and *Styles* pages must be reset manually; the **Reset** button has no effect.

Index/Table page

Use the *Index/Table* page, pictured in Figure 351, to set the attributes of the TOC.

Changing the title

To give the table of contents a different title, type it in the *Title* field. To delete the title, clear the *Title* field.

Setting the type of index/table

Be sure the *Type* is set to **Table of Contents**. See "Alphabetic indexes" on page 358 and "Other types of indexes" on page 366 for more about creating other types of indexes.

Note	You can change the type of index only when you first create it. Once you define an index type (for example, make a table of contents) you cannot change the type.

Protecting against manual changes

By default, to prevent the TOC from being changed accidentally, the **Protected against manual changes** option is selected, the TOC can only be changed by using the right-click menu or the Insert Table/Index dialog. If the option is not selected, the TOC can be changed directly on the document page, just like other text. However, any manual changes will be lost when you update it.

Changing the number of levels included

Writer uses 10 levels of headings when it builds the table of contents (or the number of levels used in the document, whichever is smaller). To change the number of levels included, enter the required number in the *Evaluate up to level* box. For example, the TOC in this book includes only the first four heading levels.

Choosing the scope of the table of contents

The *for* drop-down list in the *Create index/table* area, allows you to select whether the TOC will cover all the headings of the document (**Entire document**) or just the headings of the chapter where it is inserted. Writer identifies a "chapter" as all the headings between two first level outline headings (normally *Heading 1*).

Creating a table of contents from an outline

The third section of the *Index/Table* page is used to determine what Writer should use to create the TOC. The available choices (not mutually exclusive) are:

- Outline
- Additional styles
- Index marks

By default Writer uses the outline levels; that is, paragraphs formatted with the paragraph styles associated with outline levels in **Tools > Outline Numbering**. In the default document, *Heading 1* has outline level 1, *Heading 2* outline level 2 and so on up to *Heading 10*.

You can change the paragraph styles included in the outline as described in "Defining a hierarchy of headings" in Chapter 6, Introduction to Styles. You can include other paragraph styles in the TOC by assigning an outline level to those styles. To do this, modify the paragraph style definition: go to the Outline & Numbering page for the style, and select the required outline level. Click **OK** to save the change.

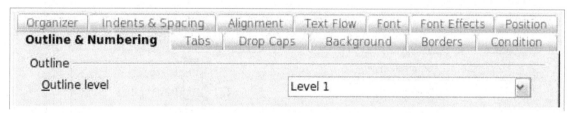

Figure 352: Specifying an outline level on the Outline & Numbering page for a paragraph style

Creating from additional styles

By selecting the *Additional Styles* option on the *Index/Table* page, you can add more paragraph styles to the TOC. This can be useful when you want to include in the TOC an annex (appendix). If the *Outline* option is also selected, the additional styles will be included in the table of contents together with the ones defined in the outline numbering. However, headings included in the TOC using this feature are **not** hyperlinked to the headings in the document body as are headings assigned to outline levels.

Creating from index marks

This selection adds any index entries that you have inserted into the document by using **Insert > Indexes and Tables > Entry**. Normally you would not use this selection for a table of contents. However, if you do wish to use it, be sure to select **Table of Contents** from the drop-down list in the Insert Index Entry dialog (see Figure 359) when you are entering the index entries for use in a TOC, so that Writer can distinguish between them and any index entries intended for inclusion in an alphabetic index.

Entries page

Use the *Entries* page (see Figure 354) to define and format the text of entries in the TOC. The text of each outline level can be styled independently from the other levels by adding and deleting elements.

Click on a number in the *Level* column to select the outline level whose elements you want to format. The *Structure* line contains the elements included in the entries for that level. Elements that can be added to the structure line are displayed just below the structure line, and are grayed out if they cannot be included:

- The **E#** button represents the "chapter number", which means the heading number value assigned in **Tools > Outline Numbering** to a heading style, not just for chapters but also for other levels of headings (Chapter level and level 2 values are illustrated in Figure 353).

- The **E** button represents the chapter (or sub-chapter) text: That is the text formatted with the paragraph style used for each level. In Figure 353, Heading 1 is used for Level 1, Heading 2 for Level 2.

- The **T** button represents a tab stop.

- The **#** button represents the page number.

- The **LS** button represents the start of a hyperlink. (This button appears on the default *Structure* line.)

- The **LE** button represents the end of a hyperlink. (This button appears on the default *Structure* line.)

The **LS** and **LE** buttons are part of the **Hyperlink** button set-up. Each white field on the *Structure* line represents a blank space where you can add custom text.

Figure 353: Assigning a chapter number value (the E# value). The assigned Level 2 value also shows in the preview pane.

| Note | In the Outline Numbering dialog, if you have included any text in the *Separator* **Before** or **After** text input boxes for any given level, then that text will be part of the E# field for that level. You should take care when building the structure line not to create any unwanted effects in the appearance of your TOC. |

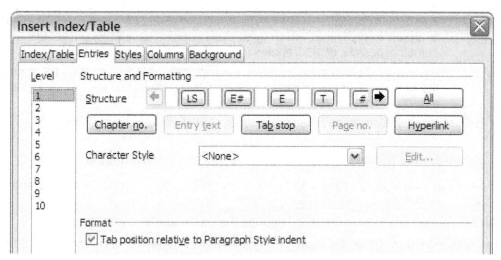

Figure 354: Entries page of Insert Index/Table dialog

Adding elements

To add an element to the *Structure* line:

1) Click in the white field where you want to insert the element.

2) Click one of the active buttons just below the *Structure* line. For example, to add a tab, click the **Tab stop** button. A button representing the new element appears on the *Structure* line.

3) To add custom text, such as the word *Chapter*, type the text in the white field. Don't forget a trailing space.

Changing elements

To change an element in the *Structure* line, click the button representing that element and then click a non-grayed out element that you want to substitute it for, in the row of buttons just below the *Structure* line. For example, to change a chapter number to a tab stop, click the **E#** button on the *Structure* line (it shows then as being pressed) and then click the **Tab stop** button in the row of available elements. To cancel before swapping an element, click in one of the white spaces.

Applying changes to all outline levels

To apply the displayed structure and formatting to all outline levels, click the **All** button.

Deleting elements

To delete an element from the *Structure* line, click the button representing that element and then press the *Delete* key on your keyboard. For example, to delete the default hyperlink setting, click the **LS** button and then press the *Delete* key (*Function+Delete* on a Mac). Repeat this for the **LE** button.

Applying character styles

You might want an element to be a bit different from the rest of the line. For example, you might want the page number to be bold. To apply a character style to an element:

1) Be sure you have defined a suitable character style.

2) On the *Structure* line, click the button representing the element to which you want to apply a style.

3) From the *Character Style* drop-down list, select the desired style.

To view or edit the attributes of a character style, select the style from the *Character Style* drop-down list and then click the **Edit** button.

	The default character style for hyperlinks is *Internet Link* (such as those inserted by **Insert > Hyperlink**), which by default is underlined and shown in blue. The default hyperlinks of TOC entries are set to the *Index Link* character style.
Tip	If you want them to appear underlined and blue, you can select the **LS** button on the Structure line and change the character style selection for TOC entries to *Internet Link*.
	You can also change the attributes for *Index Link* to what you want.

Tab parameters

Clicking on the Tab stop button on the structure line brings up two controls: *Fill character* and *Tab stop position*:

- **Fill character**: select from the three options the tab leader you wish to use.
- **Tab stop position**: Enter the distance to leave between the left page margin and the tab stop.

Tab position relative to Paragraph Style indent

When this option is selected, entries are indented according to the settings of their individual formats. Where a paragraph style specifies an indent on the left, tab stops are relative to this indent. If this option is not selected, tab stops are relative to the left margin position.

Styles page

Use the *Styles* page (Figure 355) to change which paragraph style is assigned to display the text of each level in the table of contents. In most cases, the best strategy is to keep the assigned styles but change their settings as needed to make the TOC appear the way you want.

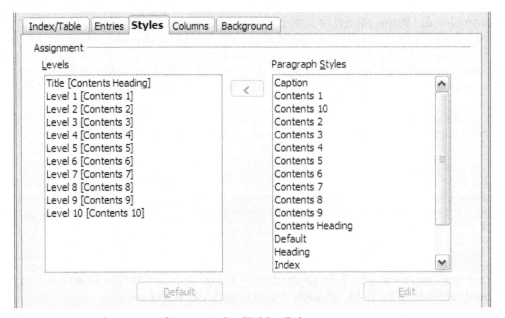

Figure 355: Styles page of Insert Index/Table dialog

To apply a custom paragraph style to an outline level:

1) In the *Levels* list box, select the outline level.
2) In the *Paragraph Styles* list box, click the desired paragraph style.
3) Click the **<** button to apply the selected paragraph style to the selected outline level.

The style assigned to each level appears in square brackets in the *Levels* list.

To remove paragraph styling from an outline level, select the outline level in the *Levels* list box, and then click the **Default** button.

To view or edit the attributes of a paragraph style, click the style in the *Paragraph Styles* list box, and then click the **Edit** button.

Note	Changes to a paragraph style will affect any text in the document that is formatted using this style, not just the format of the table of contents.

Columns page

Use the *Columns* page to change the number of columns for the TOC. Multiple columns are more likely to be used in an index than in a TOC, so this page is described in the section on indexes. See Figure 363.

Background page

Use the *Background* page to add color or a graphic to the background of the TOC.

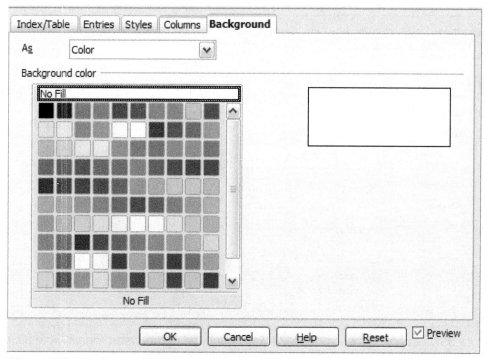

Figure 356: Background page, showing Color choices.

Adding color

To add color to the background of the table of contents, select from the color grid.

Note	By default, the background to the TOC is shaded gray. This setting is in **Tools > Options > LibreOffice > Appearance**, then, in the *Text Document* area, **Index and table shadings** is selected.
	Deselect this option to remove the gray background. Note that by adding a background color, you overwrite this setting anyway.

Adding a graphic

To add a graphic to the background of the table of contents:

1) From the *As* drop-down list, select **Graphic**. The *Background* tab now displays the graphics options, as shown below.

2) Click the **Browse** button. The Find graphics dialog opens.

3) Find the graphic file you want and then click the **Open** button. The Find graphics dialog closes and the selected graphic appears in the graphic preview box on the right-hand side of the *Background* tab. (If you do not see the graphic, select the **Preview** checkbox.)

4) To embed the graphic in your document, clear the **Link** checkbox. To link the graphic to the document but not embed it, select the **Link** checkbox.

5) In the **Type** area of the *Background* tab, choose how you want the background graphic to appear:

   - To position the graphic in a specific location, select **Position** and then click the desired location in the position grid.
   - To stretch the graphic to fill the entire background area, select **Area**.
   - To repeat the graphic across the entire background area, select **Tile**.

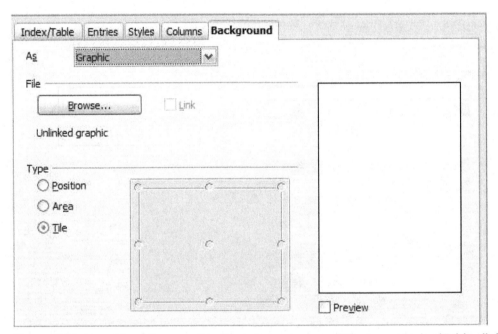

Figure 357: Graphic options on the Background page of the Insert Index/Table dialog

Deleting a color or graphic

To delete color or a graphic from the table background:

1) From the *As* drop-down list, select **Color**.

2) Click **No Fill** on the color grid.

Maintaining a table of contents

This section shows you how to:

- Edit an existing TOC
- Update a TOC when changes are made to the document
- Delete a TOC

Editing a table of contents

To edit an existing TOC:

1) Right-click anywhere in the TOC.
2) From the context menu, choose **Edit Index/Table**. The Insert Index/Table dialog (Figure 351 on page 349) opens and you can edit and save the table as described in the previous section.

	If you cannot click in the TOC, it is probably because it is protected. To disable this protection, choose **Tools > Options > LibreOffice Writer > Formatting Aids**, and then select **Enable** in the *Cursor in protected areas* section. If you wish to edit the TOC without enabling the cursor, you can access it from the Navigator.
Tip	

You can also access the *Index/Table* dialog from the Navigator (Figure 358).

1) Open the Navigator (press *F5*).
2) Click the expansion symbol (**+** sign or triangle) next to **Indexes**.
3) Right-click on **Table of Contents1** and choose **Index > Edit**.

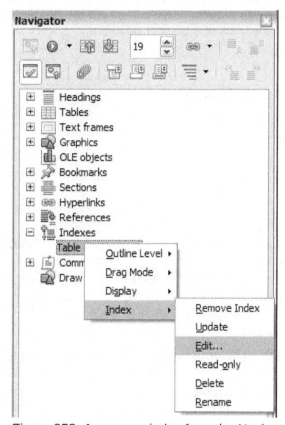

Figure 358: Access an index from the Navigator

Updating a table of contents

Writer does not update the TOC automatically, so after any changes to the headings, you must update it manually. To update a TOC when changes are made to the document:

1) Right-click anywhere in the TOC.
2) From the context menu, choose **Update Index/Table**. Writer updates the TOC to reflect the changes in the document.

You can also update the index from the Navigator by expanding **Indexes** and right-clicking on **Table of Contents1** and choosing **Index > Update**.

Deleting a table of contents

To delete the TOC from a document:

1) Right-click anywhere in the TOC.
2) From the context menu, choose **Delete Index/Table**. Writer deletes the TOC.

Note	Writer will not prompt you to confirm the delete! Use caution when deleting a TOC.

You can also delete the index from the Navigator by selecting **Index > Delete** from the menu shown in Figure 358.

Alphabetic indexes

An alphabetical index (referred to as an index) is a list of keywords or phrases used throughout a document that, if listed in order with page numbers, may help the reader find information quickly. Generally an index is found in the back of a book or document.

This section describes how to:

- Add index entries.
- Create an alphabetic index quickly.
- Customize the display of index entries.
- Customize the appearance of the index.
- View and edit existing index entries.

Adding index entries

Before you can create an index, you must create some index entries.

1) To add a word to the index, place the cursor anywhere in that word. If you want to add multiple words as one entry, select the entire phrase.
2) Choose **Insert > Indexes and Tables > Entry** to display a dialog similar to that shown in Figure 359. When the dialog opens, the selected text appears in the *Entry* text input box. You can accept the word or phrase shown, or change it to whatever you want.
3) Click **Insert** to create the entry.

You may of course open the dialog before selecting text, and then select the text required. After selecting the text, click on the dialog to enter the text into the Entry text input box.

Note	A cursor placed immediately before the first character of a word, or immediately after the last character of a word if it is followed by a space, counts as being in that word.

See "Customizing index entries" below for an explanation of the fields on this dialog.

You can create multiple entries without closing the dialog. For each one:

1) Click at the location in the document that you want to index.
2) Click again on the dialog.
3) Change the entry if needed, and click **Insert**.
4) Repeat steps 1–3 until you have finished with the entries, then click **Close**.

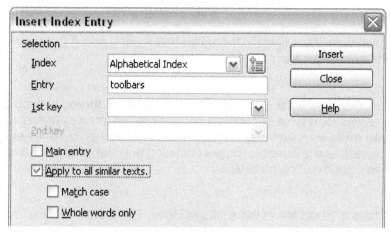

Figure 359: Inserting an index entry

Note	If field shading is active (see **Tools > Options > LibreOffice > Appearance > Text Document > Field shadings)**, when a selected word or phrase has been added to the index, it is shown in the text with a gray background. If the text of an index entry has been changed from the text of the word selected, the index entry is marked by a small gray rectangle at the start of that word.

Tip	You can also open the Insert Index Entry dialog by clicking the Entry icon on the Insert toolbar, as shown in Figure 360.

Figure 360: Entry icon on Insert toolbar

Creating an alphabetic index quickly

Now that you have some index entries, you can create the index.

Although indexes can be customized extensively in Writer, most of the time you need to make only a few choices.

To create an index quickly:

1) Click in the document where you want to add the index and click **Insert > Indexes and Tables > Indexes and Tables**.

2) In the *Type* box on the *Index/Table* page (Figure 361), select **Alphabetical Index**.

3) In the *Options* section, you may want to uncheck **Case sensitive** (so that capitalized and lower-case words are treated as the same word) and uncheck **Combine identical entries with p or pp**.

4) Click **OK**. The result will be a typical index.

Writer does not update an index automatically. If you add, delete, or change the text of index entries, you need to update the index. To do this, follow the steps outlined in "Updating a table of contents" on page 357.

Customizing index entries

Below is a brief explanation of the fields in the Insert Index Entry dialog (**Insert > Indexes and Tables > Entry**) and how to use them.

Index

The type of index this entry is for. The default is **Alphabetical Index**, but you can use this field to create extra entries for a table of contents or user-defined indexes or lists of almost anything. For example, you might want an index containing only the scientific names of species mentioned in the text, and a separate index containing only the common names of species. See "Other types of indexes" on page 366.

Entry

The word or phrase to be added to the selected index. This word or phrase does not need to be in the document itself; you can add synonyms and other terms that you want to appear in the index.

1st key

An index *key* is an entry that has no associated page number and has several subentries that do have page numbers. Using keys is a useful way of grouping related topics. (See "Example of using an index key" below.)

2nd key

You can have a three-level index, where some of the first-level keys have level-2 entries that are also keys (without page numbers). This degree of index complexity is not often necessary.

Main entry

When the same term is indexed on several pages, often one of those pages has more important or detailed information on that topic, so you want it to be the main entry. To make the page number for the main, or most important, entry stand out, select this option and then define the character style for the page number of a main index entry to be bold, for example.

Apply to all similar texts

Select this option to have Writer automatically identify and mark any other word or phrase that matches the current selection. The **Match case** and **Whole words only** options become available if this option is selected. Use this option with care, as it may result in many unwanted page numbers (for minor uses of a word) being listed in the index.

Example of using an index key

An *index key* is a primary entry under which subentries are grouped. For example, you might want to create a grouping similar to this:

```
LibreOffice
        Calc...........10
        Impress......15
        Writer...........5
```

In this example, *LibreOffice* is the *1st key*. The subentries (with the page numbers showing) are the indexed entries. To insert an index entry for the topic *Writer*, on the Insert Index Entry dialog (Figure 359 on page 359), type *Writer* in the **Entry box** and *LibreOffice* in the *1st key* box.

Customizing the appearance of an index

To customize an existing index, *right-click* anywhere in the index and choose **Edit Index/Entry** from the context menu.

LibreOffice 4.2 Writer Guide

The *Insert Index/Table* dialog (Figure 361) has five pages. Any or all of them can be used to customize the appearance of an index.

- Use the *Index/Table* page to set the attributes of the index.
- Use the *Entries* and *Styles* pages to format the entries in the index.
- Use the *Columns* tab to put the index into more than one column.
- Use the *Background* tab to add color or a graphic to the background of the index.

The preview box, located on the left-hand side of the dialog, shows as you work how the index will look. (If you do not see the preview box, select **Preview** in the lower right-hand corner of the dialog.)

After making your changes, click **OK** to save the index so it appears in your document.

Note	The preview box only shows the appearance from settings made on the *Index/Table*, *Entries* and *Styles* pages. The *Columns* and *Background* pages each have their own preview panes.

Index/Table page

Use the *Index/Table* page to set the basic attributes of the index.

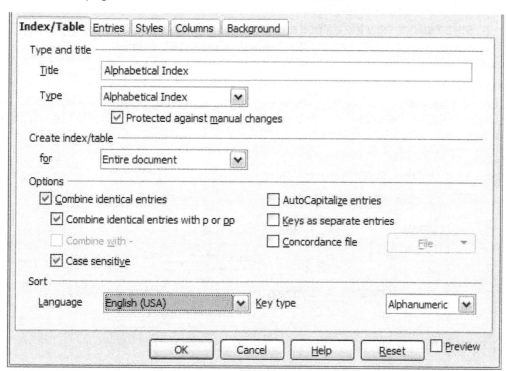

Figure 361: Index/Table page of Insert Index/Table dialog

1) To give the Index a different title, type it in the **Title** field. To delete the title, clear the **Title** field.
2) Be sure the type of index is set to **Alphabetical Index**.
3) To prevent the index from being changed accidentally, select **Protected against manual changes**. If this option is selected, the index can only be changed using the right-click menu, or the *Insert Index/Table* dialog. If the option is not selected, the index can be changed directly on the document page, just like other text, but any manual changes to an index are lost when you update it.

---

4) From the drop-down list in the *Create index/table* section, select **Entire document**. You can also choose to create an index for just the current chapter.

5) Various other options determine how the index handles entries:

- **Combine identical entries.** Defines how identical entries are dealt with. Normally each page number of an indexed word or phrase will be shown in the index; however these can be combined using the **Combine identical entries with p or pp**. If you want a page range displayed, select **Combine with –** (which will produce something similar to 23–31). If you want different entries based on what letters are capitalized, select **Case sensitive**.

- **AutoCapitalize entries.** Automatically capitalizes the first letter of each entry regardless of how they show within the document itself.

- **Keys as separate entries.** For the keys to have their own page numbers, select this option.

- **Concordance file.** Enables a list of words in an external file to be imported (select using the **File** button) and then used within the index. The concordance file has a special file format; for further information, refer to **concordance file** in **Help > LibreOffice Help**. Using a concordance file can speed up production of an index, but unless the words are very carefully selected and you edit the index afterwards, the resulting index can be full of entries for minor mentions of a term, making it less useful than a more selective index.

- **Sort**. Defines how the entries are sorted when displayed. The only option is alphanumeric, but you can define which language alphabet will be used.

Entries page

Use the *Entries* page to set exactly how and what will be displayed for each of the entries. The page is similar to Figure 362. Note that hyperlinking from the index to the location of entries in the text is not available.

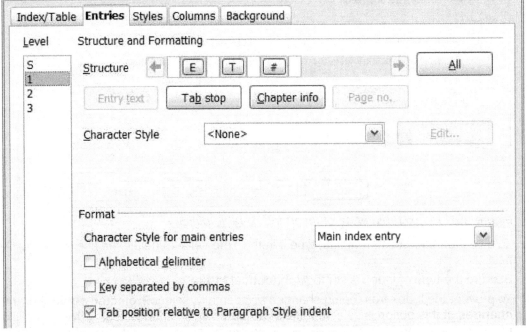

Figure 362: Entries page for creating an alphabetical index

To begin, in the *Level* column select the index level whose elements you want to format. Level "S" refers to the single letter headings that divide the index entries alphabetically when the **Alphabetical delimiter** option is selected in the *Format* section. (You will be able to apply your changes to all index levels later.) The *Structure* line displays the elements for entries in that level. Each button on the *Structure* line represents one element:

- The **E** button represents the entry text.
- The **T** button represents a tab stop.
- The **#** button represents the page number.
- The **CI** button represents chapter information. This is not present by default, but can be added by selecting the **Chapter info** button.

Each white field on the *Structure* line represents a blank space. You can add custom text if you desire.

Adding elements

To add an element to the *Structure* line:

1) Place the cursor in the white field to the left of where you want to insert the element.
2) Click one of the active buttons below the *Structure* line. (For example, to add a tab stop, click the **Tab stop** button.) A button representing the new element appears on the *Structure* line.
3) To add custom text, click in the white space at the position you want to insert it, and type the text. Don't forget a trailing space.

Changing elements

To change an element in the *Structure* line, click the button representing that element and then click the element that you want to substitute it for in the row of buttons just below the *Structure* line. For example, to change entry text to a tab stop, click the **E** button on the *Structure* line (it shows then as being pressed) and then click the **Tab stop** button in the row of available elements.

Deleting elements

To delete an element from the *Structure* line, click the button that represents that element and then press the *Delete* key on your keyboard. For example, to delete a tab stop, click the **T** button and then press the *Delete* key (*Function+Delete* on a Mac).

Chapter Info

This button inserts chapter information, such as the chapter heading and number. The information to be displayed is selected from the **Chapter entry** box menu. This data is determined in the *Outline Numbering* dialog (**Tools > Outline Numbering**).

Applying character styles

Each of the items that can be added to the *Structure* line may be given additional formatting. For example, you may want the page number to be a different size from the rest of the index text. To do this, apply a character style to one of the elements in the *Structure* line.

To apply a character style to an element:

1) On the *Structure* line, click the button representing the element to which you want to apply a style.
2) Select the desired style from the *Character Style* drop-down list. Writer applies the style to the selected element.

To view or edit the attributes of a character style, select the style from the *Character Style* drop-down list and then click the **Edit** button.

Formatting entries

Apply additional formatting using the options in the *Format* section.

- **Alphabetical delimiter**. This separates the index entries into blocks that start with the same first letter, using that letter as a header. For example, if your index begins:

  apple, 4
  author, 10
  break, 2
  bus, 4

  then selecting this option will give you:

  A
  apple, 4
  author, 10

  B
  break, 2
  bus, 4

- **Key separated by commas.** Arranges the entries in the index on the same line but separated by commas.

- **Tab position relative to Paragraph Style indent.** When checked, entries are indented according to the settings of their individual formats. Where a paragraph style with an indent on the left is in use, tab stops will be relative to this indent. If this option is not selected, tab stops will be relative to the left margin position.

Styles, Columns and Background pages

Refer to "Styles page" on page 354 and "Background page" on page 355 for detailed information on these pages.

Columns page

Use the **Columns** page (Figure 363) to change the number of columns for the index.

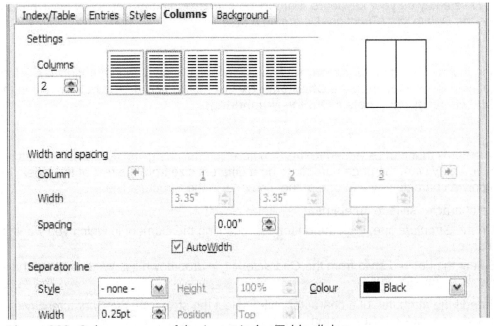

Figure 363: Columns page of the Insert Index/Table dialog

To display the index in more than one column:

1) Either enter the number of columns desired in the box labeled *Columns* or select the icon representing the number of columns.

2) To evenly distribute the columns according to the page width, check the **AutoWidth** box. If it is unchecked, you can manually set each of the following:

    • *Width* of each of the columns

    • *Spacing* between the columns

3) You can choose to have a separator line between the columns:

    • *Style:* The default is *None*, or select from three choices of line style.

    • *Width*: The width (thickness) of the line. The default is *0.25pt*.

    • *Height*: The height of the line, as a percentage of the full column height. The default is *100%*

    • *Position*: Position of the line relative to the columns (top, centered, or bottom) if the height is less than 100%.

    • *Color:* Allows the color of the separator line to be set.

Maintaining an index

To modify the appearance of an index:

1) *Right-click* anywhere in the index.

2) From the context menu, choose **Edit Index/Table**. The *Insert Index/Table dialog* opens and you can edit and save the index using the five tabs described in the previous section.

To update or delete an index, *right-click* anywhere in the index and select **Update Index/Table** or **Delete Index/Table** as required.

Viewing and editing existing index entries

Once you have added the initial entries, you can make some amendments. You can view and edit these using the following steps:

1) Ensure that field shading is active (**View > Field shadings** or *Ctrl+F8*), so you can locate index entries more easily.

2) Place the cursor in the field shading of an existing index entry in the body of your document and select **Edit > Index Entry**. In the case of a changed-text entry, the field shading is immediately before the word. Placing the cursor immediately before a word marked as a text entry will satisfy both selection criteria. Alternatively, right-click at those positions and from the context menu select **Index Entry**.

3) A dialog similar to Figure 364 appears. You can move through the various index entries using the forward and back arrow buttons. If there is more than one entry for a single word or phrase, a second row of buttons with a vertical bar at the point of the arrow head is displayed allowing you to scroll through each of these entries.

4) Make the necessary modifications or additions to the index entries, and then click **OK**.

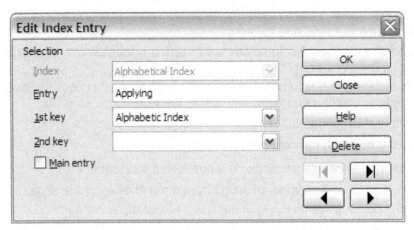

Figure 364: Viewing and editing index entries

Other types of indexes

An alphabetical index is not the only type of index that you can build with Writer. Other types of indexes supplied with Writer include those for illustrations, tables, and objects, and you can even create a user-defined index. This chapter does not give examples of all the possibilities.

To create other indexes:

1) Place the cursor where you want the index created.

2) Select **Insert > Indexes and tables > Indexes and tables** from the menu bar.

3) On the *Insert Index/Table* dialog, in the **Type** drop-down list, select the index wanted.

4) Modify the various pages, which are very similar to those discussed in previous sections.

5) Select **OK** when everything has been set.

Example: Creating an index of figures

Creating an index (list) of figures or tables is easy if the figure captions were created using **Insert > Caption** or manually using a number range variable as described in Chapter 14, Working with Fields.

1) On the *Insert Index/Table* dialog, in the **Type** drop-down list, choose **Illustration Index**. You can change the title of the index to something else; we have used `Table of Figures` as our title.

2) Be sure **Captions** is selected in the *Create from* section, and choose the category of caption. The default for **Category** is *Illustration*; in our example we have used *Figure* for the figure captions.

(The category *Figure* is not supplied with LibreOffice; however, if you have defined it when creating a caption in your document, it will appear on this list. See Chapter 8, Working with Graphics, for more about creating captions.)

3) Under **Display**, you can choose **References** (to include the category, number, and caption text), **Category and Number**, or **Caption Text**. We have chosen **References**.

4) The other pages of this dialog are similar to those described for tables of contents.

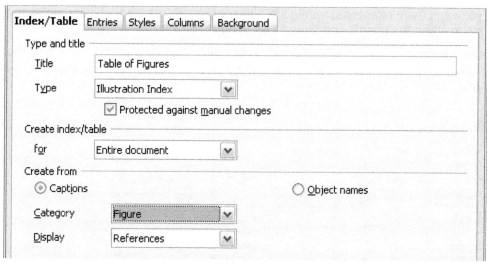

Figure 365: Creating other types of indexes

5) Click **OK**. The result is shown below.

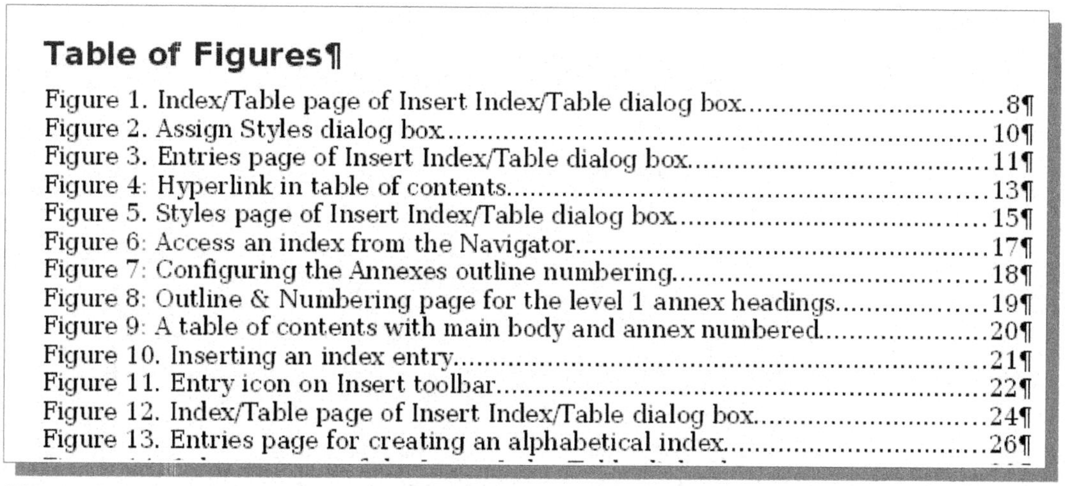

Table of Figures¶

Figure 366: Resulting index of illustrations

Bibliographies

A bibliography is a list for displaying references used throughout a document. These references are either stored in a bibliographic database or within the document itself.

This section shows you how to:

- Create a bibliographic database; add and maintain entries.
- Add a reference into a document.
- Format the bibliography.
- Update and edit an existing bibliography.

Creating a bibliographic database

For most of this section, the database table used is the sample one that comes with Writer. For information on creating a new table in the bibliographic database, see Chapter 8, Getting Started with Base, in the *Getting Started* guide.

Although you can create references within the document itself, creating a bibliographic database allows reuse in other documents and saves a lot of time.

Select **Tools > Bibliography Database**. The *Bibliography Database* window similar to that in Figure 367 opens. The upper part of the page shows all of the records, in a table layout similar to that of a spreadsheet. The lower part of the page shows all the fields of the selected record.

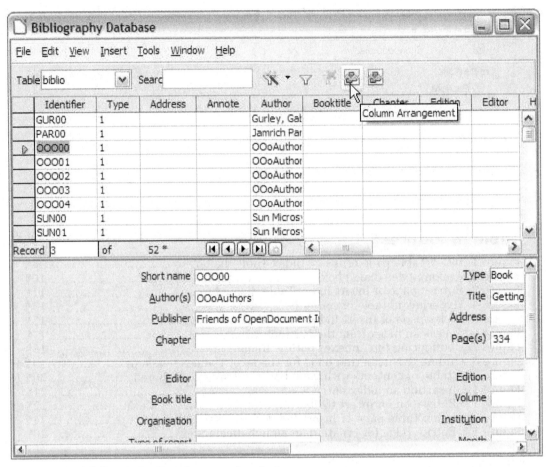

Figure 367: Bibliography Database main window

Filtering records

To set up a filter for specific records within the bibliographic database, select **Tools > Filter** from the Bibliographic Database menu bar. On the *Standard Filter* dialog (Figure 368), choose the fields, conditions and values for the filter and click **OK**.

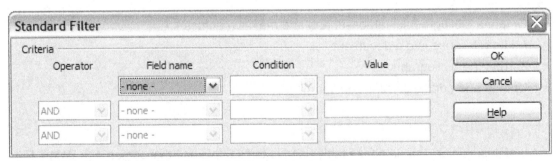

Figure 368: Setting up a filter for the bibliographic database

Changing column details

To change the details of columns in the bibliographic database, select **Edit > Column Arrangement** from the menu bar, or click the **Column Arrangement** button near the top of the window (see Figure 367). The *Column Layout for Table biblio* dialog (Figure 369) is displayed. This allows you to change which fields are allocated to which columns. As an example, you can select to have *Author* data go into the *Identifier* column, by changing the destination in the drop-down list. The *Short name* data column destination sets to *None* automatically, as you can't set duplicate destinations for data.

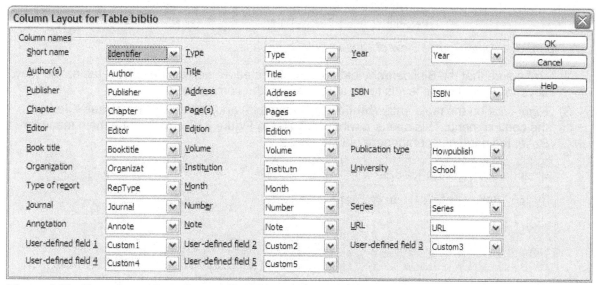

Figure 369: Changing column layout for bibliographic database

Changing the data source

To change the data source in use (for example, if you have more than one bibliographic database for different purposes), select **Edit > Choose Data Source** from the menu bar, or click the **Data Source** button near the top of the window. The *Choose Data Source* dialog (Figure 370) is displayed.

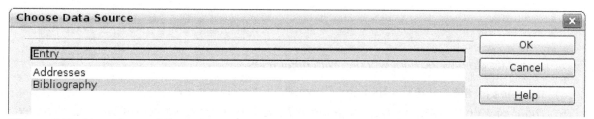

Figure 370: Choosing a different data source for the bibliographic database

Changing field details

You can make changes to the bibliography database (for example, rename fields or change the length of fields) by doing the following:

1) In the main document (not the Bibliography Database window), press *F4* or click **View > Data Sources** to open the data source window, similar to Figure 371.

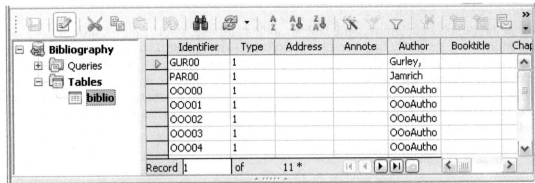

Figure 371: Data Source view of Bibliography database

2) Make sure that the Bibliography database is selected as well as the correct table. You may have to expand some levels to be able to select the correct ones.

3) *Right-click* on the table entry (**biblio** in the example) and select **Edit Database File** from the context menu. This opens a window similar to Figure 372, which is the main menu for Base, the database component of LibreOffice.

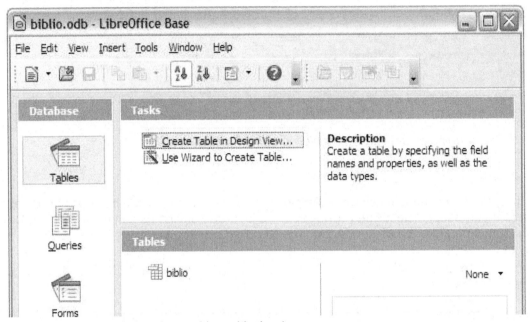

Figure 372: Main window for working with databases

4) If **Tables** (in the *Database* section) is not selected, select it now.

5) *Right-click* on the **biblio** table name in the *Tables* section and select **Edit** from the context menu to display the *Table Design* window similar to that shown in Figure 373.

6) You can now select each of the fields. You can select the text in the **Field Name** cell and change the entry as required. Clicking in the **Field Type** cell, allows you to open a selection menu to change the data type in that cell. In the *Field Properties* section, the data properties can be modified. For each data field selected, an explanation of that field appears in a window to the right of the section.

7) When finished, you will be asked to confirm that you want the changes saved.

| **Note** | For more information on how to use LibreOffice's database features, see Chapter 8, Getting Started with Base, in the *Getting Started* guide. |

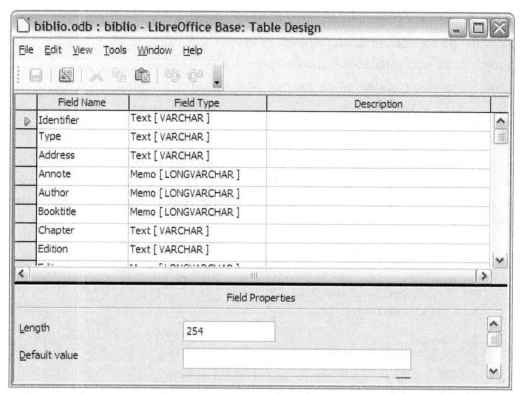

Figure 373: Modify table properties window

Adding entries to the database

Use the *Bibliography Database* dialog (**Tools > Bibliography Database**) to add entries to the database:

1) You can add records directly into the database using the fields in the lower section of the dialog shown in Figure 367 on page 368.

2) Select **Insert > Record** from the menu bar of the *Bibliography Database* dialog, or click the **Insert Record** icon ( ) to the left of the horizontal scroll bar.

3) Enter a name for the entry in the **Short Name** box. Complete other fields as required. Use the *Tab* key to move between fields.

    It is best to use a unique name in the *Short name* field. This field is used when inserting entries into documents.

4) To complete the entry, move to the last field and press *Tab* once more.

If your document requires [Author, date] style citations, use the *Short name* field of the database to record the information in the required format.

Maintaining entries in the database

To maintain entries in the database, use the *Bibliography Database* dialog (**Tools > Bibliography Database**). Click on the appropriate record and modify the fields as appropriate.

Modified entries are saved automatically to the database when the cursor moves off the record.

Adding references (citations) into a document

Writer supports two methods of adding references to your document:

- From a bibliography database, such as the one built in to Writer.
- Directly from the keyboard when you may have documents in front of you.

Entering references from a database

To add references from the bibliographic database into a document:

1) Place the cursor where you want the reference to appear.
2) From the main menu, choose **Insert > Indexes and Tables > Bibliographic Entry**.
3) In the *Insert Bibliographic Entry* dialog, choose **From bibliography database** at the top of the dialog.

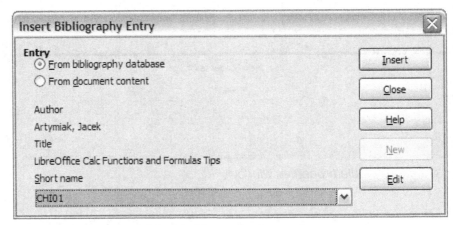

Figure 374: Inserting bibliographic entries into a document

4) Select the reference from the *Short name* drop-down list near the bottom of the dialog. The Author and Title of the selected reference are shown in the middle of the dialog, to help you verify that it is the reference you want.
5) To insert the reference into the document, click **Insert**.
6) You can keep the dialog open and insert another reference into the document; you don't need to close and reopen it.
7) When you have finished inserting all the references, select **Close**.

Entering references from documents

You may choose to enter your bibliographic entries directly into the document, instead of from an external database. For example, you may not be working on your own computer.

Click in the document where you want to add the entry.

1) Select **Insert > Indexes and Tables > Bibliography Entry**.
2) In the dialog that opens, select the **From document content** option.
   a) Select **New.**
   b) In the *Define Bibliography Entry* dialog, complete all the fields which are relevant to your entry. Type a unique name in the *Short name* text entry box, because the *Insert Bibliography Entry* dialog uses this entry for the citation.
   c) An entry must be selected from the menu in the **Type** input box in order to enable the **OK** button.
   d) Click **OK** when all the fields wanted are completed.

e) Click **Insert** to add the *Short name* field to the document

f) Click in each location you wish to add an entry and repeat this sequence

3) Click **Close**.

You may of course re-use an entry in your document, by restarting the sequence above, and then selecting the *Short name* required, from the current list of entries, instead of selecting to add a new entry

Editing a reference

You can edit a reference in the following manner:

1) *Right-click* on the entry (the cursor then displays to the left of the entry).

2) From the context menu which opens, select **Bibliography Entry**.

   The Edit Bibliography Entry dialog opens, similar to below.

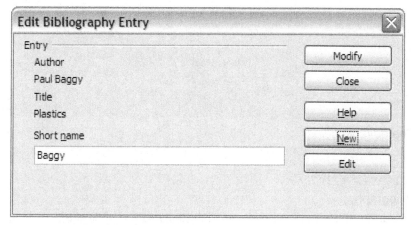

Figure 375: Edit the citation entry

3) To quickly edit only the *Short name*, click on the text box, alter the entry and then click **Modify**. The dialog saves the change and closes.

4) To edit more of the entry, click on **Edit** to open the *Define Bibliography Entry* dialog similar to the graphic shown below (Figure 376).

5) You can change the citation to attribute by choosing a different Short name from the drop-down list.

6) Make any changes required and then click **OK** to return to the dialog of Figure 375.

7) If you are satisfied with your changes, click **Modify** to accept the changes and exit the dialog.

Whatever the source of the citation, the modified references are stored in the document. If the source was a bibliography database, that database remains unmodified.

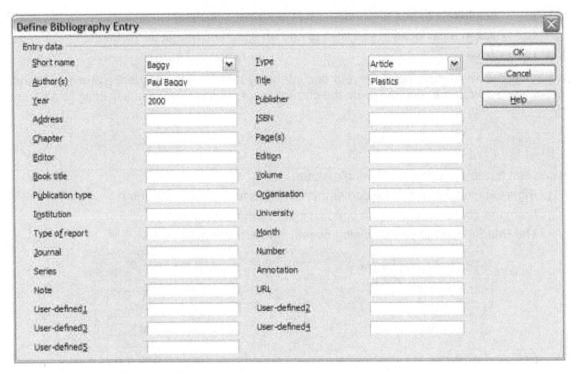

Figure 376: The editable fields

Creating the bibliography

To create the bibliography:

1) Place the cursor at the point where you wish to insert the bibliography.

2) Select **Insert > Indexes and Tables > Indexes and Tables** and change the *Type* to **Bibliography**, to display a dialog similar to that shown in Figure 377.

The *Insert Index/Table* dialog has five pages.

Index/Table page

Writer supports two ways of displaying references (citations) in the text of a document:

- Using the text recorded in the *Short name* field of each bibliographic entry, for example [GUR00].

- By numbering the referenced documents in the sequence they occur in the text, for example [1].

Tip	To specify which citation style is used in the document, use the **Index/Table** page on the *Insert Index/Table* dialog, described on page 375.

Formatting the bibliography involves choices made in two places:

- *Insert Index/table* dialog (covered in this section)

- *Bibliography 1* paragraph style (see page 377)

The basic settings are selected on this page.

1) To give the bibliography a title, enter it in the **Title** field. (A title is not required.)

2) You can protect the bibliography from being changed accidentally, by checking **Protected against manual changes**. If this option is selected, the bibliography can only be changed

using the right-click menu or the *Insert Table/Index* dialog. If the option is not selected, the bibliography can be changed directly on the document page, just like other text, but any manual changes will be lost when you update the bibliography.

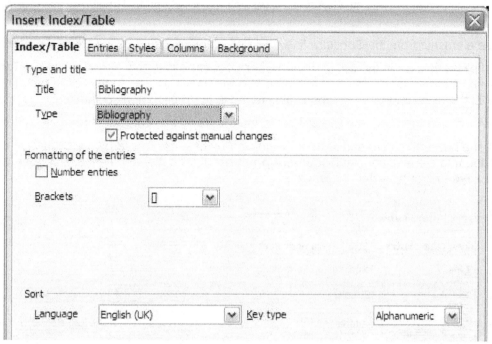

Figure 377: Inserting a bibliography

3) To have the bibliographic entries (citations) numbered within the body of the document (for example, [1], [2]...), select **Number entries**. If, however, you wish to have the *Short name* field contents (from the database) appear in the document, deselect this option.

4) Select the type of brackets that you want for the referenced entries shown within the body of the document.

5) Define the sorting you require. Currently only alphanumeric sorting is supported. Sorting by the sequence that entries appear in the text is done on the *Entries* page.

Entries page

The structure of this page (see Figure 378), is similar to that for tables of contents and for indexes.

Each type of source that you use when creating your document will have its own unique works cited format. The Modern Language Association (MLA) documentation format sets out the recommended order for these citations. For example, see http://www.mattawanschools.org/.

You can define how the entry will appear, based on its source, by selecting from the **Type** list of entries, or simply apply the same format to all entries by selecting the **All** button.

Each entry in the *Type* list has a default structure format.

The *Structure* of the entry is based on the fields available in the bibliographic database. The ones shown by default for *Article* in the **Type** list are:

Sh – Short name

Au – Author

Ti – Title

Ye – Year

Note	In this current release of LibreOffice Writer, version 4.0.2, only **Book** from the **Type** list is editable. Although you can add and remove items from the structure line for other types, as described in the instructions below, it has no effect on the index created. The index will be created with the default entries shown above. Bug 63511.

To remove elements from the *Structure* line, click the element then click the **Remove** button.

To add an element, click in the *Structure* line where it is to be inserted. Select either the **Tab stop**, or an element in the drop-down list to the left of the **Insert** button, and then click **Insert**. The elements in the drop-down list are those fields found in the *Bibliography Database*.

All the elements on the *Structure* line can be formatted using the **Character Style** selection list.

To determine how entries are sorted, modify the *Sort by* options. To sort by the sequence that entries appear in the text, choose **Document position**. To sort alphanumerically, choose **Content**. Use **Sort keys** to group similar references.

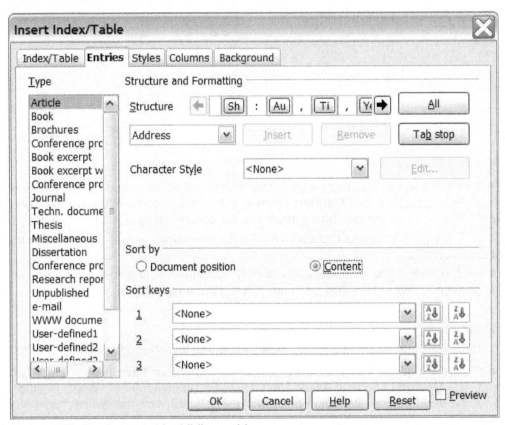

Figure 378: Entries page for bibliographies

Styles, Columns and Background pages

Refer to "Styles page" on page 354, "Columns page" on page 364 and "Background page" on page 355 for detailed information on these pages.

Generating the bibliography

To generate the bibliography so that it appears in your document, click **OK.** The *Insert Index/Table* dialog closes and the bibliography appears in your document.

Defining the paragraph style for the bibliography

You can modify the *Bibliography 1* paragraph style to suit your requirements. For example, to number the entries in the bibliography list, you need to define a numbering style and link that numbering style to the *Bibliography 1* paragraph style. To do this:

1) On the *Styles and Formatting* window, click on the **List Styles** icon. You can either define a new list style or modify one of those supplied. In this example, we will modify the *Numbering 1* style. *Right-click* on *Numbering 1* and choose **Modify** from the context menu.

2) On the *Numbering Style* dialog, go to the **Options** page. In our example we want to have the numbers enclosed in square brackets. To do this, type **[** in the **Before** box and **]** in the **After** box, as shown in Figure 379.

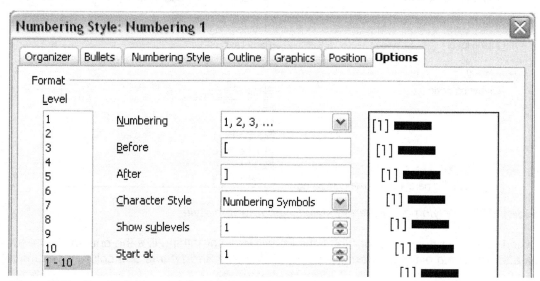

Figure 379: Specifying square brackets before and after the number in a list

3) Now go to the **Position** page of the *Numbering style* dialog. In the **Spacing to text** box, specify how much indentation you want for the second and following lines of any item in the bibliography list of your document. Often you will need to experiment a bit to see what is the best setting. In our example (Figure 380), we have chosen **1 cm.**

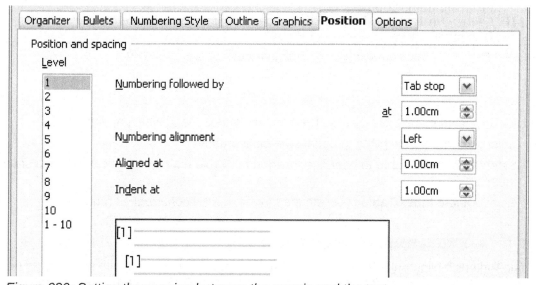

Figure 380: Setting the spacing between the margin and the text

---

4) Click **OK** to save these settings and close the *Numbering Style* dialog. Return to the **Styles and Formatting** window, click on the **Paragraph Styles** icon, choose **All Styles** from the list at the bottom of that window, then *right-click* on **Bibliography 1** and choose **Modify**.

5) On the *Paragraph Style* dialog, go to the **Outline & Numbering** tab and select **Numbering 1** from the drop-down list. (See Figure 381.) Click **OK** to save this change to the *Bibliography 1* paragraph style.

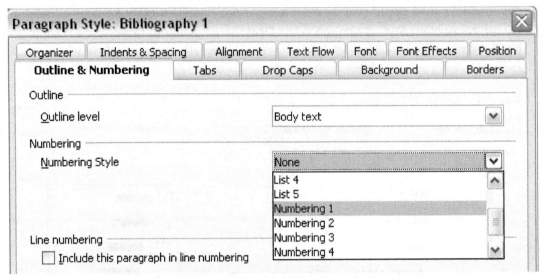

Figure 381: Applying a numbering style to a paragraph style

Now when you generate the bibliography, the list will look something like the one shown below for a book after removing elements from the structure line (the *Short name* and colon, for example).

Bibliography

[1] Gurley, Gabriel, A Conceptual Guide to OpenOffice.org 2 for Windows and Linux, 2007
[2] OOoAuthors, Getting Started with OpenOffice.org 2.x, 2007
[3] Bain, Mark Alexander, Learn OpenOffice.org Spreadsheet Macro Programming, 2006
[4] Leete, Gurdy; Finkelstein, Ellen; Leete, Mary, OpenOffice.org for Dummies, 2003

Figure 382: Result of changing settings for Bibliography 1 paragraph style

Updating, editing and deleting an existing bibliography

Right-click anywhere in the bibliography. Then, in the context menu which opens:

- Select **Update Index/Table** to update the bibliography.
- Select **Edit Index/Table** to open the *Insert Index/Table* dialog so you can edit and save the table.
- Select **Delete Index/Table** to delete the table *without a confirmation request*.

Tools for working with bibliographies

If you find Writer's bibliography feature too limited, try Bibus (http://bibus-biblio.sourceforge.net/wiki/index.php/Main_Page) or Zotero (http://www.zotero.org/). Both programs are free and open source and are reported to work well with Writer.

Chapter 13
Working with Master
Documents

Why use a master document?

A master document (*.ODM) can be considered as a container that joins separate text documents (*.ODT) into one larger document, and unifies the formatting, table of contents (TOC), bibliography, index, and other tables or lists. Master documents are typically used for producing long documents such as a book, a thesis, or a long report.

A master document is especially useful in these situations:

- When graphics, spreadsheets, or other material cause the file size or number of pages to become quite large; writing, reviewing, and editing may be easier when done on subsets of the full document.
- When different people are writing different chapters or other parts of the full document.
- When files will be published as stand-alone documents as well as becoming part of a larger document. The chapters of this Writer Guide are an example of this.
- When subdocuments are used in more than one final document.

You can use several methods to create master documents. Each method has its advantages and disadvantages. Which method you choose depends on what you are trying to accomplish. The different methods are described in this chapter, along with suggestions on when to use each one.

Tip	A master document is not always the best method to use in any of the situations given above. You may find that an ordinary document (.ODT) containing sections linked to other files may do the job just as well. For more about using sections to combine files, see Chapter 4, Formatting Pages.

Styles in master documents and subdocuments

A stand-alone document becomes a subdocument when it is linked into a master document. A document can be used as a subdocument in several master documents. Each master document may have different style definitions (font, type size, color, page size, margins, and so on), which affect the appearance of the final document, but the individual documents retain their original characteristics.

The relationship between styles in a master document and its subdocuments is as follows:

- Custom styles used in subdocuments, such as paragraph styles, are automatically imported into the master document.
- If more than one subdocument uses a custom style with the same name (for example, myBodyText), then only the one in the first subdocument to be linked is imported into the master document.
- If a style with the same name exists in the master document and in the subdocuments (for example, Default Style), then the style is applied as defined in the master document.
- The styles in the subdocuments are only changed in the master document, so when a subdocument is opened for editing the original styles are not affected.

Tip	If you use the same document template for the master document and its subdocuments, the subdocuments will look the same when they are loaded into the master document as they do when viewed as individual files. When you modify or create a style, make the change in the template (not in the master document or any of the subdocuments). Then when you reopen the master document or a subdocument, the styles will update from the template.

Creating a master document: scenarios

Which you choose from the three most common scenarios for creating a master document depends on the current state of your document:

- You have one existing document (a book) that you want to split into several subdocuments (chapters) that will be controlled by the master document.

- You have several existing documents (chapters) by one or more authors that you want to combine into one book, controlled by the master document.

- You have no existing documents but intend to write a long book containing several chapters, possibly by multiple authors.

We will look at each of these scenarios in turn.

Splitting a document into master and subdocuments

When you have one existing document that you want to split into a master document and several subdocuments, you can have Writer split the document automatically at headings with an outline level of your choice.

Although this method is quick and easy, some cleanup work may be necessary:

- The page style of the first page (and possibly all pages) in each subdocument reverts to Default Style. If you are using custom page styles and you want the subdocuments to use the same page layout, whether part of the master document or standalone, you will need to reapply at least the first page style.

- The automatically generated file names for the subdocuments are *maindocnameX.odt*, where X is 1, 2, 3, and so on. If you have a Preface or other "chapter" starting with a *Heading 1* before Chapter 1, the file names will not directly correspond to the chapter numbers. You may wish to rename the subdocuments; see "Adding, deleting, or renaming subdocuments" on page 391.

- If the original document is associated with a template, the .ODM file will also be associated with that template, but the subdocuments will not. The subdocuments will inherit the styles in the original document, but their association with the template will be lost.

How to do it:

1) Open the document and choose **File > Send > Create Master Document**.
2) On the Name and Path of Master Document dialog (Figure 383):
   a) Navigate to the folder where you want to save the master document and its subdocuments (or create a new folder).
   b) Type a name for the master document in the *File name* box.
   c) In the *separated by:* list , choose the outline level where the file should be split into subdocuments. Usually this is **Outline: Level 1** for a chapter heading, but your document may be structured differently. For more information about outline levels, see "Defining a hierarchy of headings" in Chapter 6, Introduction to Styles.
   d) Leave the *Automatic file name extension* option selected, and click **Save** to split the document into subdocuments and create the master document.

If you selected *Outline: Level 1* and the paragraph style at that level is *Heading 1*, each of the subdocuments begins with a *Heading 1* paragraph.

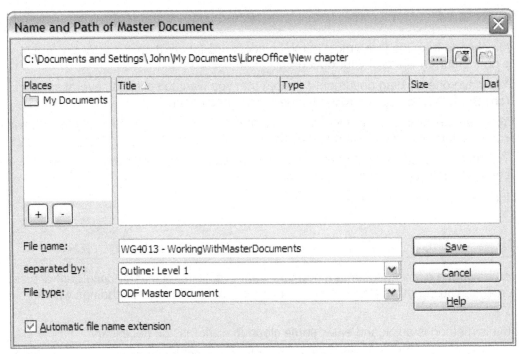

Figure 383: Splitting a document into master and subdocuments

Combining several documents into a master document

When you have several existing documents, you can combine them into one document controlled by a master document.

This method works best when all of the documents were created from the same template, but you can also use it when the documents have been created from different templates. This method is especially useful when the subdocuments are created or maintained by multiple writers. For example, you might be creating an anthology of short stories, a book of symposium papers or compiling a set of separate widget test results with a standard company front page.

How to do it:

We will go with the widget test results scenario as a very simple example.

1) Open the test results front page document being used as the master document. To avoid creating too many subdocuments from this document when it is converted to a master document, have only one level 1 heading present. If there are more, temporarily change them to lower level headings and note which they are (add, for example, an asterisk at the end of each heading to remind you which have to revert to level 1 headings later).

2) Select **File > Send > Create Master Document,** name and save this master document (see "How to do it:" on page 381 for full information).

   Let us assume our original document was named FrontPage with a single Level 1 heading, and that when we created the master document (ODM file) we named it TestFile.
   The master document is a blank file containing only one section. This can be seen by opening the ODM file and declining to update the links. Also created at the same time was a subdocument named TestFile1, an ODT file containing the text from the FrontPage file. When opening the ODM file and clicking **Yes** to update all links, this file is linked in to the master document to provide the original content.
   The original FrontPage file is left intact in its folder.

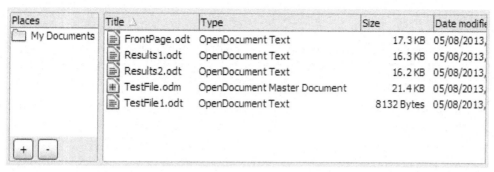

Figure 384: TestFile documents created from FrontPage

3) Open the master document and click **Yes** to update links. The master document opens with the Navigator open by default (see "Using the Navigator" on page 394 and "Step 6. Insert the subdocuments into the master document" on page 387 for more detailed information).

4) Click and hold on the **Insert** icon, move the cursor down to **File** and release the button.

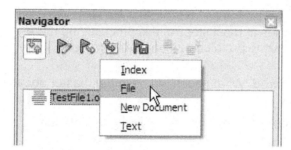

Figure 385: Adding files to the master document

5) Navigate to the location of the test results files (Results1, Results2 and so forth). Select the first file to insert, Results1 for example, and click **Insert**. The file is inserted above the existing entry.

6) Click the **Move Up** icon to have the TestFile text above the Results1 text (file contents are inserted above the selected file in the master document).

7) Repeat from step 4 as often as required. It does not matter which file is highlighted in the master document when you insert the next one, just select the inserted file and use the **Move Up** or **Move Down** icons to position it as required.

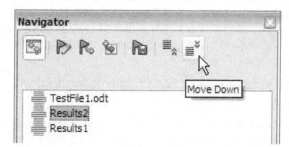

Figure 386: Moving subdocuments

8) To edit the master document, to perhaps add a widget serial number and a client's name, in the master document right-click TestFile1 and select **Edit** from the context menu. Add the required content to the file which opens, save and close the file (see "Editing a master document" on page 390 for more detailed information).

9) Select **Tools > Update > Links** from the Menu bar, or click and hold on the **Update** icon in the Navigator and move the cursor to **Links** and release the button. All the edits in the master document will now show.

Starting with no existing documents

When you start with no existing documents, you can set up everything the way you want from the beginning. Follow these steps, in the order given. Each step is explained in detail in the following subsections.

Step 1. Plan the project

Step 2. Create a template

Step 3. Create the master document

Step 4. Create subdocuments

Step 5. Add some pages to the master document

Step 6. Insert the subdocuments into the master document

Step 7. Add table of contents, bibliography, index

Step 1. Plan the project

Although you can make changes at most steps in this process, the more you can plan before you start, the less work you will have to do to correct any problems later. Here are some things you need to plan.

Parts of book or report required. What pages will be in the master document and what will be in the subdocuments?

Consider as an example a book with the parts given in the table below.

Part	*Location*
Title (cover) page	In master document
Copyright page	In master document
Table of contents (TOC)	In master document
Preface (Foreword)	Subdocument
Chapters 1 to 7	Subdocuments
Index	In master document

Page, paragraph, character, frame, and numbering styles. Determine the styles you wish to use. See Chapter 6, Introduction to Styles, and Chapter 7, Working with Styles, for instructions on how to create or modify styles and examples of the use of styles in book design. Pay particular attention to setting up headings using styles, as described in "Defining a hierarchy of headings" in Chapter 6, Introduction to Styles.

Fields and AutoText entries, as required. See Chapter 3, Working with Text, and Chapter 14, Working with Fields, for ideas.

One or more templates for master and subdocuments. If you are starting a new project, create the master document and all the subdocuments from the same template. Not using the same template can create style inconsistencies that could cause your document not to look as you expect. For example, if two subdocuments have a style with the same name that is formatted differently in each document, the master document will use the formatting from the first subdocument that was added.

Page numbering. In our example, the pages are numbered sequentially from the title page. (The title page style can be defined not to show the page number, but it will still count as page 1.) Therefore the first chapter begins on a higher number page, for example page 5. To create a book in which the page numbering restarts at 1 for the first chapter, you need to do some additional work. See "Restarting page numbering" on page 389.

Step 2. Create a template

You can create your template from an existing document or template that contains some or all of the page, paragraph, character, and other styles you want for this document, or you can create the template from a blank document. For more about templates, see Chapter 10, Working with Templates.

Be sure to use **File > Save As Template** when creating the template.

Note	A master document (.ODM) created from a template is associated with that template, but the name of the template is not shown in the Document Properties dialog (**File > Properties**) as it is for .ODT files. It can be added as a custom property if you want to record it as a reminder.

Step 3. Create the master document

It does not matter in what order you create the master and subdocuments, and you do not have to create all the subdocuments at the same time, when you are starting the project. You can add new subdocuments at any time, as you need them.

Follow this process to create the master document:

1) Open a new document from the template you created in Step 2, by choosing **File > New > Templates**, opening **My Templates** (or other location), then selecting the template you created. Be sure the first page of this new document is set to the page style you want for the first page of the final document; if it is not, change it. In our example, the style for the first page is *Title page*.

2) If any text or page breaks came into this document from the template, delete the text. (The TOC, index, and any fields in headers and footers can stay.)

3) Click **File > Send > Create Master Document**. Save the master document in the folder for this project. We will return to this master document later. For now, you can either leave it open or close it.

Note	Using **File > New > Master Document** will create a master document file (.ODM) associated with the default template. If your document is, or will be, based on a custom template, use the method described above.

Step 4. Create subdocuments

A subdocument is no different from any other text document. It becomes a subdocument only when it is linked into a master document and opened from within the master document. Some settings in the master document will override the settings in a subdocument, but only when the document is being viewed, manipulated, or printed through the master document.

Create a subdocument in the same way as you create any ordinary document:

1) Open a blank document based on the project template (very important) by choosing **File > New > Templates**, opening **My Templates** (or other location), then selecting the required template.

2) Delete any unwanted text or other material that was brought in from the template, and set the first page to the page style you specified for the first page of a chapter.

3) Click **File > Save As**. Give the document a suitable name and save it in the folder for this project.

If you already have some of the chapters written, the files are probably not based on the template you just created for this project. You will need to change the template attached to the existing files.

You can do this manually by opening the required template and copying and pasting content into the blank template.

Step 5. Add some pages to the master document

To assist you, do the following:

- Make sure paragraph marks are showing. You can set them in **Tools > Options > LibreOffice Writer > Formatting Aids**, or click the **Nonprinting Characters** icon 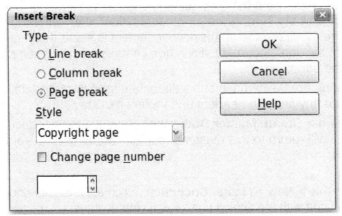 on the Standard toolbar or press *Ctrl+F10*.

- Show text boundaries, table boundaries, and section boundaries (**Tools > Options > LibreOffice > Appearance**).

If your master document does not contain any required "front matter" such as a title page, copyright page, or TOC page, add them now. The example in this section uses the sequence of page styles given in "Step 1. Plan the project" on page 384.

1) Type the contents of the title page (or leave placeholders and fill in later). With the insertion point in the last blank paragraph on the page, click **Insert > Manual Break**. On the Insert Break dialog, select **Page break** and the page style for the second page (*Copyright page* in our example), and leave the **Change page number** option deselected. Click **OK**.

Figure 387: Inserting a page break between the title page and the copyright page

2) Type the contents of the copyright page (or leave placeholders). With the insertion point in the last blank paragraph on the page, insert another manual page break, this time setting the page style to *Table of Contents page*.

3) On the Table of Contents page, leave a blank paragraph or two or insert a TOC (**Insert > Indexes and Tables > Indexes and Tables**). The TOC will not have any contents until you add the subdocuments, but you should see a gray mark or box indicating its location. For more about inserting and formatting TOCs, see Chapter 12, Tables of Contents, Indexes, and Bibliographies.

Note	Depending on the style definitions for the first paragraph (usually a heading) on the Copyright and TOC pages, you may not need to insert manual page breaks.

Step 6. Insert the subdocuments into the master document

Now we are ready to add the subdocuments.

Tip	Subdocuments are inserted into a master document *before* the item highlighted in the Navigator. If you insert the *last* subdocument first, and then insert the other subdocuments before the last one, they will end up in the correct sequence without the necessity of moving them up or down in the list.

1) Display the Navigator (click **View > Navigator**, or press *F5*, or click the **Navigator** icon ⊘.

2) Be sure the Navigator is showing the master view (see "Using the Navigator" on page 394). Click on the **Toggle** icon at the upper left to toggle between regular and master views.

3) On the Navigator, select **Text**, then click and hold on the **Insert** icon, move the mouse pointer down, and click **File**.

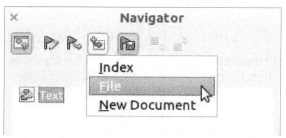

Figure 388: Inserting a subdocument into a master document using the Navigator

A standard File Open dialog appears. Select the required file (which you created in Step 4) and click **Insert**. This example uses 7 chapters and a preface; we will load Chapter 7 first, as suggested in the Tip above.

The inserted file is listed in the Navigator *before* the Text item, as shown in Figure 389.

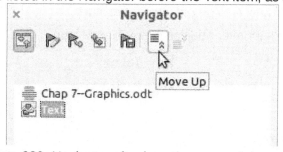

Figure 389: Navigator after inserting one subdocument

4) Because the *Text* section contains the title page and other material, highlight it and click the **Move Up** icon to move it to the top of the list.

5) Highlight the subdocument you just inserted (Chapter 7), then click and hold on the **Insert** icon, move the mouse pointer, and click **File** to insert the *first* subdocument; in this example, Preface. Chapter 7 remains highlighted. Repeat with Chapter 1, Chapter 2, and so on until all the subdocuments have been added to the list. The Navigator will now look something like Figure 390.

6) Save the master document again.

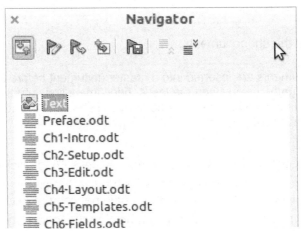

Figure 390: The Navigator showing a series of files in a master document

Step 7. Add table of contents, bibliography, index

You can generate a table of contents, bibliography, or index for the book, using the master document. You must insert these items into a text section in the master document. For more about these document elements, see Chapter 12, Creating Tables of Contents, Indexes, and Bibliographies.

Put the insertion point on the page in the first text section where the table of contents is to go and choose **Insert > Indexes and Tables > Indexes and Tables** to create the table of contents.

If you do not have a Text section at the end of the master document, insert one before the last subdocument, then move it down so it is after the last subdocument. Now, if you have included bibliographic entries in your subdocuments, you can put the insertion point on the page in this last text section where the bibliography is to go and create the bibliography.

If you have included index entries in your subdocuments, put the insertion point on the page in the last text section where the index is to go and create the index.

Figure 391 shows the Navigator after addition of a TOC and index.

Figure 391: Navigator showing subdocuments, table of contents, and index in a master document

Restarting page numbering

The example in the previous section showed a very basic collection of files with sequential page numbering. This is useful for many documents, including e-books, but a typical printed book has the following sequence of page numbers:

- No page numbers on cover page or copyright page
- Lower-case roman numerals in the front matter, starting with i
- Arabic numerals in the body of the document, starting with 1
- Page numbering sequential through the rest of the book

To set up a master document to produce such a book, you need to define a different paragraph style for the heading of the first chapter and assign two special characteristics to it.

Example

Each chapter may start with a *Heading 1* paragraph, set up on the Text Flow tab of the Paragraph Style dialog to start on a new page (Figure 392). The Page number is set to 0, with the effect that numbering continues from the number of the previous page.

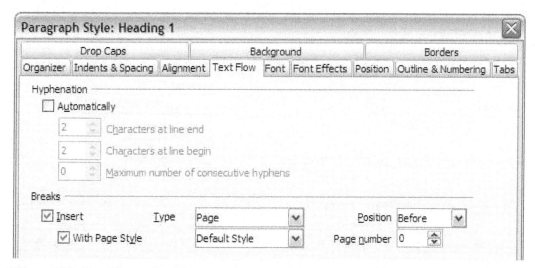

Figure 392: Text Flow tab of Paragraph Style dialog for Heading 1

Look on the Outline & Numbering tab (Figure 393) of this dialog to see what outline level *Heading 1* is assigned to. Usually this will be Outline Level 1. The level cannot be changed here because it has been set in **Tools > Outline Numbering**.

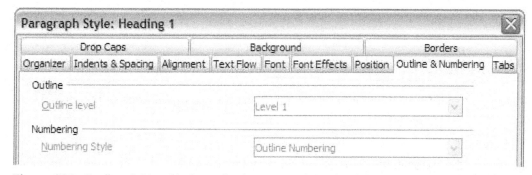

Figure 393: Outline & Numbering tab of Paragraph Style dialog for Heading 1

Only one paragraph style can be assigned to Outline Level 1 through **Tools > Outline Numbering**. However, you can assign additional paragraph styles to any outline level by using the Outline & Numbering tab on the Paragraph Style dialog.

Therefore, you want to define a style called *Heading 1 Chapter 1* that is identical in appearance to *Heading 1* but has one essential difference: on the Text Flow tab, set the Page number to 1 (Figure 394). Then, on the Outline & Numbering tab, set the Outline level to Level 1 (Figure 395). This ensures that the heading will appear in the Table of Contents along with the other chapter headings. (The Numbering Style for this heading is None, as it was not assigned an outline level through the Outline Numbering dialog.

Now, assign the new style to the first paragraph of Chapter 1, and you're done.

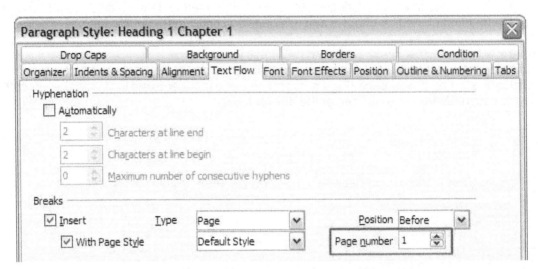

Figure 394: Set the page number to restart at 1 for this heading style

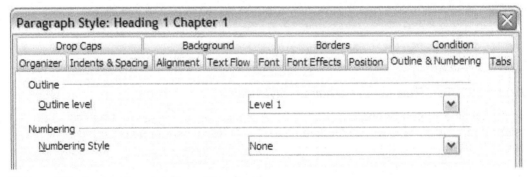

Figure 395: Assign the style to outline level

Editing a master document

After creating a master document, you may want to change its appearance or contents.

Changing the appearance of the master document

You can change the styles in the template as your project develops. Do not make changes to styles in the master document or in any of the subdocuments—make those changes in the template.

To update the master document (and all of the subdocuments) with changes to the template, just open the master document. You will get two messages: first, to ask if you want to update all links; and second, if you want to apply the changed styles. Answer *Yes* to both of these messages.

Editing subdocuments

You cannot edit a subdocument from within the master document. Instead, you must open the subdocument, either by double-clicking on it in the master document's Navigator, or by opening it from outside the master document. Then you can edit it just as you would edit any other document.

If, while editing a subdocument, you want to make changes to the styles that apply to the master document, follow the recommendations in "Changing the appearance of the master document" above.

If you change the contents of any subdocument, you need to manually update the table of contents, bibliography, and index from within the master document.

Adding, deleting, or renaming subdocuments

To add a subdocument, follow the method described in "Step 6. Insert the subdocuments into the master document" on page 387.

To delete a subdocument, right-click on its file name in the Navigator and choose Delete.

If you rename a subdocument by changing its file name, the next time you update links in the master document, that subdocument will show up as a broken link (shown in red). You can fix this by right-clicking on it in the Navigator, choosing Edit Link, and selecting the renamed file; however, the file name shown in the Navigator does not change (only the link changes). This can be quite confusing, so a better strategy is to delete the subdocument from the Navigator and then add the renamed file.

Cross-referencing between subdocuments

The methods described earlier in this chapter are all most writers will need when using master documents. However, you might want to include automatically updated cross-references between subdocuments. This section describes how to do this.

The process to create cross-references between subdocuments is time consuming, but it works.

Preparing items as targets for cross-referencing

Before you can insert a cross-reference to anything that is not automatically shown on the Cross-*references* tab of the Fields dialog, such as a heading, you must prepare or "set" that heading as an item to be referenced. To do this, you can either use bookmarks or set references.

When you set references, be sure to select the entire text you want to use as the reference, such as a heading or figure number. Keep a list of your names for the reference fields, and be sure each name is unique. One way to keep track of this information is to save it in a separate file.

The field names are case-sensitive. You can check the field name by holding the cursor over the referenced item. In our example (Figure 396), the heading has the field name *word count*.

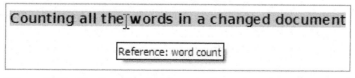

Figure 396: Finding the field name for a heading

Using bookmarks

Bookmarks are listed in the Navigator and can be accessed directly from there with a single mouse click. To insert a bookmark:

1) Select the text you want to bookmark. Click **Insert > Bookmark**.

2) On the Insert Bookmark dialog, the larger box lists any previously defined bookmarks. Type a name for the new bookmark in the top box. Click **OK**.

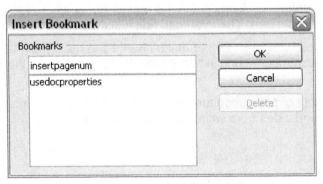

Figure 397: Inserting a bookmark

Setting references

Open the subdocument in which you want to set references.

1) Click **Insert > Cross-reference**.

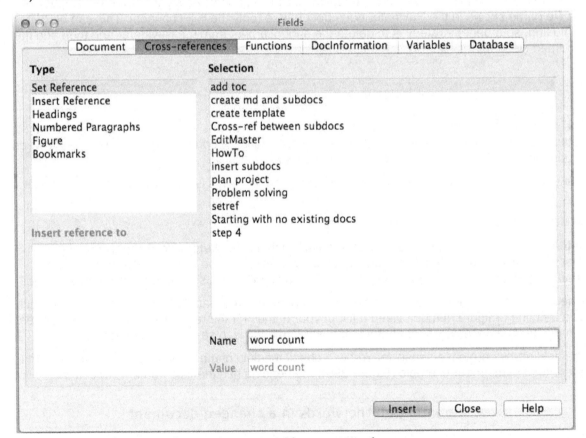

Figure 398: Setting text to be used as a target for a cross-reference

2) On the *Cross-references* tab of the Fields dialog (Figure 398), click **Set Reference** in the *Type* list. The *Selection* list shows any references that have been defined. You can leave this page open while you set many headings as references.

3) Click in the document and highlight the text of the first heading to be used as a target for a cross-reference. Click on the Fields dialog. The text of the heading will appear in the *Value* box in the lower right of the dialog. In the *Name* box, type some text by which you can identify this heading.

4) Click **Insert**. The text you typed in the *Name* box now appears in the *Selection* list.

5) Repeat steps 3 and 4 as often as required, keeping a note of your references as needed.

6) Repeat for other subdocuments if wanted. Save and close.

Inserting the cross-references

1) Open the master document. In the Navigator, select a subdocument, right-click and choose **Edit** from the context menu. The subdocument opens for editing.

2) In the subdocument, place the cursor where you want the cross-reference to appear. Click **Insert > Cross Reference**.

3) On the *Cross-references* tab of the Fields dialog (Figure 399), select **Insert Reference** in the *Type* list on the left hand side. The *Selection* list in the middle column shows only the reference field names for the subdocument you are using, so ignore that list and check the list you created manually in "Setting references". Select **Reference** in the *Insert reference to* list.

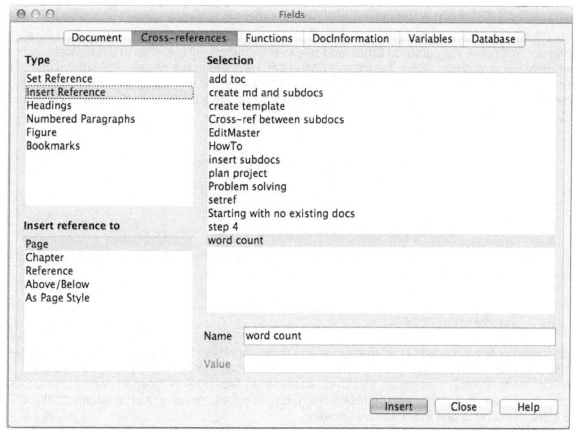

Figure 399: Fields dialog showing manual entry of field name

4) In the **Name** field in the lower right hand column, type the name of the reference you set in the subdocument you are referring to. In our example, the reference is in Chapter 3, and its name is *word count.*

5) Click **Insert,** type any text you want to appear between the reference and page number (such as "on page"), and then insert another reference with **Page** from the *Insert reference to* list. The cross-references will show an error as shown in Figure 400. When you hover the mouse pointer over one of these fields, you will see the field name.

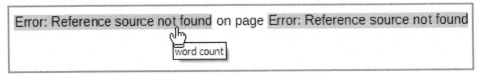

Figure 400: Viewing the field name

(You can turn on the display of field codes by clicking **View > Field Names.** The two error fields shown in Figure 400 now look like Figure 401.)

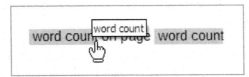

Figure 401: Displaying field codes

6) After you have inserted all the cross-references required in the subdocument, save and close it and return to the master document window.

Select **Tools > Update > Links** from the Menu bar, or click and hold on the **Update** icon in the Navigator and move the cursor to **Links** and release the button. All the edits in the master document will now show. Within the master document, navigate to the page of the subdocument on which you inserted the cross-reference field. You should now see the text of the cross-reference appear in the spot where you inserted it. If it does not work, save the master document, close it, and open it again, updating the links.

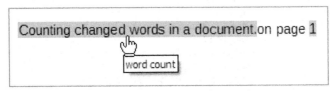

Figure 402: Field contents visible

This technique also works if you open a subdocument directly in step 2 (that is, not from within the master document) and insert a cross-reference field.

Using the Navigator

The Navigator is a very useful tool that helps you move quickly to specific parts of your document. It also provides information about the content of the document and enables you to reorganize some of the content. For example, if each chapter in your final book is a separate document, then in the master document they can be reordered; the references are renumbered automatically and the table of contents and index can be updated.

In Writer, the Navigator has two distinct forms. One form is used in ordinary text documents and the other in master documents.

In an ordinary text document, the Navigator displays lists of the graphics, tables, index entries, hyperlinks, references, and other items in the document, as shown on the left hand side of Figure 403. Click the indicator (+ sign or triangle) by any list to display the contents of the list. You can double-click an entry in the Navigator and jump immediately to that place in the document.

In a master document, you can toggle between the regular and master views by clicking on the **Toggle** icon at the upper left. In the master view, the Navigator lists the subdocuments and text sections, as shown on the right hand side of Figure 403. The use of the Navigator in a master document is covered in more detail later in this chapter (see "Step 6. Insert the subdocuments into the master document" on page 387 and "Cross-referencing between subdocuments" on page 391).

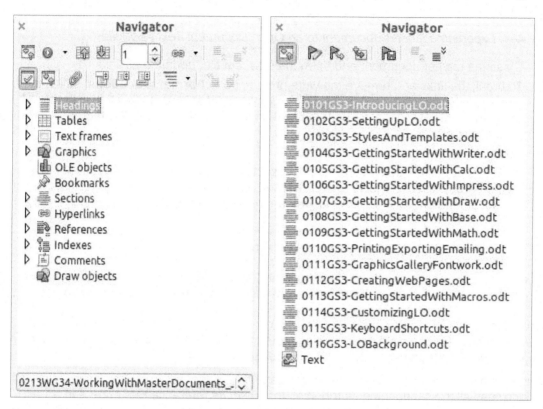

Figure 403: The Navigator for a text document (left) and for a master document (right)

Creating one file from a master document and its subdocuments

Master documents are .odm files containing linked subdocuments, which are in .odt format. Although linked files are very useful when writing and editing a large document such as a book, sometimes you might need to have a copy of the entire book in one file.

To export a master document to a .odt file (without affecting the original .odm file):

1) Open the master document. Choose **File > Export** from the menu bar.

2) On the Export dialog (Figure 404), type a name for the exported .odt file and choose **ODF Text Document (.odt)** from the *File format* list (it should be the default choice). Click **Export**. This step creates from the .odm file, a write protected .odt file, with each subdocument in a separate section.

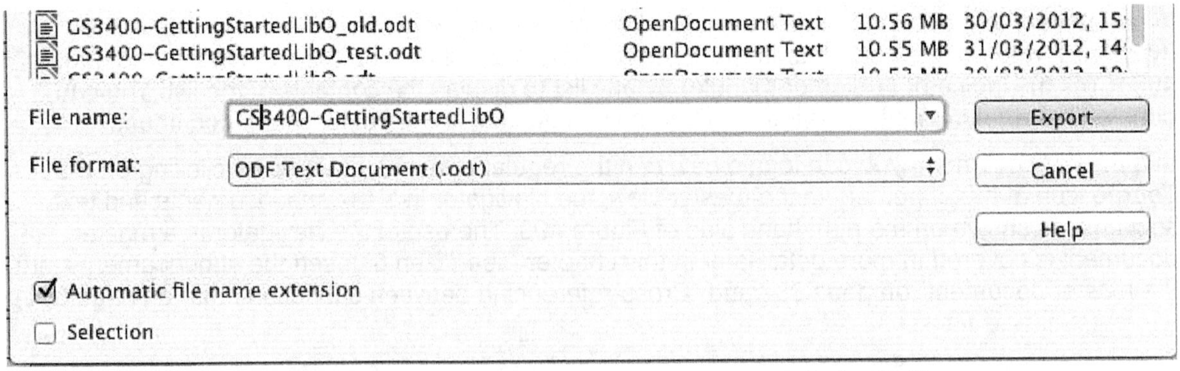

📄 GS3400-GettingStartedLibO_old.odt	OpenDocument Text	10.56 MB 30/03/2012, 15:
📄 GS3400-GettingStartedLibO_test.odt	OpenDocument Text	10.55 MB 31/03/2012, 14:

File name: GS3400-GettingStartedLibO ▼   Export

File format: ODF Text Document (.odt) ⬍   Cancel

                                                       Help

☑ Automatic file name extension

☐ Selection

Figure 404: Exporting a master document to an Open Document Text (.odt) file

3) Close the master document and open the new .odt file, updating all links.

4) To break the links and remove the write protect, go to **Format > Sections**, select the first item in the *Section* list, then press *Shift+click* on the last item in the list in order to select all the items in the list. Deselect both the **Link** in the *Link* section and **Protected** in the *Write protection* section.

5) Click **OK**.

6) If you wish to eliminate some or all of the sections to have a plain text document, select the sections you wish to remove, and click **Remove**. The contents of those sections remain in the document; only the section markers are removed. Click **OK**.

Problem solving: Anchoring pictures to a page

Some combinations of choices do not work together, and some techniques that affect master documents are not at all obvious. This section describes one problem and what to do about it.

The problem

A picture (graphic) anchored "to page" in a subdocument is not displayed in the master document although it always appears correctly in the subdocument.

Because the master document reorganizes the page flow, page numbers, and cross-references when it collates all the subdocuments together, the absolute reference to a page X in a subdocument is lost in the master document. The picture loses its anchor reference and simply disappears.

The solution

To avoid this problem but keep pictures positioned precisely on a particular page, anchor the pictures as follows:

1) Right-click on the picture and choose **Picture** from the context menu.

2) On the *Type* tab of the Picture dialog (Figure 405), set the anchor to *To character* or *To paragraph*.

3) Under *Position*, choose suitable horizontal and vertical references to the page. Click **OK** to save the changes.

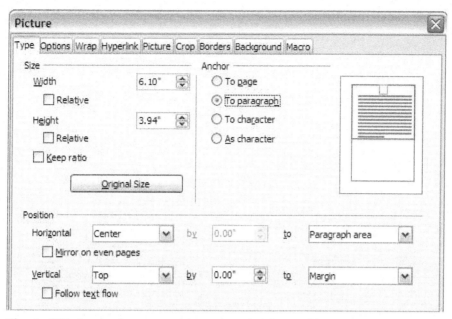

Figure 405: Anchoring a graphic and setting its position on a page

Chapter 14
Working with Fields

Introduction to fields

Fields are extremely useful features of Writer. They are used for a variety of purposes; for example, data that changes (such as the current date or the total number of pages) or might change (the name of a product or book under development), user-defined numbering sequences, automatic cross-references, and conditional content (words or paragraphs that are visible or printed in some conditions but not others). Index entries are also fields.

This chapter describes some common uses of fields. A full discussion of fields and their use is beyond the scope of this book. Power users can find more details in the application Help.

Tip	Fields have a gray background when viewed on screen, unless you have deselected the **Field shadings** option or changed the color of field shadings on the *Appearance* page of the **Tools > Options > LibreOffice** dialog. This gray background does not show when you print the file to hard copy or PDF. To turn field shadings on or off quickly, choose **View > Field Shadings** or press *Ctrl+F8*.

Quick and easy field entry

You can quickly insert common fields into your document by choosing **Insert > Fields** from the menu bar and selecting the required field from the list, as shown in Figure 406.

Figure 406: Inserting common fields

Using document properties to hold metadata and information that changes

The Properties dialog (**File > Properties)** for a document has six tabs. The information on the *General* page and the *Statistics* page is generated by the program. Other information (the name of the person on the Created and Modified lines of the *General* page) is derived from the *User Data* page in **Tools > Options > LibreOffice**.

The *Internet* page is relevant only to HTML documents (Writer/Web). The file sharing options on the *Security* page are discussed elsewhere in this book.

Use the *Description* and *Custom Properties* pages to hold:

- Metadata to assist in classifying, sorting, storing, and retrieving documents. Some of this metadata is exported to the closest equivalent in HTML and PDF; some fields have no equivalent and are not exported.

- Information that changes. You can store data for use in fields in your document; for example, the title of the document, contact information for a project participant, or the name of a product might change during the course of a project.

This dialog can be used in a template, where the field names can serve as reminders to writers of information they need to include.

Later in this chapter, we will see how to use this information in fields. You can return to this dialog at any time and change the information you entered. When you do so, all of the references to that information will change wherever they appear in the document. For example, on the *Description* page (Figure 407) you might need to change the contents of the *Title* field from the draft title to the production title.

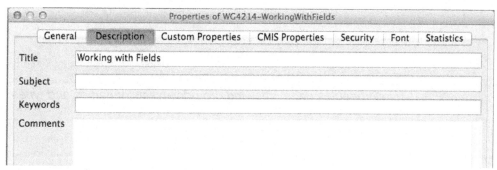

Figure 407: The Description page of the document's Properties dialog

To open the Properties dialog, choose **File > Properties**.

Use the *Custom Properties* page (Figure 408) to store information that does not fit into the fields supplied on the other pages of this dialog.

When the Custom Properties page is first opened in a new document, it may be blank. (If the new document is based on a template, this page may contain fields.)

Click **Add** to insert a row of boxes into which you can enter your custom properties.

- The *Name* box includes a drop-down list of typical choices; scroll down to see all the choices. If none of the choices meet your needs, you can type a new name into the box.

- In the *Type* column, you can choose from text, date+time, date, number, duration, or yes/no for each field. You cannot create new types.

- In the *Value* column, type or select what you want to appear in the document where this field is used. Choices may be limited to specific data types depending on the selection in the Type column; for example, if the Type selection is Date, the Value for that property is limited to a date.

- To remove a custom property, click the button at the end of the row.

Tip	To change the format of the Date value, go to **Tools > Options > Language Settings > Languages** and change the Locale setting. Be careful! This change affects all open documents, not just the current one.

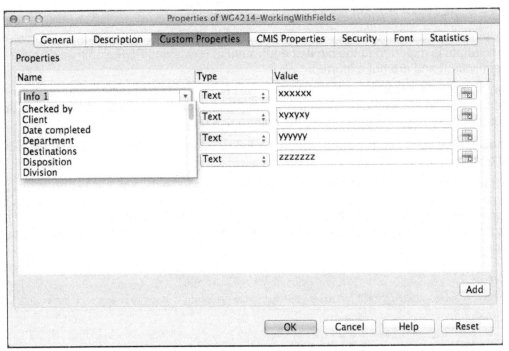

Figure 408: Custom Properties page, showing drop-down lists of names and types

Using other fields to hold information that changes

One way that people use fields is to hold information that is likely to change during the course of a project. For example, the name of a manager, a product, or even your entire company may change just before the document is due to be printed. If you have inserted the changeable information as fields, you can change the information in one place, and it will automatically change in all the places where that field occurs.

Writer provides several places where you can store the information referred to by a field. We will look at some of them here.

Seven document properties (Date, Time, Page Number, Page Count, Subject, Title, and Author) are on the **Insert > Fields** menu (Figure 406). To insert one of these fields, click on it in the menu. Some of these fields get their information from the Document Properties dialog (Figure 407.)

Other document properties are on the *DocInformation* and *Document* pages of the Fields dialog (Figure 409 and Figure 410), reached by choosing **Insert > Fields > Other** or pressing *Ctrl+F2*. Notice the *Custom* item in the *Type* list of the *DocInformation* page; this is derived from the *Custom Properties* page of the Document Properties dialog (Figure 408).

To insert one of these fields, select it in the *Type* list and then select from the *Select* and *Format* lists if choices appear. Finally, click **Insert**.

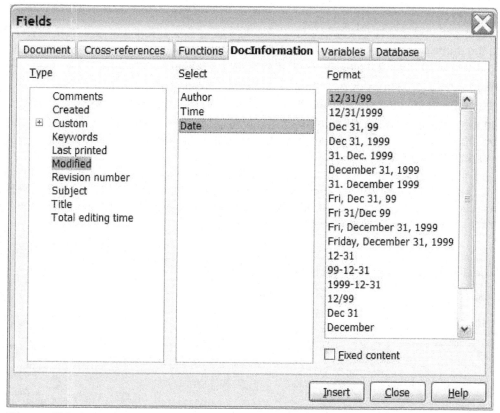

Figure 409: Inserting a Date Modified field using the DocInformation page of the Fields dialog

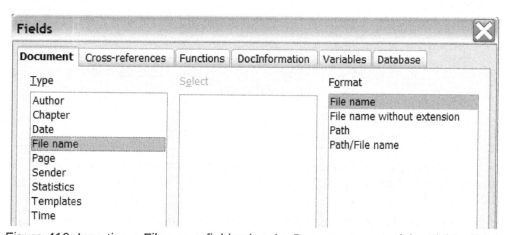

Figure 410: Inserting a File name field using the Document page of the Fields dialog

Some of these items are picked up from the *User Data* page of the **Tools > Options > LibreOffice** dialog (covered in Chapter 2, Setting up Writer), so make sure the information on that page is correct.

Tip	Although these fields are often used to hold information that changes, you can make the content unchangeable by selecting the **Fixed content** option (visible in Figure 409, lower right) when inserting the field. If necessary, you can come back to this dialog later and deselect this option to make the field variable again.

Using AutoText to insert often-used fields

If you use the same fields often, you will want a quick and easy way to insert them. You can use AutoText for this purpose. To define an AutoText entry for a field:

1) Insert a field into your document, as described previously.

2) Select the field you inserted, and then choose **Edit > AutoText** (or press *Ctrl+F3*).

3) On the AutoText dialog, choose the group where this new entry will be stored (in this example, it is going into *My AutoText*), type a name for the entry, and change the suggested shortcut if you wish.

4) Click the **AutoText** button and click **New** to have the entry inserted as a field. Do not choose **New (text only)** because the AutoText entry will be plain text, not a field. (The selection *New* does not appear until you have selected a group and typed a name for the entry.) Click **Close** to close the AutoText dialog.

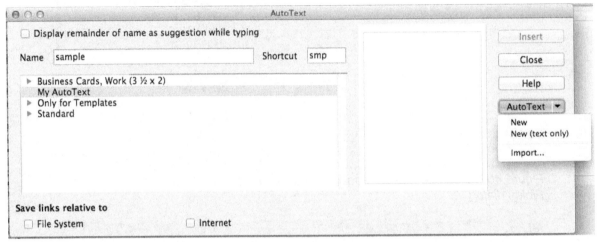

Figure 411: Creating a new AutoText entry

Now whenever you want to insert this field at the cursor position, type the shortcut, and then press *F3*.

Defining your own numbering sequences

You may want to define your own numbering sequences, for example to use in situations where you do not always want the number at the start of the paragraph or where you want more control than the built-in numbering choices give you.

This topic describes how to create and use a numbering sequence, using a "number range variable" field.

Create a number range variable

To create a number range variable using Arabic (1, 2, 3) numbers:

1) Place the insertion point in a blank paragraph in your document.

2) Choose **Insert > Fields > Other** or press *Ctrl+F2* and select the *Variables* page.

3) In the *Type* list, select **Number range**. In the *Format* list, select **Arabic (1 2 3)**. Type whatever you want in the *Name* field. (We have used **Step** in this example.)

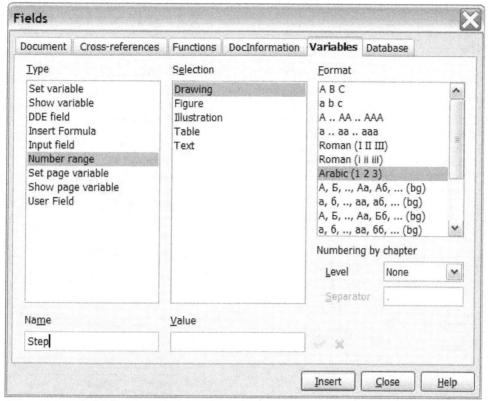

Figure 412: Defining a number range variable

4) Click **Insert**. The name of the variable (**Step**) now appears in the *Selection* list, and a number field (showing **1**) appears at the insertion point in your document. The Fields dialog remains open, so you may need to move it out of the way to see the field in the document.

5) If you click several more times on the **Insert** button in the Fields dialog, the numbers **2, 3, 4**, and so on will appear in the document.

Now you may want to change the Step sequence to a different number, forwards from the current value, or backwards to a previous value, so you can use the same sequence name more than once in your document (for example, to begin each set of instructions). To do that, you need to insert a new field of the same name, while instructing LibreOffice to force the value to the new choice.

1) Open the Fields dialog to the *Variables* page. Make sure the variable name **Step** appears in the *Name* box.

2) In the *Value* box, type **1** (we will illustrate a numbering restart here, but any number will work), as shown in Figure 413. Click **Insert**.

3) To continue with the normal sequence (that is, to have the next Step value be **2**), you need to delete the contents of the Value box after inserting at step 2.

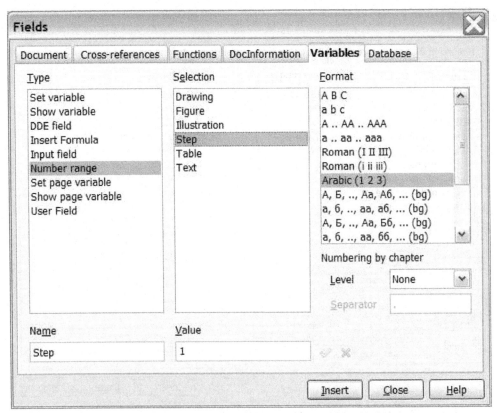

Figure 413: Defining a field to restart a number range variable

Use AutoText to insert a number range field

You certainly do not want to go through all of that every time you want to put in a Step number. Instead, create two AutoText entries, one for the *Step (Value=1)* field (call it **Step1**, for example) and one for the *Step = Step+1* field (**StepNext**). Then insert the fields in the same way you would insert any other AutoText. See "Using AutoText to insert often-used fields" on page 404.

You can create similar fields for substeps or other sequences that you want to be numbered with letters (a, b, c), Roman numerals (i, ii, iii), or some other sequence. In the Fields dialog, choose the required format in the *Format* list when creating the field codes.

Tip	If a user-defined variable is not in use in the document, the ![icon] icon next to the *Value* box is active. You can delete the variable by clicking this icon. To remove a variable that is used in the current document, first delete from the document all fields using that variable (or convert them all to text, as described on page 412), and then remove the variable from the list.

Using automatic cross-references

If you type in cross-references to other parts of the document, those references can easily get out of date if you reword a heading, add or remove figures, or reorganize topics. Replace any typed cross-references with automatic ones and, when you update fields, all the references will update automatically to show the current wording or page numbers.

| Tip | Some people use Writer's Hyperlink feature for cross-references, but it has the major disadvantage that the visible text of the hyperlink does not change if you change the text of the item to which it links. For that reason, you are advised to use cross-references in most situations. |
| | The exception is when you are creating a document to be saved as HTML; cross-references do not become hyperlinks in an HTML document. |

The *Cross-references* page of the Fields dialog (Figure 414) lists some items, such as headings, numbered paragraphs, and bookmarks. If figure captions, table captions, user-defined number range variables, and some other items have been defined in a document, that type also appears in the list.

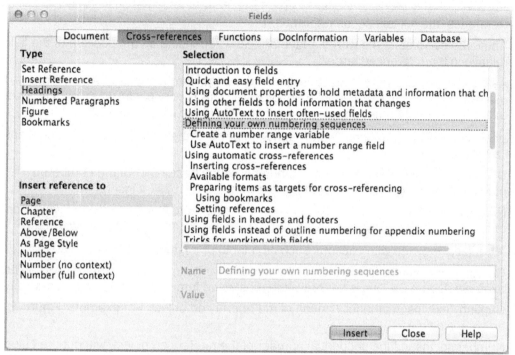

Figure 414: The Cross-references page of the Fields dialog

Inserting cross-references

To insert a cross-reference to a heading, figure, or other item shown on the *Cross-references* page:

1) In your document, place the cursor where you want the cross-reference to appear.

2) If the Fields dialog is not open, choose **Insert > Cross Reference** or press *Ctrl+F2*. On the *Cross-references* page (Figure 414), in the *Type* list, click the type of item you are referencing (for example, Heading or Figure).

3) You can leave this page open while you insert many cross-references.

4) Click on the required item in the *Selection* list, which shows both automatically created entries (for example Headings) as well as user-defined references (for example bookmarks).

5) In the *Insert reference to* list, choose the type of reference required. The choices vary with the item being referenced.

For headings, usually you will choose **Reference** (to insert the full text of the heading) or **Page** (to insert the number of the page the heading is on).

For figures, you will usually choose **Category and Number** (to insert the word "Figure" and its number), **Reference** (to insert the word "Figure" with its number and the full text of the caption), **Page** (to insert the number of the page the figure is on), or **Numbering** (to insert only the figure number).

6) Click **Insert**.

For a full list of the reference formats available, and their use, consult the Help.

Available formats

For all the types of reference, you can select one of the following formats:

- Page: the page number of the target
- Chapter: the number of the chapter where the referenced target is located.
- Reference: the full text set as reference.
- Above/Below: Inserts the words above or below depending on the position of the field relative to the referenced target.
- As Page Style: similar to Page, this inserts the page number where the reference is, but using the formatting specified in the page style. This is very useful when putting a reference to a page in the front matter where roman numerals are usually employed.

If you select Headings or Numbered Paragraphs as the type, the following two additional options become available:

- Number (no context): inserts only the number of the heading or of the numbered paragraph. For example, if referencing a numbered item 2.4, it inserts 4.
- Number (full context): inserts the full number including higher hierarchical levels. For example, if referencing a numbered item 2.4, the full numbering (2.4) is inserted.

Finally, for objects inserted with captions such as a table or a figure, you can choose:

- Category and Number: inserts both the category and number of the referenced object (for example, Figure 6). This is generally the most used formatting for figures and tables.
- Caption Text: inserts the full caption of the referenced object. For example, Figure 6: This is an example figure.
- Numbering: inserts the sequential number of the referenced object, without the category (for example, if referencing Table 2, the field will contain only the number 2).

Preparing items as targets for cross-referencing

Occasionally you might want to insert a cross-reference to something that is not automatically shown on the *Cross-references* page. Before you can insert a cross-reference to such an item, you must prepare the item as a target to be referenced. To do this, you can either use bookmarks or set references.

After a target has been defined, you can cross-reference to it as described on page 407. For an example of the use of this technique, see "Solving the page count problem" in Chapter 4, Formatting Pages.

Using bookmarks

Bookmarks are listed in the Navigator and can be accessed directly from there with a single mouse click. In HTML documents, bookmarks are converted to anchors that you can jump to using a hyperlink.

1) Select the text you want to bookmark. (You can also insert a bookmark to a location without selecting text, by clicking in the required place in the text.) Choose **Insert > Bookmark**.

2) On the Insert Bookmark dialog, the larger box lists any previously defined bookmarks. Type a name for this bookmark in the top box. Click **OK**.

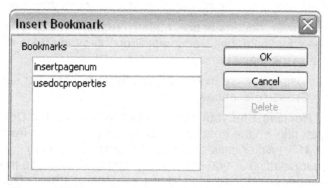

Figure 415: Inserting a bookmark

Setting references

1) Choose **Insert > Cross reference** or press *Ctrl+F2*.

2) On the *Cross-references* page of the Fields dialog (Figure 416), select **Set Reference** in the *Type* list. The *Selection* list shows any references that have been defined. You can leave this dialog open while you set many items as references.

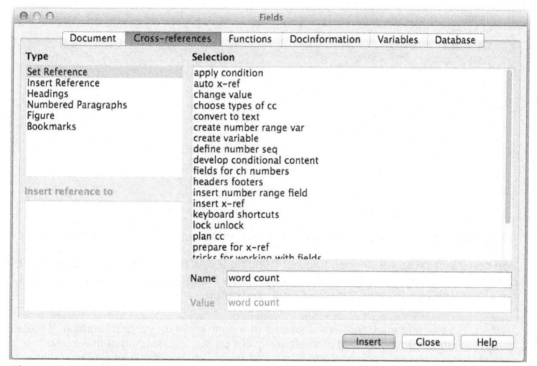

Figure 416: Setting text to be used as a target for a cross-reference

3) Click in the document and highlight the text of the first item to set as a target for a cross-reference. Click on the Fields dialog. The text of the item will appear in the *Value* box in the lower right. In the *Name* box, type some text by which you can identify this item.

4) Click **Insert**. The text you typed in the *Name* box now appears in the *Selection* list.

5) Repeat steps 3 and 4 as often as required.

Using fields in headers and footers

You can insert fields into headers or footers, using techniques described earlier in this chapter:

- To insert a page number, document title, author, creation date and time, current date and time, or total page count field, use Document Properties (see page 400) or choose **Insert > Fields > [item]** from the menu bar.

- You can insert a cross-reference to a bookmark, heading, or other item from **Insert > Fields > Other > Cross-references**.

- If you have used *Heading 1* for your chapter titles, you can use a Document field to insert the current chapter title, so the header or footer contents change from one chapter to the next. See Figure 417. (Writer calls chapter titles *Chapter names*.) If you have used outline numbering on your *Heading 1*, you can choose whether to include these numbers in the field (*Chapter number and name*). Use **Insert > Fields > Other > Document**.

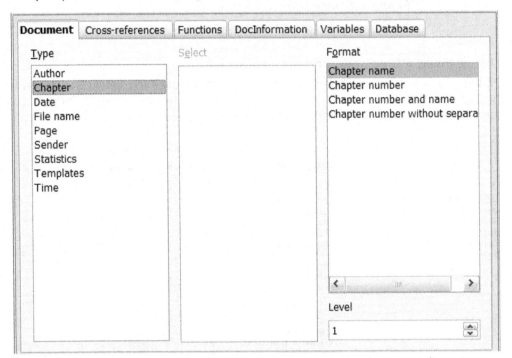

Figure 417: Inserting the current chapter name and number into your document

- You can insert cross-references to other heading levels by specifying a value in the *Level* box in the lower right of the *Document* page of the Fields dialog (Figure 417). That is, Level 1 = Heading 1, Level 2 = Heading 2, and so on.

Note	A cross-reference field in the header of a page picks up the *first* heading of that level on the page, and a field in the footer picks up the *last* heading of that level.

- To include the chapter number with the page number, position the cursor just before the *Page* field you inserted. Choose **Insert > Fields > Other**. On the *Document* page of the Fields dialog, select **Chapter** in the *Type* column and **Chapter number without separator** in the *Format* column. Click **Insert**.

  Go to the header or footer where you inserted this field, type the character you want to appear between the chapter number and the page number—for example, a period or a dash.

The table of contents will not automatically pick up these chapter numbers, so you will need to make a change on the **Indexes and Tables** menu item, as described in Chapter 12, Creating Tables of Contents, Indexes, and Bibliographies.

- You can add a page count to the footer—for example "Page 9 of 12". Type the word "Page" and a space in front of the *Page* field. Type a space, the word "of", and a space after the *Page* field. Then choose **Insert > Fields > Page Count**.

Using fields instead of outline numbering for appendix numbering

Chapter 6, Introduction to Styles, describes how to use paragraph styles to define a hierarchy of headings to be included in a table of contents.

This method has one major limitation: only one numbering sequence can be specified in **Tools > Outline Numbering**. However, many books contain Appendixes (typically designated A, B, C) in addition to the chapters (typically designated 1, 2, 3).

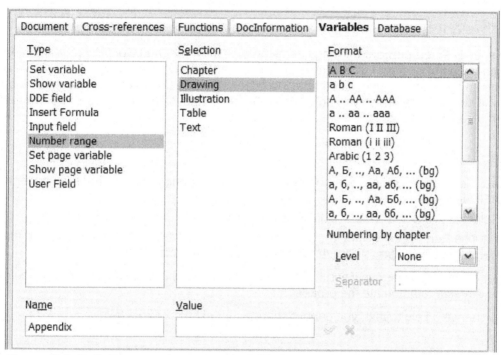

Figure 418: Defining a number range variable for Appendixes

To solve this problem, you can use one paragraph style (Heading 1) for both chapter and appendix names, and define two number range fields for the chapters and appendixes respectively. The number range field for chapters will use numbers, and the number range field for appendixes will use letters. You can then use the same field in the header or footer of chapters and appendixes.

1) Define the first number range variable, in this example *Chapter*, as described in "Defining your own numbering sequences" on page 404. To insert the field into your *Heading 1*, type **Chapter<space>**. Choose **Insert > Fields > Other**. On the *Variables* page, select **Number range**, **Chapter, Arabic (1 2 3)**. Click **Insert**. You will need to do this manually for each *Heading 1* that is to be a chapter title.

2) Define and insert a second number range variable for the appendixes, using **Number range**, **Appendix, A B C**), as shown in Figure 418. Type **Appendix<space>** and then insert the variable. Do this for each *Heading 1* that is to be an appendix title.

3) When you create the table of contents, the chapters and appendixes will be designated correctly.

Tricks for working with fields

Keyboard shortcuts for fields

Here are some handy keyboard shortcuts to use when working with fields:

Ctrl+F2	Open the Fields dialog.
Ctrl+F8	Turn field shadings on or off.
Ctrl+F9	Show or hide field names.
F9	Update fields.

Note: In KDE on Linux, *Ctrl+Fx* brings up Desktop #X, so the shortcuts mentioned above do not work in LibreOffice as they do in other operating system and desktop environments.

Fixing the contents of fields

You can specify **Fixed content** for many items on the *Document* and *DocInformation* pages so the field contents do not update. For example, you might use a field to insert the creation date of a document, and you would not want that date to change. In another place you might use a date field to show the current date, which you do want to change; in that case, deselect **Fixed content** when you insert the field.

Converting fields into text

Writer does not provide an easy way to convert a field into regular text, so that it is no longer updated. However, you can do this as follows:

1) Select the field and choose **Edit > Cut** or *Ctrl+X*.
2) Choose **Edit > Paste Special.** Click "Unformatted text" in the **Selection** list, and then click **OK**. Alternatively, press *Ctrl+Alt+Shift*+V to paste unformatted text.

This is not a very good solution if you have hundreds of fields that you want to change, but you could use a macro to automate the process.

After you change a field to text, you cannot change the text back into a field.

Developing conditional content

Conditional content is text and graphics that are included or excluded depending on a condition you specify.

A simple example is a reminder letter for an overdue account. The first and second reminders might have a subject line of "Reminder Notice", but the third reminder letter might have the subject "Final Notice" and a different final paragraph.

A more complex example is a software manual for a product that comes in two versions, Pro and Lite. Both product versions have much in common, but the Pro version includes some features that are not in the Lite version. If you use conditional content, you can maintain one file containing information for both versions and print (or create online help) customized for each version. You do not have to maintain two sets of the information that is the same for both versions, so you will not forget to update both versions when something changes.

Choose the types of conditional content to use

This section describes several Writer features that can help you design and maintain conditional content. You can use one or any combination of these features in the same document.

Conditional text

With conditional text, you can have two alternative texts (a word, phrase, or sentence). One text will be displayed and printed if the condition you specify is met, and the other will be displayed and printed if the condition is not met. You cannot include graphics or edit the text except in the field dialog (not in the body of the document). You also cannot format part of the text (for example, bolding one word but not the others), but you can format the field to affect all of the field contents (for example, bolding all of the words). You cannot include a cross-reference or other field in the text.

Hidden text

With hidden text (a word, phrase, or sentence), you have only two choices: show or hide. If the condition you specify is met, the text is hidden; if the condition is not met, the text is displayed. The disadvantages are the same as for conditional text: you cannot include graphics, edit the text in the body of the document, format part of the text, or include a field.

Hidden paragraphs

Hidden paragraphs are like any other paragraphs, but you can specify a condition under which the paragraph is not displayed or printed. A blank paragraph can also be hidden—for example, if a database field has no content for the current record. This is very useful when merging an address into a letter: if you allow two lines for the street address and the database record uses only one line, you can prevent the blank line from appearing in your document. You can include graphics, edit the text in the body of the document, format any part of the text, and include fields.

Hidden sections

Hidden sections are like hidden paragraphs, but they can include more than one paragraph—for example, a heading plus one or more paragraphs. However, a section cannot contain less than a paragraph, so you cannot use this method for single words or phrases. The contents of a hidden section behave just like the contents of any other part of the document, but you can specify a condition under which the section is not displayed or printed. In addition, you can password protect a section.

Plan your conditional content

Conditions are what programmers call *logical expressions*. You must formulate a logical expression for each condition because a condition is always either true (met) or false (not met). You can use the same condition in many places in your document, for different types of conditional content.

To make conditional content work, you need to:

1) Choose or define a variable.
2) Define a logical expression (condition) involving the selected variable.

Choose or define a variable

You can use the following variables in your condition:

- User-defined variables
- Predefined LibreOffice variables, which use statistical values from the document properties
- User data
- Database field contents—for example from your address book

You cannot use internal variables (for example, page number or chapter name) to formulate conditions.

The examples in this chapter use user-defined variables.

Define a logical expression (condition) involving the selected variable

The condition compares a specified fixed value with the contents of a variable or database field.

To formulate a condition, use the same elements as you would to create a formula: operators, mathematical and statistical functions, number formats, variables, and constants. The possible operators are given in the online help; look in the index under "operators: in formulas". You can define quite complex expressions, but in most cases a simple condition will do the job.

Create the variable

To create your variable, choose **Insert > Fields > Other** or press *Ctrl+F2*. You can use choices found on the *DocInformation*, *Variables*, and *Database* pages.

DocInformation fields

"Using document properties to hold metadata and information that changes" on page 400 described how to set up a custom document property. You can use that document property as the variable in your condition statement, or you can create another document property field specifically for conditions.

User-defined variable field

To set up a variable or user field:

1) Place the cursor where you want the field to be inserted.
2) On the Fields dialog, select the *Variables* page.

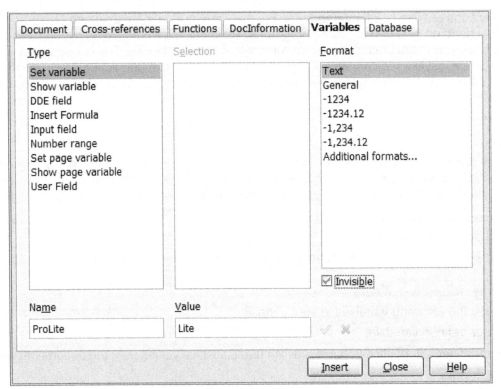

Figure 419: Defining a variable to use with conditional content

3) Select **Set variable** in the *Type* list and **Text** in the *Format* list. Type a name for the variable in the *Name* box, and a value in the *Value* box. I have chosen **ProLite** for the name (to remind me that this variable is related to the two product versions), and I set the value as **Lite** because I can remember "If it is the Lite version, then this text should be hidden."

4) Select **Invisible** so the field does not show in the document. Click **Insert**, then click **Close**.

5) A small gray mark should be visible where you inserted the field. We will come back to this field later.

Tip	Because the gray mark is so small, you may have trouble finding it again, especially if you have other fields in the document. You may prefer to leave the variable field visible while you work, and change it to invisible just before you create final copy.
	At any time, you can place the insertion point just before the field and choose **Edit > Fields** or right-click the field, and then click **Fields** on the context menu. On the Edit Fields dialog (Figure 423), select or deselect the **Invisible** option.

Apply the condition to the content

Now that you have defined the variable, you can use it in a condition statement. This topic describes some of the possibilities.

Conditional text

First, let us set up some conditional text that will insert the words **Great Product Lite** into the Lite version and **Great Product Pro** into the Pro version of the manual. You would use this field whenever you want to mention the name of the product.

1) Place the cursor where you want one of these phrases to appear. (You can move or delete it later, if you wish.)

2) Open the Fields dialog by clicking **Insert > Fields > Other**, select the *Functions* page, and select **Conditional text** in the *Type* list.

3) As shown in Figure 420, type **ProLite EQ "Lite"** in the *Condition* box, **Great Product Lite** in the *Then* box, and **Great Product Pro** in the *Else* box.

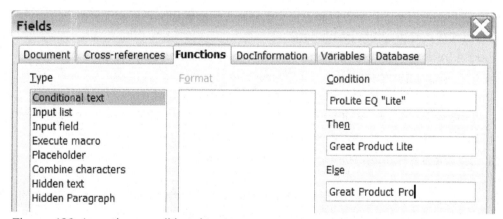

Figure 420: Inserting conditional text

Note	These fields are case-sensitive, and quotation marks are required around a text value such as **Lite**.

4) Click **Insert** to insert the field, then click **Close**. You should see **Great Product Lite** in your text.

Tip	If you want to insert this field into your text in many places (as you probably would for a product name), create an AutoText entry for it. See "Using AutoText to insert often-used fields" on page 404 for instructions.

Hidden text

You might use hidden text for words or short phrases that describe features of Great Product Pro that are not found in the Lite version. You can reuse the same field in several places in your document—for example, by copying and pasting it.

To create a hidden text field:

1) Choose **Insert > Fields > Other** and select the *Functions* page.
2) Select **Hidden text** in the *Type* list, as shown in Figure 421.
3) Type **ProLite EQ "Lite"** in the *Condition* box and type the required text in the *Hidden text* box. Remember, this is the text that is *hidden* if the condition is true.
4) Click **Insert** to create and insert the field.

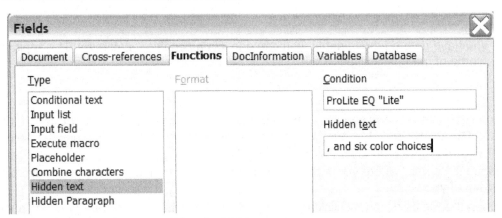

Figure 421: Creating a condition for hidden text

Hidden paragraphs

A paragraph is hidden if the condition is true. To hide a paragraph:

1) Click in the paragraph to be hidden.
2) Choose **Insert > Fields > Other** and select the *Functions* page (Figure 421).
3) Select **Hidden paragraph** in the *Type* list.
4) For this example, type **ProLite EQ "Lite"** in the *Condition* box.
5) Click **Insert** to create and insert the field. If an extra paragraph mark appears, delete it.

To show hidden paragraphs so you can edit them, do one of the following:

- Choose **View > Hidden Paragraphs** from the menu bar, so it is checked (shows all hidden paragraphs).
- On the **Tools > Options > LibreOffice Writer > Formatting Aids** page, select the *Fields: Hidden paragraphs* option (shows all hidden paragraphs).
- Double-click in front of the variable that you used to define the condition for hiding the text, and enter a different value for the variable (shows all hidden paragraphs).
- Double-click in front of the hidden text field or the hidden paragraph field, and change the condition statement (changes only the selected hidden paragraph).

Hidden sections

A conditional section is hidden if the condition is true. To create a conditional section:

1) Select the text that you want to be included in the conditional section. (You can edit this text later, just as you can edit any other text.)

2) Choose **Insert > Section**. On the Insert Section dialog (Figure 422), select the *Section* tab, then select **Hide** and enter the condition in the *with Condition* box. You can also give the section a name, if you wish (strongly recommended, so you can find it again easily if you have several sections in your document).

3) Click **Insert** to insert the section into your document.

To show a hidden section so you can edit it:

1) Choose **Format > Sections**.

2) On the Edit Sections dialog (similar to the Insert Section dialog), select the section from the list.

3) Deselect **Hide**, and then click **OK**. You can now edit the contents of the section. Afterwards, you can choose **Format > Sections** again and select **Hide** to hide the section again.

To show all the hidden sections so you can edit them, change the value of the variable to something that the conditions will not recognize. In our example, you could change the value to **1**.

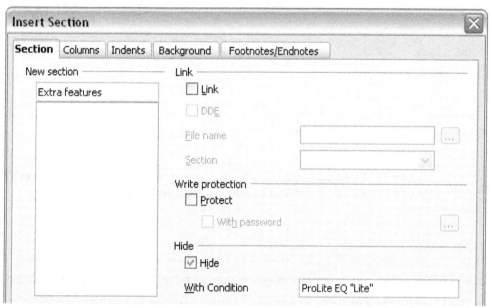

Figure 422: Creating a section to be hidden when a specified condition is met

To make the hidden section a normal part of the document (that is, to remove the section markers, but not the contents of the section):

1) Show the hidden section, as described above.

2) On the Edit Sections dialog, select the section from the list.

3) Click **Remove**. The contents of the section are now a normal part of the document.

Change the value of the variable

1) Find the variable field you created in "Create the variable" on page 414.

2) Click once just in front of this field, then right-click and click **Fields** on the context menu.

3) On the Edit Fields: Variables dialog (Figure 423), change the value of the variable to **Pro**.

---

4) If you have set fields to update automatically, all of the conditional and hidden text that uses this variable as a condition will change.

Tip	Conditional text and hidden text can only be edited in the Edit Fields dialog.

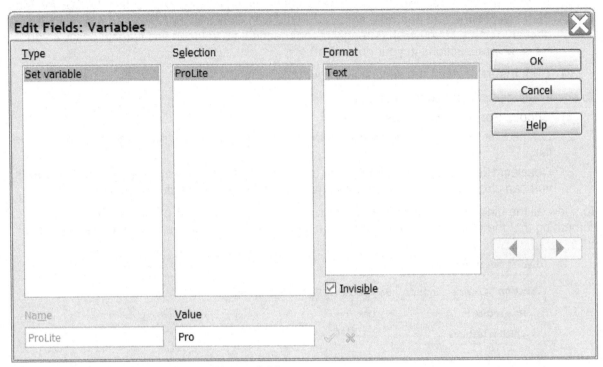

Figure 423: Changing the value of the variable

Tip	To turn on automatic updating of fields, choose **Tools > Options > LibreOffice Writer > General**, and select **Fields** under **Update: Automatically**.

Using placeholder fields

A placeholder field prompts you to enter something (text, a table, a frame, a graphic, or an object).

To insert a placeholder field into a document:
1) On the *Functions* page of the Fields dialog, select **Placeholder** in the *Type* column and select what the placeholder is for in the *Format* column.
2) In the *Placeholder* box, type the text that you want to appear in the placeholder field.
3) In the *Reference* box, type the text that you want to display as a help tip when you rest the mouse pointer over the field.

Figure 424 shows the results of inserting a placeholder field for a graphic.

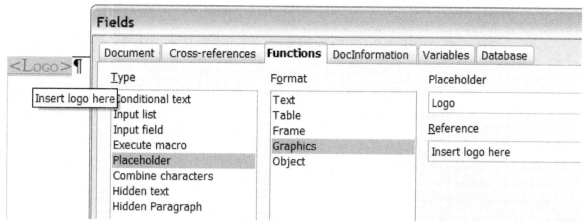

Figure 424: Inserting a placeholder field

Because the *<Logo>* field is a graphics placeholder, when you click on the field in the document, the Insert picture dialog opens, prompting you to select a graphic (picture). When you select a picture and click **Open**, the picture replaces the field in the document.

Similarly, clicking on a table placeholder field opens the Insert Table dialog, clicking on a frame placeholder field opens the Frame dialog, and clicking on an object placeholder field opens the Insert OLE Object dialog. The text placeholder field is different: you simply click on it and type some text in the *Placeholder* box, which replaces the field.

Using input fields and input lists

Input field

An *input field* is a variable that you can click in a document to open a dialog where you can edit the text displayed in the field. To insert an input field:

1) Choose **Insert > Fields > Other** and choose the *Functions* page.
2) Choose **Input field** in the *Type* list (Figure 425).
3) Optionally type some text in the **Reference** box. This text will appear as a tooltip when the users hover a mouse cursor over the field.
4) Click **Insert**. In the small dialog that opens, type some text for the variable (for example, a brief instruction to the user regarding the purpose of the field); this text can be the same or different from the text in the Reference box in the previous step.
5) Click **OK**.

To edit an input field, click on it in the document. In the small dialog that opens, edit the text of the field.

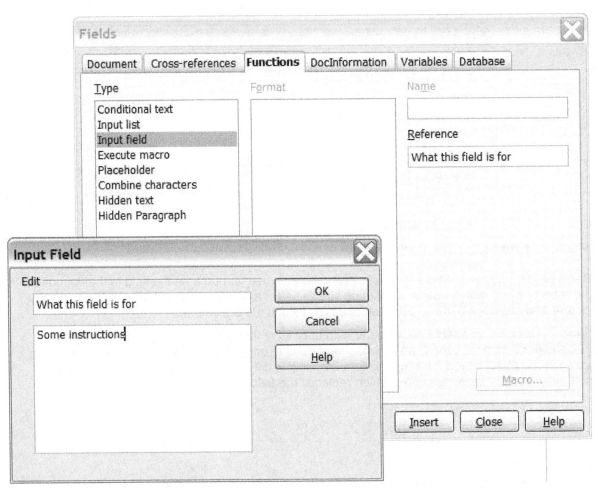

Figure 425: Inserting an input field

To edit the field's reference, right-click on the field and choose **Fields** from the context menu. This opens the Edit Fields: Functions dialog.

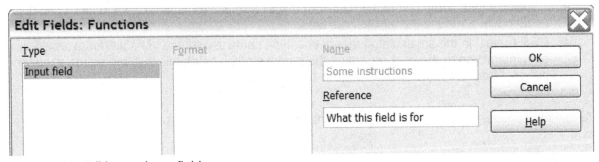

Figure 426: Editing an input field

Input list

An *input list* is a text field that displays one item from a list. To insert an input list field into a document:

1) Choose **Insert > Fields > Other**; on the *Functions* page, choose **Input list** in the *Type* list (Figure 427).

2) Type the names of the list items in the **Item** box on the upper right, clicking **Add** after each item. The items then appear in the **Items on list** box. To change the order of the items, select an item and click the **Move Up** or **Move Down** buttons.

3) Type the name of the list in the **Name** field on the lower right.

4) Click **Insert**.

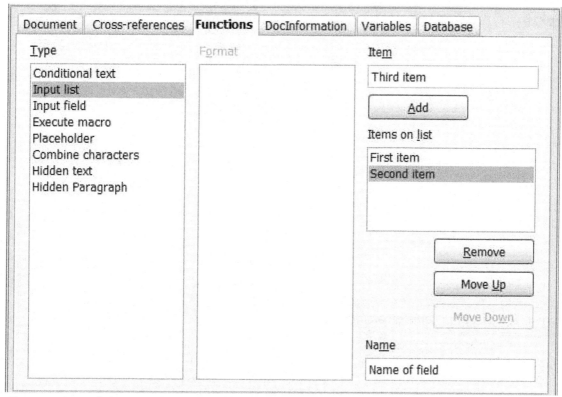

Figure 427: Defining an input list field

To display the Choose Item dialog, click the Input list field.

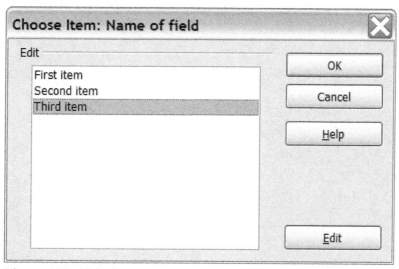

Figure 428: Choosing an item from an input list

To add, edit, and remove items from this list, and change their order in the list, click the **Edit** button in the Choose Item dialog. This displays the Edit Fields: Function dialog (Figure 429).

To quickly edit all input fields and lists in a document, press *Ctrl+Shift+F9*. The first input field or list in the document opens. Clicking **OK** or **Next** moves to the next input field or list. After the last input field or list, clicking **Next** or **OK** returns you to the document.

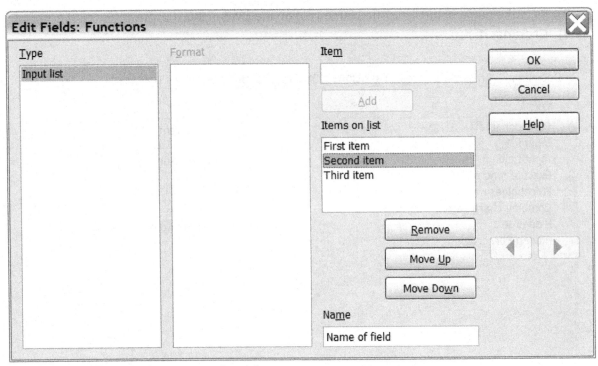

Figure 429: Editing the items on an input list

Chapter 15
Using Forms in Writer

Introduction to forms

This chapter covers the use of forms within Writer documents. Most of the information here also applies to forms in other LibreOffice components, but there are some differences.

The chapter presents information on using forms in four main sections: setting up a basic form, an example for creating a form, linking a form to a data source, and finally some advanced techniques.

LibreOffice forms cover a lot of ground and not everything is included here. Notable omissions are using forms in HTML documents and writing macros to link to form controls.

When to use forms

A standard text document displays information: a letter, report, or brochure, for example. Typically the reader may edit everything or nothing in the document. A form has sections that are not to be edited, and other sections that are designed for the reader to make changes. For example, a questionnaire has an introduction and questions (which do not change) and spaces for the reader to enter answers.

LibreOffice offers several ways to enter information into a form, including check boxes, option buttons, text boxes, pull-down lists, and other items, collectively known as *form controls*.

Forms are used in three ways:

- To create a simple document for the recipient to complete, such as a questionnaire sent out to a group of people who fill it in and return it.
- To link into a database or data source and allow the user to enter information. Someone taking orders might enter the information into a database using a form.
- To view information held in a database or data source. A librarian might call up information about books.

Using forms to access a database offers a fast and easy way to build up complex graphical front ends. Your form can include not only the fields that link up to the data source but also text, graphics, tables, drawings and other elements.

A typical way to use a simple form is:

1) You design the form, then save it when you are happy with it.
2) You send the form to others (for example, by email).
3) They fill in the form, save it and send it back to you.
4) You open the form and see what their answers are.

Tip	By using a data source, or setting a form to update over the web, you can automatically gather data. However, both of those are more complex and you might prefer to keep things simple.

Alternatives to using forms in Writer

In LibreOffice, the Base component provides an alternative way to access a data source. There are a lot of similarities between forms in Base and Writer, but one may be better for a particular task than the other. Base is appropriate only if the form accesses a data source; you would not use it for simple forms.

LibreOffice Calc, Impress, and Draw also support forms in almost the same way that Writer does.

Creating a simple form

This section explains how to create a simple form without any links to a data source or database and without advanced customization.

Create a document

There is nothing special to be done when creating a document to use as a form. Create a new Writer document with **File > New > Text document**.

Open the form toolbars

Two toolbars control form creation: Form Controls and Form Design. Select **View > Toolbars > Form Controls** and **View > Toolbars > Form Design** to show them both. The Form Controls toolbar has a button for each of the most commonly used types of control.

You can also open the Form Design toolbar from the Form Controls toolbar. Some of the less commonly used controls are on a third toolbar—More Controls—also opened from the Form Controls toolbar.

You can dock these toolbars in different places on the Writer window, or leave them floating. Figure 430 shows the three toolbars floating. When they are floating, you can also change them from vertical to horizontal and change the number of tools on a row; to make these changes, drag a corner of the toolbar.

See "Form controls reference" on page 427 for descriptions of the tools on these toolbars.

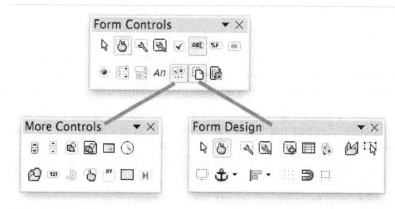

Figure 430: The Form Control, More Controls, and Form Design Toolbars

Activate design mode

Click the **Design Mode On/Off** button (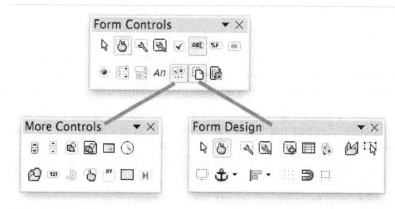) on the Form Controls toolbar to turn design mode on. (Click it again when you want to turn it off.) This activates the buttons for inserting form controls and selects controls for editing.

When design mode is off, the form behaves as it would for the end user. Buttons can be pressed, check boxes selected, list items selected, and so on.

Insert form controls

1) To insert a form control into the document, click the control's icon to select it. The mouse pointer changes to look like this: ⌐□

2) Click in the document where you want the control to appear. (You can move it later.)

3) Holding the left mouse button down, drag the control to size it. Some controls have a fixed size symbol followed by the name of the control (for example, *Check Box* or *Option Button*).

4) The control button remains active, so you can insert several controls of the same type without needing to go back to the toolbar.

5) To change to another tool, click its icon on the toolbar.

6) To stop inserting controls, click on the **Select** button ( ) on the Form Controls toolbar, or click on any of the controls you have just inserted. The mouse pointer changes back to its normal appearance.

Tip	Holding down *Shift* when creating a form control makes the control square. If you press *Shift* when resizing an existing control, its proportions are kept the same.

Note	When you insert a group box, list box, or combo box, a wizard is launched to guide you through the setup. If you prefer not to run the wizard, click the **Wizards On/Off** button ( ) on the Form Controls toolbar.

Configure controls

After inserting the controls, you need to configure them to look and behave as you want. Right-click on a form control within your document and select **Control** from the context menu to open the Properties dialog for the selected control. Double-clicking on a form control also opens this dialog.

The Properties dialog has three pages: General, Data, and Events. For simple forms, only the General page is of any interest. On this page you can set the look and feel of the control. See "Configure form controls" on page 434 and "Form control formatting options" on page 444 for more information, and the descriptions in the Help for details. Configuration for use with a database is discussed in "Creating a form for data entry" on page 439.

The fields on this dialog vary with the type of control. For example:

- Some controls have visible labels, such as Push Button and Option Button. The label text can be set.
- The List Box contains a list of options to choose from. Set these in the List entries box.

Notice the scroll bar in this dialog. You can use the scroll bar or enlarge the dialog to see additional fields.

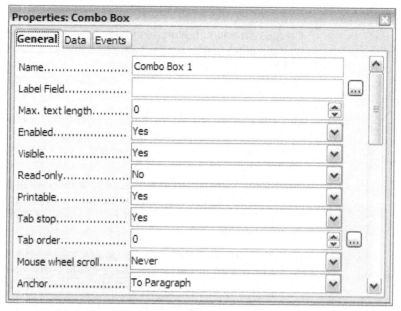

Figure 431: Example of the Properties dialog for a form control

Use the form

To use the form, leave design mode by clicking the **Design Mode On/Off** button (⏻) to deactivate it. Save the form document.

Form controls reference

Form Control toolbar	
⬉ Select	Selects a form control to perform some other action on it.
⏻ Design mode on/off	Toggles between design mode on (to edit forms) and design mode off (to use forms).
✎ Control	Launches form control properties dialog. This dialog can be kept open as different controls are selected.
▦ Form	Launches form properties dialog, controlling properties for the form as a whole, such as which data source it connects to.
☑ Check Box	A box that can be selected or deselected on the form. You can label the box.
ABC Text Box	A control to create a box into which the form user can type any text.
%F Formatted Field	A control allowing numeric formatting options. For example, you can set maximum and minimum values for the number entered, or the number type (decimal places, scientific, currency).
OK Push Button	Creates a button that can be linked to a macro. The label is the name that appears on the button.

⊙	Option Button	Creates an option button (also known as a *radio button*). When multiple buttons are grouped together, only one can be selected at a time. The easiest way to group multiple buttons is to use the Group Box button on the More Controls toolbar, with wizards enabled.
▤	List Box	Creates a list of options as a pull-down menu that the user can choose from. If wizards are on, creating a list box launches the List Box Wizard. This wizard is only useful if your form is linked to a data source. If the form is not linked to a data source, turn wizards off and create an empty list box. Then click the control button and, in the *List Entries* option on the *General* tab, enter the options you want to appear on the list.
▤	Combo Box	As with a List Box, you set up a list of choices. In addition, a panel at the top either displays the choice made or allows the form user to type in something else. This works the same as the List Box.
An	Label Field	A text label. The difference between this and just typing on the page is that, as a control, you can link a label field to macros so, for example, something happens when the mouse passes over it or clicks on it.
▦	More Controls	Launches the More Controls toolbar.
▤	Form Design	Launches the Form Design toolbar, which can also be opened with **View > Toolbars > Form Design**.
▤	Wizards On/Off	Some form controls (List Box and Combo Box) have optional wizards. If you do not want the wizard to launch when you create one of these controls, use the **Wizards On/Off** button to switch wizards off.

More Controls toolbar

▤	Spin Button	Allows form users to choose a number by cycling through the list of numbers. You can specify maximum, minimum, default, and the step between numbers. This control is not commonly used in Writer, as the number is not displayed. In Calc, however, a Data tab appears on the Control Properties dialog, so you can link the spin button to a cell.
▤	Scrollbar	Creates a scrollbar, with a number of options to define the exact appearance. This control is not commonly used in Writer. In Calc, a Data tab appears on the Control Properties dialog, allowing you to link the scroll bar to a cell.
▣	Image Button	Behaves exactly like a push button, but displays as an image. Choose the image in the Graphics option on the *General* tab in the Control Properties dialog.
▣	Image Control	Only useful when the form is connected to a data source and a field in the data source exists that can hold images. You can add new images to the database or retrieve and display images from it.

More Controls toolbar

Date Field	Stores a date. You need to configure the earliest and latest dates the field will accept, the default date, and the date format. You can add a spinner.
Time Field	Works like a date field but specifies a time.
File Selection	Allows a user to select a file, either by typing the path and name directly or by clicking on a Browse button and choosing the file from a dialog.
123 Numeric Field	Displays a number. You need to specify formatting, maximum, minimum and default values. You can add a spinner.
Currency Field	Works like a numeric field; additionally you can add a currency symbol.
Pattern Field	Pattern fields are useful when the form links into a data source. Specify an Edit Mask to restrict what a user can enter into the field. Specify a Literal Mask to restrict which data is displayed from the data source.
Group Box	The group box control has two different uses depending on whether wizards are on or off. If wizards are on, creating a group box launches the Group Element wizard. This creates a group of options buttons (in which only one may be selected at a time). In most cases, using a group box is the best way to create a set of option buttons. If wizards are off, a group box is simply a visual box to group together different controls. It has no effect on the way the controls operate.
Table Control	Table Control is only useful with a data source. If no data source is specified, you will be prompted to choose one in the Table Element Wizard. You then pick the fields to display and, when design mode is off, the data appears in the table. The table also includes controls to step through the records. Records can be added, deleted, and modified in the table.
Navigation Bar	A navigation bar is the same as the Form Navigation toolbar (**View > Toolbars > Form Navigation**), but can be placed anywhere in the document and be resized.

Form Design toolbar

Select	Selects a form control to perform an action on it.
Design mode on/off	Toggles between design mode on (to edit forms) and design mode off (to use forms).
Control	Launches form control properties dialog. This dialog can be kept open as different controls are selected.
Form	Launches form properties dialog, controlling properties for the form as a whole, such as which data source it connects to.

Form Design toolbar

Form Navigator	The Form Navigator is a utility displaying all the forms and controls in the current document. It allows you to edit and delete them easily.
	If you use the Form Navigator, it's recommended that you give your controls names (in the properties dialog). The name appears in the navigator so, for example, if you have ten text boxes, you can tell which is which.
Add Field	Add Field is only useful if you have specified a data source for the form. If no data source is specified, an empty box opens.
	If you have specified a data source, Add Field opens a list of all the fields in the specified table, which you can then drag and drop onto the page. The fields are placed on the page with the name of the field before them.
	This is a quick and easy way to create a form from a data source.
Activation Order	Allows you to specify the order in which focus shifts between controls. You can test the order by leaving design mode and using *Tab* to switch between the controls.
Open in Design Mode	Opens the current form in design mode (to edit the form rather than entering data into it).
Automatic Control Focus	If activated, focus is set to the first form control.
Position and Size	Launches the Position and Size dialog, allowing you to specify both by typing in precise values, rather than dragging the control. You can also lock the size or position, so they do not get changed accidentally. For some controls, you can rotate and set the slant and corner radius.
Change Anchor	Just as with a frame, any form control can be anchored to page, paragraph or character and also anchored as a character (meaning that it behaves like any other character on the page).
Alignment	The Alignment button is disabled unless the control is anchored as a character. You can align a control in different ways, for example so the top of the control lines up with the top of the text or the bottom lines up with the bottom of the text.
Display Grid	Displays a grid of dots on the page, to help you line up controls.
Snap to Grid	When a control is brought close to a grid point or line, it will snap to the grid. This makes it is easier to line up controls.
Guides when Moving	When a control is being moved, lines extend from the control horizontally and vertically to help you position it accurately.

Example: a simple form

Create the document

Open a new document (**File > New > Text Document**). It is a good idea to write down the outline of the document, without form controls, though of course it can easily be changed later.

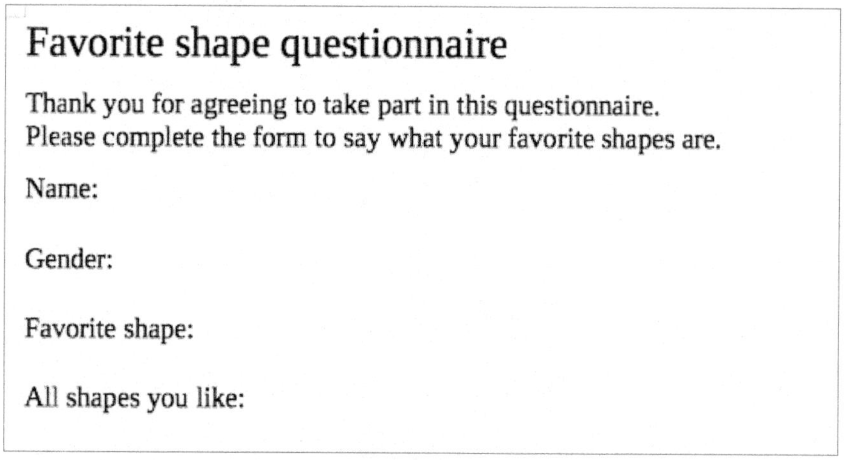

> # Favorite shape questionnaire
>
> Thank you for agreeing to take part in this questionnaire.
> Please complete the form to say what your favorite shapes are.
>
> Name:
>
> Gender:
>
> Favorite shape:
>
> All shapes you like:

Figure 432: Initial document without form controls

Add form controls

The next step is to add the form controls to the document. We will have four controls:

- **Name** is a text box.
- **Gender** is three option buttons: male, female, or other.
- **Favourite shape** is a list of options.
- **All shapes you like** is a series of check boxes.

To add these controls:

1) Select **View > Toolbars > Form Controls** to open the Form Control toolbar.

2) If the tools are not active, click the **Design Mode On/Off** ( ) button to activate them.

3) Click the **Text Box** button ( ), then click in the document and, with the left mouse button held down, drag the shape of the Name text box to approximately the size you want.

4) Make sure the **Wizards On/Off** button ( ) is on (shown with a border). Click the **More Controls** button ( ) to launch the More Controls toolbar.

5) On the More Controls toolbar, click the **Group Box** button ( ). Draw a group box by the Sex: entry. The Group Element Wizard opens.

   a) On the first page of the wizard, enter three names for the options fields: **Male**, **Female**, and **Other**. Click the **>>** button after each entry. Click **Next >>**.

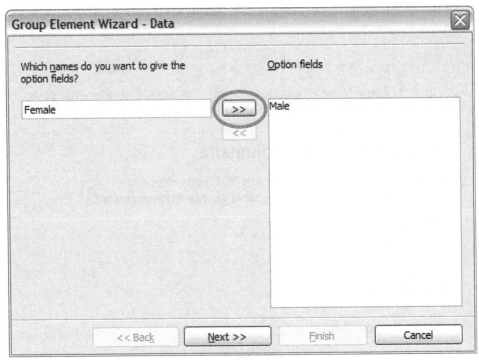

Figure 433: Specifying names for option fields

b) On the next page, select the option **No, one particular field is not going to be selected**. Click **Next >>**.

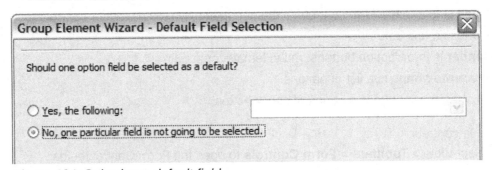

Figure 434: Selecting a default field

c) Give a value to your fields. Typically, you would give one field the value 1 and the other field the value 2. If there are more than 2 option fields, you would give them values of 3, 4, and so on. Click **Next >>**.

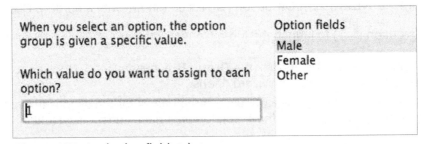

Figure 435: Assigning field values

d) You can either delete the caption or give a caption to your Group Box. In this example, delete the caption. Then click **Finish**.

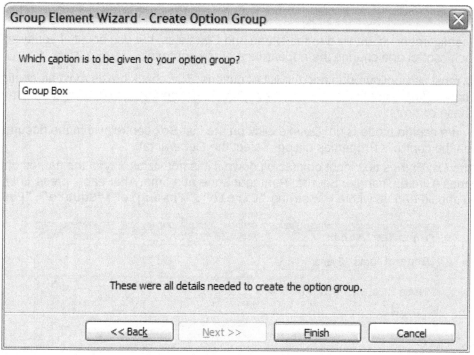

Figure 436: Create Caption Option

6) Now create the list box. On the Form Controls toolbar, click the **Wizards On/Off** button ( )
to turn wizards off. Click the **List Box** button ( ) and draw a list box by *Favourite Shape*
in the document. This will just be an empty pane for now.

7) Finally create four check boxes by *All shapes you like*. Click on the **Check Box** ( )
button and then draw four check boxes, side by side across the page.

You should now have a document looking something like Figure 437.

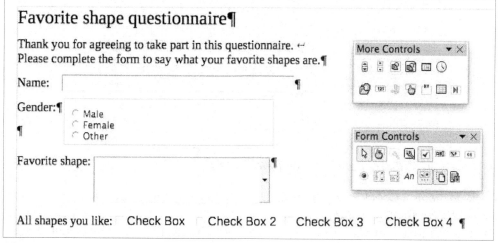

Figure 437: Document with form controls

Configure form controls

No further configuration is required to the Name and Sex fields, but you could, if you wish, give a name to each control and change the appearance of the controls.

The list box must be configured to add the list of options. The check boxes must be configured to add in the names (instead of Check Box, Check Box 2, and so forth). Following are instructions to configure these controls:

1) Be sure design mode is on. Double-click on the List Box control within the document to open the control's Properties dialog. Select the *General* tab.

2) In the *List Entries* text input box (scroll down if it is not visible), type the names of the shapes (Circle, Triangle, Square, Pentagon) one at a time. After each, press *Shift+Enter*. You should end up with a line saying **"Circle";"Triangle";"Square";"Pentagon"**.

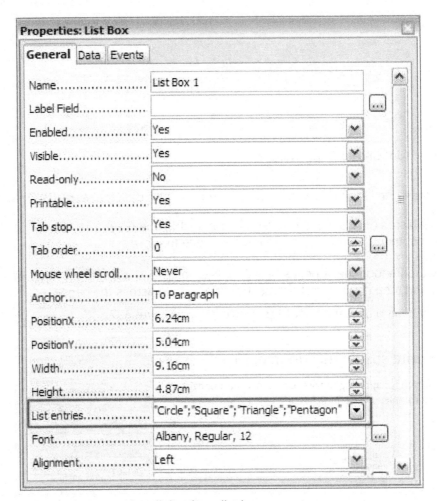

Figure 438: Properties dialog for a list box

3) Click on the first Check Box. The Properties dialog stays open but changes to show the properties for the check box.

4) Change the text in the *Label* text input box from **Check Box** to **Circle** and press *Enter.* The cursor moves to the *Label Field* text input box, and the label on the check box in the document changes immediately.

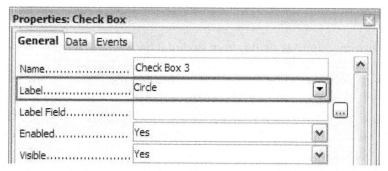

Figure 439: Top part of Properties dialog for a check box

5) Click on each of the other three check boxes in turn. Change the text in the *Label* text input box in the Properties dialog to Triangle, Square, and Pentagon in turn.

6) Close the Properties dialog.

7) Turn design mode off (⬚) and close the two Controls toolbars.

You have now completed the form, which should look something like Figure 440.

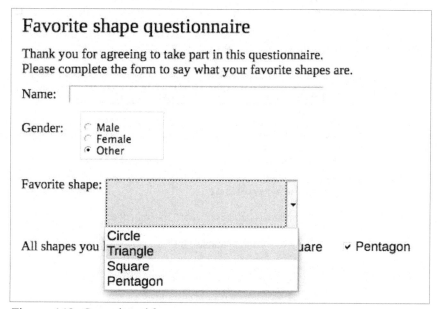

Figure 440: Completed form

Finishing touches

The form is complete, but you are free to make further changes to the document. If you were sending this out to other people to complete, you would probably want to make the document read-only. The effect would be that users would be able to fill in the form but not to make any other changes to the document.

To make the document read-only, select **File > Properties**, select the *Security* tab and enable the **Open file read-only** option.

Note	If the document is read-only, anyone filling in the form will need to use **File > Save as** to save the document.

Accessing data sources

The most common use for a form is as the front end of a database. You can provide a form that allows users to enter information into a contacts database and, because it is part of a Writer document, the form can contain graphics, formatting, tables, and other elements to make it look just the way you want. Modifying the form is as simple as editing a document.

LibreOffice can access numerous data sources. These include ODBC, MySQL, Oracle JDBC, spreadsheets and text files. As a general rule, databases can be accessed for read and write; other data sources (such as spreadsheets) are read-only.

Tip	To see the list of supported data source types for your operating system, choose **File > New > Database**. On the first page of the Database Wizard (Figure 444), select **Connect to an existing database** and then open the drop-down list. An example is shown in Figure 445.

Creating a database

Chapter 8, Getting Started with Base, in the *Getting Started* guide covers in more detail how to create a database. Here we give a short guide to creating a very simple database with LibreOffice Base.

1) Select **File > New > Database** to start the Database Wizard.

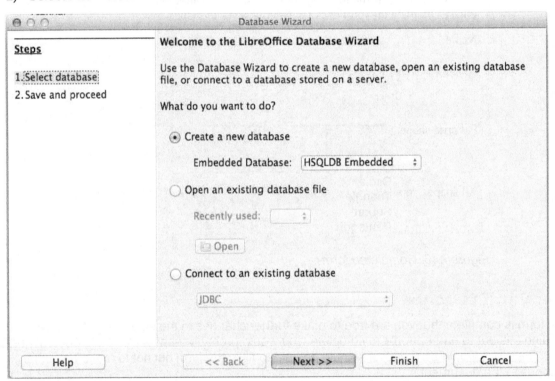

Figure 441: Database Wizard

2) Select **Create a new database** and click **Next >>**.

3) On the next page, select **Yes, register the database for me** and **Open the database for editing**. Registering the database means that it can be accessed from other LibreOffice components such as Writer and Calc. You need to do this if you want to link forms into it.

4) Click **Finish** and save your new database, giving it a name. Unlike creating other documents in LibreOffice, databases must be saved when you first create them.

After saving the database, you should see the main Base window (Figure 442), which contains three panels. The left-hand panel is Database, with icons for Tables, Queries, Forms and Reports.

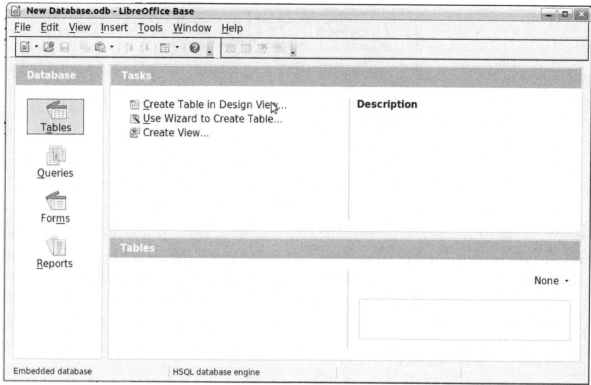

Figure 442: Main Base window

The next step is to create a table. Again, this is covered in more detail in Chapter 8, Getting Started with Base, in the *Getting Started* guide. Here we are going to create a small table as an example.

1) Choose **Tables** in the left-hand column, then choose **Create Table in Design View** under Tasks.

2) Use the Table Design window to tell Base which fields to create. We will have three input data fields: Name, Address, and Telephone.

3) On the first line, enter under Field Name, `ID`, and set the Field Type to `Integer` `[INTEGER]`. In the box at the left of the line, right-click and select **Primary Key**, bringing up a key icon in the box. In the **Field Properties** at the bottom of the window is an **Auto Value** option; change this to **Yes**. Optionally, type `Primary key` in the Description column. See Figure 443.

Tip	Setting up the Primary Key field with Auto Value set to **Yes** is an important step. If this is not done, the form you create later will be much trickier to use and may generate errors for the user. It could even prevent the user from saving the records in the form. Make sure you get this step right!

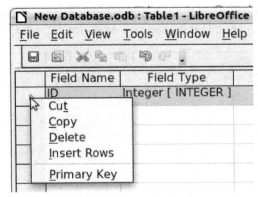

Figure 443: Setting a primary key

4) On the next three lines, enter under Field Name **Name**, **Address** and **Telephone**. Accept the default Field Type of Text [VARCHAR] and leave Description blank.

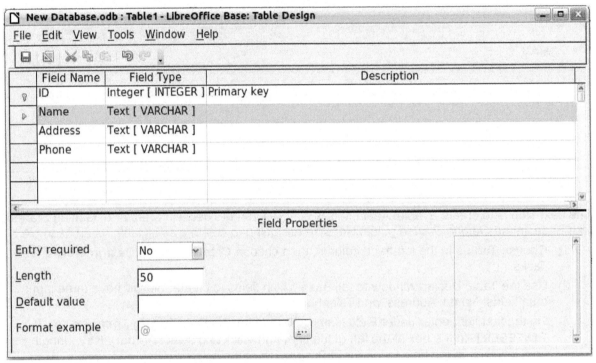

Figure 444: Database table design

5) Save the table (**File > Save**). You will be prompted to name it. The name can be anything you like. Click **OK**.

6) Finally, close the table design window to return to the main Base window. If **File > Save** is available, select it to save the whole database.

Accessing an existing data source

If you have an existing data source, such as a spreadsheet or database, you simply need to tell LibreOffice about it. This is called registering a data source.

To register an existing data source:

1) Select **File > New > Database** to launch the Database Wizard.

2) Select **Connect to an existing database** and choose the type from the drop-down list.

LibreOffice 4.2 Writer Guide

3) Click **Next** and follow the instructions to select the database to register (the exact process varies between different types of data source).

4) In Step 3: Save and proceed, check that **Yes, register the database for me** is selected. Deselect **Open the database for editing**; you just need to register it, not edit it through Base.

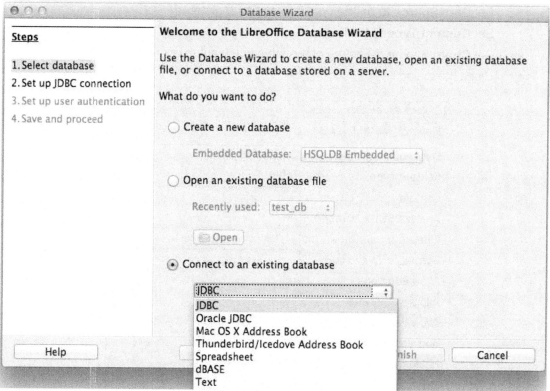

Figure 445: Using the Database Wizard to connect to an existing database

Creating a form for data entry

Whether you created a new database, or already had a data source, it must be registered with LibreOffice (see above). Once it is registered, linking your form to the data source is simple. Follow these steps to create a new form and link it to a registered data source.

1) Create a new document in Writer (**File > New > Text Document**).

2) Design your form, without putting in the actual fields (you can always change it later).

3) Show the Form Controls toolbar (**View > Toolbars > Form Controls**).

4) Click the **Design Mode On/Off** button ( ) to put the document into design mode, if necessary. With design mode off, most of the toolbar buttons are grayed out. If the Design Mode button is also grayed out, click on the **Select** button to activate it.

5) Click the **Text Box** button ( ). Click in the document and, holding down the left mouse button, drag the mouse to create a text box for the first form field (for example, Name, if you are linking to the database created above).

6) Click the **Text Box** button ( ) again and drag the mouse to draw another field. Additional fields, of any type, can be added in the same way (click and drag).

So far you have followed the same steps used before when creating your first form. Now you will link the form with the data source you registered.

1) Click the **Form** button (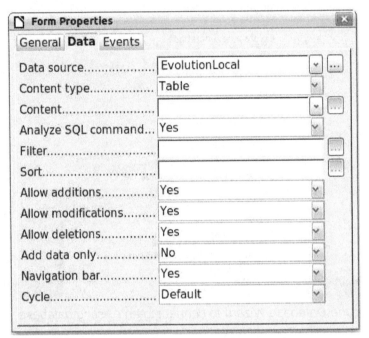) in the **Form Controls** toolbar, or right-click on any of the fields you inserted and select **Form**, to open the Form Properties dialog.

2) In the **Form Properties** dialog, click on the **Data** tab.

- Set **Data Source** to be the data source you registered.

- Set **Content Type** to be Table.

- Set **Content** to be the name of the table you want to access.

- Close the dialog.

Figure 446: Form properties, connecting to a data source

3) For each form control in turn, click on the control to select it (so small green boxes appear around it), then launch the **Properties** dialog: either right-click and select **Control** or click on the **Control** button ( ) on the **Form Controls** toolbar.

4) In the **Properties** dialog, click on the **Data** tab (Figure 447). If you set up the form correctly, the **Data Field** option will contain a list of the different fields in the data source (for example, Name, Address and Telephone). Select the field you want.

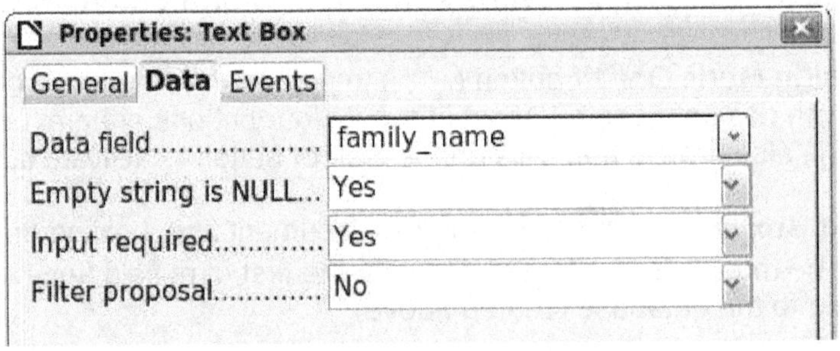

Figure 447: Form control properties, Data tab

5) Repeat for each control in turn until every control that should be assigned to a field has been assigned.

Tip	If you created a database in LibreOffice Base and your Primary Key field had **Auto Value** set to *Yes*, that field does not need to be part of the form. If **Auto Value** was set to *No*, you will have to include it and have your users enter a unique value into that field whenever they make a new entry—not something that is recommended.

Entering data into a form

Once you have created a form and tied it to a database, you want to use it to enter data into your data source, or modify data already there.

1) Make sure that the form is not in design mode. In the **Form Controls** toolbar, click on the **Design Mode On/Off** button ( ). If design mode is off, most of the buttons on the toolbar will be grayed out.

2) Make sure that the Form Navigation toolbar is on (**View > Toolbars > Form Navigation**). This toolbar normally appears at the bottom of the window.

Figure 448: Form Navigation toolbar

3) If there is existing data in the data source, use the control buttons on the Form Navigation toolbar to look at different records. You can amend data in a record by editing the values in the form. To submit the changes, press the *Enter* key with the cursor in the last field. The record is saved and the next record is displayed.

4) If there is no data in the form, you can start entering information by typing into the fields of the form. To submit the new record, press the *Enter* key with the cursor in the last field.

5) Other functions can be performed from the Form Navigation toolbar, including deleting a record and adding a new record.

Tip	If a user tries to fill in the form and receives the error "Attempt to insert null into a non-nullable column", then the form designer should go back to the database and confirm that the Primary Key field has the Auto Value set to Yes. This error will prevent the form user from saving the records.

Advanced form customization

Linking a macro to a form control

You can set any form control (for example, text box or button) to perform an action when triggered by some event. To see the full list of events, right-click on the form control when the design mode is on, select **Control** and click on the **Events** tab.

To assign a macro to an event:

1) Create the macro. See Chapter 13, Getting Started with Macros, in the *Getting Started* guide.

2) Be sure the form is in design mode. Right-click on the form control, select **Control** and click on the **Events** tab.

3) Click the **browse** ( ) button to bring up the **Assign action** dialog (Figure 450).

4) Click the **Macro** button and select the macro from the list in the Macro Selector dialog. You return to the Assign action dialog. Repeat as needed, then click **OK** to close the dialog.

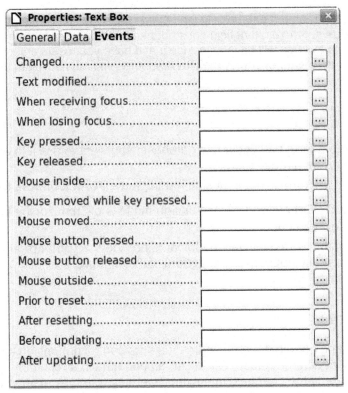

Figure 449: Control properties, Events tab

Macros can also be assigned to events relating to the form as a whole. To assign these, right-click on a form control in the document, select **Form** and click on the **Events** tab.

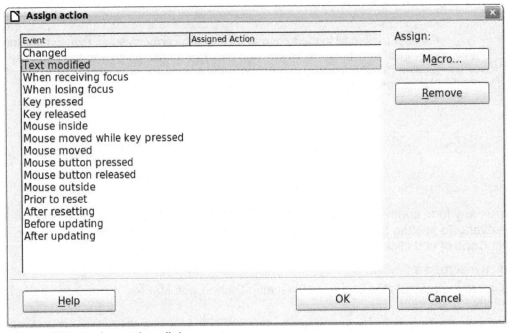

Figure 450: Assign action dialog

Read-only documents

Having created your form, you want whoever is using it to be able to access the information stored in the database, or complete the form, without changing the layout. To do this, make the document read-only by choosing **File > Properties > Security** and selecting the **Open file read-only** option.

Fine-tuning database access permissions

By default, when a database is accessed from a form, any changes can be made to it: records can be added, deleted, and amended. You may not want that behavior. For example, you may want users to be able only to add new records or to be prohibited from deleting existing records.

In design mode, right-click on a form control and select **Form** from the context menu. On the *Data* tab of the Form Properties dialog are a number of options: Allow additions, Allow deletions, Allow modifications and Add data only. Set each of these to *Yes* or *No* to control the access users have to the data source.

Individual fields can also be protected. This might be useful if you wanted a user to be able to modify some parts of a record but only view others, such as a stock list where item descriptions are fixed and quantities can be modified.

To make an individual field read-only, in design mode, right-click on the form control within the document and select **Control** from the context menu. Select the *General* tab and set **Read-only** to **Yes**.

Figure 451: Data Properties of a form

Form control formatting options

You can customize the way form controls look and behave in a number of ways. These are all accessed in design mode. Right-click on the form control, select **Control** from the context menu and select the **General** tab in the **Properties** dialog.

- Set a label for the control in the *Label* box (not to be confused with the box called *Label Field*). Some form controls, such as push buttons and option buttons, have visible labels that can be set. Others, such as text boxes, do not.

- Set whether the form control will print out if the document is printed with the Print option.

- Use the Font setting to set the font, typeface, and size for a field's label or for text typed into a field. This setting does not affect the size of check boxes or option buttons.

- For a text box, you can set the maximum text length. This is very useful when adding records into a database. Every database text field has a maximum length and, if the data entered is too long, LibreOffice displays an error message. By setting the maximum text length of the form control to be the same as that of the database field, this error can be avoided.

- You can set the default option for a form control. By default, a control is blank, or has every option unselected. You can set the control to start with a particular option or list item selected.

- For controls where a password is being entered, setting the Password character (for example to *) displays only that character, but saves what the user really types.

- You can add additional information and help text for a form control.

- Other formatting controls such as background color, 3-D look, text formatting, scroll bars, and borders allow you to further define how the control appears.

XForms

XForms are a new type of web form, developed by the World Wide Web Consortium (W3C). LibreOffice supports the XForms 1.0 open standard for creating web forms with XML.

In LibreOffice, an XForms document is a special type of Writer document. XForms use the same controls as the ordinary forms described in this chapter.

After you create and save an XForms document, you can open the document, fill out the form, and submit the changes to a server.

A detailed discussion of XForms is beyond the scope of this chapter, as it is related more to databases than word processing.

Chapter 16
Customizing Writer

Introduction

This chapter describes some common customizations that you may wish to do.

You can customize menus, toolbars, and keyboard shortcuts in LibreOffice, add new menus and toolbars, and assign macros to events. However, you cannot customize context (right-click) menus.

Other customizations are made easy by extensions that you can install from the LibreOffice website or from other providers.

Note	Customizations to menus and toolbars can be saved in a template. To do so, first save them in a document and then save the document as a template as described in Chapter 10, Working with Templates.

Customizing menu content

In addition to changing the menu font (described in Chapter 2, Setting up Writer), you can add to and rearrange categories on the menu bar, add commands to menus, and make other changes.

To customize menus:

1) Choose **Tools > Customize.**
2) On the Customize dialog, go to the **Menus** page.

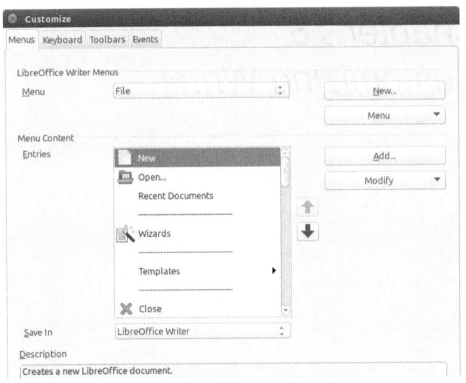

Figure 452: The Menus page of the Customize dialog

3) In the *Save In* drop-down list, choose whether to save this changed menu for the application (Writer) or for a selected document.
4) In the section *LibreOffice Writer Menus*, select from the **Menu** drop-down list the menu that you want to customize. The list includes all the main menus as well as submenus, that is menus that are contained under another menu. For example, in addition to *File, Edit, View,*

and so on, there is *File | Send* and *File |Templates*. The commands contained in the selected menu are shown in the central part of the dialog.

5) To customize the selected menu, click on the **Menu** or **Modify** buttons. You can also add commands to a menu by clicking on the **Add** button. These actions are described in the following sections. Use the up and down arrows next to the *Entries* list to move the selected menu item to a different position.

6) When you have finished making all your changes, click **OK** to save them.

Creating a new menu

In the *Menus* page of the Customize dialog, click **New** to display the Move Menu dialog, shown in Figure 453.

1) Type a name for your new menu in the *Menu name* box.
2) Use the up and down arrow buttons to move the new menu into the required position on the menu bar.
3) Click **OK** to save.

The new menu now appears on the list of menus in the Customize dialog.

After creating a new menu, you need to add some commands to it, as described in "Adding a command to a menu" on page 448.

Figure 453: Adding a new menu

Modifying existing menus

To modify an existing menu, either user-made or inbuilt, select it in the *Menu* list and click the **Menu** button to drop down a list of modifications: **Move, Rename, Delete**. Not all of these modifications can be applied to all the entries in the *Menu* list. For example, **Rename** and **Delete** are not available for the supplied menus, and **Move** is not available for submenus.

To move a menu (such as *File*), choose **Menu > Move**. The dialog shown in Figure 454 opens. Use the up and down arrow buttons to move the menu into the required position.

Figure 454: Moving a menu

To move submenus (such as *File | Send*), select the main menu (**File**) in the *Menu* list and then, in the *Menu Content* section of the dialog, select the submenu (**Send**) in the *Entries* list and use the arrow keys to move it up or down in the sequence. Submenus are easily identified in the *Entries* list by a small black triangle on the right hand side of the name.

To rename a custom menu, selecting it in the *Menu* list, click the **Menu** button in the upper section of the page, and select **Rename**.

To rename supplied menu items, supplied submenus, and custom submenus, select the item in the *Entries* list, click the **Modify** button in the *Menu Content* section of the dialog, and select **Rename**.

Note	Changes to the menus are not immediately displayed. Changes saved to LibreOffice Writer's menu are displayed the next time Writer is opened. Changes saved to a document's menu are displayed the next time the document is opened.

In addition to renaming, you can allocate a letter in a custom menu's name, which will become underlined, to be used as a keyboard shortcut, that allows you to select that menu when you press *Alt* + that letter. Existing submenus can be edited to change the letter which is used to select them from the keyboard once the menu is open.

1) Select a custom menu or a submenu in the *Menu* drop-down list.
2) Click the **Menu** button and select **Rename**.
3) Add a tilde (~) in front of the letter that you want to use as an accelerator. For example, to select the **Send** submenu command by pressing <u>S</u> (after opening the File menu using *Alt+F*), enter **~Send**. This changes it from the default <u>d</u>.

Note	It is possible to use a letter already in use in the menu list (for example, in the Insert menu, the letter *v* is used in *Envelope* and in *Movie and sound* as an accelerator). However, you should use an unused letter if possible, to make it simpler for the user to navigate.

Adding a command to a menu

You can add commands to the supplied menus and to menus you have created. On the Customize dialog, select the menu in the *Menu* list and click the **Add** button in the *Menu Content* section of the dialog. The Add Commands dialog is displayed.

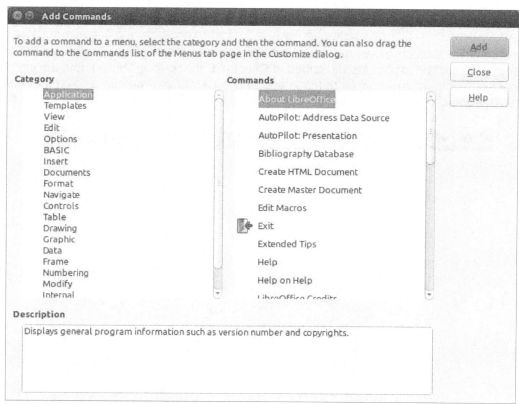

Figure 455: Adding a command to a menu

On the Add Commands dialog, select a category and then the command, and click **Add**. The dialog remains open, so you can select several commands. When you have finished adding commands, click **Close**. Back on the Customize dialog, you can use the up and down arrow buttons to arrange the commands in your preferred sequence.

Tip	You can also add a command to a menu by clicking on it and dragging to the Menu list on the Customize dialog. Choose the menu you want to modify before dragging the command. Thus, you can also place the command in your preferred location.
	This procedure works too when you add a command to a toolbar (see "Adding a command to a toolbar" on page 451).

Modifying menu entries

In addition to changing the sequence of entries on a menu or submenu, you can add submenus, rename or delete the entries, and add group separators.

To begin, select the menu or submenu to be modified, from the *Menu* list near the top of the Customize page, then select the entry in the *Entries* list under *Menu Content*. Click the **Modify** button and choose the required action from the drop-down list of actions.

Add Submenu does just that. After adding a submenu, it can be selected in the *Menu* list in the top section of the page and another submenu can be nested within it.

Add Separator adds a separator line after the highlighted entry.

Rename allows you to rename the entries and to modify the accelerator letter used in the menu entry for items other than submenus (see "Modifying existing menus" on page 447).

Delete removes the selected entry from the *Entries* list.

Customizing toolbars

You can customize toolbars in several ways, including choosing which icons are visible and locking the position of a docked toolbar (as described in Chapter 1, Introducing Writer), and adding or deleting icons (commands) in the list of those available on a toolbar. You can also create new toolbars. This section describes how to create new toolbars and add or delete icons on existing ones.

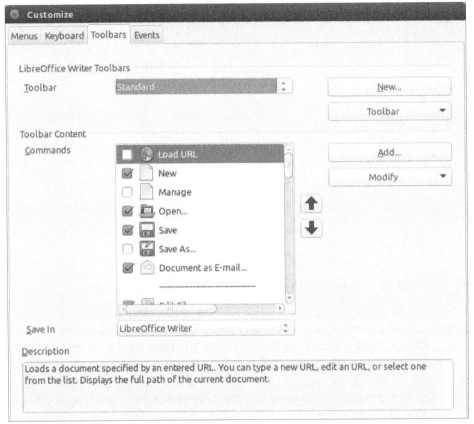

Figure 456: The Toolbars page of the Customize dialog

To get to the toolbar customization dialog, do any of the following:

- On the toolbar, right-click in the toolbar and choose **Customize Toolbar**.
- Choose **View > Toolbars > Customize** from the menu bar.
- Choose **Tools > Customize** from the menu bar and go to the *Toolbars* page.

Modifying existing toolbars

To modify an existing toolbar:

1) In the *Save In* drop-down list, choose whether to save this changed toolbar for the application (Writer) or for a selected document.
2) In the section *LibreOffice Writer Toolbars*, select from the *Toolbar* drop-down list the toolbar that you want to modify.
3) Click on the **Toolbar** or **Modify** buttons to edit or remove items on the toolbar, and add commands to a toolbar by clicking on the **Add** button. You can also create a new toolbar by clicking on the **New** button. These actions are described in the following sections.
4) When you have finished making all your changes, click **OK** to save them.

Adding a command to a toolbar

If the list of available buttons for a toolbar does not include all the commands you want on that toolbar, you can add commands. When you create a new toolbar, you need to add commands to it.

1) On the *Toolbars* page of the Customize dialog, select the toolbar in the **Toolbar** list and click the **Add** button in the *Toolbar Content* section of the dialog.

2) The Add Commands dialog (Figure 455) is the same as for adding commands to menus. Select a category and then the command, and click **Add**. The dialog remains open, so you can select several commands. When you have finished adding commands, click **Close**. If you insert an item which does not have an associated icon, the toolbar will display the full name of the item: the next section describes how to choose an icon for a toolbar command.

3) Back on the Customize dialog, you can use the up and down arrow buttons to arrange the commands in your preferred sequence.

4) When you are done making changes, click **OK** to save.

Tip	You can also add a command to a menu by clicking on it and dragging to the toolbar on the Customize dialog. Choose the toolbar you want to modify before dragging the command. Thus, you can also place the command in your preferred location.

Choosing icons for toolbar commands

Toolbar buttons usually have icons, not words, on them, but not all of the commands have associated icons.

To choose an icon for a command, select the command in the *Toolbar Content – Commands* list in the Customize dialog, and click **Modify > Change icon**. On the Change Icon dialog, you can scroll through the available icons, select one, and click **OK** to assign it to the command.

To use a custom icon, create it in a graphics program and import it into LibreOffice by clicking the **Import** button on the Change Icon dialog. Custom icons must be 16×16 in size and cannot contain more than 256 colors.

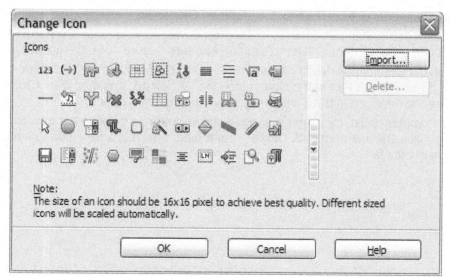

Figure 457: Change Icon dialog

Example: Adding a Fax icon to a toolbar

You can customize LibreOffice so that a single click on an icon automatically sends the current document as a fax.

1) Be sure the fax driver is installed. Consult the documentation for your fax modem for more information.

2) Choose **Tools > Options > LibreOffice Writer > Print**. The dialog shown in Figure 458 opens.

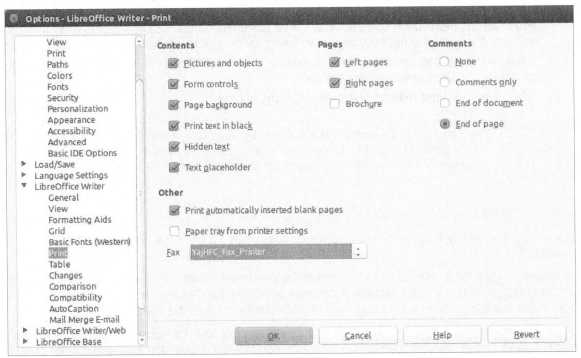

Figure 458: Setting up LibreOffice for sending faxes

3) Select the fax driver from the **Fax** list and click **OK**.

4) Right-click in the Standard toolbar. In the drop-down menu, choose **Customize Toolbar**. The *Toolbars* page of the Customize dialog appears (Figure 456). Click **Add**.

5) On the Add Commands dialog (Figure 459), select **Documents** in the *Category* list, then select **Send Default Fax** in the *Commands* list. Click **Add**, and then click **Close**. Now you can see the new icon in the *Commands* list of the *Toolbars* page.

6) In the *Commands* list, click the up or down arrow button to position the new icon where you want it. Click **OK** and then click **Close**. Your toolbar now has a new icon to send the current document as a fax.

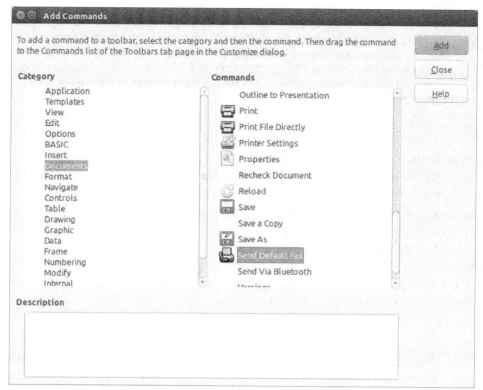

Figure 459: Adding a Send Fax command to a toolbar

Creating a new toolbar

To create a new toolbar:

1) Choose **Tools > Customize > Toolbars** from the menu bar.

2) Click **New**. On the Name dialog, Figure 460, type the new toolbar's name and choose from the *Save In* drop-down list where to save this changed menu: for the application (Writer) or for a selected document.

Figure 460: Create a new toolbar

The new toolbar now appears on the list of toolbars in the Customize dialog. After creating a new toolbar, you need to add some commands to it, as described above.

Assigning shortcut keys

In addition to using the built-in keyboard shortcuts (listed in Appendix A), you can define your own. You can assign shortcuts to standard LibreOffice functions or your own macros and save them for use with the entire LibreOffice suite.

Caution	Be careful when reassigning your operating system's or LibreOffice's predefined shortcut keys. Many key assignments are universally understood shortcuts, such as *F1* for Help, and are always expected to provide certain results. Although you can easily reset the shortcut key assignments to the LibreOffice defaults, changing some common shortcut keys can cause confusion, especially if other users share your computer.

To adapt shortcut keys to your needs, use the Customize dialog, as described below.

1) Choose **Tools > Customize > Keyboard**. The Customize dialog opens.

2) To have the shortcut key assignment available in all components of LibreOffice, select the **LibreOffice** button; to have it available only in *Writer*, select the **Writer** button.

3) Next select the required function from the *Category* and *Function* lists.

4) Now select the desired shortcut key in the *Shortcut keys* list at the top of the page and click the **Modify** button on the right. The selection now appears in the *Keys* list on the lower right.

5) Click **OK** to accept the change. Now the chosen shortcut key will execute the function chosen in step 3 above whenever it is pressed.

Repeat as required.

| Note | All existing shortcut keys for the currently selected *Function* are listed in the *Keys* selection box. If the *Keys* list is empty, it indicates that no key combination has been chosen for the selected function. If it is not empty, and you click Modify, the shortcut key combination is added to the shortcut key(s) already assigned to the currently selected function.

Shortcut keys that are grayed-out in the listing on the Customize dialog, such as *F1* and *F10,* are not available for reassignment. |
| --- | --- |

Example: Assigning styles to shortcut keys

You can configure shortcut keys to quickly assign styles in your document. Some shortcuts are predefined, such as *Ctrl+0* for the *Text body* paragraph style, *Ctrl+1* for the *Heading 1* style and *Ctrl+2* for *Heading 2*. You can modify these shortcuts and create your own.

1) Click **Tools > Customize > Keyboard**. The *Keyboard* page of the Customize dialog (Figure 461) opens.

2) To have the shortcut key assignment available only for Writer, select **Writer** in the upper right corner of the page; otherwise select **LibreOffice** to make it available to every component.

3) Choose the shortcut key you want to assign a style to. In this example, we have chosen *Ctrl+9*. This enables the **Modify** button.

4) In the *Functions* section at the bottom of the dialog, scroll down in the *Category* list to *Styles*. Click the ▶ (or **+** sign, depending on your operating system) to expand the list of styles.

5) Choose the category of style. (This example uses a paragraph style, but you can also choose character styles and others.) The *Function* list will display the names of the available styles for the selected category. The example shows some of LibreOffice's predefined styles.

6) To assign *Ctrl+9* to be the shortcut key combination for the List 1 style, select *List 1* in the *Function* list, and then click **Modify**. *Ctrl+9* now appears in the *Keys* list on the right, and *List 1* appears next to *Ctrl+9* in the *Shortcut keys* box at the top.

7) Make any other required changes, and then click **OK** to save these settings and close the dialog.

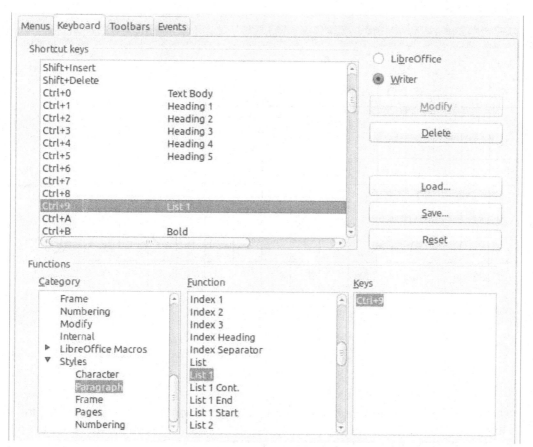

Figure 461. Defining keyboard shortcuts for applying styles

Example: Assigning macros to shortcut keys

A common use for assigning macros to shortcut keys is to enable quick and easy insertion of special characters. This example shows how to set up keyboard shortcuts for inserting en-dashes and em-dashes.

Note	To enable macro recording, go to **Tools > Options > LibreOffice > Advanced** and select the **Enable macro recording** option. By default, this feature is turned off when LibreOffice was installed on your computer.

First, you need to record a macro for inserting each type of dash. Then, you need to assign those macros to shortcut key combinations.

1) Choose **Tools > Macros > Record Macro** to start recording a macro.
2) A small window is displayed, Figure 462, so you know that LibreOffice is recording. (This window may look slightly different on different operating systems.)

Figure 462: Record macro

3) Choose **Insert > Special Characters** to open the Special Characters dialog. Scroll down until you find the en-dash (U+2013), Figure 463, and em-dash (U+2014) characters. Select one of them and click **OK.**

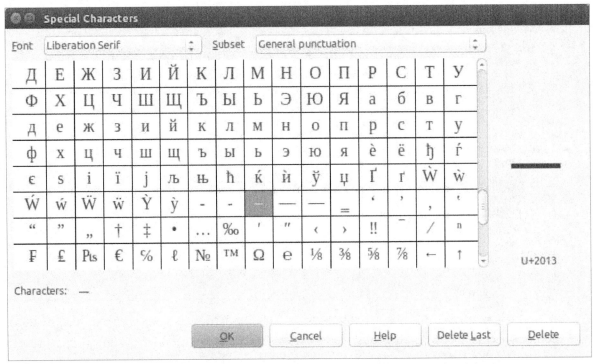

Figure 463: Find and choose the en-dash

4) Click the **Stop Recording** button to stop recording, save the macro, and display the LibreOffice Basic Macros dialog (see Figure 464). Type a descriptive name for the new macro in the **Macro name** box on the upper left.

5) Be sure to open the library container named **My Macros**. Find the library named **Standard** under **My Macros**. Select **Module1** and click **Save**.

6) Repeat steps 1–4 to create other macros, for example to insert an em-dash.

7) Choose **Tools > Customize > Keyboard** tab (Figure 465). In the *Shortcut keys* list, pick an unused combination (for example, *Ctrl+Shift+N* for an en-dash). In the *Category* list, scroll down to **LibreOffice Macros**, click the ► (or **+** sign, depending on your operating system), click the ► (or **+**) next to **user**, then click the ► (or **+**) next to **Standard** and choose **Module1**. In the *Function* list, choose **en_dash** and click the **Modify** button on the upper right. The selected key combination now appears in the *Keys* list on the lower right, and **en_dash** appears next to *Ctrl+Shift+N* in the *Shortcut* keys list.

8) Repeat for the em-dash macro, selecting perhaps *Ctrl+Shift+M* for the shortcut key and then click **OK.**

Tip	For inserting en- and em-dashes, and other special characters, you may find extensions such as Compose Special Characters useful. See "Adding functionality with extensions" on page 459.

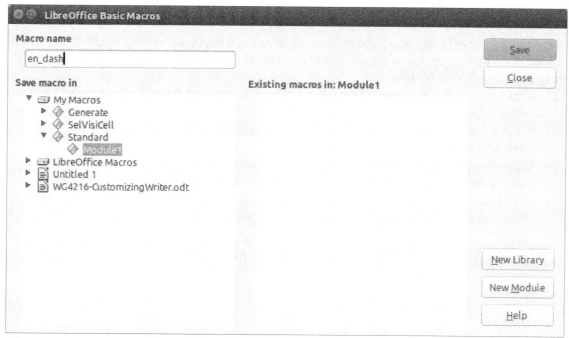

Figure 464: Naming the new macro and storing it

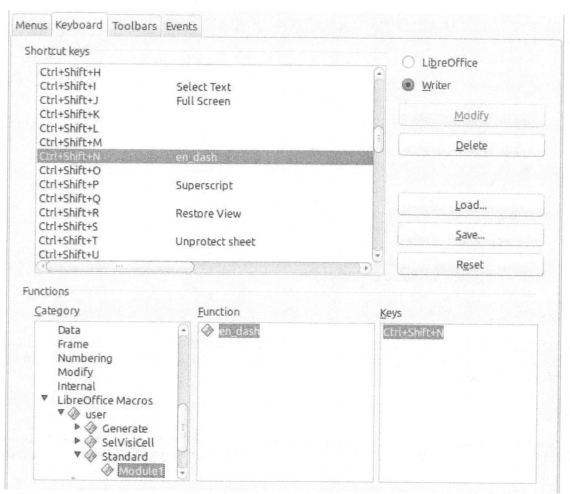

Figure 465: Defining keyboard shortcuts for running macros

Saving changes to a file

Changes to the shortcut key assignments can be saved in a keyboard configuration file for use at a later time, thus permitting you to create and apply different configurations as the need arises. To save keyboard shortcuts to a file:

1) After making your keyboard shortcut assignments, click the **Save** button on the Customize dialog (Figure 461).

2) In the Save Keyboard Configuration dialog, Figure 466, select *All files* from the **Save as Type** list.

3) Next enter a name for the keyboard configuration file in the **File name** box, or select an existing file from the list. If you need to, browse to find a file from another location.

4) Click **Save**. A confirmation dialog appears if you are about to overwrite an existing file, otherwise there will be no feedback and the file will be saved.

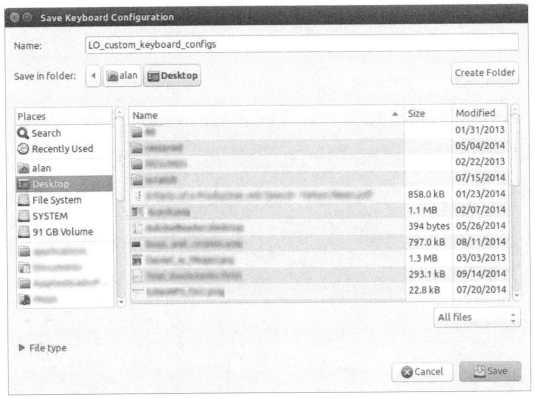

Figure 466: Save Keyboard Configuration

Loading a saved keyboard configuration

To load a saved keyboard configuration file and replace your existing configuration, click the **Load** button on the Customize dialog, and then select the configuration file from the Load Keyboard Configuration dialog.

Resetting the shortcut keys

To reset all of the keyboard shortcuts to their default values, click the **Reset** button near the bottom right of the Customize dialog. Use this feature with care as no confirmation dialog will be displayed; the defaults will be set without any further notice or user input.

Assigning macros to events

In LibreOffice, when something happens, we say that an event occurred. For example, a document was opened, a key was pressed, or the mouse moved. You can associate a macro with an event, so the macro is run when the event occurs. For example, a common use is to assign the "open document" event to run a macro that performs certain setup tasks for the document.

To associate a macro with an event, use the *Events* page of the Customize dialog. For more information, see Chapter 13, Getting Started with Macros, in the *Getting Started* guide.

Adding functionality with extensions

An extension is a package that can be installed into LibreOffice to add new functionality.

Several extensions are shipped bundled with LibreOffice and are installed with the program. Others can be downloaded from various websites. The official extension repository is located at http://extensions.libreoffice.org/. These extensions are free of charge.

Some extensions from other sources are free of charge; others are available for a fee. Check the descriptions to see what licenses and fees apply to the ones that interest you.

Installing extensions

Extensions can be installed in any of three ways.

1) Directly from the *.oxt file in your system's file browser.
2) From your web browser if it can be configured to open this file type from a web page hyperlink.
3) Directly from **Tools > Extension Manager** by clicking **Add**.

To install directly from a saved *.oxt file on your system, double-click the file.

To install from a suitably enabled web browser, select the hyperlink, and then select to Open the file.

To install directly from Extension Manager:

1) In LibreOffice, select **Tools > Extension Manager** from the menu bar. You can deselect the *Installation* option (which covers extensions bundled with LibreOffice) to easier view those extensions that have been added by a user.
2) In the Extension Manager dialog (Figure 468), click **Add**.
3) A file browser window opens. Find and select the extension you want to install and click **Open**.
4) Users with administrator or root privileges will see a dialog where they can choose to install extensions "for all users" (**shared**) or "only for me" (**user**). Normal users without those privileges can install, remove, or modify extensions only for their own use (**user**).

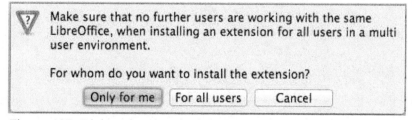

Figure 467: Dialog showing the installation choices

5) The extension begins installing.

6) In all three cases, during the process you may be asked to accept a license agreement. When the installation is complete, the extension is listed in the Extension Manager dialog.

Tip	To get extensions that are listed in the repository, you can open the Extension Manager and click the **Get more extensions online** link. You do not need to download them separately.

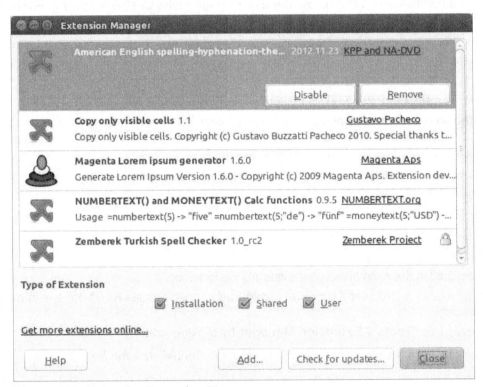

Figure 468: Using the Extension Manager

Appendix A
Keyboard Shortcuts

Using Writer Without a Mouse

Introduction

You can use LibreOffice without requiring a pointing device, such as a mouse or touchpad, by using its built-in keyboard shortcuts.

LibreOffice has a general set of keyboard shortcuts, available in all components, and a component-specific set directly related to the work of that component. This appendix lists the default set for Writer. For general shortcuts, see Appendix A of the *Getting Started* guide.

For help with LibreOffice's keyboard shortcuts, or using LibreOffice with a keyboard only, search the LibreOffice Help using the "shortcut" or "accessibility" keywords.

In addition to using the built-in keyboard shortcuts listed in this Appendix, you can define your own. See Chapter 16, Customizing Writer, for instructions.

Note	Some of the shortcuts listed here may not work if your operating system uses the same shortcuts for other tasks.
	To get around this problem, assign different keys to these shortcuts by reconfiguring either LibreOffice (see Chapter 16) or your operating system (see system documentation).

Tip for Macintosh users

Some keystrokes are different on a Mac from those used in Windows and Linux. The following table gives some common substitutions for the instructions in this book. For a more detailed list, see the application Help.

Windows or Linux	Mac equivalent	Effect
Right-click	Control+click and/or right-click depending on computer system	Open a context menu
Ctrl (Control)	⌘ (Command)	Used with other keys
F5	Shift+⌘+F5	Open the Navigator
F11	⌘+T	Open theStyles and Formatting window

Opening menus and menu items

Shortcut Keys	Result
Alt+<?>	Opens a menu where <?> is the underlined character of the menu you want to open. For example, *Alt+F* opens the menu **File.** With the menu open, you will again find underlined characters. You can access these menu items directly by simply pressing the underlined character key. Where two menu items have the same underlined character, press the character key again to move to the next item. *Example*: to access the **Printer Settings** item of the **File** menu after opening it, press *R* twice to move from the initial **Digital Signatures** selection to **Printer Settings**. *Exception*: **Language** in the **Tools** menu has no underlined characters.
F6	Repeatedly pressing *F6* switches the focus and circles through the following objects: • Menu bar • Every toolbar from top to bottom and from left to right • Every free window from left to right • Document
Shift+F6	Switches through objects in the opposite direction.
Ctrl+F6	Switches the focus to the document.
F10 or Alt	Switches to the Menu bar and back.
Esc	Closes an open menu.

Accessing a menu command

Press *Alt* or *F6* or *F10* to select the first item on the menu bar (the **File** menu). With the *right-arrow*, the next menu to the right is selected; with the *left-arrow*, the previous menu. The *Home* and *End* keys select the first and the last item on the Menu bar.

The *down-arrow* opens a selected menu. An additional *down-arrow* and *up-arrow* moves the selection through the menu commands. The *right-arrow* opens any existing submenus.

Press *Enter* to execute the selected menu command.

Executing a toolbar command

Press *F6* repeatedly until the first icon on the toolbar is selected. Use the right and left arrows to select an icon on a horizontal toolbar. Similarly, use the up and down arrows to select an icon on a vertical toolbar. The *Home* key selects the first icon on a toolbar and the *End* key, the last.

Press *Enter* to execute the selected icon. If the selected icon normally demands a consecutive mouse action, such as inserting a rectangle, then pressing the *Enter* key is not sufficient: in these cases press *Ctrl+Enter*.

• Press *Ctrl+Enter* on an icon for creating a draw object. A draw object will be placed into the middle of the view, with a predefined size.

- Press *Ctrl+Enter* on the Selection tool to select the first draw object in the document. If you want to edit, size, or move the selected draw object, first use *Ctrl+F6* to move the focus into the document.

If a toolbar is longer than can be displayed on screen, it shows an icon at the right or lower edge. Select the toolbar and press *PageUp* or *PageDown* to display the remaining icons.

Navigating and selecting with the keyboard

You can navigate through a document and make selections with the keyboard.

- To move the cursor, press the key or key combination given in the following table.
- To select the characters under the moving cursor, additionally hold down the *Shift* key when you move the cursor.

Key	Function	Plus Ctrl key
Right, left arrow keys	Moves the cursor one character to the left or to the right.	Moves the cursor one word to the left or to the right.
Up, down arrow keys	Moves the cursor up or down one line.	(*Ctrl+Alt*) Moves the current paragraph up or down.
Home	Moves the cursor to the beginning of the current line.	Moves the cursor to the beginning of the document.
End	Moves the cursor to the end of the current line.	Moves the cursor to the end of the document.
PgUp	Scrolls up one page.	Moves the cursor to the header.
PgDn	Scroll down one page.	Moves the cursor to the footer.

Controlling dialogs

When you open any dialog, one element (such as a button, an option field, an entry in a list box, or a checkbox) is highlighted or indicated by a dotted box around the field or button name. This element is said to have the focus on it.

Shortcut Keys	Result
Enter	Activates the selected button. In most cases where no button is selected, *Enter* is equivalent to clicking **OK**.
Esc	Closes the dialog without saving any changes made while it was open. In most cases, *Esc* is equivalent to clicking *Cancel*. When an open drop-down list is selected, *Esc* closes the list.
Spacebar	Toggles a checkbox on or off.
Up, down arrow keys	Moves the focus up and down a list. Increases or decreases the value of a variable. Moves the focus vertically within a section of a dialog.
Right, left arrow keys	Moves the focus horizontally within a section of a dialog.
Tab	Advances the focus to the next section or element of a dialog.

Shortcut Keys	Result
Shift+Tab	Returns the focus to the previous section or element in a dialog.
Alt+Down-arrow	Shows items in a drop-down list.

Macros

Shortcut Keys	Result
Ctrl+* (multiplication sign: on number pad only)	Runs a macro field.
Shift+Ctrl+Q	Stops a running macro.

Shortcut keys for controlling documents and windows

Shortcut Keys	Effect
Ctrl+O	Opens a document.
Ctrl+S	Saves the current document.
Ctrl+N	Creates a new document.
Ctrl+Shift+N	Opens Templates and Documents dialog.
Ctrl+P	Opens the Print dialog.
Ctrl+F	Activates the Find toolbar.
Ctrl+H	Opens the Find & Replace dialog.
Ctrl+Shift+F	Searches for the last entered search term.
Ctrl+Shift+J	Toggles the view between full-screen mode and normal mode.
Ctrl+Shift+R	Redraws the document view.
Ctrl+Shift+I	Enables or disables the selection cursor in read-only text.
F1	Starts the LibreOffice Help. In the LibreOffice Help: jumps to main help page.
Shift+F1	Opens Context Help.
Shift+F2	Turns on Extended Tips for the currently selected command, icon or control.
F6	Sets focus in next subwindow (for example, document/data source view).

Shortcut Keys	Effect
Shift+F6	Sets focus in previous subwindow.
F10	Activates the first menu (File menu).
Shift+F10	Opens the context menu.
Ctrl+F4 or Alt+F4	Closes the current document (closes LibreOffice when the last open document is closed).
Ctrl+Q	Exits application.

Function keys for Writer

Shortcut keys	Effect
F1	Opens Writer Help at the Home page. Pressing *F1* again opens the home page of the active tab.
Shift+F1	Enables the extended help tips under the mouse pointer until the next click.
F2	Opens or closes the Formula Bar.
Ctrl+F2	Opens the Fields dialog.
Shift+F2	Displays tips for the currently selected command, icon, or control.
F3	Inserts the AutoText entry corresponding to the typed shortcut.
Ctrl+F3	Opens the AutoText dialog, where you can edit an AutoText entry or create a new entry from the selected text.
F4	Opens or closes the View Data Sources window.
Shift+F4	Selects the next frame.
F5	Opens or closes the Navigator.
Ctrl+Shift+F5	Opens the Navigator with cursor in page number field.
F7	Starts the spelling and grammar checker.
Ctrl+F7	Opens the Thesaurus.
F8	Turns Extension Selection mode on or off.
Ctrl+F8	Turns field shadings on or off.
Shift+F8	Turns Multiple Selection mode on or off.
Ctrl+Shift+F8	Turns Block Selection mode on or off.
F9	Updates fields.

Shortcut keys	Effect
Ctrl+F9	Shows or hides field names.
Shift+F9	Calculates Table.
Ctrl+Shift+F9	Opens a dialog for editing input fields and lists.
F10	See "Opening menus and menu items" on page 463 for details.
Ctrl+F10	Displays or hides non-printing characters.
F11	Opens or closes the Styles and Formatting window.
Shift+F11	Creates a new style from a selection.
Ctrl+Shift+F11	Updates a style.
F12	Turns paragraph numbering on or off.
Ctrl+F12	Inserts or edits a table.
Shift+F12	Turns bullets on or off.
Ctrl+Shift+F12	Turns numbering/bullets off.

Shortcut keys for Writer

Shortcut Keys	Effect
Ctrl+A	Selects all content in a document, unless the cursor is in a table (see "Shortcut keys for tables" on page 470).
Ctrl+D	Double underlines selected text or text typed afterward. Press again to turn off.
Ctrl+E	Centers the paragraph.
Ctrl+F	Opens the Find toolbar.
Ctrl+H	Opens the Find and Replace dialog.
Ctrl+J	Justifies the paragraph.
Ctrl+L	Aligns the paragraph to the left.
Ctrl+R	Align the paragraph to the right.
Ctrl+M	Removes direct formatting from the selected text or objects (as in **Format > Clear Direct Formatting**).
Ctrl+[	Decreases the size of the selected text.
Ctrl+]	Increases the size of the selected text.
Ctrl+Shift+B	Subscripts selected text or text typed afterward. Press again to turn off.

Shortcut Keys	Effect
Ctrl+Shift+P	Superscripts selected text or text typed afterward. Press again to turn off.
Ctrl+Y	Redoes last action.
Ctrl+Plus Key(+)	Calculates the selected text and copies the result to the clipboard.
Ctrl+Hyphen(–)	Inserts a conditional hyphen.
Ctrl+Shift+Hyphen (–)	Inserts a non-breaking hyphen (not used for hyphenation).
Ctrl+Shift+X	Stops applying direct character formats whilst typing, from the cursor point onward.
Ctrl+/ (slash)	Inserts a no-width optional line break.
Ctrl+Shift+Space	Inserts a non-breaking space (not used for hyphenation and not expanded if text is justified).
Shift+Enter	Inserts a line break without paragraph change.
Ctrl+Enter	Inserts a page break.
Ctrl+Shift+Enter	Inserts a column break in multi-column texts.
Alt+Enter	Inserts a new paragraph without numbering.
Alt+Enter	Inserts a new paragraph directly before or after a section or a table.
Arrow Left	Moves cursor to left.
Shift+Arrow Left	Moves cursor with selection to the left.
Ctrl+Arrow Left	Goes to beginning of word.
Ctrl+Shift+Arrow Left	Selects to the left word by word.
Arrow Right	Moves cursor to right.
Shift+Arrow Right	Moves cursor with selection to the right.
Ctrl+Arrow Right	Goes to start of next word.
Ctrl+Shift+Arrow Right	Selects to the right word by word.
Arrow Up	Moves up one line.
Shift+Arrow Up	Selects lines in an upwards direction.
Arrow Down	Moves cursor down one line.
Shift+Arrow Down	Selects lines in a downward direction.
Home	Goes to beginning of line.
Shift+Home	Goes and selects to the beginning of a line.
End	Goes to end of line.

Shortcut Keys	Effect
Shift+End	Goes and selects to end of line.
Ctrl+Home	Goes to start of document.
Ctrl+Shift+Home	Goes and selects text to start of document.
Ctrl+End	Goes to end of document.
Ctrl+Shift+End	Goes and selects text to end of document.
Ctrl+PageUp	Switches cursor between text and header.
Ctrl+PageDown	Switches cursor between text and footer.
Insert	Turns Insert mode on or off.
PageUp	Moves up one screen page.
Shift+PageUp	Moves up one screen page with selection.
PageDown	Moves down one screen page.
Shift+PageDown	Moves down one screen page with selection.
Ctrl+Del	Deletes text to end of word.
Ctrl+Backspace	Deletes text to beginning of word.
Ctrl+Shift+Del	Deletes text to end of sentence.
Ctrl+Shift+Backspace	Deletes text to beginning of sentence.
Ctrl+Tab	Uses next suggestion with automatic word completion.
Ctrl+Shift+Tab	Use previous suggestion with automatic word completion.
Alt+W	In the spelling checker dialog: Calls back the original unknown word into the text box.
Ctrl+double-click or Ctrl+Shift+F10	Docks or un-docks the Navigator, Styles and Formatting window, or other windows.

Shortcut keys for tables

Shortcut Keys	Effect
Ctrl+A	If the active cell is empty, *Ctrl+A* selects the whole table; otherwise, it selects the contents of the active cell. Press *Ctrl+A* a second time to select the entire table.
Ctrl+Home	If the active cell is empty, *Ctrl+Home* moves the cursor to the beginning of the table. Press *Ctrl+Home* again to move the cursor to the beginning of document. If the active cell is not empty, *Ctrl+Home* moves the cursor to the beginning of the active cell. A second press of *Ctrl+Home* moves the cursor to the beginning of the current table. A third press moves the cursor to the beginning of the document.
Ctrl+End	If the active cell is empty, *Ctrl+End* moves the cursor to the end of the table. Press *Ctrl+End* again to move the cursor to the end of document. If the active cell is not empty, *Ctrl+End* moves the cursor to the end of the active cell. A second press of *Ctrl+End* moves the cursor to the end of the current table. A third press moves the cursor to the end of the document.
Ctrl+Tab	Inserts a tab stop (only in tables). Depending on the Window Manager in use, *Alt+Tab* may be used instead.
Ctrl+Shift+Arrow Up	Jumps to start of table.
Ctrl+Shift+Arrow Down	Jumps to end of table.
Alt+Arrow keys	Increases or decreases the size of the column or row on the right or bottom cell edge.
Alt+Shift+Arrow keys	Increases or decreases the size of the column or row on the left or top cell edge.
Ctrl+Alt+Shift+Arrow keys	Like *Alt*, but modifies only the active cell.
Alt+Insert	Provides 3 seconds in Insert mode, during which time pressing an arrow key inserts a row or column, or *Ctrl+Arrow Key* inserts a cell.
Alt+Del	Provides 3 seconds in Delete mode, during which time pressing an arrow key deletes a row or column, or *Ctrl+Arrow Key* merges the active cell with the neighboring cell.
Ctrl+Shift+T	Removes cell protection from all selected tables. If no table is selected, then cell protection is removed from all of the tables in the document.
Ctrl+Shift+Del	If nothing is selected, the contents of the next cell are deleted. If cells are selected, the whole row(s) of the selection are deleted. If all rows are selected completely or partially, the entire table is deleted.

Shortcut keys for paragraphs and heading levels

Shortcut Keys	Effect
Ctrl+0 (zero)	Applies Text Body paragraph style.
Ctrl+1	Applies Heading 1 paragraph style.
Ctrl+2	Applies Heading 2 paragraph style.
Ctrl+3	Applies Heading 3 paragraph style.
Ctrl+4	Applies Heading 4 paragraph style.
Ctrl+5	Applies Heading 5 paragraph style.
Ctrl+Alt+Up Arrow or Ctrl+Up Arrow	Moves the active paragraph or selected paragraphs up one paragraph.
Ctrl+Alt+Down Arrow or Ctrl+Down Arrow	Moves the active paragraph or selected paragraphs down one paragraph.
Tab	When the cursor is at the beginning of the heading text, moves a heading in format *Heading X* (X = 1–9) down one level in the outline. Does not affect the applied paragraph style.
Shift+Tab	When the cursor is at the beginning of the heading text, moves a heading in format *Heading X* (X = 2–10) up one level in the outline. Does not affect the applied paragraph style.
Ctrl+Tab	At the start of a heading: Inserts a tab stop. Depending on the Window Manager in use, *Alt+Tab* may be used instead.

Shortcut keys for moving and resizing frames, graphics, and objects

Shortcut Keys	Effect
Esc	Cursor is inside a text frame and no text is selected: *Esc* selects the text frame. Text frame is selected: *Esc* clears the cursor from the text frame.
F2 or Enter or any key that produces a character on screen	If a text frame is selected: positions the cursor to the end of the text in the text frame. If you press any key that produces a character on screen, and the document is in edit mode, the character is appended to the text.
Alt+Arrow Keys	Moves the selected object.
Alt+Ctrl+Arrow Keys	Resizes an object by moving the lower right corner.
Alt+Ctrl+Shift+ Arrow Keys	Resizes an object by moving the top left corner.

Shortcut Keys	Effect
Ctrl+Tab	Selects the anchor of an object (in Edit Points mode).

Shortcut keys in the Gallery

Shortcut keys	Result
Tab	Moves between areas.
Shift+Tab	Moves between areas (backwards)

Shortcut keys in the New Theme area of the Gallery

Shortcut keys	Result
Up Arrow	Moves the selection up.
Down Arrow	Moves the selection down.
Ctrl+Enter	Opens the Properties dialog.
Shift+F10	Opens a context menu.
Ctrl+U	Refreshes the selected theme.
Ctrl+R	Opens the Enter Title dialog.
Ctrl+D	Deletes the selected theme.
Insert	Inserts a new theme.

Shortcut keys in the Gallery preview area

Shortcut keys	Result
Home	Jumps to the first entry.
End	Jumps to the last entry.
Left Arrow	Selects the next Gallery element on the left.
Right Arrow	Selects the next Gallery element on the right.
Up Arrow	Selects the next Gallery element above.
Down Arrow	Selects the next Gallery element below.
Page Up	Scroll up one screen.

Shortcut keys	Result
Page Down	Scroll down one screen.
Ctrl+Shift+Insert	Inserts the selected object as a linked object into the current document.
Ctrl+I	Inserts a copy of the selected object into the current document.
Ctrl+T	Opens the **Enter Title** dialog.
Ctrl+P	Switches between themes view and object view.
Spacebar	Switches between themes view and object view.
Enter	Switches between themes view and object view.
Step backward (only in object view)	Switches back to main overview.

Selecting rows and columns in a database table (opened by F4)

Shortcut keys	Result
Spacebar	Toggles row selection, except when the row is in edit mode.
Ctrl+Spacebar	Toggles row selection.
Shift+Spacebar	Selects the current column.
Ctrl+Page Up	Moves pointer to the first row.
Ctrl+Page Down	Moves pointer to the last row.

Shortcut keys for drawing objects

Shortcut keys	Result
Select the toolbar with *F6*. Use the *Down Arrow* and *Right Arrow* to select the desired toolbar icon and press *Ctrl+Enter*.	Inserts a Drawing Object.
Select the document with *Ctrl+F6* and press *Tab*.	Selects a Drawing Object.
Tab	Selects the next Drawing Object.
Shift+Tab	Selects the previous Drawing Object.
Ctrl+Home	Selects the first Drawing Object.
Ctrl+End	Selects the last Drawing Object.

Shortcut keys	Result
Esc	Ends Drawing Object selection.
Esc (in Handle Selection Mode)	Exit Handle Selection Mode and return to Object Selection Mode.
Up/Down/Left/Right Arrow	Move the selected point (the snap-to-grid functions are temporarily disabled, but end points still snap to each other).
Alt+Up/Down/Left/Right Arrow	Moves the selected Drawing Object one pixel (in Selection Mode). Re-sizes a Drawing Object (in Handle Selection Mode). Rotates a Drawing Object (in Rotation Mode). Opens the properties dialog for a Drawing Object. Activates the Point Selection mode for the selected drawing object.
Spacebar	Select a point of a drawing object (in Point Selection mode) / Cancel selection. The selected point blinks once per second.
Shift+Spacebar	Select an additional point in Point Selection mode.
Ctrl+Tab	Select the next point of the drawing object (Point Selection mode). In Rotation mode, the center of rotation can also be selected.
Ctrl+Shift+Tab	Select the previous point of the drawing object (Point Selection mode).
Ctrl+Enter	A new drawing object with default size is placed in the center of the current view.
Ctrl+Enter at the Selection icon	Activates the first drawing object in the document.
Esc	Leave the Point Selection mode. The drawing object is selected afterwards. Edit a point of a drawing object (Point Edit mode).
Any text or numerical key	If a drawing object is selected, switches to edit mode and places the cursor at the end of the text in the drawing object. A printable character is inserted.
Alt key while creating or scaling a graphic object	The position of the object's center is fixed.
Shift key while creating or scaling a graphic object	The ratio of the object's width to height is fixed.

Index

CPSIA information can be obtained
at www.ICGtesting.com
Printed in the USA
LVOW03s1615060416

482440LV00016B/463/P

9 789881 4435